LOST PASSPORT

THE LIFE AND WORDS OF EDWARD LACEY

Fraser Sutherland

BookLand
press

TORONTO, CANADA

Published by BookLand Press
6021 Yonge Street, Suite 1010, Toronto, Ontario, Canada M2M 3W2
www.booklandpress.com

Printed and bound in Canada.

Library and Archives Canada Cataloguing in Publication

Sutherland, Fraser
    Lost passport : the life and times of Edward
Lacey / Fraser Sutherland.

ISBN 978-1-926956-06-0

    1. Lacey, E. A. (Edward A.), 1937-1995. 2. Poets, Canadian (English)--20th century--Biography. 3. Translators--Canada--Biography. 1. Title.

PS8523.A225Z78 2011   C811'.54   C2011-905713-1

MIX
Paper from
responsible sources
FSC® C004071

ANCIENT FOREST ™
FRIENDLY

We acknowledge the support of the Canada Council for the Arts
which last year invested $20.1 million in writing and publishing
throughout Canada.
Nous remercions de son soutien le Conseil des Arts du Canada,
qui a investi 20,1 millions de dollars l'an dernier dans les lettres
et l'édition à travers le Canada.

Canada Council   Conseil des Arts
for the Arts   du Canada

On Definitions

And if they ask you, are you straight or gay?
Say "Boys, I'm stray."

~ Edward A. Lacey

TABLE OF CONTENTS

Part Three
PASSPORT CANCELLED
1984-1995

EPILOGUE IN PLACE OF A PROLOGUE

THE NEAREST RIVER, LAKE, OR SEA

July 1995

In my lap was a bag. In the bag was a box. In the box was another bag, which held the remains of Edward Allan Lacey, almost 58. He had died a month earlier. The box had lay, a brown rectangular reproach, atop a filing cabinet in my basement. His will, whose form he'd copied from legal boilerplate six years earlier, was clear. He did not want his body to be returned to, interred in, or otherwise retained in his birthplace, the town of Lindsay, Ontario, an hour and a half's drive northeast of Toronto. His body was offered to medical science. If it were deemed unacceptable, it was to be cremated, and the ashes scattered on the nearest river, lake, or sea. The Don River was perhaps closer to my home than Lake Ontario, but I didn't want to deposit the last of an old friend in a toxic trench. Better the wide expanse of what the Iroquois had called the lake of shining waters.

Up to now my tasks as executor had been simple. A few days after Edward had died of a heart attack, I'd cleaned out the small dim room where the government had housed him.

The Filipino boy-of-all-work helped me sift and sort the bits of shaving gear, the untaken Prozac tablets, the empty notebooks. The rest I lugged home in the tatty vinyl suitcase that three years earlier had partnered Edward from Bangkok.

He had not specified what kind of funeral he wanted. A few of us gathered in a big, near-empty yellow brick church on the edge of Chinatown: the publisher of one of his books, with a friend; two women friends traceable to his university days; a cousin and her daughter; a cousin of his father who'd tumbled to Edward's presence in the city. A long-lost maternal uncle, a roly-poly septuagenarian priest, conducted the service. The uncle belonged to the Redemptorists, famous for hellfire sermons, but Edward's uncle did not declare that his nephew was slowly turning on a rotisserie; he said a few mild kindly words. A ghetto blaster served in lieu of a choir. A few souls edged forward to take the sacrament.

Now the streetcar bumped and lurched my wife, 11-year-old son, and I toward Lake Ontario. The rear doors parted where the lakeshore skirted a hurtling boulevard. We looked for an inconspicuous spot, but people thronged the strip of parkland this cloudless Sunday afternoon of high summer. A few dogs competed in the 100-metre dash. Canada geese stomped across our path, mugging bread crusts from the picnickers who organized cookouts and spread blankets by the boles of maples and elms. A heat-haze lay on the lake. My wife, a believing Christian, was cheerful and reverent. Our son was unreadable. Maybe he thought that what I was about to do I did to all my friends, once I had finished with them.

On a sparsely peopled bend of the lake I removed shoes and socks, rolled up trousers, undid the sturdy metal clasp that clenched the bulging opaque plastic bag. Seeing me, a Canada goose flotilla swerved on their wave crest and veered near, anticipating lunch. Scattering them, I waded in, soggy sand underfoot.

Since the next act would flagrantly violate several municipal bylaws, I nervously glanced around. Atop a knoll loomed a knot of tall Africans, curious. To hell with it. I gingerly disgorged the bag of gritty sand into the murk, afraid that the backwash would cling to my legs. Edward's friend and publisher in San Francisco had asked that a few ashes be sent to him-for use in a Buddhist ceremony. I wasn't up to it. I carefully shook out the bag.

The waters of Lake Ontario swirl clockwise like the contents of a giant sink or toilet bowl. Assuming that Edward escaped the predations of *Branta canadensis*, maybe he would wash among the clinkers and slag of the steelmaking city to the west, or in the east deliver himself to the town of Port Hope. Maybe he'd be swallowed by the citizens of Toronto as part of their water supply. Or maybe some part might journey from the Great Lakes into the St. Lawrence River, thence far down to the Atlantic, and, infinitesimal, end in a tropical sea.

I splashed ashore and dropped the emptied bag in a waste bin. My wife had said a short prayer that Edward might find rest. I said to her that he'd always sought adventure. Recalling the true nature of heaven, she said he'd find adventure there. We went for supper at a Hungarian restaurant, dining on roast duck. It was a meal that Edward might have enjoyed.

Part One

PASSPORT ACQUIRED
1937-1961

... far from concern, need or love, your departure:
the rushing river carried you to sea.

~ The Flaw

1

THE LINDSAYITE

July 1937-September 1955

What does the child see behind the mirror?
He merely relives his past, which becomes his future.

~ The Closet

Lindsay, Ontario, someone said, had "the widest streets and narrowest minds in North America." On a July morning of 1937, the "Glorious Twelfth," the *Lindsay Daily Post* reported that members of the Orange Lodge marked the day by marching to the train station to the "stirring strains" of the "Protestant Boys" played by the Citizens Band. They presented "a very smart appearance as they paraded to the station, accompanied by a new gleaming satin banner, displaying King Billy to the eyes of the world..." That good Catholic, Allan Tasker Lacey, did not take much notice of William III. He was rushing his wife Alex to Ross Memorial Hospital. On that hot, partly cloudy day someone other than King Billy would be displayed to the eyes of the world.

Nearly 39 years earlier Allan's father, of Irish descent, had been born on rapids-encircled Ile aux Allumettes in Québec, on the north shore of the Ottawa River. About 1911, the thriving merchant William Lacey took his family and business a few

miles down the road to Pembroke, Ontario. By his first wife
Julia, he had a son. After Julia died, his second wife, the convent-
educated Marion, produced a daughter, Helen, and two sons.
One of them, Allan, was born in 1899. After matriculating in
1917, Allan entered St. Michael's College at the University
of Toronto, but in May 1918 he impulsively enlisted in the
Canadian Expeditionary Force. Without having faced enemy
fire, he resumed his studies, graduating in 1921. He articled in
law, and moved to Lindsay, Ontario, where he became junior
partner in a two-man firm. In the decade after his graduation,
the Pembroke phase of his life closed. The store owned by his
father burned down, his mother died in early 1926, and in 1931
William Lacey died.

Thin, long-faced, solemn, Allan met a suitable Catholic
girl in Marion Alexandrine Blanchard, "Alex," at a Newman Club
dance in Toronto. Born in 1901, she was the eldest daughter of
Dr. Fabian Blanchard and his wife Marion, née Benson, a slim
dark-haired teacher with a bulge on her upper lip incurred
when she fell as a baby. She painted over it with lipstick. To
some it passed unnoticed, to others it suggested the lip of a fish
that had been deformed from exposure to toxic waters. After a
long courtship, she and Allan wed on a Monday in September
1934, the sacrament performed by a cousin. The Toronto *Globe*
reported that she wore a tweed travelling suit with fur trimmings
and a felt hat. After the couple was feted, they left on a motor
trip to the Eastern United States.

When Dr. Blanchard died the following year there was
no shortage of survivors. Besides his wife, they included Alex
and her younger siblings, in order of age, Marie-Camille, Marion,
Fabian, Alice, Grace, Phyllis, and Edward ("Bud") — the last
a 16-year-old at the time of the wedding. Besides a substitute
hometown, Allan had acquired a new family that was half mutual aid society, half round-the-clock surveillance network.

Lindsay spans the Scugog River, a link in the Trent-Severn
Waterway's chain of channels and locks that winds between
Lake Ontario and Georgian Bay. Europeans arrived in the area
in 1615, when Samuel de Champlain touched down, followed by

fur traders, hunters, and trappers during the next two centuries. After the War of 1812, English, Scots, and Irish, assisted by grants of rations and implements, canoed down the meandering Scugog past tall pines, wild roses, and beaver meadows. The business of naming and claiming went on in a cedar swamp. At first, Lindsay was called "Purdys Mill," after William Purdy and his sons, who had been granted the surrounding acreage. A survey plotted two streets that bisected the town from east to west and from north to south. When a surveyor named Lindsay died from an infection that set in after a gun accident, "Lindsay" was marked on the town plan. Street names doffed the cap to royalty — Victoria, and Kent, after her father, the Duke of Kent. The streets north and south were named for her uncles, including William IV. Albert was called after Prince Albert, her consort, and Adelaide after Queen Adelaide, William's wife. Streets east and west favoured British prime ministers and colonial office-holders.

William Purdy got a cash bonus to erect a mill, siting a dam to secure the headwaters he needed to grind flour, but not before their pressure swept the dam away. Rebuilt, deluging the countryside, the dam raised the level of Lake Scugog and the ire of the local farmers. During the Upper Canada Rebellion of 1837, a rumour circulated that the rebel leader, William Lyon Mackenzie, was hiding in Lindsay. A dispatched detachment of Peterborough militia bivouacked at a log tavern, possibly the one whose notice, posted over the bar, oddly warned, "Keep sober or keep away." Mackenzie was nowhere near.

As time went on, unsightly stumps of felled pines marred the Scugog's sylvan banks. Meanwhile, Lindsay grew more Catholic; new streets were named after saints. One part of town housed Irish fugitives from the Potato Famine, another, French-Canadian lumberjacks. A fire in July 1861 consumed mills, shops, and the railway station, clearing the way for a brick frontage that came to range for nearly a mile on both sides of Kent Street. In 1877 a "Vigilance Committee" set about burning down brothels: each time it happened, newspapers crowed, "another rookery gone." Until the end of the 1880s, the leading municipal question was whether to prevent "the poor man's cow" from browsing in gardens. Eventually free-grazing cows were banished. As an 1892 history of the town pointed out, "In Lindsay, then as today, deception and wrong doing recoil with swift vengeance on the wrong doer."

With its handsome wooden portico, Kent St.'s most imposing structure was the Benson Hotel, erected by an English immigrant, Edward Benson. Lindsay had become the chief town in Victoria County. Canvas awnings sheltered store doorways, and "silent policemen," emplacements that allowed traffic to make U-turns, stood at intersections. By the early 1920s, the Trent-Severn Waterway was completed, having taken 90 years to finish, and railway lines radiated. Victoria and Grey Trust had become Ontario's biggest rurally based finance company. In the gabled and turretted homes lived the North Ward's "Proddies": the Orangemen, the Imperial Order Daughters of the Empire, the WASP first families. The Catholic South Ward had the Frogs and the Black Irish — the lace-curtain Irish, too. In 1924, Old Home Week was rung in by a song, "Lindsay (My Home Town)," specially composed for the midsummer event:

> Lindsay is my hometown,
> No matter where I roam
> There's no place just like Lindsay,
> My dear old childhood's home.

The chorus:

> There are dear old friends in Lindsay,
> None others can compare,
> With childhood's early friendships,
> Most beautiful and rare.
>
> I'll ne'er forget my old home,
> While memory shall last,
> But always treasure in my heart,
> Fond memories of the past.

Edward Allan Lacey was born in 1937. Main-street reminders of his family included the corner offices of Weldon & Lacey; the Hotel Benson; and a few doors away the "House of Quality" maintained by Allan's friend George Beall ("Watchmaker, Jeweller, Optician, Watch Inspector and Eye Specialist for

Canadian National Railways.") Virtually across the street was the Tangney Furniture Co.: Edward's Aunt Alice had married its proprietor, Joe Tangney. Fabian Blanchard *fils* worked in Lindsay; Alex, Alice, and Phyllis became wives and mothers there; Marie-Camille joined the Sisters of St. Joseph, Marion joined the Franciscans. Phyllis tried out the Sisters of the Precious Blood in Peterborough but settled for marriage to Clair Murtha. Grace, neither married to husband nor church, took care of their mother in the family home at 11 Ridout St., an old brick house shrouded by maples.

Nephews and nieces gave these omnipresent aunts and uncles nicknames. Alexandrine was "Alex." Marion's junior siblings called her "Super," after Superman — she was mannish, sharp-tongued, formidable. Marion herself called Marie-Camille, the gentle one who taught at the convent school, "Tim." In keeping with local custom, Fabian, the oldest son of a doctor, was "Doc"; the independent-minded Phyllis became "Tuss." For Edward, Marie-Camille became "Mill"; Grace was "*Tante.*"

Family ties were knotted at dinners, parties, wakes, and weddings, which Toronto cousins, the DeGuerres, sometimes attended, at summer cottages and shoreline excursions. The Tangneys' cottage was at Kennedy Bay on Sturgeon Lake, as was the Laceys' at Snug Harbour, near where the Conservative lawyer and politician Lesley Frost summered. The oldest, and for a decade the only, boy among the cousins, Edward was a brown-haired, dark-eyed child. To open the family album was to see him, aged two, spoon-fed by Tuss on a lakeshore; armed with a snow shovel next to his two-years-older cousin Janet, the eldest daughter of Joe and Alice, equipped with a broom; a year later, a birthday party, and he's holding a balloon.

10 Mill St., telephone 546W, was a brown-shingled, sharp-roofed, square beige house with a tool shed at the back. A front door opened off a big verandah. The living room fronted west; a closet connected an upstairs bedroom to the bathroom. Next to the Laceys, an impoverished family rented a house that Allan owned, but the south-facing Lacey kitchen offered a good view of the corner house at 12 Russell St., three maples up. The Wilfords lived there. Their daughter Susan, a year younger than Edward and, like him, a singleton, was his

first and closest friend. Much of his early childhood was bound up with the Wilfords: picnicking, boating, and berry-picking at a property with a trout-stocked lake. The Wilfords' home had once housed a branch of the Bank of Upper Canada, whose manager lived in what became the Lacey home. Edward's grandmother Marion told him that underground passages connected them but, despite lots of looking, he never found them. He did find earth-blackened coins, one a big fat penny of 1837 showing the new Queen's laurel-crowned profile. Each Victoria Day, the Monday preceding May 24, the Wilfords and Laceys set off firecrackers. With Susan, he played in the attic and corners of her home, and the closet at the foot of his bed, handy for playing hide-and-seek or for dressing up in feather boas. Dining with the Wilfords, one had to wait until the meal's end to drink one's milk, a regulation that appalled him: he was never able to consume food without something to wash it down.

When the Laceys dined, Alex would exclaim, "There's Grace at her kitchen window again; she's got eyes like a hawk!" The Wilfords were Anglican, though sometimes, as an act of piety or from pedagogical instinct, Edward took Susan into St. Mary's Church (full name, Purification of the Blessed Virgin Mary Church), to follow the Stations of the Cross. Grace moved in the circle of the wealthy, North Ward, Protestant families, yet lived in the Catholic South Ward. There were limits — she would not have lived in Punkin Hollow, the poverty-stricken Catholic section leading to the river. For himself and Susan, Edward invented an imaginary family. Susan was "Momma Leelee," whose formal name was "Mrs. Finlay," Edward was "Mr. Leelee," and their child was "Baby Leelee." Ignoring jibes, they dragged the baby's carriage up and down the street.

When Edward had been five, a dentist pulled out a tooth without anyone's telling him what was about to happen, inducing an intractable terror of dentists. He endured the quarantines of whooping cough and scarlet fever. One midsummer morning, his father called him out to the cool whitewashed tool shed arched by Virginia creeper. Allan had trapped something inside a bottle. His father — long lean frame, huge face, precisely trimmed moustache, glasses with gold rims and plastic nosepieces — bent down beside him, showing what spun within the bottle's walls like an emerald top: a hummingbird.

Allan and Alex were so unlike each other that opinion varied as to whether they were ill-assorted, or splendidly compatible. It was proverbial that "a party doesn't start until Alex arrives." Overanxious, fussing, always in a hurry: that was Alex. Sedate, stern, perfectionist, scrupulous, fond of rituals: that was Allan. People said that he'd have made a good bishop, though they agreed that Alex possessed more genuine piety. Perhaps that was why she dared irreverence. She'd say, "It seems so stupid for this damn Lent to come right in the coldest months of the year, when people need their strength."Allan would say, "Now, Alex, don't talk like that." Alex's birthday often inconveniently fell during Lent. During it, her scales fascinated Edward. Small, bell-like, delicate, of polished bronze, they stood on the kitchen table. A good Catholic might eat only one full meal a day with the combined weight of the other two meals not to exceed eight ounces. She weighed breakfast: two ounces of toast, one ounce of eggs, one ounce of butter and marmalade. At noon, two ounces of potatoes, two ounces of fish or vegetable.

The church bells jangled the Angelus at 6, 12, and 18 hours. In the Lacey home, vigil lights burned in the grotto of the Virgin, and the sword-impaled Sacred Heart of Jesus hung on a wall, blazing like a tattoo. Edward went to Mass every Sunday, and every Saturday night to confession. He ate fish every Friday, and on Ember Days and the Holy Days of Obligation. The Laceys' overnight guests tended to be clergy.

They enrolled Edward in a primary school, St. Dominic's, run by the Sisters of St. Joseph, a "separate school," publicly funded, but administered by the Roman Catholic Church. Though it was arguable whether the hovering nuns were stricter than teachers in nondenominational schools, red-faced, bleating Sister Aloysius was wrathful when she caught Edward with his hand under his underpants. Mostly, he was a junior intellectual who'd only look at you sideways, and spoke out of turn. Two chums, Clayton Paquette and Larry Murphy, competed with him academically, though they soon realized they'd never match his vocabulary. He hero-worshipped the feisty Bernard Daigneault who, when a nun shoved him against a wall, told her, "Fuck off!" — an oath virtually unheard of in Lindsay, at least in that school.

One schoolmate, Pat Walker, saw him after mass at St. Mary's, looking small and forlorn in an old windbreaker. On school days he seemed to her head-down lonely, dragging his worn leather bag along the street. When, one day, he brought flowers to a teacher, boys chased him round the school. On winter mornings they lowered him into a sewer, toppled him headfirst into snowdrifts, polished his cheeks with snow and made him eat it. He forgot his lines in a Christmas pageant and burst into tears. His mother forced him into scratchy long woollen underwear, stockings within stockings, boots over shoes, coats inside coats, sweaters on sweaters, mitts, muffs, galoshes, scarves, and earmuffs.

For the cousins, Alex organized costume and Halloween parties. The Tangney children created an imaginary family, "the Buguses." Edward was "Father Bugus," Jan was "Mother Bugus," Marg was "Nuisance Bugus," and the youngest Tangney girl, Marion," Baby Nuisance Bugus." They'd go boating on a lake or take winter rides in a sled that Uncle Joe had fitted out with a noisy motor. In a family album, there was Uncle Joe with a huge muskellunge looped on a stick; the kids and Aunt Marion, espaliered on a ladder.

Winter brought moonlight blue on snow, the red of rosehips on icicled bushes, snowberries' white against whiteness. Edward's breath silvered the air as cold slapped his face. Snowdrifts sometimes rose as tall as houses. At Christmas, he came in to thaw his fingers, and find a tree glowing with lights, tinsel, and orange globes. Under the tree was a pomegranate. He tore the shell open for the translucent bits and pieces, wondering where pomegranates grew.

Nights, the kitchen was warm but in his corner bedroom the wind crept through cracks, frost ferns on the windowpanes. Saturday nights he begged to listen to Foster Hewitt's play-by-play when the Maple Leafs were playing — any excuse to stall bedtime: he sought a cup of cocoa and graham wafers, cajoled his father to tell him another story. But then he had to head upstairs, peel off shirt, sweater, long underwear. The cold floorboards shrank his bare feet as he got into flannelette pajamas, kneeling on goose-pimpled knees to pray to Jesus, Mary, and Joseph, in fine shape for night terrors.

Sugaring parties in early spring brought the congealing of maple syrup on the crust of snow that you ate, cold and warm sweetness mixed. Hating the little mounds of dirty ice that lingered, he sallied out with a hatchet to chop them up. The first butterfly of spring was the Mourning Cloak, cream-and-chestnut, sporting a row of violet dots. In the backyard he dug a little garden in which he managed to transplant the nodding delicate bloodroot. He searched in nooks at the foot of the convent walls for the yellow violet, the rare white violet.

He began to practise the small dispassionate cruelties of childhood. To turn a painted turtle on its back and watch it struggle, to torch a writhing web of tent caterpillars. In June, the lobe-leaved locust tree, showering its little white flowers on him, was his favourite, more than the May-candles of the horse chestnut, more than the scent-heavy lilac. He picked wild strawberries, and later raspberries dangling from dusty roadside bushes. Summers he'd be down in the swamp by the cottage, deep in the alder thickets. Each year he saw a mossback procession on an abandoned road. Once he caught a young one on a log, keeping it in a refrigerated tray where it ate raw hamburger from a matchstick. After a year he released it in the swamp and it swam away, diving, doing what it had to do.

Aged nine, he became a keen lepidopterist, loping across fields with net and poison bottle. One day a tiger swallowtail —a bright yellow-and-black zoot suit with a spot of blue — fluttered over the high walls of the convent behind which, among wimples and endless corridors, he had learned to play the piano. The Tiger Swallowtail drifted to the asters and snapdragons. His net descended. Trapped, the butterfly beat against the muslin. Then came the crisp voice of Marie-Camille: "Édouard, how dare *you* — a gentle boy like you that likes to run and roam and swim in the river — be putting any of the good God's creatures who loves his liberty as much as you to such torture?" Unheeding, he transferred the swallowtail to the cyanide bottle. It subsided, wings still fluttering. Ten seconds later the delicate wings shuddered and stiffened, the sleek body hardened. He pinned it on his mounting board.

Along the jungly river, hobos jumped off and on the freight trains that slowed on the iron bridge. Winos slapped together cardboard huts amid junk bushes and Manitoba maples. There, unspeakable people committed unnameable acts — so Edward told his terrified cousins. Unimpressed, Jan thought that he didn't pull his weight. When Joe Tangney made the girls bring in firewood, Edward was excused; Alice was always making excuses for him, too. One day Edward, 12, Jan, 10, and Marion, 3, were out walking. Marion sentimentally picked a trillium for her mother. Edward belted her, yelling, "You don't pick trilliums!" Jan, not the sort of girl to put up with guff, much less abuse of her little sister, belted him on the nose, breaking his glasses. His feeble response: "You shouldn't hit someone who wears glasses."

To his cousins, the fact that he didn't learn to tie his shoes until he was 8 seemed a tactic to outwit his parents, or just to get attention. He had a cruel side, too. He'd administer nasty pinches, and abandon little cousins in a scary patch of woods for a finely calculated length of time, or leave them alone in a hidden passage of a house, then pretend to be a monster. He threatened to torture their adored pets. It was just talk, but....

For her birthday, Jan got a device to cut up potatoes into thick chips ready for deep-frying. They'd eat monstrous plates of them, which Edward consumed with mayonnaise. His cousins were amazed, though they admitted they tasted all right that way. His aunts and uncles treated him with amused or bemused tolerance. He most liked Grace of the frizzy, mouse-coloured hair, the grey clothes, and huge grey eyes. Grace loved children, infant birds and animals, and couldn't bear to kill even a cockroach or a spider. Spoiling her nieces and nephews, she could be more shrewish than mousy to others; no family gathering was complete without *Tante*'s storming off in mid-meal, enraged by a careless remark or sly verbal thrust.

Meanwhile, Edward's school readers were stuffed with stories of stoicism — the boy on the burning deck, or with his finger in the dyke, or parables involving the industrious beaver. He worshipped a comic strip involving one Invisible Scarlet O'Neill, who solved crimes by gathering evidence while unseen. The nuns of St. Dominic's directed his palpable talents toward holy ends. Aged 11, in a competition in the Peterborough Diocese, he won a prize from Father Peyton's World Rosary Crusade for the best poem on the subject of the rosary in which he mentioned nearly every precious stone in the dictionary. The prize was a rosary blessed by Father Peyton.

Edward had never seen his parents naked. Until the age of 8, he believed that possessing a penis was a personal misfortune, a feeling reinforced when Alex bathed him. But when the Laceys vacationed on Lake Simcoe, he saw people in bathing suits — a revelation. From his parents, he'd gleaned that the relationship of body, sex, and human being was something mysterious and sacred. He gathered only fragmentary information from old medical and legal textbooks. But one day when he was 12, a boy in class said, apropos of nothing, "Go fuck a football player!" Suddenly, for no reason he could fathom, he understood everything: the act of conception, how children were born. "So that's what *it's* for! And that's how they do it! How bizarre!" Before he discovered muscle magazines, he liked to browse through illustrated books on mythology and classical Greek profiles and physiques. Yet he couldn't understand what other boys' sexual agitation was about. Surely masturbation was safer and more satisfactory.

It was 1952 and the program was called *"Les Visites Interprovinciales,"* an exchange of teenagers from Québec and Ontario designed to bring together the French and English solitudes. Edward's exchange partner was Michel, about two years older. Arriving from Lac St. Pierre, Michel was their guest for a month. He ate a lot, drank huge quantities of milk, and grew about an inch in the month. Edward's jabber about poetry didn't mean a thing to him. He asked Edward if he was interested in girls, *filles*, or knew much about them, or if there were any around Lindsay. Edward always answered no.

Then it was Edward's turn for a *visite interprovinciale.* Packed on a bus to Montréal, they arrived too late to catch a connection to Lac St. Pierre. At least that was what Michel said. This was exciting: a night in Montréal. They found a tourist guesthouse on Mountain Street. When the landlady asked, "One bed or two?" Michel was going to say "two" but Edward chimed in that economy dictated one. When they went out, Michel shook him off, but he was happy to be free in a big city. He walked east along Ste-Catherine Street, then down St-Laurent toward the port, sniffing, listening, taking in the neon lights. When he returned, it was two a.m. Michel was apparently asleep. He undressed and slipped into bed beside him. Half an hour passed and Edward's heart was knocking. He knew that Michel was awake, waiting for something to happen. Inch by furtive inch he willed his fingers to creep outward. No hand slapped his away. His hand passed through the vent of shorts, touched something warm and hard. Tentatively he began to stroke it. Then he felt Michel's rough hand brushing the down on his legs, moving upward. Their hands moved faster. He smelled something sharp and yeasty. They slept. In the morning Michel shook him gently awake, smiled at him, and put a finger to his lips.

In the small town by a cold river-lake, he gabbled to Michel's mother, who made breakfasts that began with pea soup and ended with apple pie. He picked berries with Michel's sister. He watched, scandalized and envious, as men and boys walked out of Sunday mass during the sermon to smoke. He learned to sing "A Guy Is a Guy" in French. Michel told his pals about all the *filles* he'd had back in Ontario. Back home, Edward wrote poems alluding to boys whom he secretly loved, with veiled allusions to the hobo jungle by the iron bridge, the scene of furtive sexual experiments. His parents found and destroyed them.

Clayton Paquette, his friend at St. Dominic's, had drowned in the river after he'd dived off a bridge and was trapped in the metal junk at the bottom — Larry Murphy had tried to rescue him. Edward could not believe in his own death. He burned up the concession roads on his bike on moonlit summer nights, dismounting to balance on a snake fence that twitched along a cornfield between sandy hills. The air was warm and windless as he sat, a boy in dark jersey and blue jeans, thin legs dangling, hands crossed, thumbs under his belt. Cars passed on the distant highway, their lights against the sky's pale edge, the darker edge of the woods. The moon crept up the road. He smelled vetch and sweet clover, heard the crickets, and brief laughter from a carful of joyriders. More laughter from camps and cottages, from spits of sand and groves of cedar on far shores. In a small-town dance hall or hotel a party was going on.

He started high school at the three-storey, double-winged, redbrick Lindsay Collegiate Institute — the "Collegiate" signified that it readied its students for university. There, his Aunt Marion had been star of the girls' basketball team. Larry Murphy noticed that Edward would be friendly one on one with him, but grew distant when others joined them. Edward's friend Reg Truax had a cousin, a pretty girl who lived 10 miles out in the country. When she had to stay home because of a broken leg Edward walked out to see her, not, Reg thought, out of romantic interest, but just because he was lonely.

Heading home from school, he'd pass the Victoria Park Armoury, the post office with its clock tower, and then, hitting the main stride of wide Kent St., weaving west in and out among the parking meters, passed the Benson Hotel, his uncle's furniture store, the Chinese restaurant, the Italian grocery, the funeral home. The shopkeepers said, "Here comes Ed."

He lingered in the Carnegie-endowed public library, a redbrick building with limestone foundations and pillars on Kent St., a few steps from a wrought-iron fountain that looked like a hip bath, erected by a temperance society half a century earlier. He'd begun to read books by the time he was 5. He got drunk on homemade cider and became an apprentice kleptomaniac. More than coveting an object, it was the excitement of the criminality, the concealment, the dare, the possibility of being caught and the euphoria of escape, the defiance and outwitting of the organized adult world. Besides a treasured album of Johnny Cash ("The Man in Black"), he played race music on his old monaural: B.B. King, James Brown, Muddy Waters, Howling Wolf — unassimilated outsiders.

He drifted apart from his old friends. They liked hockey; he didn't — his excuse for avoiding it was weak ankles. He told Reg, a superb player, "You are very adjustable. You can adjust to anything." Along with hated compulsory math, one thing Edward could not adjust to was mandatory cadets. In protest, he'd march with right arm and right leg in concert — the way he walked out of uniform. The Physical Education teacher knew that allowances had to be made for so exceptional a student, and made sure he passed. Head down, he beetled fast through the high school halls. Acned, he looked undersized but pugnacious, even with his big dark-rimmed glasses. Sandy Wansbrough, a student friend who, because of dyslexia, was also an unhappy outsider, saw him drop into the school newspaper office after classes ended for the day, not because he was interested, simply to avoid going home. Of whatever happened in the hobo jungle his friends were unaware.

On the *The Tattler* yearbook's literary staff, he contributed poems about dying years, ashen skies, and wind-shaken nights. Kids called him "Denny Dimwit," but also labelled him an egghead; he was the kind of kid who'd protest at getting 98 instead of 100. He disconcerted a teacher, who had 30 years' experience, by correcting her French and Spanish. One evening, guests were calling on Allan and Alex. Suddenly Edward appeared from upstairs. He curtly told them that they'd have to leave since they were disturbing him. He addressed his mother, "You stupid cow!" He applied a self-designed IQ test to his cousins, grading them at the low end. They thought that he set one against another, alternating between niceness to belligerence. He would bang out a piece called "I Can't Sit Down," hooting and hollering, his hands all over the place, the piano practically falling apart. Or his long graceful fingers traced out a medley that somehow ended up as the Moonlight Sonata.

In 1954 the laboured prose in Edward's yearbook-published "Retrospect" mirrored the longueurs of the school year, or perhaps the tedium of having to write a "First Prize Senior Essay." World-weary, it spoke of "dun-deary facts" and "duil slate-grey winter days." Because of study, December was "a period of penance and mortification, obscuring the joy of the normally fresh and healthy Christmas season...", then came "cruel, smiling January," "pale February," and "sodden March." When students emptied lockers, "the winds of June blow dust-whirls on the roads, and flying pollen from the linden trees in flower fills the air, you will think, with a dim, obscure pang of regret, `This, then, is the End'" except "the manifold tasks and occupations which are your inheritance and your duty..."

Everyone agreed that Allan Lacey was dutiful. He'd been practicing law alone after the death of his partner. A little frail —he'd been diagnosed with a heart condition in his 40s — he was careful and conscientious. He dabbled in real estate. He sat on the separate-school board and the public library board. He belonged to the Knights of Columbus. At Christmas he'd disappear to bestow quiet benefactions. In some respects, Edward felt pity for this duty-driven man. He believed that when Allan ran away to enlist in the army it was his sole act of self-liberation. He was a lawyer. He believed in wills.

Sometimes Allan and Alex took Edward to Toronto, an hour and a half away, staying at the Westminster Hotel, whose smorgasbord was Toronto's first. It amazed him that he could go back to fill his plate as many times as he wanted. From Toronto he imported precious records — sometimes for Marg, his favourite cousin. Allan and Alex were kind to Marg, the daughter they didn't have. Marg realized that something wasn't right, that Edward didn't seem like other boys. Allan, perhaps realizing that unless something changed, his family life was in a downward spiral, became more tolerant. He had sought to mould his son, but Edward was unmouldable.

Bishop Fulton J. Sheen had told them on TV that "The family that prays together stays together." Uncle Edward had become a Redemptorist priest who, when he returned to Lindsay from the prairies, stayed with the Laceys. Edward argued at length with him about religion. He contended that one should love life and people for themselves, but Father Bud countered that one should love them only because they were God's creations: God came first. He began to quarrel violently with Allan about where he should attend college. Top of his class, he refused to apply to St. Michael's College at the University of Toronto, Allan's alma mater. Instead, he chose nondenominational University College.

He was now equipped with permanent parts of his vocabulary: "strange," "for some reason," "alien," "odd," "peculiar," and "anyhow." He packed away his treasured alarm clock, and consigned his butterfly collection box to the cool cellar. Up to then, he thought, he'd been watching human beings for cues as to how he should behave. If they were obsessed with sex, he would follow their example, but his fascination lay in their fascination. To live with another human being to share a bed for the rest of his life, seemed to him intolerable. It was as though he had to teach himself, act by act, lesson by lesson, how to be a human being. On his own, the only emotion he felt was pity. Births, birthdays, anniversaries, marriages, deaths left him unmoved. Even though he ate, excreted, slept, needed money and company, he felt neither in, nor of, the world. He didn't have the slightest competitive instinct. Politics he held in contempt. He did not hunt. He did not fish. He had not learned to drive a car. He never watched TV. College was next... and then what? In this year, 1959, bearing scars disguised to others but undisguisable to himself, he was on the cusp, the brink, the trembling lip of manhood.

2

MAN ON CAMPUS

September 1955-September 1959

Twitching on crossed wires
of sex and ambition
this young man academic and delinquent
walks astigmatic streets.

~ Portrait of Someone Familiar

Hair flying, arms akimbo, he hurtled across the campus. But if there was purpose in his hurry, some imperative destination, he could not have defined it. At present, the long strides took him from residence to classroom. He roomed in Hutton House in the males-only Sir Daniel Wilson Residence, opened a year earlier. Sir Daniel Wilson, not that Edward much cared, had been the Scots polymath who, arriving in 1853, became President of University College, founded as a nondenominational redoubt against its clerical neighbours: Trinity, St. Michael's, and Victoria, respectively Anglican, Roman Catholic, and Methodist, uneasily cohabiting within the federated pattern that Wilson had pioneered. UC, which tended to attract minorities, especially Jews, had a muted tradition of dissent, sometimes expressed by prickly campus newspaper editors who resigned or were sacked. Yet to attend UC could be a rung on the career ladder. Two graduates, the political archrivals Mackenzie King and Arthur Meighen, became Canadian Prime Ministers.

Hutton House, three-storeyed, gabled, copper-roofed, its brick a becoming shade of dull mustard, raised an unbroken façade along St. George Street just south of Hoskin Avenue. Beyond a stone arch, six houses comprised it, each with a resident don: the 183 undergraduates dined in the north wing. The houses were disposed around a small park that funnelled into the wider campus and closest, stone-clad, grey, lumpish UC. Inside it was a rotunda, two upper-storey halls, a library, and the Junior Common Room, a smoky den for card players. In a ground-floor corner a spiral staircase was marked by the college's mascot, a lavishly carved dragon. Oak doors of classrooms led off tall dim wood-panelled corridors configured in a rectangle whose ogival windows gave onto a pillared quad known as the "Cloisters."

South of UC, drab squat buildings formed stations of a grassy arc, or a uniformly glum wall along College Street between Spadina and University Avenues. North was Hart House, a grey mullioned combination of medieval abbey and YMCA, endowed by the farm-machinery money of the Massey family. North across Hoskin Avenue, before it devolved into Queen's Park Crescent and the rear of the provincial legislature, was the neo-Gothic, Oxonian face of Trinity College, with its framed portraits of robed Anglican bishops and begowned students. Further afield, on the eastern edge of Avenue Road, were wholesome Victoria, and the Basilian bulk of St. Michael's.

In this monochrome setting, UC had its share of eccentrics. But even among them, Student No. 550474 was exceptional. For example, how he dressed: the big round dark-tinted glasses, the seldom-changed plaid shirt, pockets stuffed with soiled Kleenex, which he often pulled out and rolled into fuzzy balls. A fellow student, an anthropologist in the making named Bruce Trigger, noted Edward's Sunday ritual: he would ceremoniously drop a metal statuette of the Virgin Mary from his bedroom window. Retrieving it one day, he found that a piece of the Virgin had broken off, and announced that she'd given birth. He regaled people about his project to record graffiti poems in men's washrooms — not always about sex — for linguistic analysis. What he actually analyzed were other students' personal letters that he'd winnowed from the Hutton trash. But he closely guarded his own privacy.

By 1955, all the World War II veterans had graduated. A breakthrough generation replaced them, divided between those bent on becoming judges or taking over Dad's business, and those who considered themselves outside, or forming a new, mainstream. White and male, Edward was exempt from the prejudice black students faced — or the segregation of women. Hart House once invited Jay Macpherson, then making a name as a poet, to give a talk, under the impression that she was a man. They might have checked: she was Dean of Women at Victoria College. Women, those dangerous creatures, were allowed in only through the Hutton front door during restricted hours, but the more permissive dons let them at other times, by the back door.

Having plunked down $340 tuition, Edward recorded his Lindsay address as 42 Russell St. E., which was not his home, nor that of any of his family. In opting for a major in Modern Languages & Literatures, he made the right, indeed inevitable, choice. Totalling 13 firsts and two seconds, his Grade XIII marks, among them a near-perfect 98 in French Composition, qualified him for the Edward Blake Scholarship, worth $100 plus $100 against tuition for up to four years. A Hutton group photo from the start of the year shows him in the second row, got up in jacket, shirt, and tie. In the front row are young men with crossed legs and baggy socks, his friend Bob McCaldon, in second-year Pre-Med, at the end. Grinning next to Claude Bissell, the Dean of Residence, was Paul Weingarden, a final-year student from Windsor. Before Christmas, Paul was ejected from residence for aiming a bank of film floodlights at a nearby nurses' residence. Bob, a co-conspirator, escaped penalty. Paul rented an apartment and hosted Sunday beer parties. On weekends they'd stuff themselves at $1.50-a-head buffets at the Town and Country. Edward became a regular on Monday nights for a binge of horror movies. When he drank in beverage rooms, laws decreed where, when, what, and how you could drink. But on Bloor Street, taking advantage of the King Cole Room's lax enforcement, students still managed to get drunk.

Although he grumbled against a diet of useless classics, Edward conceded that he had excellent teachers. His French professor, the poet Robert Finch, had written:

Think of each house you live in as a tent
That holds you insecure from wear and tear
And do not let its neighbourhood grow dear
And never call its welcome permanent...

Finch, born on Long Island in 1900 to English parents, had studied piano with Alberto Guerro, the teacher of Glenn Gould, and harpsichord under Wanda Landowska. He kept a piano in his office. On occasion he limped slightly, which his more imaginative students attributed to his having contracted, while travelling in France, a disease that had been unknown since the Middle Ages. A quiet, reticent, precise man with a velvety, Vincent Price-like voice, he was soberly conspicuous in black homburg and three-piece suit. He advised Edward that hard work habits would evade despair. Teaching German was pale, tense, chain-smoking Laura Hofrichter, a Jewish survivor of Shoah and an authority on Heinrich Heine, who made her office open house to Edward. She lived on Willcocks Avenue, where a neighbour was Barker Fairley, a craggy Yorkshireman who, after teaching at the raw new University of Alberta in Edmonton, had became Professor of German Literature here. He had performed the mind-bending task of translating Goethe's *Faust*.

Behind Edward's vindictive mask was a gentle face that he showed to a few, like Roslyn Paleff, the daughter of immigrant Russians, a fellow student in French and German. To her, he was unfailingly helpful, with a sweet warm smile. She sensed he'd come from a terrifically good background. He always called her "Miss Paleff." When she despaired at not being able to complete a task he was kindly, empathetic. A friend in French class, another daughter of immigrants, was a Jewish girl of vivid intelligence named Ruth Brown, who he liked to tease for having the same name as one of his favourite rhythm 'n' blues artists. To her, he was a bit like a martinet schoolmaster: given a foreign word, he'd supply several spellings and pronunciations. He had the small child's facility for learning languages. But she wondered whether he'd ever grow up.

For Robert McCaldon, he was a guy who could attend the first day of class to learn what was being covered, skip classes all year, and still get an A. What Bob, his girlfriend Jane, and everyone else noticed that what he pounded out on the residence piano, was not the hit parade of Patti Page ("How Much is that Doggie in the Window?"), Doris Day, and Pat Boone, or the sonatinas he'd learned to play as a boy, but rhythm 'n' blues and rock 'n' roll — Little Richard, Chuck Willis, Bo Diddeley.

Deciphering his obsessions and stories was like peeling an onion. He reported to Bruce that he'd rebuffed priests from St. Michael's College, likely his father's delegates, who'd urged him to transfer. His first-year marks in English (modern American and British poetry), French, German, and Spanish were First Class. Only Geology, which he had to take to dispose of a science requirement, was substandard: he garnered a meagre 57, not quite failing but, in quaint U. of T. terminology, "Below the Line."

He plainly considered below the line two poems, "Snowflakes" and "The Tiger" which, written at age 13, and now appeared in the anthology *First Flowering: A Selection of Prose and Poetry by the Youth of Canada*. On learning of their impending publication, he furiously blamed their disinterment on his mother and insisted that a note be inserted: "I wish to dissociate my present self from these two poems as they represent an emotion excrescence of my adolescence, of which I am now neither proud nor ashamed, but which I consider neither to be good poetry, nor to give promise of better, unless in the very narrow vein of the nature lyric. — E. L." But he met and liked the editor, Anthony Frisch, who, like Robert Finch, happened to be gay. Northrop Frye amiably reviewed the collection under the headline, "First Deflowering."

Global events in the autumn of 1956 triggered a nervous crisis. After Nasser had seized the Suez Canal, the British and French bombed Egyptian airfields and Israel invaded the Sinai Peninsula. Then the Soviet Union stomped out any chance of democracy in Hungary. Edward could not explain why these events upset him so, unless it was because they demonstrated how Authority crushed Hope. Some 60,000 cold, hungry Hungarian refugees came to Canada.

As his own revolt against authority, he mimeographed a manifesto denouncing university deans, dons, and donors, and affixed copies across the campus. Hearing of this — so the

story went — Claude Bissell got the dons up at 6 a.m. to remove
them. After Edward assaulted a don or two — without inflicting
much in the way of physical damage — he was expelled from
Hutton House. With his parents' consent, he was consigned to
the psychiatric wing of Toronto Western Hospital. When Allan
and Alex came to clear out Edward's room, Bruce Trigger met
them, who he thought resembled grandparents more than parents. Edward had often ridiculed them, mocking his mother's
piety and her attempts to teach catechism to "Mongoloid idiots."
Doctors ascribed schizoid tendencies to him, and one prescribed
the heavy-duty tranquillizer chlorpromazine. When his friends
visited him he showed them a sock he'd filled with pills when
the nurses weren't looking. Upon his release, he was assigned
to a psychiatrist in the university's Faculty of Medicine. Edward
made sure to maintain ascendancy over him.

The traumas of autumn 1956 did not drastically affect
his marks: he won a book prize given by the Federal Republic
of Germany but his course average slipped. When he resumed
studies in September 1957, he lived on Huron, a street of rooming
houses on the campus's western edge. A resolute non-joiner,
he lacked the college spirit of student-paper headlines ("U.C.
Enthusiasm Unprecedented.") He preferred, not TV, but the
dark enveloping ambiance of the movie-house, to read a play
rather than see one performed, to listen to a recording rather
than hear a live orchestra. He found nothing in the strained
voices and rubbishy libretti of opera. He saw no special virtue in
poetry readings: reading in private better permitted a wealth of
alternative versions. He wanted to live in a world of books.

There was something warlock-like about him. Indeed,
he claimed that he was a witch. He stood too close to people,
menacing their personal space. He acquired the nickname, "The
Road Runner," for his habit of rapidly weaving head-down
among dining-hall tables. Attending his odd progress, students
looked up from their dinners and called "Beep! Beep!" Among
the vendettas he pursued, one target was Walter Bowen, a young
cousin of Claude Bissell. He took to entering dining hall just
behind Walter, using him as a screen to avoid the Beep-Beeps.
He stalked or shadowed him to class, or to his relatives' home,
where he would camp on the lawn. After Bruce Trigger had

stomach cramps on the day he had to write two exams, Edward put it about that he'd cast a spell on him. Bruce passed his year anyhow.

Ruth Brown had introduced him to her boyfriend, John Robert Colombo, a third-year Arts student. Serenely leonine in profile but given to flares of temper if tweaked, John was waist-deep in small-press work and fine printing. On their first encounter, Edward talked for hours about poetry. John published him in magazines, chapbooks, and broadsheets, and caused others to publish him, too. Edward could quote at length and at will from any poem he had ever read. Until he met him, John had never heard of Lindsay, but from what Edward said, the town beggared Sodom and Gomorrah. Hypersensitive, self-dramatizing, he proclaimed that he wished to die of venereal disease in his mother's arms. John thought he was Toronto's Rimbaud, though destined to become, not a slave-trader and arms-dealer, but their victim. When John asked him for a poem, he would produce a crumpled bulging grocery bag and extract paper scraps with multiple versions of a poem written in snub-nosed pencil. There were a lot more where they came from. Often in strict verse-forms, they were full of puns, closeted gay allusions, archaisms like "carven" and "curven."

The well of influence into which he dipped included a few canonical greats — Heine, Walt Whitman, and Emily Dickinson—but mainly the lesser known: Trumbull Stickney, Ernest Dowson, Dunstan Thompson. His private anthology of American poetry contained large tracts of Dickinson and Edgar Allan Poe, as well as Conrad Aiken, the Cranes — Stephen and Hart — Delmore Schwartz, and Muriel Rukeyser. What moved him most were the R & B heirs of the ballad tradition, epitomized in Chuck Willis's version of "C. C. Rider." Among Canadians, he admired the cerebral style of Robert Finch, not the visceral Irving Layton. When Edward attended a Layton reading and the poet delivered the line "as for the wife, a little alcohol parts her thighs," a student in the front row guffawed. To Edward's disgust, Layton revelled in the laugh. Forgiving Layton his ego-mania, mindful of the rebuffs he'd endured in his battle for free speech, at least he kept awake, unlike during the lecture Stephen Spender gave on Friedrich Schiller — it was not so much that

Spender was soporific, he said: it was the combined effect of him *and* Schiller.

He only knew glancingly the sibylline Jay Macpherson, author of the acclaimed poetry collection *The Boatman.* To his delight, she once remarked that his poems were "all gems, and all of them flawed." Although Macpherson and James Reaney, teacher-poets who had studied under Northrop Frye, were contrary indicators, he thought that English studies harmed the creative writer. Among the aspiring writers in the vicinity, David Helwig seemed to him versatile, talented, full of lively appetites, yet an intelligent conformist destined to join the literary-academic establishment. Disdaining careerism, Edward quoted Dickinson that one should "reduce no Human Spirit / To Disgrace of Price..." However diffident he seemed to be about publication, he seemed to beg for it. He claimed to rigidly separate poems from personal life, yet they were full of "I." Like John Colombo, he loved pseudonyms, submitting a batch of poems to *The Fiddlehead* literary quarterly as "N. B. Carr."

When he turned up one night at a meeting of a writers' group, he met Henry Beissel. A 16-year-old at the end of World War II, Henry had studied in battered Cologne, then at the University of London. Coming to Canada, he completed a B.A. in a year, and proceeded headlong into studies for a Ph.D. in English. He had left his Spanish first wife, and moved in with a woman from Danzig, Ruth Heydrasch, who was pregnant with their child. Laura Hofrichter, who taught both Henry and Edward, told the former that Edward had "an uncanny ability to get at the heart of linguistic problems." To Edward, Henry seemed, like Anthony Frisch, a cultivated European lost in the Canadian Barrens. Their loathing of Roman Catholicism was a further link. Edward, Henry thought, had a vision of a world in which God had died, everything was now permitted, and people had again become mere animals.

In the spring of 1958 *Gargoyle*, a UC student journal, published Edward's translations of André Chénier, the classicist poet guillotined during the French Revolution. Written under the guidance of Robert Finch, they won the Norma Epstein Award in Creative Writing. The *Varsity* noted that Lacey did not wish to comment on his work except to express gratitude and to call his work "a sort of pastiche." Come exam time, Edward's marks in his Honours subjects remained safely First Class, though he slumped in Greek and Roman History, withdrew from Oriental Lit, and reaped an ignominious 37 in Economics, its substitute. He had to redo an exam in August, which he passed, barely.

Barker Fairley had retired in 1957. Decades earlier, Barker had consorted with the Group of Seven painters, in whom Expressionism met the Precambrian landscape. A Communist fellow traveller, he wrote for the *Canadian Forum* of the 1920s, taking part in one of Canada's cyclical eruptions of cultural nationalism. Encouraged by Robert Finch, he began to paint. For him, a portrait was collaboration between artist and sitter: he had collaborated with Laura Hofrichter, John Colombo, and Henry Beissel. In 1958 it was Edward's turn. He went to Barker's home to sit in a captain's chair in a little studio on the second floor. Barker, putting on a painter's smock and a pair of glasses, drew a charcoal outline on the primed Masonite surface, and then put in colour — there were not many colours. Against a dull brown background, Edward wears a dull green sweater, his facial tones brown and cream. The man-boy looks studious, his shoulders emerge sharply from a boatnecked sweater, the arms angular against the curve of the chair. A dark crow's wing slightly angles across his forehead, the face is a triangle, glasses clamped on a Roman nose. The eyes are oval, dark, acute, troubled behind their lenses. His lips are pursed.

He was about to enter his final UC year. That summer he lived on Harbord St., One Sunday, at Ruth Brown's request, he took her to mass; ecumenically he'd also attended synagogue with John. Edward was late in calling for her, and proceeded to get lost around Dundas and Queen Streets, looking for, and missing, the 11 a.m. High Mass at St. Michael's Cathedral. They did make it to the noon Low Mass. He pencilled a letter to John to tell him "what you already know — that I think she's a perfectly lovely girl."

John inspired envy. Edward was awed by his rate of output, range of reading, and burgeoning reputation as a man of letters. When Edward was moderately happy he didn't want to write, which made him feel guilty. He wrote John:

Having nothing else to do these last weeks —
tho' I must soon begin looking for work — or
sleeping in parks — I've been going over what
poetry I've written... in the past 8 years or so,
trying to establish what is good — if anything...
I can find scarcely 40 pieces I like; and not more
than a dozen that are printable. If I believed in
inspiration—and in waiting unperturbed for
the afflatus — in ripening slowly like a medlar
tree, this w'd be all right. Again, if I believed in
poetry as work; or in poetry as a combination
of inspiration & work, I c'd proceed tranquilly,
knowing that in the end, by mere mathematical
laws, I'd produce a good poem. Unfortunately, I
believe in poetry as language in a state of crisis,
as a morbid secretion...."

On his rare returns to Lindsay, he partook of downtown snacks with Aunt Grace. His long-widowed grandmother,
Marion Blanchard, had died. In the aftermath, Grace moved out
of the house they shared. Grace once told him that everyone had
just one chance in life, and she had bungled hers. Men on street
corners whistled at her shapely legs, an attention she pretended
to deplore but, he thought, actually enjoyed. Her life consisted
of masses, rosaries, novenas, family, and work at the Hydro office. She was waiting, he thought, for someone to save her from
herself. Once they walked an abandoned road and stumbled on
a patch of wild strawberries. Getting down on their knees, staining their clothing, they crawled to pick the fragrant elusive little
berries.

When home, Edward slept up to 11 hours a day, thinking that he could, if he willed it, become all things, yet had no
will to become anything. Was homosexuality a matter of *will*?
Gusts of existentialism from the Left Bank were blowing across
the Atlantic. The existentialists, not the rebels without a cause
or the Beats, attracted him, especially Jean Genet and his ideas
about criminality. He took heart from Genet's *Thief's Journal*, and
translated for himself a passage from Sartre's *Saint Genet*:

... what remains of the book, once closed? An
impression of emptiness, of shadows and of

monstrous beauty, an "eccentric" experience which we cannot fit into the framework of our lives, and which will always be marginal, unassimilable, the memory of a night of debauchery in which we gave ourselves to another man, and found pleasure. There are books which speak to the all in each of us, and we feel that we are *the* crowd when we dip into them. Genet's are brothels into which one glides by a swinging door, hoping against hope to meet no one, and when one is inside, one finds oneself all alone.

When he headed back after a weekend home, his mother always bade him farewell from the veranda.

In Toronto, he had cousins on his mother's side, the DeGuerres, and undertook to teach Latin to their pretty daughter Marion, aged about 13. Their lessons abruptly ended when he told her, "You're getting to be the age when I can't stand women!" Though he had little to do with Lindsay friends who were living or learning in Toronto, an exception was Susan Wilford, now training as a nurse. Her mother had always thought that she and Edward should marry; indeed, he once raised the possibility himself — he may even have been serious. Pat Walker, another Lindsayite, was attending St. Michael's College. One evening, wearing a long dark cloth coat, she encountered him on a sidewalk. "That's a nice coat," he said crisply, and strode on.

One Saturday night he enjoyed watching a riot at the corner of Spadina Avenue and College Street, in which, to his great pleasure, a crowd attacked two rookie policemen. He was picked up, not by the police but by a French-speaking visitor from Montréal. The man invited Edward, posing as a Francophone tough, to come home with him, but when they got to his door, Edward told him that, though he needed money, he didn't want to beat up a compatriot. The man bade him a hasty goodbye.

He told friends that his father could not understand why he didn't want to lead a serious life and do something useful. His friends thought that, as an only child of well-off parents, he'd not have to make his way in the world. Although he wasn't quarrelling with his parents at present, they — particularly his father — could not be expected to understand the allure of the outlaw. He wrote John:

> My search for the criminal, which seems to you merely a romantic & half-hearted essay at slumming—is to be extremely serious; given certain facts of my background, and past life, of which you are unaware, I sh'd have been a criminal long ago...the only escape from certain difficulties of my childhood & early adolescence; and the right escape; since I did not or c'd not take it then, I must do so now. Soon or later. And residence mi't interfere with the delicate balance of my gradual transformation. I have said I consider myself a defeated, and invisibie person. I sh'd not like to consider myself a dead person.

Residence might help make him, of all horrors, a respectable academic. Despite that fear, he returned to Hutton House in September, having assured the Dean, Ian MacDonald, that scuffles would not recur. Several Hutton Housers pledged to attend a reunion on the twenty-fifth anniversary of their graduation. Edward refused to sign up, saying that he found the thought of seeing everyone old and decrepit — at age 40 — too appalling to contemplate.

During Thanksgiving dinner in the dining-hall, the festive spirit was snuffed out when the headwater stopped a graduate student named Vladimir (sometimes called Walter) Degen from taking a second helping. Edward promptly took a second meal himself. Harsh words were said; chastisement followed. The self-governing student Caput next day decreed that Degen's eating privileges were withdrawn for three days and Lacey's for a week. Edward promptly posted a notice on his door saying that he would abstain from "all solid nourishment and all possible liquid nourishment" if his penalty was not revoked or "reduced to within reasonable limits." Reading the works of Gandhi, he would take to his bed in order to conserve energy.

Edward's supporters held hushed conclaves, and the administration conferred behind closed doors. Edward posted a note that he would consider legal action for breach of contract should his punishment not be revised. He then posted a notice suggesting a retroactive suspension of meals for three days, and compensation for all other meals missed. His friends circulated his mimeographed "abbreviated" statement: he would "try to make these few remarks in a spirit of temperance, as I have neither sufficient energy to indulge in vituperations, nor sufficient time and space to make a detailed accusation. As one concerned in the case, I can only say that, to the present evils of Deans, Dons, and donors, this building has added a fourth, irresponsible student government." He noted, "Judgements should be based on facts and ascertained motives, not uncertainties and suspicions. In this case, evidence of a temporal and spatial connection between the two crimes was made proof of a causal connection." He ringingly ended with a quotation from Thomas Jefferson: "IN QUESTIONS OF HUMAN RIGHTS, LET NO MORE BE SAID OF CONFIDENCE IN MAN BUT BIND HIM DOWN BY THE CHAINS OF THE CONSTITUTION."

Dean MacDonald now told his fractious eloquent hunger striker that he'd have to leave residence. In a welcome change from its usual diet of federal politics, intercollegiate football, and intramural fisticuffs, the *Varsity* headlined, "Resident Student Expelled by Dean Following Two-Day Hunger Strike." The photo of a bespectacled, longhaired, tweed-jacketed Edward with a mildly impish grin bore the cutline, "Expelled and hungry, UC honour languages student Edward Lacey contemplates future." Doug Marshall, the *Varsity*'s editor, weighed in: "The case of Edward Lacey, the University College student expelled from residence last Tuesday, is a tragedy of contradictions, person-alities, puerile behaviour and student ineptitude." Lacey bore "the hall-mark of eccentricity which is neither affected on the one hand nor harmful on the other." His "past was exhumed, his `probationary' period declared over, and his future clouded. That is the essence of tragedy.... the protagonist departs form the stage and the audience remains silent."

The next day the *Varsity* devoted a page to Edward's poems put together by John Colombo, accompanied by a crude pencil portrait. An editorial note advised readers that the news-paper chose "to overlook his conflict with his community and concentrate on the contribution he has made.... It is in an at-tempt to acknowledge that contribution that we publish some of his poetry." John wrote that "Lacey is more than a poet — he is an artist whose expression is his way of life. " Preferring Little Richard to William Shakespeare, Lacey "cultivates the experiences of life as the gardener his narcissus, as the street cleaner his daily toil" and "somehow manages to resolve the chaos of the Great City with the insidious solitude of the pastoral." He was "a man who feels that the world without and the world within are strange, beautiful, fascinating — sees existence in its frightening intensity."

Meanwhile, Edward had tucked a suitcase under each arm and taken temporary lodgings in the Sigma Alpha Mu frat house. In the January 1959 issue of *Gargoyle*, UC's literary magazine, John profiled Edmund Carpenter, an expert on Eskimo art and collaborator of Marshall McLuhan, asking him about the Lacey incident. Comparing Edward to Oliver Twist, Carpenter concluded, "Things are getting pretty bad around here when a guy can't steal a turkey dinner!"

Edward drunkenly pounded a residence don on the chest, denouncing him as a "prick." He later explained that since everyone called him a prick behind his back, he thought it was time someone said it to his face. He threatened to rape one of his Modern Languages classmates, a prim-and-proper girl of spectacular academic achievement, though it was doubtful that she was in any danger. He warred with a Trinidadian student named Michael Sylvester. Tall, lean, dangerously good-looking, Michael had a reputation for racial touchiness, brawling belligerence, and for preying on white girls. Edward reported that Michael had threatened to expose him as a homosexual and had plotted to kill him. To David Lewis Stein, a campus journalist, he was all moderation and good sense, stating that "Most of the benefits of the university have been largely incidental. I have not always found the courses stimulating but the staff of University College has been almost always helpful." He merely asked leeway to follow his own path: "I have found that the best way to be left alone is to go underground and remain completely passive. Unfortunately, this is almost impossible in the academic world. I have fought, on matters of principle, administrators who did not show humour and a sense of proportion in dealing with me."

Impressed by their daughter's sensitive intelligent friend, Roslyn Paleff's parents offered him a place to stay after his residence expulsion. He declined. Roslyn had been going through angst and anomie, wondering why she was in university at all. Edward convinced her that study was worthwhile. He also impressed another female undergraduate and daughter of immigrants, Haide Polacsek, who'd been born in Austria. Taking languages at UC, she was smitten by this gentle attentive boy — a contrast to her authoritarian father. She'd meet him in the library stacks, where she had a part-time job. Although they didn't date, they had long talks about books, a little German varying their English. But, reading his poems, she realized she and he could have no romantic future.

On April 15 in the national weekly, *Maclean's Magazine*, Barbara Moon's "University of Toronto: Can it survive sheer size?" noted that Edward's expulsion from residence was "curiously suggestive" about UC — not only because Lacey had "embarked on a one-man rebellion but also because he went away and made a sonnet out of fresh memory":

> *The yellow residence was not built of bile*
> *But bricks, not bones but beautiful bequests.*
> *Behold it, golden in the sinking west,*
> *The lordly, godless and endowèd pile;*
> *Dons stroll its broad green lawns, bereft of guile,*
> *Kindly men, light of learning, free of jest;*
> *And students dream by, clad in Ivy best,*
> *And elm leaves tilt down softly all the while.*
> *There was a time when I once roamed those halls*
> *Innocent in my light and laughing morning,*
> *Knew friendship, treason and autocracy;*
> *But now I hear, without an unseen wall,*
> *The soundless voice again of my first warning,*
> *"All shalt thou have, who hast hypocrisy."*

The horse chestnuts and lilacs were coming into bloom as he wrote his final exams. He placed first in the French and German Division of Modern Languages and Literatures, a standing that he'd achieved for three of four years, and won a Woodrow Wilson Fellowship for graduate study.

Ruth, John, and Roslyn were to graduate with him. The UC convocation came on May 28. An hour before the event, students in black gowns and mortarboards assembled. When a candidate was to receive a degree, each was to mount the platform and kneel upon a stool before the Chancellor, and place hands within his hands. He would then intone "*Admitto te ad gradum.*" Simultaneously, a bedel would place a hood on his shoulders. The candidate was to rise, the hood having been removed by the bedel, and depart. Before this execution-like procedure could take place, however, an incident in the UC quadrangle astonished the throng. They saw a silver-haired man, a white shirt draped across his arm, chasing his son in an attempt to make him wear the shirt instead of the one he was wearing: wide-collared, black, and patterned with a gold spider-web. The father was Allan Tasker Lacey, the son was Edward Allan Lacey.

After three decades of lawyering, Edward's father had done well. He collected Victorian antiques and travelled abroad for the first time. In 1959, his summer-cottage neighbour, Leslie Frost inherited the premiership of Ontario. Frost, whom the Toronto newspapers liked to call "Uncle Leslie" and "the Laird of Lindsay," boasted that the view from a Kent Street barber's chair was all a premier needed in order to know the province. The long run of Conservative governments Frost served and led was a political desert for Allan Lacey, an hereditary Liberal. He had hoped to become a judge but, shut out, had to settle for a King's Counsel honorific.

Reading Lindsay headlines like "353 Dogs, 198 Cats Receive Vaccination" that summer of 1959 made Edward comatose. He got a job as a research assistant in archives dealing with the musty Ontario past, and wrote a scholarly piece for the *Ontario Historical Review*, "The Trials of John Montgomery," about an obscure incident, an obscure figure, and an obscure event in world history, the Upper Canada Rebellion of 1837. Closer in time, it seemed to him that he had learned nothing in four years that he didn't know already, or couldn't have picked up. Poets could never be academics, nor could travellers. That summer Bruce Trigger encountered him limping along the street. The injury had happened the previous night, he said, while he was drinking.

Edward's friends debated whether he posed as a homosexual—his nun teachers made him one, he claimed, by forcing him to play female parts in plays—or to maintain an image of outrageousness. During his first year at UC, he'd remarked that he thought of joining a drama society but found he could not tolerate the "bitchy fairies." With straight friends, he never discussed his cruising, though a few, like John Colombo, guessed at it. Edward would typically talk about some "person" he was attracted to. This was to be expected. His friends might be tolerant or oblivious, but homosexuality was popularly deemed a crime or a disease. Gay public encounters were furtive — fear of the law alone made them so, though the risk could add its own erotic frisson. A campus path known as "Philosopher's Walk" was known to gays as a relatively safe trysting place (though on one occasion some rowdies from Trinity College embarked on a self-appointed mission of street-clearance), and harassment was mostly confined to someone jumping out from behind a bush with a "Boo!" Gays did not comprise an organized community, much less a political force, and a middle-aged bachelor of artistic inclinations like Robert Finch was not automatically assumed to be gay.

Pick-ups could occur in a bar for the older set or in one for young "refined" men, in a few beer halls and hotel beverage rooms, the darkness of certain movie theatres. Quick sex could happen in Queen's Park near the legislature and the university, Allen Gardens downtown, and High Park, much further west. On campus there was Philosopher's Walk, and the dark recesses of Varsity Stadium's indented outer wall. Campus police neglected university washrooms. In the Greyhound Terminal and all-night restaurants, washroom walls bore provocative or enigmatic messages. In Union Station, a sporadic mating dance involved teenagers' stares and pivoting hips in tight jeans. Edward would stand by the ramp and pretend to look up the Sunday trains to Stratford, buy a morning paper and pretend to read it. One of the boys would glide over.

Such encounters speckled his poems with snatches of overheard exchanges. He wrote a poem, "Interlude," after a winter trip to New York, when he said he'd wandered the streets and prostituted himself: "Night came, and I shall never know / who stood beside me in the snow..." During his final year he had become obsessed with Mirvyn Hanna, a sociology major a year junior, who lived in Hutton House. Mirvyn would get poisonously drunk, and lean out windows, calling into the night things like, "What is understanding? Do you understand? You're all I have left, Edward."

One day in late summer his high school friend Reg Truax, who'd been attending UC but had seen nothing of him other than his picture in a newspaper at the time of his residence expulsion, spotted him heading south on Yonge St. in the general direction of Union Station. When Reg hailed him, Edward said, "I'm leaving for Mexico." But perhaps Reg had misheard the destination. Perhaps he had said "Texas."

3

LONE STAR STATE

September 1959-April 1961

I came; I was an alien; why should Texans
understand a creature from another planet?
Enough, they tolerated me, in their odd way.

~ Tejas

The recipient of a Woodrow Wilson Fellowship at the University of Texas arrived by train in a thunderstorm. It was 100° F. in Austin. He got a room at the YMCA and took a cab to the cowboy bars. After a shared bottle of peach brandy, a Louisianan took him home, but painful drunken pawing drove him out. A taxi took him to the tiny Manhattan, where the bartender asked for I.D. Edward startled him by pulling out of his pocket the underwear he'd hurriedly stuffed there. Drunker, he fell into talk with a thin rangy young man named Charles Heyden. Together, they walked under a big moon to Charles's place near the university. Though Charles plied him with drinks, he regained his room at the Y. Thinking of Charles, he masturbated and fell asleep. When he got up, the washbowl was full of sphinx moths that had died in the night.

Austin was in central east Texas, with Houston and San Antonio a vertex of a triangle. People told him that he'd arrived in "the squarest little town in the southwest." He soon moved

into Charles's apartment on San Antonio St., one of four rooms
built above garages behind the home of the aged Miss Maude
Cartledge. Climbing over the garages was a juanmecate vine
with red, heart-shaped flowers, which Miss Maude called the
"queen vine." She was intrigued by Edward's growing collection of empty wine bottles, among them his favoured Zlatni's
Yugoslavian Muscat.

Charles Gervin Heyden, a year younger, had been born
in Maryland but mainly grew up in Florida. After living in New
Jersey, he attended Washington and Lee University, and then
transferred to the University of Texas, major in psychology, minor in sociology. During his first days with Charles, Edward
thought he'd found affection and protection. But Charles, he
thought, stalled him from becoming more active, or at least,
more reciprocal, in sex, bullied, nagged, and ragged him, invaded his privacy, and tyrannized him. This egomaniac, Edward
thought, foisted his views of others on them, disappointed when
they didn't conform. Yet Charles, who kept looking for mean-
ings long after other people had given up, impressed him. The
intense relationship, equally conflicted for Charles, intermingled
love and hate. One morning after Edward came home incapably
drunk, Charles said, "I raped you last night." Edward said, "Oh,
how charming."

He abhorred Charles's fem affectations. He couldn't
reconcile them with Charles's active role in sex; it was like a
woman's doing him with a dildo. Charles thought he was a
self-hating "anti-homosexual homosexual" who hugged Roman
Catholic values. Edward considered that Charles's concept of a
gay community was synthetic: there were only human beings
— why did Charles retreat into this silly little corner of life and
make such a big deal of it? Only stupid Americans would do
that.

Supercilious about how Charles wrote and spoke, he
thought his problem was metathesis — the spelling and speech
disorder that enriched the world with spoonerisms — clinically
noting that Charles's inverted letters and clipped words followed a pattern. His first clue came when Charles called himself
a "human hatrack." He'd meant "packrat." In turn, Charles disliked the fact that Edward wore the same reeking towel around

his neck for months. But in such an oppressive, oppressed place, where rightwing Christians assailed anybody who did not conform to their mean brand of righteousness, Edward was free of class and race constraints. He built no barriers against people. He was a free spirit, and Charles needed freeing.

Charles tried — or Edward thought he'd tried — to set his room on fire. After consulting a campus psychiatrist, he moved to an apartment one next door. On campus, he took dawn sunbaths on the Batts Hall lawn below the statue of Thomas Jefferson — or maybe it was Jefferson Davis. When he walked across the flat burning space of the mall in cloudless noonday heat, he had the feeling that the tower was an altar readied for a sacrifice. Meanwhile, his friend John Colombo was contemplating a spuriously posthumous *Complete Poems of E. A. Lacey.* In a tongue-in-cheek introduction, he wrote:

> Edward Lacey died suddenly on June 6, 1960, in Texas at the age of twenty-two. His death came as a shock to his close friends in Toronto and Lindsay and was regretted by those who knew his work and had admired his poems. Lacey had many times expressed the fear that he would die suddenly at an early age, and at one point he told me that in the case of his death I was to do what I wished with any of his poetry.

John added, "It is to be regretted that Lacey wrote what he did in such a disorganized fashion with no thought to possible publication." In real life, not fictional biography, Edward thought that in publishing his gay poems, John had shown courage. Toronto, the "Queen City," was still very much a closet queen. The poet and professor Jay Macpherson advised that some of Edward's poems were publishable, but not enough of them to make a book. Edward had some sport with John's role as a campus poetry editor by submitting work allegedly from undergraduates in Public Health Nursing, Mechanical Engineering, and Forestry. He also wrote Bruce Trigger, now in graduate school at Yale, to ask why the best universities were in uninteresting towns like "this god-damn insular little German-fundamentalist clean college and legislature town, with 12 churches within a block of the university."

Among professors in the Linguistics Department were E. Bagby Atwood, with a bloodhound face and bloodshot eyes, hard-drinking, kindly, and helpful, and A. A. Hill, "an old mummy," who was his graduate adviser and who, Edward said, owned the copyright to "Happy Birthday to You," composed at the turn of the century by two maiden aunts. Edward soon learned to play off Hill against W. P. Lehmann, another eminent teacher. Linguists, he thought, tended to have speech defects, oral fixations, and personality disorders. Any linguist he knew who wasn't homosexual was unhappily married. Or both. Yet linguistics seemed the most logical and rational of disciplines.

When he went home for Christmas break, his father was abruptly called from the dinner table with the news that his office was burning down. He and his father stood in the cold dark as flames rose and the firemen's snakes of water hissed. He watched his father's long grey face tighten and his white fists clench as wills, deeds, and law books went up in smoke. The next day everything was icicles, ashes, and paper debris.

Back in Austin, he wrote Paul Weingarden, thanking him "for the use of your apt., which I guess you didn't know you would be lending me. I slept well, & would have re-vomited, out of gratitude and a desire to be remembered by you, purely, on our bedspread, had I been able to find it." In January, Edward wrote that Texas beer gave him bad hangovers, although that day's had been caused by having drunk a fifth of Grandpa Meier's Old-Fashioned American Apple Wine. He'd been celebrating completion of an end-of-term exam. He'd enjoyed the course in American society, but the exam depressed him with finicky true-false questions. He'd then shifted roles from student to academic, invigilating a German exam. Luckless freshmen sweated over the complexities of

Der Vater unseres Landes is

> *A - Sam Houston*
> *B - George Washington*
> *C - Fritz Kreisler*
> *D - Fidel Castro*

Soon the students began to find errors in the exam itself. They established such a talkative rapport that he had to remind them that the paper had a time limit.

Next term he would teach elementary German for one semester, five hours a week. He had told the German Department
head that he did not intend to wear a tie to class. The man said
that perhaps it would be a good discipline for him. Edward said
that he had many mental hair shirts already. The head remarked
that tie-wearing put a useful distance between teaching assistants and students, and Edward answered that his bleak personality would enforce all the distance necessary. The head said
that if it was a financial problem he could give him some ties.
Edward declined. Meanwhile, he had to sign and have notarized
a form sent out by the State Legislature, swearing that he was
not, and had never been, a member of the American Lithuanian
Women's Literary Society and about 400 other Commie-front
groups.

February brought the hillside-blooming bluebonnet,
the state flower of Texas, Lady Bird Johnson's favourite. That
month, fuelling his prejudices against queens, a fat Republican
cross-dresser named John Coffman became his new neighbour.
On midnights, he heard Coffman's large feet thunder up the
outside staircase, and the light feet of young hustlers. One day
Coffman appeared on the balcony of his room, wearing mas-
cara and women's underwear. This offended Edward's sense of
decorum, especially since a nearby schoolyard was filled with
grade-school children. He pointed out, "One lives in society,
you know, not in one's own little pigpen."

He'd befriended Mary Jane Cook, a divorced Bryn
Mawr graduate two years away from getting a doctorate in
English. They would sit under a live-oak tree and discuss her
thesis, while crows added their comments. He liked to frequent
a campus patio to eat the best pecan and peach pies ever baked,
but it was in a long-closed restaurant with red-felt flooring that
he copulated with a boy named Gómez, who had the key to
the place. Afterwards, they decided they'd enjoyed it so much
they went back for another turn. At 21, he felt that his Texas
experience was just beginning, and sex and gay life, too. Life
was an open prairie, and might always be.

The previous fall he'd met a student from Dallas named
Reese Copeland with sapphire blue eyes, spun-gold hair, and
uncertain sexuality. Turning 22, Reese brooded about how

he'll look as an old man: spare, wrinkled, mean-looking. A
distraction from his involvement with Reese was the revolving
cast of characters clustered around Miss Maude's apartments.
Roosevelt, black, married, and with children, turned up to have
sex with the white boys. He had the largest penis anyone had
ever seen, or could imagine. The notoriously promiscuous Victor,
a large-nosed Mexican boy, was sometimes called "Victoria" or
"Ramona." Both were objects of derision around the place; they
might be grabbed but you wouldn't want your friends to know
about it.

One of Edward's fellow linguistics students was Byron
Black, son of a much-posted U.S. Army Air Corps Lieutenant
Colonel. About age 15, Byron had seen his drunken father beat
up his mother while he and his younger brother sat on the floor
in pajamas screaming and his mother tried to brain their father
with Byron's plastic clock radio. Accepting himself as gay,
he realized that marriage and children was not a protective-
cover option. He, like Mary Jane, thought of their institution of
learning as the "University of Texas for the Criminally Insane."
Byron was horrified by Edward's predilection for Latino jailbait
and the Black bars of East Austin. Edward insisted that he only
patronized practitioners of three professions: shoeshine boys,
cab drivers, and bartenders.

In March, he was in Galveston on the boardwalk, where
he took a $1 room. Everything, he wrote Paul Weingarden,
was "half-wide-open, half-prohibition." There was "overt
prostitution, yet the `clubs' which serve hard liquor, in one
of which I spent last nite, have locked doors, & peephole, or
window to peer out thro' when a caller comes. But what a relief,
after purer-than-thou Austin! I spent most of the nite listening to
a blind negro piano player; then, when he left at 5 a.m., took over
the piano myself till 9."

On March 25, he wrote the Colombos on the occasion
of John's birthday and of the Feast of the Annunciation. Robert
McCaldon had sent him a copy of the literary issue of the *Varsity*
newspaper: work from "Earwig" (David Helwig) was "a little
better than usual," and 'A Long Story' by "M.E. Atwood"
sounded "apocalyptic, but mildly interesting. "Austin wasn't
the sort of city where you felt like writing poetry. Some tree

was always losing its leaves or budding; just now the live oaks were turning, the elms were in small green leaf, and bees buzzed in the cloud-blue wisteria. "Result — no poetry on the change of seasons, the mutability of things, man's life linked with the changing year." The town wasn't big enough to boast many teenage gangs or bikers. "Result — no urban poetry." You could find plenty of squalor and vice in the Black or Hispanic slums, but you had to look for it.

His letter was interrupted. He had spilled bock beer over hundreds of little cards with rhymes on them, material for his thesis. He taught, he wrote, according to two main principles "(1) keep things hopping; don't spend all period on the same thing; have them at the board, doing dictation, translating German to English and vice versa, and freely conversing in one period (2) stress blackboard work and speaking practice, even at the risk of making the class seem a little juvenile for university." They were shy, so he had to spend far too long prying answers out of them. He thought he would pass them all.

Escapes from academe began in San Antonio, at the end of the old Chisholm Trail, where the Alamo was a little fort-chapel with a bullet-riddled door. From there, he once hitched a ride south with someone he met in the park, who had helped him look in bars he'd visited the night before for eyeglasses he'd lost. They ended up across the river from Del Río in Ciudad Acuño, a little adobe place with a *zona de tolerancia*, a red-light district: the prostitutes roared when he confused Spanish words and asked for a toothbrush instead of a match. On weekends, he and his friends would speed for the nearest Mexico entry point, Laredo, 220 miles away, driving the plunging line of Highway 35 to San Antonio. Then the violet sky and orange landscape of South Texas; the eroded half-human, half-saurian forms of mesas and buttes; the flowers of prickly pears and yuccas; Dilley, watermelon capital of the world, with its cement sculpture of the world's most useless fruit — except, perhaps, for sexual purposes. Finally, Laredo. They crossed to Nuevo Laredo by a bridge over the Rio Grande, waved on by Texas Rangers. Then languid, violent Mexico, carnivalesque bars, and boys. He never affected an effeminate manner: Mexicans didn't call him a *maricón*. According to Byron, they merely assumed he was crazy.

A sociologist, Gideon Sjoberg, sometimes echoed by Charles, angered Edward by accusing him of "getting his kicks from the monetary and intellectual poverty of inferior races," someone who battened "on the physical and intellectual poverty of others." He thought Gideon was condescending and hypocritical. For Edward, sociology was *the* American pseudo-science, a faintly ridiculous way of stratifying and classifying existence. He *did* prefer the "primitive," he declared, but not so he could get his jollies from others' misery, or by slumming. They were simply more fun. A friend, after watching his drunken interactions in cantinas, told him that he should never be sober. "When you're drunk, you're generous, you're open, you communicate with people, you attract them, you charm. When you're sober, you simply retreat into yourself."

On one occasion in San Antonio, Charles found him drunk by a canal, and said that, if he kept doing it, he'd roll him in and leave him to drown. Back in Austin, Edward told a university counselor that he was living next to a madman who'd threatened to kill him. The counsellor went to Arno Nowotny, the nebbish Dean of Student Life, reporting that a patient alleged Charles, running for student president, was a "homosexual homicidal maniac." This seemed odd, because Charles's public image was macho, and he'd been profiled in the *Texas Ranger* student magazine under the headline "Arise! The Thrilling Story of One Man's Fight against the Forces of Virtue, Peace, and Complacency." He was to some, the story said, "a comic mascot. To others a sharp-fanged, slavering villain." He'd got up a petition against the administration's ban of *Playboy* magazine; he'd led a march on the state legislature against the doubling of tuition fees, which turned into a riot and got him thrown into a fountain, from which he surfaced to make a speech.

Anyone the administration suspected was gay was told that he had two choices: (1) Drop out of school within two weeks, with nothing negative put on his record or (2) Go to a Texas Rangers post to take a lie-detector test. If he failed it, he was expelled. When Edward brought Charles a summons to a dean's office, Charles was in bed with another student. Charles managed to outface the dean but suspected that Edward had betrayed him. After losing the student council election, he graduated with his M.A. Edward fought with him again just before he left Austin. Afterwards, he sent Charles a tiny onyx frog. It was a sign, Charles thought, that they'd stay friends.

Edward took a new place, leaving behind two dozen empty Zlatni bottles. He wrote Paul Weingarden that he was "so fucking tired of Austin that it isn't funny, and am just on the point, at times, of packing up and going to Mexico for good... somewhere where people are alive. This little old Southern hick town just sleeps in the sun. It wd require only very little further irritation than I've been feeling lately to make me take some step."

Drinking Champale instead of the watery Texas beer, he liked to talk French at a bar with a Cajun druggist, who told him that John F. Kennedy was a good President precisely because he was a bad Catholic. June 19 passed, "Juneteenth" — the date the Emancipation Proclamation was declared after the Civil War — less significant for most Texans than March 2, the date when the Republic of Texas declared its independence in 1836. He took summer courses, attended the meeting of the Linguistic Institute of America, and briefly returned to Lindsay. When the fall term began, he became a teaching assistant in the English Department. A postcard to Paul declared, "The U. of Texas seems more than unbearable to me now. I'm at the end of my, or somebody's rope." He resolved to hitchhike back to Canada after he'd talked to Reese in Dallas, which made him believe that they'd be better off far apart. But his professors persuaded him to stay. He had aced his courses in Descriptive Linguistics, Externals of Poetic Form, Phonemics and Phonotactics, Field Methods Linguistics, Morphology and Syntax, and the Semantics of Poetic Style, and gained a respectable B in Urbanization in World Society.

During the fall his essay, "The Trials of John Montgomery," the fruit of his summer job a year earlier, appeared in the scholarly journal *Ontario Historical Review*. Montgomery

> ... was the proprietor of the famous tavern which
> the rebels of 1837 made as their base for the
> intended assault on Toronto, and when that

desperate enterprise failed his hotel was burned
to the ground. He himself faced a spectacular trial
for high treason which ended with his calling
hellfire down upon judge, jury and witnesses.
Condemned to die on the scaffold, he escaped
to the United States, eventually was amnestied,
and returned to resume his profession on the site
of his former inn. His career thus presents to the
amused and distant eye of history a fairly ironic,
even comic aspect. But closer study reveals much
more than irony or comedy both in Montgomery
the man and in his chequered career — rather
it discloses the subtle play of conflicting
responsibilities and loyalties, attractive but not
unheroic traits of personality, and elements of a
personal tragedy.

In the evidence at Montgomery's trial much was
"confused and often contradictory," and was beset with partiality
and bias. "After all, what else could have been expected from a
trial conducted at such a time, in such surroundings, and raising
questions so laden with emotional overtones?" But he noted,
"One can hardly help admiring the man, John Montgomery, inn-
keeper and host, for the dignity, humanity, courage, good sense,
and lack of self-pity with which he faced his many ordeals."
Perhaps Edward identified with him.

When he was found drunkenly *hors de combat* the police, learning
he was a Woodrow Wilson scholar, usually let him go. A charge
of sleeping in a public place was dropped, though Nowotny
placed him on probation. Now, when police found him asleep
on the grass in front of City Hall, they threw him in jail. He had
no reason to suppose that the deans would hear about it. After
spending all one night drinking, he got a summons from the
Assistant Dean of Student Life. Edward lectured his students on
the evils of state universities, and the dangers of falling into the
hands of deans.

The dean asked him, "Mr. Lacey, are you an alcoholic?"
Edward answered that (1) his drinking was his private business,

(2) he paid money for his degree, and viewed his relationship with the university as a contract of minds, not involving extra-curricular activities (3) he was of age, and self-supporting and (4) far from bringing disgrace on the university, he was, by his presence, bringing honour to it, because he represented a national fellowship, few of whose recipients had ever come here. After some shouting, the dean set a discipline committee trial for the following Thursday. Edward told him that he was quite prepared to be expelled. Perhaps it would be the best thing, at such a university. He slammed the door.

He now learned that a tentatively planned trip to Mexico with friends was on. On Saturday they left. Very early the next day in Nuevo Laredo, he wandered off alone. With a young fellow unhappy over a girl, he formed one of those tremendously empathetic, generous, beer-buying friendships of which he was capable. After he woke that afternoon in a worker's remote hut, he dispatched Charles an incoherent postcard partly in Spanish, vowing to "insult and defy" the disciplinary committee. Meanwhile, his friends had given up on him and gone back to Austin.

Towards evening, very drunk, he heard a little man dangling pornographic images of the Blessed Virgin murmur about marijuana. It struck him that it would be the perfect revenge on the deans if tried to take weed across the border. If he succeeded, it would be a joke; if he were caught, either the troubles of life would dissolve him, or he'd dissolve them. It would be so beautifully definite.

He tucked two ounces of marijuana into his crotch. At the bustling border, an elderly American customs officer spotted him as someone needing a period of recovery and suggested that he rest for a few minutes. He took a seat, and then abruptly announced to the astonished officer, "You're looking for marijuana, aren't you? Well, take this: I don't know whether it's marijuana or not. "After they stripped him, anally probed him, muttered over the many cryptic papers in his wallet, and vainly tried to get him to say whom he came down with, who gave him the grass, and whether he smoked it habitually, they packed him off to Webb County Jail. Among his tank companions were a pretty little cutthroat of 16, in for robbery; a Mexican barber due for deportation; and a tattooed guy, in for being under the influence of narcotics.

From the moment he was jailed, he began to plot about how to get out. He had no American money, but the druggie gave him some to use the pay phone. He phoned his parents; at this remove, they were less upset than he thought they'd be. After a local lawyer contacted them, he was released on a bond of $1,500 over Customs protests — he was an alien, he was very nervous, he was a bad risk.

In Austin, Edward's disappearance had taken on the shape of a murder mystery. He had promised his English Dept. boss to meet on Monday while Mary Jane rounded up character witnesses for the Discipline Committee hearing. But he did not turn up. A teaching assistant had committed suicide a week earlier, and the English Department head feared that Edward had, too. People began to ask Mary Jane, "Have you heard from Edward?" In her hands were two strands of the plot: she knew where he lived, and why he was disturbed, but didn't know where he'd gone. Byron knew where he'd gone, but nothing else. On Monday afternoon, Edward's landlady said that he'd disappeared, and owed her a week's rent. By Wednesday, his Arabic professor told Mary Jane that he hadn't seen him for a month. Mary Jane assured all that Edward had just panicked, and would turn up. The other teaching assistants were told that Edward was no longer employed; his classes were told that their teacher had vanished.

That evening, readers of an Austin newspaper were enjoying the comics when they saw a small item, "Student Charged In Dope Case," which gave Edward's name, nationality, age (wrongly), amount of fine (wrongly), and other details of his "capture." The episode seemed so typical that half his friends believed it was one of his jokes, while the other half thought he was an innocent victim. A. A. Hill offered to pay his bail. A Presbyterian department secretary thought he was in jail for Driving While Intoxicated, until she learned that he didn't have a car, and said, "Why the poor boy; he just must have been screwed." Another Presbyterian secretary said, "The paper says 'semi-refined marijuana', and there are lots worse things than that. What if it had been refined marijuana? Or even heroin?

Why, the people in Mexico grow it all over the hills, and smoke it all the time." Some were prepared to send food. Meanwhile, Edward was in a Laredo bar waiting for a bus to Austin, arguing with an Indian about the rival merits of marijuana and peyote.

He reached Austin to find an overflowed mail slot and his apartment door plastered with notes. When Mary Jane saw him, she paled. The Discipline Committee meeting was cancelled. Everyone stared at him as though he were the undead. The next day Mary Jane was so fearful he was going to be grabbed by the police that she stood guard while he went to the Austin Barber College for a hair trim. With people marshalled on his side, the deans couldn't just suspend him. He was to meet them on Friday morning.

At the meeting, Nowotny said, "Have a chair, my boy." The assistant dean apologized for having lost his temper. All concurred that the Austin papers were foul rags. Nowotny said he hoped, and Dr. Hill, his friend, had told him that he, too, hoped, that Edward would stay on and pick up the pieces. He would be happy if Edward would consent to see a psychiatrist just once — why here on the university staff they had some of the finest doctors in the country. Edward agreed to see one. If the man found him raving mad, so much the better for his impending trial. They all shook hands.

In some respects, Edward plainly enjoyed the fuss of which he was the cynosure. To his students, he murmured, "All I know is what I read in the papers." He went to San Antonio, Dallas, or Houston every other weekend, even daring a trip to the Mexican border, though not across it. Writing Charles in early November, he noted that, besides his own case, this year one English Department teaching assistant had killed himself, one had been twice arrested and jailed, one had been once arrested and almost jailed, two had their houses burn down, and one professor had disappeared into Mexico. As a department secretary put it, "My, what an interesting sort of semester this is turning out to be!"

About Reese, he regretted that he had wasted the chance to experience tenderness with one of the rare creatures you could love. The Cartledge home was being torn down: the garage apartments were extant, sitting grotesquely in midair, the staircase stopping above the ground. Perhaps they were going to move them, as they had the tarpaper shacks, in one of which Reese had lived. When Reese returned to the campus, he'd find nothing to remind him of Edward.

His academic career seemed to him over. But his father's career was flourishing. Allan, about whom Edward had sewn hints that he might have set his own office fire, was able to piece together his practice and make more money than before. He was almost rich. Edward's legal troubles a closely guarded secret in Lindsay, Allan came to see his son. On a December day warm as summer, they walked across a bridge to a jungle of live oak and Spanish moss, and a ravine where forest fell away to mesquite and cactus-scrub. In a Mexican bar, the barman asked, "You 21, boy?" Edward said, "This is my father." The barman said, "Oh, well, if you with your daddy you can drink at any age. No problem." Allan had never seen live mistletoe which, with its stiff leaves and white berries, still greened the branches of sycamores, a harmless parasite. He left Austin with an armful of it.

On December 16, 1960, Edward faced Judge Ben Connally in U.S. District Court, Southern District of Texas, in the city of Houston, charged with three counts of possession of marijuana, a criminal offence. The sun fell on the dwarf palms and slanted through high windows. Grey-eyed Judge Connally, who had hunted dove and deer on his friend Lyndon Baines Johnson's ranch, leant forward, his chin on his palm. His eyes bored into Edward's, then shifted to his papers. His leaf-dry voice crackled and twanged, "Three years internment, suspended for five years." Then he said to Edward alone, "The law was made for and by normal people, and abnormal people have to abide by it as best they can." The next case was called.

Hill and others encouraged him to go on for a Ph.D. — at some other school of course — but all he only wanted to stop studying and start learning. Only marijuana solaced him. Feeling unwell ever since his father left, he went to the Health Center. A doctor ordered him to bed. On his way home to pick up clothes, he saw in a newspaper that a friend, Ted Estrada, had been charged with stealing a book. He chased over town trying to find him. Two days later the Health Center sent out a campus-wide watch for Edward, warning that he was dangerously contagious with hepatitus. When he returned, they tried to put him in isolation. He threatened to call a lawyer, pointing out that no one had proved he was ill. After much acrimony, they agreed to run a test for hepatitis. When they reported he had it, he refused to enter hospital, but his allies made him. He was now feverish. For someone who had resisted it so much, he enjoyed his enforced isolation. No one could penetrate it except his probation officer, who came from Houston every month.

Ted was to be tried soon. Arno Nowotny had asked him, "Do you know Edward Lacey?" "Yes." "What do you know about him?" Ted, wanting to protect his friend, said, "Well, uh, many things." Nowotny said, "Edward Lacey is a heeroe. Do you know he risked his life for you? You ought to be proud to have someone like that risk his life for you. Yes, he is a heeroe. He was in danger, and he stayed out of a sickbed to help you." But there was little he could do for Ted. He'd confessed.

Edward now sported a long, drooping moustache. Upon release from hospital, he had sex with a black guy on a stone bridge in a park, under the blue light of the moon while huge wreathed live oaks cast humpbacked shadows over them.

Bored, he'd begun to stand up in the stand-ins that called on movie theatres to integrate. Goons heckled a woman friend, calling, "I'll bet she's a nigger, with all them big ol' teeth," and "Bet she'd sleep with one," "Naw, she's married to one." A man said he wouldn't eat with niggers, he wouldn't sleep with niggers, he wouldn't talk with niggers, and he wouldn't walk with niggers, so Edward asked him why he didn't leave the South. All in all, it was a satisfying day.

He slept half the time; the rest of it he laboured over his thesis on prosody. He had only a little more to go, but he was tired. He yearned for affection. One night a young Hispanic, his brother scheduled for the electric chair, came home with him — the boy claimed he had nowhere to stay — and was so affectionate Edward could have cried. When the boy woke up the next morning, he couldn't remember anything he'd done, and was affectionate all over again.

One night he got drunk. and saw a handsome youth in front of a café. The boy was from Abilene, waiting for friends. He said he'd spend the night with Edward, but wanted $20. Edward held firm at $10. The boy suggested they go down by the creek and have a quickie for $5. Edward said it was too dangerous. Finally, despairingly, he said, "Come on over to the car." They got in, and he pulled out his small erect penis, shoved it towards him, and said, "Well, it isn't much but the girls all seem to like it pretty good." Edward just sat there. He said, "Come on, suck it for me." Edward said, "You don't understand, kid, I just don't want it any more." The boy zipped up his fly. His friends came out of the café, and they rolled off to Abilene.

Edward asked himself why he'd behaved as he had. Maleness, he thought, was a combination of pride, sensuality, brutality, and tenderness. Men were so sad and so lovely. The erect penis, the badge of maleness, was the boy's pride, and he had injured his pride. Down the street, he met a Mexican kid. They went into a huge abandoned bar, stumbling in the dark. This boy, on probation, had done eight months of a sentence for armed robbery. He thought sex with men was a sin, and cringed and winced when his body was touched. He said he liked it: that was what he was afraid of.

Another night, he met someone named Jesse. They got friendly with a charming prostitute. Jesse had it off with her in the back seat of his car while Edward slept in the front. Then Jesse moved him to the back seat, and had it off in the front. He and Edward drove to Houston to see Jesse's regular girl, waking her and her family up. Back in Austin, they spent the next day drinking. Edward fell asleep in a café. When they woke him up, Jesse was gone. He upbraided the staff, who called the police. When the policemen cursed him, he said, "Who do you think you're talking to?" He refused to give his name at the station and yelled for a lawyer. They took off his shoes and belt while he kicked them. They roughed him up, and chucked him in a cell. When morning came, he paid a fine.

He was living in the basement of a crumbling mansion, which its owner wanted to half-demolish. A rain left an inch of water on the floor. Everything important was high up, so Edward let the water settle and had clean feet for a day or two.

Reese had come back to campus, and Edward discovered that he was looking for him. When they finally met, Edward recalled the previous Saturday, when he'd been disturbed to see him lying asleep in the sunlight on a playing field. Now Reese told him that he was adjusting to being heterosexual.

When, at the beginning of March, an Immigration official came to interview Edward, he couldn't be found. Mary Jane refused to give his address, and rushed to warn him. The police were called out. After he was tracked down, the official said it was a relief to deal with him, compared to the wetbacks. But he fingerprinted him, took away his visa, and gave him a form "Under Docket Control at San Antonio." Edward sped up his work.

Meanwhile, he'd been arrested for loitering, but the charges were dismissed. Afterwards, he didn't dare stroll downtown after midnight, much less hang around the bus terminal. He was likely the only student to have been dropped four times from the rolls in one semester and reinstated thrice. When Nowotny gave him a tongue-lashing, he slammed down his books and rushed out, and sent a stream of people over to say that he'd had an attack of hepatic nausea. Later Nowotny told him he was a fine boy, and all he had to do now was "lick that dad gum Government exam." On March 21, while drunk, he wrote the exam for American Government 6100.

A special-delivery arrest warrant ordered him to appear in San Antonio the next day to "show cause why you should not be deported from the United States on the charges set forth." In San Antonio, he marched into a grim pentagonal building. The trial featured questions like "set forth in the charges contained herein, viz. that you are one Edward Alan Lacey, alias N.B. Carr, do you answer yes or no?" The deportation order was signed; he declined to appeal. Arguing at length, he said that he wanted to be deported to British Honduras, since he was a British subject. The judge allowed a stay of deportation till May 6. He was still technically under arrest, but they let him return to Austin. In late March, he was drinking alone at a table, and noticed that Reese was correcting papers at another. Reese went by him to the washroom, saying, "Ed." He didn't answer.

Paul Weingarden and Bob McCaldon wrote from Toronto that they'd be passing through Austin on their way to Monterrey. After furious labour, he finished his thesis, and secured a last-minute typist. Quickly completing the job, she advised him on a slip of paper, "Do try not to let your flair for the dramatic do you harm." He began to proofread the thesis, and by 6:30 a.m. on April 12 the thing was ready. He packed his belongings, sold his typewriter, left stuff with friends, and set off with Paul and Bob. It took them five hours to get to the border. He was quivering by the time they reached it, but they crossed without trouble, and he got his tourist permit the next day. The permit was marked "Entry," but not "Exit."

Part Two

PASSPORT RENEWED
1961-1984

The charm of travel is, you cannot stay.
You turn like pages cities, countries, races,
look for one moment, and go on your way.

~ **Travel Empts Unease**

4

"YOU THINK YOU'RE MEXICAN, DON'T YOU?"

April 1961-July 1963

The eternal clothes are readjusted on the dusty bodies and they,
Larks now to raise the sun, on wings of newspapers
Fly away.

~ Mexican Newsboys

On June 14, 1961, the *Lindsay Daily Post* reported, "A Lindsay man, who was the recipient of a Woodrow Wilson fellowship for graduate study in languages, has received his Master's degree from the University of Texas. He is Edward Alan Lacey, son of Mr. and Mrs. A. T. Lacey, 10 Mill Street." Lacey had received his degree on June 3. "He is now holidaying in Mexico."

Back in April, Edward, Paul, and Robert had arrived in the blast furnace of Monterrey after touring the cantinas and cathouses of Nuevo Laredo. The industrial city, capital of Nuevo León state, had four *zonas*, where in early morning the bartenders yawned, the last clients nodded, and women sat sleep-bleared in their doorways. Swearing bar-boys sloshed water on the spit and sawdust, bare-chested men slid slabs of ice into taverns, ragged children ran with newspapers, tacos, and shoeshine boxes into pastel cantinas where music still blared. Out among the weeping-willow-like huisache, desert birds sang. The trio photographed each other quaffing bottles of beer. They kept encountering a "guide" named Hector Robles Rodriguez, who demanded a fee for directing them to a bar they were going to anyway. When they gave him $5 to buy some grass, he evaporated.

After Bob and Paul left, Edward picked up with people he'd met earlier, including someone who told him that he was 80 per cent Mexican and his friends 0.0 per cent, which pleased him. By month's end he was in Mexico City, having vivid dreams of arrest, disgrace, and death. He was in a boarding house: room with another fellow plus three meals a day in a nearby restaurant for $32.50 a month. He had $45 left, and no job. In the wake of the Bay of Pigs invasion, anti-Americanism was rampant, A huge student demonstration bore signs, *Muera Kennedy* and *Cuba Si, Yanqui no*. The city seethed. For Edward, it was wonderful just to watch people in the streets, paperboys mingling with tycoons. He thought that Latinos were the loveliest people in the world. Everything— their pride, tenderness, skin colour, hair — appealed to him. But the police closed bars early, and a policeman asked him for proof of age in a *pulquería* — which amused the other drinkers of the cactus beer. He said he was a tourist, and told the policeman to go away. He did.

Signing in at hotels under false names satisfied his taste for subterfuge. Having deported himself, he worried that the Mexicans might extradite him to Texas. His college friends had refused to divulge his whereabouts. Ted Estrada, after a heart attack he'd had in Austin, and a suspended sentence for book theft, was teaching English in Torreón at the Instituto Latinamericano. Through him, Edward got a job there, though Ted soon left. In the Instituto's premises on Hidalgo Avenue he became an English-as-a-second language teacher: repeating, correcting, painfully extracting halting answers to questions. His grind began at 7:30 a.m. and ended at 3:30 p.m., with another stint from 7:30 p.m. to 9:30 p.m. In June, he wrote Paul Weingarden, "My parents are very happy that I got my degree, and all my damn relatives are writing uncomprehending congratulatory letters, to which I shall never reply." He had received A's in 10 courses, and for his Master's thesis.

Paul's letter had been bright with stamps and postmarks, a boon to the philatelists among Edward's students: "So if any unusual stamps come out in Canada lately, & you're writing to me, you could get the stamps & use them on the letter." He apologized for having put Paul to expense in the past, but "I no longer mind owing people money; in fact, I rather like it." He had yet to find out whether, if ever, and, if so, at what time, he could apply for readmission to the United States. He might soon be like John Christian Hanna, the "man without a country.... that unfortunate gentleman from Lebanon who sailed around on a ship, never being allowed to land, for so many years." He had been invited to the wedding of Vladimir Degen, the college friend he had once defended against campus authorities: "unfriendly governments and money separate me from the occasion, which I hope will be as properly spirituous."

"Sometimes I feel so weak," he wrote, "esp. if I've been drinking the night before, & have a hangover, that I can barely move. Then there is some damn Yankee factory around here that discharges arsenic or some compound of arsenic into the air, with complete impunity. The combination of arsenic, and chalk dust in the classrooms, and dust from the dust storms which, until the rains started, come almost daily, and are really impressive productions, causes me to lose my voice almost completely sometimes." Mary Jane Cook, who came to visit, thought he clearly enjoyed his subject. He was incredibly patient and sympathetic with his students. She was astounded how, after having only been in Mexico for a few months, he sounded like a native speaker.

Torreón, a little bigger than Austin, was the largest city in La Laguna. Aeons ago, a big inland sea dried up, leaving a seasonal lagoon, which was why it was called La Laguna. His landlady was a widow, Doña Aurelia. She was an fat old lady with iron-grey hair, warts on her cheeks, and ironclad principles that, fortunately for him, bent to curing his hangovers with shrimp broth — lemony, salty, peppery, the sovereign Mexican cure. She, like everyone else, called him *profe*, short for *profesor*. She allowed him to bring boys to his room at discreet hours. His huge bed creaked *chaca chaca* like a puritan protest.

Behind palm and eucalyptus trees, the big house on Presidente Carranza Avenue had two patios. Between them, Doña Aurelia took her noonday siestas. The rear patio had a pomegranate bush, a chinaberry tree, and a great silver fig tree, under which on Sundays an old roomer named Chevo drank mescal from a clay cup, drops from his craggy chin leaving spots on the dust. Once a carpenter, he sang: "*Cuando el pájaro canta, el indio muere.*" When the bird sings, the Indian must die. In the front patio, Doña Aurelia performed green magic with morning glory, oleander, bougainvillea, and hibiscus: everything she touched burst into bloom. Once a month she sailed out on missions of money-collection: tongues clacked that she secretly owned a string of brothels all over northern Mexico. Her late unlamented husband had been a bar proprietor. Doctors had told him to stop drinking: he'd stopped for eight long years, then resumed it, and promptly died. He had sired a fat graceless daughter, rumoured to be the offspring of a servant. But Edward doubted it. She looked too much like Doña Aurelia.

In the shade of mulberry trees, uniformed schoolgirls sucked dripping wheels of pepper-dusted pineapple, coming home for their noonday meal past iron-grilled windows in adobe walls. In the corner cantina, faded walls once blue and gold, white-aproned waiters pumped beer and bustled with the free lunch. Through swinging doors workers spilled in and out, then vanished on bicycles. Nothing else moved. The trunk and branches of the huisache were bright green, so that even when it briefly lost its fern-like leaves it didn't seem dead. It grew along riverbanks, around waterholes, and anywhere there was seasonal moisture. Next to the palm, it was his favourite tree.

In northern Mexico, the days typically were hot, suddenly cooling after sundown. When dust clouds rolled across the Coahuila desert, darkening the sky, the torreónenses scurried to close doors and windows, his students in their wine-and-white uniforms scattering for home, the housewives saying, "*Ahí vise la tierra.*" They'd hear the wind banging doors and shutters and tossing the branches of the salt cedar, while dust blew white as snow and sifted in.

In the dozen blocks of the red-light district, he particularly liked a gay whorehouse called the Gallito de Oro, the Golden Cock, with a stable of queens in drag, all expert pickpockets. They were under the protection of a motherly madam, with whom he had long conversations. She told him she preferred *putos* to *putas* because they were less trouble and had fewer fights. Saturday nights in the dirty sand-filled patio featured dancing, necking, drinking, and chattering till well after dawn. Behind the patio were the shemales' rooms, from whence disaster was always erupting: an irate young peasant who thought he was dancing with a girl till the moment of truth came, or a client rushed out screaming, claiming he'd been robbed. A little bigger than Austin, Torreón had more organized and unorganized vice than gangland Chicago.

Torreón, Gómez Palacio, and Lerdo, all with wide streets and dirty, noisy markets, was a tri-city complex, A dry riverbed ran between Coahuila and Durango, barren stone mountains glowering over them. Within a radius of 50 miles were country towns with bars and *zonas* of their own. Edward sought out towns in an arc from Chihuahua to the north to Monterrey in the east to Zacatecas state in the south. The prickly pears of the Valley of the Mesquital, the meeting-point of the states of Coahuila, Durango, and Zacatecas, were made into candy, ice cream, and wine; maguey was turned into pulque, mescal, and tequila. But the low, tap-rooted green tree from which the valley got its name was only a façade, for the mesquite was subterranean; it lived in earth, not air. For Edward, the mesquite's other name was poetry.

In northern Durango, Mapimí was almost a ghost town. Dust clouds swirled around its adobe walls. He walked around the shabby plaza, heard a burst of music from a bar, saw the shadow of a scorpion on the church wall, thought of the ruined gold and silver mines in the mountains. Here, Benito Juárez had once slept on a rusty bed while fleeing from the French occupation. Here, Father Miguel Hidalgo, who tried to introduce the idea of independence to Mexico, was imprisoned prior to his execution. Ten miles away was Ojuelas, a ghost town. There, the mountain shadowed a long swinging bridge, swaying from emptiness to emptiness.

On the way to Zacatecas, mist swirled on the Durango mountains, shepherds fluting goat-like sheep to upland meadows. He saw bullet marks on walls that dated back to when Pancho Villa roamed and ruled. Zacatecas was set among dark hills, capital of the namesake state whose pine forests had been stripped to provide lumber and charcoal for the mines. Behind the baroque façade of the cathedral, children heard mass at gold altars, bribed by the free milk in clay bowls. In bars, hard old men wore sombreros and carried guns, and young men cursed their luck. Swarms of Black Witch moths frightened old ladies on their way to mass.

On one train excursion, he sat opposite a drab long-faced boy with lacklustre eyes. He tried to engage him in conversation but it was no use. The cactus land slipped by. A small town came up under the winter sun, a stone hill in the distance, a spireless adobe church, a dog barking. "What town is this?" Edward asked. Suddenly the boy became voluble. "This is Paredón," he said excitedly. "There's the hill where Pancho Villa fought. The battle lasted three days. There's the church and our plaza, where we make our festivals. The arroyo in spring runs full of water and flowers bloom. Look, you can see our house. My dog's waiting for me. This is our home."

Once a very drunk Indian in a straw hat, white shirt, and huaraches approached him in a bar. He stared at Edward's sugarcane brandy, looked away, looked again, asked to share the bottle. He delicately poured himself a shot glass and then another. He ate some of Edward's lunch of toasted corn and chitlins. Soon the bottle was finished. He asked if Edward would stand him another. Edward said yes. Mumbling, he said that his wife had tuberculosis and badly needed to go for treatment. He needed only 100 pesos to take her from his hut in the hills for an X-ray. Could Edward lend him the money? Edward said no. One hundred pesos wasn't much, but Edward knew it would vanish in one spree, and he'd be sick and depressed for a week. They shook hands.

He couldn't count the number of boys he'd had, though he sometimes tried. He prided himself not being a sex tourist, making a smash-and-grab raid on street kids, then scurrying back to the safe purlieus of home. Mitigating his predatory stare, relaxing the grim set of his mouth, was another emotion: pity. The newsboys were little birds, sparrows perhaps, urban, brown, and humble. They owned only their clothes and their dusty bodies. One boy's father had left his mother long before and then death had taken her off. Men had taken his sisters away. The police had thrown him in jail and taken away the 50 pesos with which he'd come to the city, as well as the good black shoes and the coat he'd been so proud of.

The town's bill-collector — a mustachioed young man, with six kids — whizzed about on the Mexican national vehicle, the bicycle, which shared transportation honours with the national animal, the burro. One day he was complaining to Edward about how little he earned and how much food cost. Edward asked him why, then, he had so many children. He was surprised and said "Ah, but *profe*, you don't know the pleasure of seeing children grow — the fruit of oneself."

During Holy Week in 1962, his parents descended on him. The previous Lent his mother had turned 60. Pope John XXIII had abolished fasting and meatless Fridays, too late to be of much use to her. The trio went travelling, reaching Mazatlán and the coast. That spring he finally got *visitante* papers, which permitted him to work legally, though he was sure that the Mexicans kept their eye on him since his papers were delayed every time he sent them to be renewed in Mexico City. The immigration man in Torreón once followed him into the *zona*, searched him, and accused him of being a narcotics addict — a bribe kept him from taking action.

He began to venture far south, all the way to Chiapas and the Yucatán Peninsula. In mid-August he was in San Christóbal de las Casas, a cool high airy town of white colonial houses, red-tiled roofs, gardens, and treeless streets, enfolded by pine hills topped by churches. There, he took an excursion led by Mrs. Franz Blom, the famous anthropologist's widow, to Tenejapa: five hours by truck over a hopeless road. The Maya were exquisitely fine-featured, with lovely muscular hairless bodies; the calves of the legs especially fascinated him. However, they were highly moral and conventional, and something about the climate, the strange, beautiful landscape, and the way of life made contact impossible and sex seem unnecessary. His trips to the south left him exhausted for weeks after.

Before Christmas, he returned to Mazatlán; it was sad to see that, where used to be 24-hour bars, the women of the *zonas* now worked in restaurants. At Christmas, he headed through central Mexico to Michoacán, where he added a few more *zonas* to his collection, and then to Acapulco, hot, expensive, and crowded. The natives were nice, but you could hardly see them for the ineffable tourists. He found a cabaret in which a donkey drank beer, and where he had to spend two nights drinking before he could get a room. Wandering around with a suitcase, he caused wildest alarm to the police; he wondered if they thought he was going to blow up Acapulco.

He brought back to Torreón two young, three-foot-long iguanas, male and female, and christened them Gilberto and Muruaga. Costing four pesos each, tied, thonged, and sewn at the mouth and legs, they had been sold for meat. Rejecting that purpose, he fed them grass, alfalfa, tomatoes, and apples. They ran around his room, climbed walls, fell on people, and terrified everyone in the house. They clung to the barred window screen and drank the water he poured for them, since iguanas only drank running water. Dragonlike, they attracted staring audiences of *campesinos* in straw hats and sandals. Gilberto, the livelier and prettier of the pair, developed an infection, which, though he ate more heartily, made him sicker and sicker. One noon, Edward found him sprawled panting on the floor. He soon died. Muruaga, hiding in the patio under a bunch of palm leaves, remained fat and healthy, though she ate almost nothing. He released her near the Nazas River.

A parcel arrived with a dried snake inside that Mary Jane Cook had sent two years earlier. The snake had been all over Mexico, the United States, and Canada ever since, since it had arrived too late to reach him in Mexico City. Bounced back, it had come too late to reach her in Austin, since she had left for Chicago, whence it had chased her until it reached her in Rhode Island, whence she re-mailed it to his parents in Lindsay, who mailed it to Torreón. The snake, and other mementos of Texas, survived intact.

A Canadian political crisis was getting the full treatment from Mexican newspapers, headlining "Downfall of the anti-American government of the premier Diefenbaker." Being Latin American, the papers seemed unable to recognize that a government could fall by non-violent means. People asked him seriously if Canada was going Communist, if there would be a war with the United States, if Diefenbaker was in prison, if Edward would be able to go back to his country now.

Paul, who tantalized him with job prospects in Canada, was planning an Easter visit. In early February, in what promised to be a short letter but turned out to be the usual long one, Edward wrote, "I can't continue this kind of life forever, and crime, or a return to respectability seem the only ways out...try to tell you more definitely...All my important decisions are last-minute ones.... if you see any loose passports lying around, grab me one, so that I can get back to the US on a false name." At the moment he was

> ... sitting in the typing room of the school, surrounded by about 20 other of my stupid girl-students, all pecking away (no more successfully than I, tho they're supposed to learning the touch system) on broken-down 20-year-old typewriters, after eight-and-a-half hours of teaching to and shouting at and not being heeded by, these same stupid girl-students, makes me wish you were coming to Juárez tomorrow, so that I cd pack my things & leave Torreón tonite, & be back in Canada in a week and out of this un-air-conditioned nitemare. However, when the weekend comes, & I have time to do a bit of drinking and staying up and other activities, I'll realise, as always, that I'd give a dozen Canadas and good jobs and security, etc., for this freedom, even if it is only 2 days a week & I work like a devil the other 5.

He liked the postmark the government had stamped on Paul's letter: "Education through Philately." Almost as good as "Don't Wait for Spring — Do It Now." Paul had mentioned "a mickey of rum." He'd been away so long, and so used to thinking in *litres*, *medias*, and *cuartitos* that he'd forgotten that a mickey was a half-bottle. On March 1 he wrote that he had just "eluded going on a school picnic by explaining off a bad hangover as intestinal flu (grippe, here) to the directress, & so am free to write, but somewhat weary, as I was roaming around the Tolerant Zone till 5 a.m." For their Easter-vacation rendezvous in Juaréz, perilously at the U.S. border, he would adopt the alias "Carlos Fink."

As it happened, Carlos Fink was not called into action. He, Paul, and friends enjoyed the red-light district, fending off taxi-drivers, street-corner idlers, and 12-year-old boys. Declining

to return to Canada with his friends, he spent most of his time in
Juaréz in bed. On the train back, he encountered his landlady and
daughter. The trip lasted a day, and included four breakages of
the air-conditioning hose, each entailing a long stop. They also
outlasted a canyon landslide in a pouring rainstorm at midnight,
one car thrown off the tracks: they nearly went into the Bachimba
River, while the train hung at a steep angle. They were drinking
hot soup on the platform of the Chihuahua station when the
train started. He managed to get on the train steps and stretched
his hand to his overweight landlady: she nearly dragged him
under the wheels. He had the mug of soup between his teeth
while soup venders dragged at her purse, trying to get their
money. Finally, a station agent shoved her aboard. When they
neared Torreón, she revealed she carried a contraband shipment
of American clothes, and outfitted him with sweaters and coats.
She also threw her suitcase out the window to some red cap in
cahoots with her, and all was well.

Back home, he found Texan friends waiting for him, one
of whom had just broken off with his girlfriend, and the other
had just got a divorce. Glum himself, he tried hard to divert them.
Writing to Paul on May 7 ("we're giving a set of exams right now
& the brats need the afternoon to study, or go to the movies, or
fuck with their boy-friends & thus relieve their mental tension,
or something..."), he reported that the Juaréz photos of himself
Paul had sent him "were even more sinister than I had expected,
and show a striking resemblance to "El Piporro," a popular
Mexican cowboy actor & singer. They were the delight of my
students, who passed them around excitedly, & practically wore
them down, in fact, refused to give them back until I threatened
dire consequences." Did Bob, he wondered, know

> .... of any nerve medicine or anytime [sic] of
> therapy, massage, etc., which can cure this
> problem I have of tingling in hands, which
> successively spreads to, & seems to mock-
> paralyse (tho it does not really paralyse at all, in
> the sense that I can still move my members; they
> simply become rigid, as in a cramp of "Charley-
> horse," or any other kind of muscular spasm) my
> whole body... accompanied by a strange feeling

in my head, which I get if I try to sleep when
I have a hangover, as tho an intolerable tension
were building up within, & my head wd explode
(I superstitiously associate this with a stroke or
heart attack) if I went to sleep....I've had it for
years, in periods of stress or great fatigue, as a
recurrent nightmare while dropping off to sleep
— a dream in which I'd feel my head were going
to explode until I woke, & I cd only wake if I
moved, and I cdn't move a muscle, until finally
I jump awake with a start. This repeats up to a
dozen times, esp. if I lie on my back, which is
how I normally lie before going to sleep. Only
recently has it become associated with hangovers. Except for a violent increase in heartbeat
& pulse rate, & a slight, normal trembling of the
hands, & nausea even when I have nothing to
vomit, there are no other physical symptoms.

After Bob and Paul had left him in Monterrey back
in April 1961, they'd reported that, when they crossed the
Brownsville, Texas border, the customs people had pulled their
car apart, and even confiscated miniature bottles of liquor.
Edward now sent Bob a clipping from a San Antonio newspaper
concerning a major bust of smugglers taking drugs across the
Rio Grande. Instrumental in the bust was special agent Hector
Robles Rodriguez, posing as a Monterrey tourist guide.

One long weekend he went to Matamoros on a rain-
ruined road to join Byron and his friends down from Texas.
Matamoros, across the border from Brownsville, had a long,
surfy beach about 20 miles outside it. Byron insisted on riding
his car up and down, zigzagging in and out of the waves of the
Gulf of Mexico, at about 70 miles an hour, seagulls dodging as
they barrelled toward the mouth of the Rio Grande. About to
leave the United States soon, Byron planned to give the car to his
brother, whom Edward thought he must hate. As had to happen,
a big wave hit, the motor stalled, and the battery died. They
were stranded miles up the beach at nightfall, the tide rising.
Edward and a friend ran for miles to a beach restaurant, and
found someone to tow them out. Amid frantic efforts to rescue

the stranded car, Edward sat in salt- and sand-covered interior, refusing to budge. When the car got on dry land, luckily two *rancheros* came along and pushed it into town. It was Sunday and all the repair shops were closed. Nor was this the end of the car's misfortunes: it also got stuck in a cavernous mud-puddle in the *zona*, and had to be towed out again.

The *zona's* best bar was called *La Rata Muerta,* The Dead Rat, where they saw a performer insert a banana into his partner's vagina prior to eating it. Later, they drank in a huge empty cabaret, and in a bar with a burro in plaster with a broken-off penis at the door, from which a bird flew as they neared. Byron and his friends had to get five-day visas in nearby Reynosa; Edward idly got one for himself.

In Torreón, his Toronto days revisited him. The previous year he'd learned that Laura Hofrichter, his teacher and confidante, had committed suicide. In February, Dennis Lee, a Torontonian who'd graduated from the university a year after him, wrote to say he represented a "group of writers, mostly of the same vintage as yourself," including Margaret Atwood, who took "advice from such people as Jay Macpherson." He asked to see a manuscript that they might publish, since they sought "younger writers who had shown exceptional talent." He noted, "over the past six years we've read most of the poetry you've published with Toronto magazines and private presses; and again we're struck by the imaginative power and the technique you bring to writing." Replying at the start of May, Edward supposed that Lee had heard of him from that "grey eminence," John Colombo. Thanks to this small pod of well-wishers, it looked as if Edward's first book was going to be published. Since many of the poems were flagrantly homosexual, he said he feared for his reputation, or perhaps his reputation feared for him.

The book's publication was one reason why he had decided to return to Canada. There were others. His friends and parents were urging him to, he was paid badly for a heavy workload, he had begun to dislike teaching teenagers, and he realized that Mexican officials didn't like foreigners working in Mexico. Or maybe going back would simply test whether he really loved Mexico as much as he thought he did. He would never forget that weekend in Matamoros, he wrote Byron: it was

John Keats's "huge, cloudy symbols of a high romance," from the sonnet that most spoke to him: "When I have fears that I may cease to be…"

All June he waited for his visa renewal to arrive from Mexico City. By early July, he set off on another trip, hoping that the papers would be there when he returned. Why not cross over in Brownsville, and see if they would let him take a bus straight to Canada, saving much money and time? With his heart in his mouth and bags in his hand, he re-entered the United States. Trying to look nonchalant, he gave Customs his name and passport. An official said, "Just when and where were you deported from the U.S., son?" Sure enough, he was in the big book. But they decided that, bound for Canada, he had acted in good faith. They did pull his baggage apart, but all they found were dead seahorses, grass-spears, and sycamore balls.

After he taxied back to Mexico, officials berated him for having tried to leave the country without turning in his papers: he protested that no one had asked for them, and anyway, he had none to turn in. A functionary threatened to leave him in the middle of the bridge; Edward told him he'd jump off. They were about to let him go when they saw he had a Reynosa stamp on his passport, which seemed to contradict his story that he'd lived in Mexico for two years. The chief said his case was so complicated only Mexico City could solve it. They bundled him into a bus.

On arrival in Torreón he found that his renewal still hadn't come through. Short on funds, he set out for Mexico City, where he found the authorities their usual surly and evasive selves. It was Wednesday, and he had to catch a Sunday plane, or wait till the next Sunday, and he had only a few pesos to live on. After he booked a ticket, he browbeat the Canadian Embassy to help him. Thanks to the Ambassador, he got a Mexican exit permit issued Saturday afternoon. But his propeller plane had been cancelled and he'd have to take the more expensive jet. He managed to scrounge up enough to pay for it, with enough left over to get drunk on pulque that night. He caught his plane.

In Torreón, one of his students had been a handsome young traffic policeman who wore a gun to class. He had invited Edward to family gatherings. But Edward had failed to take advantage of the offers. He now regretted refusing this *calor humano* and overtures of friendship. It had hurt him badly when, one day, a student said to him — and that day he determined never to live more in a country where such things could be said and, worse, were *true* — "Teacher, you think you're very Mexican, don't you? But I tell you that the more Mexican you think you are, the less Mexican you'll be."

5

DEADMONTON, DULLBERTA

July 1963-April 1964

*The world was neither better nor worse than usual
while I was there, but it seemed much more distant.*

~ The Year in Edmonton or Sensory Deprivation

When he met John and Ruth Colombo in Toronto, Ruth said that his desperation was like an ongoing pose he felt he had to sustain. Neither she nor John had changed, nor had Paul Weingarden. Bob McCaldon, married to Jane, now had a child and a career. It was hard for Edward to grasp concepts like "career," "child," and "future."

At his parents' summer cottage, he wrote letters on an old typewriter that lacked a comma key, which he'd long ago replaced to make way for a now-useless phonetic symbol. There was time for family get-togethers and keepsake photos: celebrating cousin Marg's birthday at Joe and Alice's place at Kennedy Bay; someone mugging behind Allan; Aunt Phyllis ("Tuss") crooking her leg around Edward's arm.

On a cold morning on Labour Day weekend, he found a black sweater that Charles had given him before he'd left the apartment they'd shared, or had sold to him for cash — "or perhaps the price was our usual one." The sweater was his "only remaining emblem of you." This was as near as Edward would come to saying he missed him. Sorry he'd left Torreón, he was afflicted by "listlessness laissez-faire attitude fatalism" in contrast to Charles's "frenetic death-oriented youth-oriented organisation-oriented success-oriented meaningfulness-oriented hate-oriented energy."

With some excitement, he was reading John Rechy's *City of Night,* despite its "dreadful conversion scenes and the phony sequence of the woman "who's punishing herself for having turned her gay son loose on the world when actually it was the best thing prob. she could have done." He had rarely encountered Rechy's combination of magnificent resources and puny mind. The "obsession with decay loss of powers death was the best thing about the book." In a Toronto washroom, he looked up from the urinal and saw that someone had scribbled, "I want sex with young guys 25 or under. Will pay." He noted that he was only just eligible. He went to a park and sold himself—simply to prove he was still a "youngman."

Relatives turned up, ostensibly to visit, but really, he thought, so they could pass comment on him later. He spent a morning looking for puffballs in the woods and found half-a-dozen; as he ate them, he imagined that they were the hearts of relatives. Having arrived in Toronto with 25 cents in his pocket, with fall nearing and winter unemployment looming, a late unexpected job opportunity in Alberta—in part thanks to Barker Fairley—was too good to turn down. On the train west, he reflected on how innocent Canadians were. He was talking to an obviously straight fellow about blacks, and the man said, "I'm queer, you know. One of my best boyfriends is a Negro, and the things we don't do together!" He went to his sleeper, and woke up in Medicine Hat.

"I'm going out to Alberta / the weather's nice there in the fall," Ian Tyson sang in "Four Strong Winds." Sure, sure. When he arrived, leaves were already dropping. Late asters and chrysanthemums were blooming, though: funeral flowers. No one was at the airport to welcome him but, then, he hadn't bothered to announce his arrival. With a third of a million population, Edmonton was at 55°N and 115°W the northernmost city in North America. Until the end of the following April he was to be a sessional lecturer in German at the salary of $4,600.

Edmonton was *dull*, but the beer delivered between 6 and 8 per cent alcohol. The beer-halls closed between 6:30 and 7:30 p.m. — to make sure people would eat as well as drink. You sat alone at a table — no standing at the bar. Closed on Sunday, cocktail lounges were drearily respectable. Since there was no liquor-related advertising, the words "beer" and "cocktail" couldn't be used; as a result, the town was full of drinking places that called themselves "parlours," making them sound like a Victorian mansion or furniture store, or else "men's rooms" and "women's rooms," making them sound like a lavatory. He liked the latter image: clean, chrome, enamel, but with secret filth.

He had to pay $90 plus a $50 breakage fee for a bachelor suite that wouldn't be ready for him till September 28, the nearest to the campus he could find, reachable by a long walk across a bridge over the North Saskatchewan River. Suffering chills and fevers since he arrived, he considered taking the next plane to Mexico though it had been a triumph to get a university position without a Ph.D. — with his record, almost a miracle. He was to teach nine hours a week: three courses in Scientific German. Since they were morning classes, he claimed that half the time he didn't turn up and the other half the students didn't, so they got along well.

Charles had contemplated visiting him, but he did his best to dissuade him. Charles should be aware that his over-drinking, refusal to socialize, and inattention to dress passed "in eloquent pantomime." In late October, he wrote that his hangover shakes would cause him to miss his 8 a.m. class, and probably his 9 a.m. class. The German Department had been so relieved at finding someone — anyone — that it had lapsed into a coma about him. His office was in the new Education Building, remote from the German Department head, a hangdog little man. You sensed that he'd been in a concentration camp; maybe the *university* was the camp. Only three teachers remained from the previous year. Nobody knew each other, or what to do. He'd wondered at not being briefed on his duties: now he knew that there was no one to brief him.

He decided to go to his 9 a.m. class after all, assaulting his students with remarks like "That cigarette you're smoking may have given you poise, but it hasn't given you the answer to the question I'm asking, has it, my dear fellow?" His 8 a.m.

students had got up about 6:45, dressed, shat, eaten breakfast, slicked down their hair, and gone out in the bitter cold through the bright morning to a classroom. And sat in a classroom and waited. No one came. So they got up and went to the tuck shop and cursed Edward over coffee.

The university was new and going places, but not the same places he was going. Its library had good holdings of Canadian poets. He caught up on the latter, especially the work of a Vancouver group that included Lionel Kearns. He liked Kearns's poems, but thought they had prose rhythms — something like "Down by the gasworks, dead-drunk," to quote an example from A.A. Hill, his Texas mentor. After Mexicans, his students seemed painfully reticent, well-adjusted, yet unhappy. He wanted to tell half of them to go away and get a job that would fit their capacities and to screw and drink around and stop messing up the only youth they'd ever have by trying to learn things they couldn't.

Civic Edmonton was in chaos. The re-elected mayor had once been forced to resign for corruption in office and breach of public trust. Now he was returned to office. Edward's colleagues had circulated a protest petition, which he refused to sign, on the grounds that he liked corruption. Citizens unfriendly to the university made barbed comments in beer-halls, especially if he wore glasses. He explained to Charles that Alberta's neighbour, Saskatchewan, had, with its New Democratic Party, North America's only freely elected, avowedly socialist government. But since 1935, Albertans had been ruled by Social Credit, which espoused press censorship, compulsory sterilization of the mentally handicapped, and nationalization of banks. Ernest Manning, the Alberta premier, was a minister who conducted a radio show, the "Back to the Bible Hour."

Distances were so great that you had to take busses, or else walk miles. Amid suburban sprawl, the downtown was small. Skid Road, around 97th St. — all streets and avenues were numbered — was populated by some French, and a lot of Crow, Blackfoot, and Métis, the beer-halls and all-night Chinese restaurants catering to pimps, prostitutes, and hustlers, along with female-starved bush pilots and loggers from places like Lesser Slave Lake, Yellowknife, and Uranium City. You would sit at 3 a.m. in an all-night restaurant in a frozen northern city, trying to convey to a half-drunken young Crow that you were interested in him, while he was trying to convey to you that if you were interested in a $10-dollar prostitute he had one for you — both of you, as well as the prostitute, trying to look unconcerned under the bored eyes of the police.

Indians looked so much like Mexicans that he could hardly refrain from speaking to them in Spanish. In Mexico, he could have sat all night drinking in the red-light districts, amid music, bright murals, laughter, hair-pulling or knife-pulling (hair, between women; knife, between men). He was reading Oscar Lewis's *The Children of Sanchez*, which reminded him of every Mexican he'd ever known.

He went to bed late and woke early. Only beer and masturbation put him to sleep. He'd always been haunted by lines of Hart Crane, "And so it was I entered the broken world / To trace the visionary company of love..." As Charles once said, when you're a child or teenager, being homosexual was like a game, something you played at, and all of a sudden you were grown up and you were a homosexual, part of the broken world. He could understand now what Genet, or Sartre on Genet, meant by "willing one's homosexuality." Once you made the choice, it was made. Maybe he was lucky having no one he cared about, and, except for the law, nothing he feared. Once he met a man who'd remembered having seen him six years ago in a professor's office. He wondered if his penis had been dangling to make such an impression.

The days grew shorter, the leaves fewer; the last asters and Michaelmas daisies withered. Soon it snowed and the snow stayed, the sun rising at 10 a.m. and setting at 4 p.m. Since the hours assigned to him were early, he taught in darkness, on the way stopping for a pink lemonade. Miles and miles of flat land lay about. A rare reminder of the past was an empty log cabin that optimism or opportunism called a "fort." By the highway south of town an historical plaque read, "Here Passed the Thundering Herd." The city's houses were of brick and stucco, arranged in symmetrical rows on symmetrical streets in symmetrical blocks laid out like a chessboard with small symmetrical trees in front of each. The residential districts were strictly residential and the business districts, business, which a symmetrical Prussian colleague said pleased him. "So neat. None of the horrible unplanned promiscuity of Europe."

He seemed to be the only customer of a downtown chicken shack, owned by a fat American black woman whose jukebox's rhythm 'n' blues records played like echoes of his adolescence. To Dennis Lee, whom he had met in Toronto, he wrote that in a city "8/9 submerged in inertia and suburbia," his "hyperthyroidism was less hyper, but his alcoholism was running wild." On Thanksgiving, he took a bumpy bus-ride, a thousand miles over the mountains to mild, misty Vancouver. *Anything* was better, even 48 hours on a bus, than a long weekend in Edmonton. Vancouver had gay nightlife; the beer-halls had the sparkling cider he liked; Chinatown reminded him of a second-rate *zona*. After all he'd heard of Vancouver's Englishness it struck him as much more American even than Toronto. He met a handsome older guy who took him home and wined, dined, and bedded him over the weekend. It was a delightful change from Deadmonton.

After Allan Lacey had moved his law practice two years earlier, his building had nearly burned down again but, Edward wrote Paul Weingarden, had "luckily been saved at the last moment in an inferno that destroyed most of a whole building block & I am now more than ever convinced there's a firebug loose in Lindsay." He added, "I wish the pyromaniac w'd come & set fire to Edmonton: I'd throw oil on the flames & fiddle while the city burned."

He had a huge gleaming office to himself: three desks, six chairs, two phones, three bookcases, and a filing cabinet. Enough for all the splits in his personality, he thought. The walls were white, the floor and ceiling grey. No window would open; the heat had to be kept at 20° C. He tried to pry open his window, but was squelched by a memorandum. Nor could lights be turned off. Henry Beissel, last seen at the University of Toronto, defied the policy of all-lights-all-the-time: at night his window glared like a black hole. By jumping up and down often enough, Edward supposed he could cause his ceiling to collapse on Henry's office directly below.

During two years in Edmonton, Henry had founded the literary and political journal *Edge*, the first number of which had recently appeared. His office was a hive of conspiracy: people running in and out, discussed in hushed tones the latest steps to be taken against the mayor. Protestors, including Henry, had attempted to read a statement at the first city council meeting amid a crowd of mayoral friends. A near-riot ensued, police were called, and Henry and his colleagues were arrested while the Mayor, like the Red Queen, shouted, "Arrest that man," "And that one," "And that one, too." At a second council meeting, the anti-mayoral faction picketed city hall. The mayor's goons rounded up everyone they could from neighbouring beer-halls and a mob pitched down on the picketers, spitting, punching, throwing eggs, and breaking glasses. Edward had not been there. It was too cold to picket.

The cause célèbre further strained town-and-gown relations. In beer parlours, he heard hostile remarks about university fuck-ups and shit-stirrers. "Let'em go back to Russia" — ironic, since most of the commentators' forbears had come from Russia. Edward's foreign-looking moustache and dark glasses seemed to infuriate Albertans. They resembled Texans in some ways, he thought: the same glad hand and then cold shoulder for strangers, the incomprehension of how anyone could think of living anywhere else. But they were less offensively inquisitive than Texans, and they didn't say "Thenk-yéww." Alberta and Texas had parallel economies based on oil and cattle. To Paul, he wrote, "About all Texas had that this place doesn't have was its ugly race problem; & there are enuf down-trodden Indians here to be considered a race problem..."

The next day he wrote the Colombos, asking to be excused for his hangover-affected handwriting. *Tremens*, without the *delirium* yet — but that, he said, would come with time and practice. It was halfway to Christmas, and also the Day of the Dead and the anniversary of his grandmother's funeral. The anniversary of his friend and teacher Laura Hofrichter's death was impending; her and Barker Fairley's translation of Heine's poems had been published this year. He enclosed poems for John to read, adding that a Mr. Dennis Lee was still planning to do something with them. He didn't know precisely what and he preferred not to know, because it made him nervous.

He had just notified his parents, he wrote Byron Black, that he would not be home for Christmas. They were "the original vampires, the body & mind-snatchers." He did "not wish to be unkind to my parents, for they love me more than I love them, which is a sad and human situation, & they actually mean well & probably think I'd be happier in what they consider my native country." He noted that *City of Night* was maligned "among the straight, like a friend of mine in To., who knows of my tastes & can understand & approve of paying a person to blow one, but is baffled by the practice of paying a hustler so that one may blow him."

At noon on November 23, he heard a weeping woman on an icy street cry, "They've shot the President." He thought it must have been in Texas. The sky was grey and the branches, black. He hurried to a drugstore, where they confirmed that Kennedy had indeed been shot. As days passed, he saw the arrival of the body in Washington and a tired Lyndon Baines Johnson, the new President of the United States, say flat, drained words. He thought that Kennedy had been the best alternative to madmen like Goldwater or slimy professionals like Nixon. He mourned Kennedy, not so much for all he was, though one liked to see handsome, calm, poised, well-dressed, well-bred people in high office, but for all he was *not*: a force of darkness, ignorantism, and fanaticism. Even if Oswald turned out to have followed Russian orders — shades of *The Manchurian Candidate* — it was Texas that killed Kennedy. For the next few days he didn't sleep well. His apartment was near the airport and he heard the noise of planes, thinking that the first bombs could come at any time. At least the beer parlours, often in basements, made good bomb-shelters.

He spent a weekend with an Indian, a former convict who was affectionate and permissive in bed. He couldn't recall who had picked up whom. Daily he saw endless steppes from his apartment's picture window, drifts piling against snow fences. No one came to his office. The students of Scientific German handed in translations of articles with titles like "*Biologische Systeme des Titakakasees.*" They only needed him as a translation-correction machine. His textbooks dealt with such existential problems as modal auxiliaries and extended-adjective constructions, up-to-date, upbeat accounts of supersaturated solutions, and the fact that the malaria protozoon produced a remission in the symptoms of paresis, which, Edward had to admit, he hadn't known.

At the university was a machine that, if he put a dime in, dispensed hot chicken broth, steaming, salty, parsleyed, in a wax paper cup. Such whirring silver glass-and-metal robots churned out pork 'n' beans and stew in cans, and sandwiches and cakes in cellophane. The sun set earlier and rose ever later. He should have realized that when people had told him Edmonton had only six hours of darkness in summer, it meant that in winter there was six hours of daylight. Though he refused to buy galoshes, the numbness in his ears, fingers, and nose compelled him to buy gloves and a Russian lamb's wool cap that made him two inches taller. He decided not to have his hair cut until spring.

He and Charles had resolved to rendezvous in Mexico; as a meeting place he nominated Torreón, Juárez, Monterrey, or Mexico City. If necessary, he would adopt the alias, "Carlos Fink." He warned that Charles would "find only an eccentric and now completely rigid and self-communing, self-sufficient young man slowly hardening into old age and crankishness." He advised, "I shall be there to dig Mexico, and will follow my own time-table. That doesn't mean I'll drag you everywhere but I'll insist on leading my own life and if you want to see me you'll have to go with me." He flew to Mexico City on December 17 from Vancouver, bussed to Monterrey, and arrived on Christmas Day in Torreón. Meanwhile, Charles had beetled down overland. Edward had not been in his hotel 15 minutes when he arrived: they hadn't seen each other in more than three years.

Edward dragged him out to country towns in the outlying Laguna, introducing him to a bullet-riddled bar in Gregorio García, filled with drunken peasants, who Edward told to pester Charles for a drink. An eerie cowboy village consisted mostly of doorless, windowless, bars, shit-filled bars with wind and sand blowing in and out, but a town named Chávez had 8,000 inhabitants and 80 bars. In a cabaret in Francisco I. Madero, he happened upon a taxi-driver from Torreón whom he'd bedded. After listening uncomprehending for half an hour, Charles exited. Edward later found him silent and glowering in his Volkswagen, windows up, surrounded by small children throwing pebbles at his car. He was reading an essay he'd written on communication with dolphins.

Being nasty was irresistible. It annoyed him to have to rationalize, explain, and argue with people, and Charles was a great arguer. He began speaking only Spanish. He refused to take Charles to restaurants, forcing him to live on snacks from street vendors, who Edward got to raise their prices. He'd tell venders

"*Este pincha gringo es tan tacaño que vendería a su propre madre si le dieran buen pricio.*" ("This gringo prick is so cheap he'd sell his own mother if he could get a good price.") He was behaving like a real bastard, he realized, but Charles irritated him by comparing the prices of ashtrays and stuffed toads, declaiming against the outrageous price of beer in border towns, and making a scene about an extra charge for a room in a Juárez whorehouse. They parted in Chihuahua.

Alone on Saturday night in Torreón, he saw the queens out in full force in the *zona*. A crowd of *campesinos* watched from the doorway of a bar. A straight guy who'd been dancing with a queen missed his watch. When the police came, he accused his dance partner—and Edward, who'd been standing next to him. Edward also encountered one of his former amours, a taxi-driver, who got drunk and took him out at gunpoint for a terrifying predawn ride.

On the way to Canada, a dust storm forced down the plane in El Paso where, disembarking, he was briefly back in Texas. At home, a shower of letters had arrived from Charles. In tardy replies, he reflected "on all the trouble you had caused me in my life, and on how essentially unchanged, sadistic, overbearing, narrow, selfish and limited you are..." The German Department secretary, he wrote, eagerly awaited those "fascinating" envelopes from New York, covered stickers marked "Personal," "Communism Killed Kennedy," and "Pray for Pain." He usually delayed reading Charles's letters until he could go to a bar and be "nicely rocked in the arms of alcohol."

He did wish that he'd gone north with Charles as far as Juárez, where John Rechy was living. He was re-reading *City of Night*. Reviewers had misunderstood the book, he thought: straights all assumed Rechy was homosexual. But, by self-definition, hustlers were *never* homosexual. The book was about hustlers and hustled and the clash of two myths, equally false. The hustler's was that he could practice homosexual acts as long as he did them for money, food, or shelter, acted the male role with a fem, and did not become emotionally involved. The queen's myth was that he could strip the male hustler to his homosexual core. In revealing this struggle, the book succeeded brilliantly. It also succeeded in catching the gay obsession with youth, a timeless world where "there were just two kinds, youngmen and oldmen. When you're a youngman, you're paid. When you're an oldman, you pay." In this world the hero, or Rechy, by virtue of superior intelligence and education, stuck out, and could never be wholly integrated. Real hustlers drifted into hustling because of economic motives, lack of education, boredom. Rechy was not a real hustler; he'd have to abdicate intelligence to be that, and intelligence could neither be feigned nor be abdicated.

Edward's landlady, married to a blind, 95-year-old, was a 75-year-old who bestowed Baha'i tracts on him. She was baffled when he insisted that Baha'i was too perfect a religion for corrupt, fallible human beings. But he read the tracts, along with Chomsky and Southern Gothic, travel books and Boris Pasternak, Marcel Proust, Thomas Lovell Beddoes, William Burroughs, Arnold Toynbee. With the aid of barbiturates and alcohol he managed to prolong unconsciousness up to 14 hours a day until it resembled hibernation. He jotted down his dreams of travel, tropics, sex, and greenery. As time passed, even his dreams became thin, repetitive, self-mirroring.

His refrigerator was stocked with ale and wine, and his cabinet shelves groaned with liqueurs and liquors. His weekends were occupied with reading, cooking nostalgic meals of rice and beans, and drinking till often he blacked out sometime Saturday and woke up to find it was early Monday. Byron Black, now living in Japan, raved of its marvels, urged him to come over, and promised to help him find a teaching job. The temperature shot down to 40 below, yet it snowed little. A blizzard deposited about six inches in three hours at nightfall. For once, he delighted in the weather. He went tavern-hopping in it, taking the snow gusts in his face.

At the foot of main street was a mahogany-bar tavern that had once been visited by the Prince of Wales but was now frequented by Indian alcoholics. Edward brought some back to his apartment. One of them, a teenager, stayed a week, and told him how the Indian boys would go on month-long hunting trips on which they'd joyously copulate. When the boy returned to his hometown, Cold Lake, he sent Edward a letter in broken English thanking him. His name was Cardinal. They were all called Cardinal. What he spoke was mostly Cree. They all spoke Cree. In January, his boss had gently, rather embarrassedly explained that next year they would not be needing him, and Edward as gently replied that he would not be needing them.

The first time Edward visited Henry's home he didn't make a good impression on his wife Ruth. His handshake was, Henry thought, in the words of Robertson Davies, "like a rubber glove filled with porridge." When he left, Ruth said, "I don't want to see that man again." But soon he was dining with the Beissels, and playing with their three-year-old daughter Angelica. Henry introduced him to a few *Edge* contributors; he wondered how intelligent people could last lifetimes here. He would rather have been a beggar in Rio de Janeiro than a professor in Deadmonton, though, in the best of both worlds, he'd prefer to be a professor in Rio. *Edge* published three of Edward's poems in the Autumn 1963 issue, and Henry and he had fun inventing an expressionist Québécois poet they named Jacques Poignard.

Battling the Social Credit government in the pages of *Edge* wasn't the only drama in Henry's life. While visiting Munich, he had become involved with a young woman named Susanne Forster, who came to Edmonton to study and to live with the Beissels, ostensibly to help Ruth with her chores. Naturally, tension arose. Susanne and Edward became friends. One weekend, while Henry and Ruth were away in Vancouver, they spent the time drinking and exchanging emotional intimacies. When the Beissels returned, Henry found that the vodka and gin had been watered—perhaps, Edward thought, by tears.

Byron still wanted to help him exit. "God knows why," Edward wrote him, "...my nature is a solitary & self-communing one, & can't really comprehend the sort of temperament that wants actively to help others; I tend to leave alone & demand in return only that I be left alone." He quoted from an encyclopedia: "Edmonton has been described as the boom town that refuses to boom...All cities, of course, strive for glamour, but it has been more difficult for Edmonton." A graduate student had remarked that he "lived & behaved as tho Edmonton wasn't there. It mite be a bit harder to ignore Tokyo." He quoted Charles: "… the minute you have a friend…. anyone who in any way threatens to put some sort of demands on you, you flee."

About bought sex, he wrote, "…as I've remarked many times, any tenderness you get in it is so much more wonderful than in a lover-relationship, because it's above & beyond the bargain…you get only the body, and if the other person gives a little of his soul, too, what a triumph!" Several months ago, he'd sent his old professor A. A. Hill the $10 that he'd owed him in Linguistic Society dues since 1960, explaining that he hadn't sent it earlier because his "experiences in Texas had been so traumatic I'd developed a sort of mental block, or amnesia, concerning everything that had happened there." To his surprise, Hill profusely thanked him. Edward wondered why he was so affectionate, since Hill had "seemed to think of me as some scapegrace n'er-do-well who mite in a sunny day ruin the fine superstructure of public relations for linguistics that he had built up over 40 years. I suppose my return to the milkless bosom of the academic witch is what's done it, tho God knows I felt at least a little more useful to human beings when I was teaching in mi tierra."

He observed that there were other E. A. Laceys in the world. One had recently died and, after his obituary appeared in Toronto newspapers, Allan and Alex received condolences, phone calls, and letters of enquiry — "or congratulation." He'd stayed up all night reading *The Sheltering Sky*, "which half increases, half diminishes any desire I mite have to go to North Africa." He was cooking his staple meal, rice and refried beans, which together with some photos Byron had sent him ("that warm wooden door in the sun, down from the lavender cathedral, where we stood for the shot") sent him into reverie about the rackety weekend he and Byron had spent in Matamoros.

At midnight, he'd go to the movie theatre to see *Hud*, which would probably remind him of "Texass." After, he would descend to Skid Row, and see if he could pick up an Indian kid, if he hadn't already at the movie. Or maybe he'd just go home to bed. He'd been having a disturbing relationship recently with an 18-year-old half-breed — "disturbing because he didn't want

money, or anything, it wd seem, except affection & a place to
sleep every now & then. I picked him up while I was drunk one
nite by ordering him to come with me — he was standing idly
at about 3 a.m. in front of one of these cheap restaurants where
his race gathers — & he, thinking I was a policeman or detective,
obediently did so. He can hardly speak English but pretends he
doesn't know any Cree."

> The West is full of these people, half-French, half-
> Indian, the Métis...a sullen, neglected, alcoholic
> race, often physically very beautiful, living in
> squalor. He is from the north country, and is in
> Edmonton at govt. expense, being treated for an
> arm-wound caused by his brother-in-law, who
> shot him because he (my friend) was playing
> around with his sister. His face is all scarred right
> now, because an uncle beat him up for playing
> around with his aunt. He said to me when I
> came on him, "I may as well, because I jack off
> every nite anyway." He first had experience
> with men when he was fourteen, on a hunting
> trip with another Indian kid, when they got lost
> in the forest, and the other boy threatened to
> shoot him if he didn't let him fuck him. So he
> said, "At first it hurt — ooh — but then I get to
> like it — and he let me do him it too — and then
> we do it all the time — first him in, then me — he
> don't like that so much but he have to let me do
> it, 'cause he do me it."

Edward added that Indians and half-breeds seemed to
him the only human beings around. The Indians were by treaty
direct subjects of the Queen and responsible only to her. Not
being Canadian was another good thing about them.

Would he join Byron in Japan? Writing him in April,
Edward spoke of his "genius for foreseeing all poss. complications
in an affair," fretted about class and plane schedules, and the
travails of immigration, noting that his "experiences in Mexico
(even granting that the Japanese don't have the Mexican genius
for bribe, graft, official letters & confusion) getting, renewing &
holding on to my papers have made me forever wary, & I'd like

my status to be as clear-cut as possible." Meanwhile, he cleared out "six months' accumulation of débris. I sometimes think this is the only reason why I move — to escape from my débris." He reviewed recent incidents.

Sunday morning, and at 11 a.m. I am sitting in my royal purple bathrobe, sipping alternately chicken broth and my favourite Canadian liqueur (if anything Kannadian can be said to have any status with me), cherry whiskey, after having — to use yr. euphemism — played rather exhaustively all nite. And a good nite for playing, too — since the temp., which had been mild, dropped some 50 degrees & a day-long drenching rain turned to snow, which I had thot I'd not see again after the 60-degree temps. that began around Easter, and I woke, after saying goodbye to my partner in vile offences against Alberta law (that cd net us up to 20 years in Fort Saskatchewan pen, if known...at 5 a.m., again at 10 a.m., because of the unusual white snow-lite in my stuffy, book-, bottle- & paper-littered apt. Now a dreadful wind is howling & blowing snow across the landscape of my mind as it has been doing for over 5 months, and someone else must have been playing last nite, because fragments of broken bottles litter my verandah & the whole front of the house, and at about 3 a.m. a bunch of very noisy & obviously drunk Germans passed my door, raving in their rather brutal English about making a guy if the broads wdn't come across. However, at that moment I was being made, so wasn't available. I don't know why it is that I always begin to lead a life of frenzied sexual activity just before I leave a place...

He bought his ticket weeks before he marked his final exams in late April. Brush fires broke out over the flatlands, and he watched them from the non-alcoholic staff lounge. The next day he left by train without bothering with goodbyes. The ice was coming apart in the river, rhomboids bobbing and clashing. Yet

Edmonton, at 76° F that day, was the warmest place in Canada. He had sent the German Department an eight-page memo outlining their defects in course set-up and content. He spent the night choosing and discarding, packing, and answering letters, and boarded the 2 p.m. train at the last moment, taxi-driver and redcaps rushing after him with packages. He felt like a coiled spring unsprung. He settled down to sleep, and did not see the last of the city as the train pulled out through the stockyards, across the ice-rimmed river.

6

DUST TO DUST

April 1964-July 1965

Being a man, I could not show hate or heat;
if sometimes, in a word for loss, a kiss,
tenderness budded, it did not endure...

~ The Children of Sanchez

After what he'd gone through for nine months in Edmonton, the Montréal spring seemed wondrous. He sat in Ste-Catherine St. dives, where fat green bottles ranged across the bar, listening to the crossfire of *joual:* "*Donne une Mol*," "*Ouai, ouai,*" "*Trente cennes.*" Gimme a Molson. Yes, yes. Thirty cents. He went to the Club Tropitolaine; at any rate he woke up one morning in bed with someone who'd picked him up there. The El Mocambo was supposed to be gay, but, since Fats Domino, one of his culture heroes, was performing the night he went there, he concentrated on him. He lingered in the Taverne Altesse near the French edge of the bilingual dividing line. If you spoke English you would either be greeted with a blank stare and no service, or answered in French, whereas, if you spoke French, either your French would be corrected by the person you addressed, or you would be answered in English. He supposed that eventually nobody would talk to anybody. This was the year that Canada was at last to get a national flag.

While in Toronto, he picked up a copy of *Gay* magazine at a newsstand. It startled him, as much by its juvenile crassness as by its explicitness, and the very fact that it could exist. The city's homosexual population seemed to have quadrupled. All the pickup places of his college years still existed, except that the most flagrant washrooms had been closed, not for reasons of morality, but for renovations. Other haunts would go in another year or so, victims of slum clearance around the new City Hall. But there were several late-opening, theoretically private gay dance clubs. It was hard to get a good-looking hustler to oneself any more — no sooner did one walk into a bar than the guy was surrounded. Two restrained, if naive, articles appeared on "The Homosexual Next Door" in *Maclean's*. Yet he didn't like Toronto any more than he ever had.

By the start of June he had joined his parents; his cousin Marg Tangney was marrying his high school friend Sandy Wansbrough. Meanwhile, his cousin Don Blanchard, the son of Uncle Adolphe, was attending high school, much annoyed that his teachers, recalling Edward the prodigy, addressed him as "Lacey" or said, "Why aren't you as smart as your cousin?" Replying to Charles Heyden, he wrote that he was tired of calling him "Charles." The name, with its slight fruitiness — the effect of the final "s," unusual in Anglo-Saxon names and reminiscent of French ones like "Georges," and the fact that homosexuals often affected formality by using full names such as "Robert," "James," and, for that matter, "Edward" — stood for all the things he disliked in his friend.

He found a letter that Charles had sent the previous September, which his parents had opened but not forwarded, and stumbled on some that Texan teachers and friends had written to his parents, likely answering their requests to know what was happening to him. Then there was the correspondence between the U.S. authorities and his father, who had tried pulling every string — including one attached to a friend, Liberal, and fellow Catholic, Paul Martin, Sr., usefully the Minister of External Affairs — attempting to get reversed the ban on Edward's entry into the United States. Allan had even received a letter from Robert Kennedy, the U.S. Attorney General, regretting that drug smuggling cases were irrevocable, even by presidential pardon.

Evidence of Charles's "complete mental breakdown and degeneracy" was his letters to John Colombo, attempting to get information about him. John had shown them to him: their "deliciously garbed form" recalled Lewis Carroll or John Lennon. To Edward, Charles wrote that he had forgiven him for a "horrible betrayal." Under the letterhead of the Scottish Canadian Assurance Corporation, Edward stoutly denied that he had turned him in to the deans at the University of Texas or, as Charles put it, "turned me into the deans" — that would be too hideous a fate, even for Charles. He should not "think you can blackmail me into writing to you by sending drunken pleas." He cut people off when they had offended, annoyed, or upset him, and Charles had done all three. He urged him, the next time he wrote under the influence of alcohol, to put his letter aside and read it next day. Charles, he said, was strange: "you revile, abase and calumniate a person, and then expect him still to love you," indeed, expected him to love him the more. "You want to be loved," he wrote, "and you are not loveable."

Edward's first book, *The Forms of Loss*, was to come out that summer, but as it grew warmer and warmer, his feet got colder and colder. By August, he successfully applied for a Mexican teaching permit. By September, he was back in Torreón at the Instituto Latinamericano and living in a high-ceilinged, pastel blue room with a mosaic floor at Doña Aurelia's establishment. In a bar, he found a former bedmate, Leobardo, serving *botana*, the free lunch. He wrote two poems "for Leobardo" — all the names he used were actual ones; he was incapable of inventing them; fortunately most or all of the people mentioned couldn't read English — couldn't read, in fact. In them, he described a dusty face webbed in sleep, smooth arms crossed upon a hairless chest, strong legs hunched against his.

He was overworked and underpaid. Henry Beissel was now at the University of the West Indies in Trinidad under the Canadian Aid program of the Canadian Department of External Affairs, which supplied teachers to universities in developing countries. To Henry, he wrote that he supposed there was joy, interest, and some use in living in Trinidad, though maybe not, because puritanism was rampant and virulent, posing in one place as progress, in another as industrialization, in another as Americanization, in another as Communism, in another as Catholicism. Back in Canada, Isabel Perón of Argentina — or "Isabel II" as she was known in Latin America — was on a state visit. An attempt on her life was feared. Edward surmised that if she were assassinated it would be virtually the only interesting thing ever to have happened in Canadian history.

Henry's problems in Trinidad were duplicated here: the heat, the speed-demon drivers, academic disorganization, the hopeless boss. As usual, he was having trouble with his papers. The passport he'd handed in to the Canadian Embassy for renewal wouldn't be returned until he sent a baptismal certificate verifying that he was indeed Edward A. Lacey and not some imposter. This he refused to send, not only because he didn't have one, but also because it was unnecessary: he knew so, having read the rulebook. But the Embassy didn't know he knew.

A friend of his, who'd stolen a tire from another friend's car, was in jail. It turned out that Edward's friend's friend had stolen all *his* tires from other people. Edward's *amigo* was blamed for the compounded thefts. For a month, he visited his friend, bringing tortillas because Mexican jails provided almost no food. He expended much time and money on a *tinterello*, a quack lawyer, which gave him a look into the deep false bottoms of Mexican justice. Astoundingly, Mexicans asked for, and accepted, bribes openly, right in the courtroom. It was barefaced corruption, accepted as part of human nature, and as the reward and prerogative of a judicial post. Edward resorted to a *tinterello* because, he said, a quack had more influence than a real lawyer. The quack got his friend out on bond, which was tantamount to going free. The final step was to pay the judge now and then so that the case would not be "ventilated," to use the delightful Mexican euphemism. The friend was only minimally grateful: another Mexican trait, he thought, was the expectation that a *patrón* — anyone who was richer or better educated than you — would aid you. Charity was good for the giver, *ergo*, the giver should thank the beggar for the opportunity afforded him of doing good.

Rounding up papers he needed, and keeping track of them, was made problematic by the mildly malevolent presence of a *duende*, a poltergeist haunting the household. Unexplained noises occurred at night, doors flew open without warning, and stray dogs got into the patio without anyone's discovering how. He had so far lost a safety razor and a pair of prescription sunglasses. However, knowing the magpie habits of Mexican servants, and the fondness Mexicans showed for dark glasses, he surmised that human hands might have been, or aided, the *duende*. Having heard that *duendes* were fond of sweets, he bought a honeycomb and placed it on his dresser, hoping that would serve to distract them from their routine restless activities. Since then, though the honeycomb appeared to have remained untouched, nothing had been taken.

In Mexico City, papers he had sent to the Immigration Department in August had vanished: perhaps its own *duende* was at work. Since he'd sent them, the government, and all the officials, had changed. Edward's tourist card would expire in mid-December and he had to get a new card or classification, or leave the country. With his Canadian passport in Mexico City, he had no documents to identify him as anybody at all, only the word of his friends that he existed.

The quack that he'd hired to liberate his friend was dissatisfied with his fee. That they'd settled on it beforehand hardly mattered. He summoned him for unnerving appointments in dim cantinas, in which he began with honeyed flattery and ended with veiled threats that, unless he was paid more, his friend would go back to jail, or something could happen to Edward. With his armed henchmen floating around, this threat seemed real. Edward took to bringing friends along. After several such rendezvous, however, the appointments ceased: it had become apparent that the gringo milk cow couldn't, or wouldn't, be mulcted further. The quack then denounced Edward to cronies in the Secret Service. They started hanging around bars, asking questions about him. He suspected that his tire-robbing friend had skipped town.

In October, after he'd boarded a bus from Ciudad Juárez, immigration officials yanked him for interrogation. Before letting him take another bus, the officials told him that he was no longer a tourist and not yet an immigrant. Back in Torreón, he had rows with two sisters at the school, whose father burst into his class to insult and buffet him. The girls' father and brother tried to get him deported. They also placed nasty articles about him in the newspapers.

It was not really cold — in the 40s F. — but he felt it was. So did the locals. With their inborn hatred of monotony and love of drama, they ran around in bizarre makeshift clothing — rugs and blankets they'd enlisted for the occasion, calling them *serapes* though they remained rugs and blankets, and long underwear shirts under short-sleeved summer shirts, with two or three hats on the heads of the men. The women wore pillows on their heads and handkerchiefs bound around their mouths. They reminded him of picturesque Russians wearing pajamas at parties in Crimean resorts that used to be seen in *Life* magazine.

To ward off his room's chill, he ignited the low blue flame of 192-proof alcohol on his mosaic floor. The spirit cost 10 pesos a litre. Local drunks thrived on it, and it was a fairly effective, not uneconomical, way of keeping himself warm on cold nights. Smudge pots and braziers were messy, gas stoves didn't exist, and no one had ever heard of central heating. The big, one-storey, Moorish houses with their great plant-filled inner patios and dark, high-ceilinged rooms were designed for protection against dust storms and heat, and offered next to none against cold and the fine rain of the cool season. His room often reeked of the alcohol, a not unpleasant fragrance. It consumed itself and nothing else.

The town had changed with the weather. The clouds were low, grey, and Canadian, obscuring the barren chalky mountains that ringed the town. In the market were great mounds of winter fruits like pineapple, guava, tangerines, oranges, and apples, and the winter vegetables: tomatoes, chayotes, peppers, green beans, and corn. Vendors softly murmured; barefoot children trembled with the cold. Apart from the market workers, people stayed home in bed, or huddled around braziers. He'd always suspected that the loud, light-hearted, dancing, laughing Mexico was a fiction forced on the country by the *idées fixes* and wish fulfilments of tourists. A whole other Mexico was revealed just by a change in weather, probably the real Mexico, the suffering, patient, Indian one.

He was not always happy here, but people didn't laugh at him like the jackass Edmontonians. Police didn't pick him up at 3 a.m., because the streets were full of people at 3 a.m. He was never alone, and he was needed in his work. He was needed in other ways, too—not emotionally, he could never stand that—but because everyone depended on everyone else, in partnership with, for example, the little men who sold *aguas naturales* and fruit slices on the corners, as well as hot buttered corn, open-faced sandwiches, and sweet potatoes. One man sold cheeses for one peso each, big, flat, white, delicious cheeses. At noon every day the man, *vendedor* to *cliente,* expected and depended on the sale. When he said that he might be leaving soon, the man said, "Oh, *no, jefe,* don't go — what would you do there, and here, who would buy my cheeses?"

Instead of going to a supermarket once a week, you went out to buy things as many times a day as required. In hundreds of little human contacts a day, a person was treated with gravity, respect, and the friendly Mexican formality, and by each of them—from the old janitor at the school who did nothing but would expect his little Christmas offering, to the beggar who passed by the house at five p.m. and got a handful of tortillas from the señora. If he didn't attend his favourite bar or market stall for a week or two, the bartender or stall girl would stop him, concerned, to ask, "Why haven't you visited us lately?"

He knew that all this would vanish, and be replaced by standardization, modernization, and mechanization, the diabolical plot to enslave people by telling them that they were becoming freer. He knew that a stable, static folk society had its defects, horrors, and medievalisms. But he would still like to nuke the United Nations with all the heads of states and pompous nobodies, and their directors of urban renewal and abolishers of prostitution, drugs, and poverty. He accepted, and accepted guilt for, children sleeping in the streets and the starving old but he'd fight against, the eradication of poverty because the human, humane values of this culture were much more positive and important. You couldn't pick and choose with culture, he believed. You had to take it whole, or not at all.

Fearing the day that Migración would expel him from Mexico, he learned from Henry Beissel that the Spanish

Department in Trinidad was seeking a teacher under the Canadian Aid program. Filling out a Personal History form, Edward suspected that he was alternately too humble and unassuming, or too freakishly humorous. He couldn't help it; it was the way he wrote. Unfortunately, many people took the humility for lack of energy and the freakishness for arrogance. He faithfully listed his undergraduate and graduate studies and teaching experience. He mentioned his interests in literature and linguistics, and tabulated every award he'd ever won, short of the prize he received from Father Peyton's World Rosary Crusade. He was ashamed of himself for committing the loathsome mess to paper.

A three-week-long vacation over Christmas gave him the chance to see Veracruz, where Totonac Flyers performed their pre-Colombian swirling fertility rites atop tall poles. When he returned, the weather had changed to hot sunny brilliant days and cool nights. The jacarandas, chinaberries, cottonwoods, huisache, and desert willow looked barer with each passing day. He loved to watch the huge cast-iron leaves of the fig drop, and the green fronds of the mesquite that fell and exposed trunks and branches.

He was growing tired, not of this city and region, but of too many classes, too much talking, and of his students, who subjected him to perpetual run-ins and denunciations. One day he got into a fight with his *bête noir* sisters. He expelled one after she told him that he was "always explaining, explaining, you never come to the point about anything." They called him a *"maldito"* and announced they would summon their father, the man who had burst into Edward's class the previous November. He told them to bring their *Méndigo padre*—not a nice term in Spanish. They began to scream that he had kicked and beat them. They were finally locked in a storeroom until they could calm down. At an evening adult class, he was informed that the girls' father and brother were going to shoot him on sight.

That Monday he got up about five a.m. and went out to a bar to read the paper. Suddenly he could not bear another week of classes. Since he hadn't missed a day all year, he decided not to go. He headed for the red-light district, where the school wouldn't send anyone to look for him. They did send someone to his home, who found his room locked. Meanwhile, hiding out, he talked to bartenders, and had musicians sing him songs. He got a taxi-driver to call up and say he was sick. Just then a mariachi band burst into violent music about a foot from the telephone booth. The school thought he'd been kidnapped. He was back at work the next day.

The Nazas, the town's river, was seasonal in its flow, but an enormous dam had been built in the mountains to harness the water for irrigating crops. Only one year in five was "rainy." But subsoil levels were falling rapidly, making for a permanent dustbowl crisis. Beginning in March, they released water from the dam. He had never seen the water come down the dry channel and always imagined it as a wall. To greet the water, he walked over the riverbed bright with poppies. The water came creeping like fingers or a snake's tongue. When he came to a pool, he thought at first it was just last year's stagnant water. But soon the pool began to wet his feet. He heard a dull roar: the water had broken into an old natural channel and came pouring down. Suddenly, he was on an island. He quickly jumped off as his island disappeared. The water poured, soaking in, the earth began to boil and bubble. Driven out came tarantulas and scorpions, hopping and crawling over the sand, only to be reached by the water. They died swimming, or survived for a while floating on a piece of foam, sunk later as the current gathered speed. It reached a small dam, filled up behind it, and then lapped over to begin its downstream course as two different branches that later joined.

And the children. Every newsboy or street urchin was there, fighting, playing, squalling, and swearing. They ran barefoot over the sand, they rushed along the banks, trying to keep ahead of the water. They lay down in its path until it licked their feet, then jumped up and ran on. They dug ditches, trying to stop its advance. Mongrels barked wildly at the water as it passed. Further into the city, families came out to watch. Finally, the channel narrowed. All the little brown children, with the water like an angry parent now rushing threateningly behind them, raced through the floodgates under the bridge and were off like a shot down the canals, the water after them. He walked along a canal, watching the water rise and the kids throw mud and stones into it. Hats, feces, and mattresses floated on the current. Water had come to the Laguna.

It became hotter, reaching nearly 100 F. He got a letter from Charles, who had somehow got his address from his parents, though they'd been ordered not to divulge anything about him to anyone, and composed a telegram to the Beissels, which he felt sure they would never receive. No one knew what or where Trinidad was. They asked him a dozen times what country it belonged to, then when he told them the capital was Port-of-Spain, they looked under "Spain" and tried to situate it in the Balearic Isles. Then they wanted to send the wire to St. Augustine, Florida.

One day about dusk a dust storm began. The wind called the *tolvanera* began to rise, the cedars and palms sighed, and brown haze blotted out the barren hills. The dust cloud cut across the face of the sun, which turned pale platinum and vanished, now and then peering through the clouds like the ghost of a moon. Palms blew over. All the stores closed and shopkeepers rushed to take down their awnings. The corner vendors covered their wares with canvas and rushed for shelter. Cars turned on their headlights. A few hours later, all returned to normal, with the air and sky clear and a cool delicious breeze. He enjoyed these dust storms. Even when he didn't have to go out, he often strolled down an avenue of a deserted city itself made of adobe, essentially dust. The Mexicans thought he was even crazier than usual. They rushed to their brown clay-brick houses, closed every window and door, and shut themselves up for hours in stifling rooms, while the dust filtered through every crack and cranny and covered everything up anyway, having sifted into hair, food, and beds. He enraged the few students who showed up during the storm by throwing open windows and repeating the old saying, "Everyone eats a peck of dirt before he dies."

The Forms of Loss had appeared in an edition of 200 copies, published by Dennis Lee, who'd just got his M.A. from the University of Toronto. It was a slim volume barren of biographical data. On April 28, a column by Robert Fulford in the *Toronto Star* appeared, headlined "A very special poet." *The*

Forms of Loss, Fulford wrote, revealed "a personality torn apart by inner conflicts. They reflect a young man of romantic sensibility who finds himself addicted to a form of sex he regards as both brutish and shameful," the homosexual world one that he saw "as bleak and desperate — and inevitable." On seeing Fulford's column in the *Star*, Allan Lacey rushed around Lindsay buying up every copy of the paper he could find.

Fulford noted that when Edward had been "a student at the University of Toronto his contemporaries looked on him with a kind of awe. Several have described him to me as a precociously brilliant student, a poet of great skill, and an eccentric who refused to live by any of the rules of his environment." A few people who didn't know him personally, Fulford said, "sponsored the private publication of his verse because they recall it as one of the best things about those years." With the review copy went a letter in which Lee wrote: "The book is of passing interest because of Lacey's turbulent career as a student at University College, and because he is a fugitive, underground sort of figure for a number of young Canadians..." Lee had seen him the previous summer, he wrote Fulford, but hadn't heard from him since: "It's possible he's in Mexico, but I don't know for sure...."

Edward's room was invaded by a horde of small winged ants that ran over the bed, floor, and him. They had co-existed peacefully for some months, until the ants suddenly decided to sprout wings and expand into his portion of the room. They were just mating, he supposed, and multiplication was the game of the game. Who was he to stop or suppress the eternal urges that provided still human links and common ancestry with the ant? So he took a broom and swept up all the winged and wingless *asqueles*, dumping them back in their corner to mate as much as they wished. He needed to sweep his room anyway, to clear away the dust.

7

AN ISLAND OFF THE MAINLAND

July 1965-July 1967

Too briefly falls the casual rain,
the too bright sun shines forth again
and warms a carbon lover's grief
on every dripping blade and leaf.

~ Kiskidee

He spent his first night in Trinidad on the Beissels' living-room sofa in the invisible but highly audible company of the family's adopted dogs, who were whooping it up outside with their friends.

When he'd arrived that day, speeding down a highway into Port-of-Spain, he smelled the swamp. For two years he was to be Lecturer in Spanish and Linguistics at the University of the West Indies. He almost hadn't got there. From Torreón, he'd phoned Henry Beissel, embarrassed to report that he needed money sent so he could buy an air ticket. Henry sent it. After two anxious weeks passed and he hadn't turned up, Henry phoned and learned that the money hadn't arrived. Edward had stormed down to his bank and raised hell.

He moved into a secluded house provided for him in the village of Curepe. There, wild dogs wouldn't let him sleep. Avoiding the pack, he whiled his nights away at the never-closed Red Spot Bar, a gambling den on the road that led up to his place. The dogs would scent him staggering home, setting off a crescendo. One fiend named Rover lived next door. He and Henry dognapped him for release some miles away, but Rover found his way back.

Edward became a familiar face for meals at the Beissels' in nearby Tunapuna, a village of tin- or thatched-roofed bungalows where chickens, goats, or cows foraged in the yards. Scraping along in Canada, the Beissels had found themselves with a big house and servants to go with it: a Seventh-Day Adventist, Mrs. Fredericks, their housekeeper, and a skin-and-bones widower who tended their garden. Mrs. Fredericks, stern and stately, dished up banana pizza, little plates laden with odd-looking fries and tubers, and omnipresent rice and pigeon peas.

He had arrived with only the clothes on his back, so Ruth took him shopping. When Henry had to go away to South America that summer, he charged him with the task of protecting the household. Sensing someone prowling one night, Ruth dozily asked, "Edward, did you bring the mail?" He did not reply: for all his vaunted insomnia, he slept like a log while guarding the house. In the event, the intruder only took an alarm clock. Another night, hearing a thump, Ruth rushed to investigate, but discovered it was Edward, fallen out of bed. Once she heard a row, and located him outside, barking at some bemused dogs. "I couldn't sleep! I showed them!" One night he came back reeking of rum, his face bloody, his glasses smashed. Ruth took him off to get new glasses.

She was skeptical about his many maladies. On discovering a boil under his arm, he feared he'd contracted the plague. Generally, he'd give doctors a self-diagnosis and expect a cure. Ruth's opinion of his physical valour was confirmed that autumn when she went to Venezuela as his companion. During a scary cable-car trip in Caracas, he buried his head in her lap. Henry, who earlier had sent him a reproachful letter about his dereliction of duty, could not make out whether his paranoia attracted violence or was its consequence. Some part of himself decided, Henry thought, that punishment was what he deserved.

Port-of-Spain's brothels were called "hotels." Once, in the middle of a hot afternoon, he and Henry were drinking in one, while the barman and whores sprawled in torpor. Henry spoke of how, basically homeless, a German teenager in 1945-46, he'd been taken up as an interpreter by U.S. occupation troops. Suddenly, a piano piece with jazzy riffs and odd pauses came on the jukebox. Henry asked what the piece was called. Edward went over to the jukebox: it was "Cast Your Fate to the Wind."

Those first few months, Edward found that Trinidad, where more than a million people boiled around on a small island, gave him claustrophobia. It was only 10 miles off the coast of Venezuela, but no one talked Spanish. The people were about 50 per cent black, 40 per cent Hindu or Muslim, a multiracial society that didn't work, he thought. Blacks hated Indians, and Trinidadians hated other West Indians. Every day was as hot and humid, as ugly or beautiful, as the day before.

By September, he was teaching at the "College of Farts and Sciences." He got up at 6 a.m. to walk to his office along green country roads through a half-mile of wood huts and houses on stilts. By 8 a.m., the heat became unbearable. When he wasn't teaching, he had to do errands before the stores closed at 4. He recovered with rum punches in dim, air-conditioned lounges, venturing out when the sun sank and the surprisingly cool night fell. Already, he wasn't sure that he'd last out his contract. But Trinidad was a holiday steppingstone to South America: five weeks at Christmas, four at Easter, and almost four months in the summer. Whenever he could, he fled offshore. In Caracas, he found that the university campus, a little autonomous city, was rife with wall-posted propaganda in red, black, and white: "We Support You, Viet Cong." "North Vietnam and Venezuela — Brother Nations," "Murderer Johnson, Out of Vietnam." Back in Trinidad, he was sitting in his lattice-walled office when from the experimental banana-patch next door a butterfly flew in on huge iridescent blue-green wings. Then it was gone. He wished it had stayed.

In early December, he went with Henry and the young British Columbian poet and linguist, Lionel Kearns, to a country town for a *parang*, a pre-Christmas party, where singers improvised lyrics based on the nativity story in a Spanish and French patois. Like Edward, Lionel had been published in Henry's magazine *Edge*. After prior stays in Mexico and Cuba, he had arrived with his Trinidadian wife and their children to research local English. When it was time to go home from the party, Edward couldn't be found. Finally he showed up. He'd been out behind the hall with the big burly fellow who'd played the washboard.

During his Christmas break, he went to Venezuela and Colombia. The day the passport photo was taken he'd a bad hangover; his dark glasses were off, because the Venezuelan government refused to accept photos of people with glasses on, he wrote Charles Heyden, "since they distorted the shape of the face, or so the lady in the Embassy piously informed me, citing Decree No. 86749 of the Ministry of Foment." At first he thought he looked Latin-handsome, but then detected what seemed to be hyperthyroidism: thick neck, glassy eyes.

Colombia was full of surprises. He'd been unable to exchange travellers' cheques except at banks, but the banks closed for a solid week at New Year's. Street-boys ran after him throwing stones because he'd made an improper suggestion to one of them, and he had to escape in a taxi. From one city to another he took taxi-rides that lasted as long as 18 hours, in sun, dust, rain, mist, mountain, and plain. He'd had 50 unexchangeable Trinidad dollars stolen from him, while not a cent of Colombian money was touched. He'd closely trailed the thief, never quite catching up with him, the thief unable to cash the notes.

In late January, he learned that his parents, together with Uncle Joe and Aunt Alice Tangney, planned a West Indian holiday. Delegated to find rooms for them, he found nearly every one taken. He feared they'd have to stay with him. Weeks before they came, he betrayed signs of an imminent nervous collapse. Finally he found rooms, and advance tickets for Carnival functions. The night before their arrival, he disappeared. When, seeking their son, Allan and Alex came to the Beissels' home, Henry had to fetch him by force. His mother embraced Edward with what Henry termed "a glutinous hug" while he shrank with embarrassment. The Beissels thought that Allan was sober and reserved; Alex, garrulously inane. At a beach, the little family was caught in a snapshot: Edward in dark glasses and moustache, arms behind his back, the silver-moustached Allan, looking out of place, Alex on spindly legs.

To spend nearly a month with neurotic older people—
Aunt Alice, the exception, was charming and adaptable—who
complained and talked incessantly, strained his nerves and
drained his good nature. When they learned Trinidad was a
left-hand-drive country, they decided they didn't want a car,
so Edward desperately turned to Lal Kaloo, an Indian friend
and taxi driver. For a small sum, Lal agreed to chauffeur them.
During one week, they covered more than 600 miles—this on an
island only 60 miles long and 40 miles wide. Edward thought
Carnival would kill his family; instead, they lapped it up.

Carnival began on the Monday before Ash Wednesday.
The *pan* steel drums started, and the *mas'* began with its
costumed sun gods, emperors, unicorns, and devils. Sipping
ginger beer or sucking tart tamarind candles, he watched the
dancing called "jumping," and a rhythmic shuffle to tunes they
called "roadmarches." Now he knew why Trinidadians had no
energy left for the rest of the year. He had to squire the family
for weekends in Tobago, Venezuela, and Barbados. At last,
after monopolizing him for February and much of March, they
departed. He thought they'd enjoyed themselves, but he had
never been so glad to see anyone leave. Nor, once they'd gone,
had he enjoyed his solitude more.

March 20, St. Joseph's Day, arrived, an important feast
in Trinidad. He kept waking to the sound of dogs, roosters, and
steel bands. Through Charles, he renewed contact with Byron
Black, writing him that he was "tired, having got in at 6 a.m. (it
is now 11) and written several letters, aided by a few puffs of
ganja." The West Indies was "perverse, exasperating, dull and
provincial." He hated sugarcane, two-storey stilt houses with
gingerbread and balconies, and Angostura bitters. "The heart for
all intents & purposes, is in Britain. Besides the Carnival, cricket
and afternoon tea are the two basic national ceremonies." Though
Trinidad had just gained its independence, the government
building was still called "Whitehall." People suffered angst
about the "brain drain": Edward sympathized with a woman
who wrote to a newspaper that the true crime was bringing
brains back to this drain.) In this society, "nothing and none
works as it or he should," "mails are never delivered, or arrive
late, or are never sent..." The lights never worked properly, and

"one's office phone goes out of order in December and is still out of order in March, despite half-a-hundred complaints to insolent people who say, `sorry, gentleman, there are others ahead of you on your repair list'." Books ordered took three weeks to get from Port-of-Spain, eight miles away.

Violence lurked: "I've already been beaten up twice, and my pockets picked countless times; I fear to go to bars here, refuse to carry a wallet because its bulge can be detected....I'd carry a gun but it's not allowed, & they'd prob. rob me to get the gun, or kill me with it." He told Byron, "Trinidad shd have an active volcano, or an earthquake which wd cause it to sink into the sea, or should be made a preserve for tropical insects."

When he boozed, he began at noon, when the teenagers came out to drink. He had plenty of chances with the black boys, but he disliked the "huge ebony-and-rose penises, bodies that smelt of sour milk, the wiry, sponge-like hair." He got stock approaches from diseased slatterns, even though they'd seen him dozens of times: "What ship you really from, darling?", "Buy me a Coke, dear." When he took along a dark-skinned slumming academic, they thought he was a cab driver showing round a rich tourist and offered him a rake-off if he'd persuade Edward to "brush" with them. He found Indians more compatible, though, due to a Hindu prohibition, they didn't swallow semen. They were shy and distant, but, once he made contact, there was no supply problem: there might be a dozen brothers in a family.

He brooded on his Texas legal difficulties. To enter the United States again, he'd have to convince the Customs people that he was not an enemy alien. Moreover, they'd never let him work there. Meanwhile, Allan continued his hopeless attempt to obtain a Presidential pardon. Edward didn't think he'd take a pardon now if it were offered; he'd reject it on the grounds that he didn't consider what he'd done to be a crime.

Ganja grew wild in Trinidad, but it didn't release his inhibitions. Sometimes it made him euphoric; sometimes it relieved him of a hangover; sometimes, it filled him with dark delusions. But alcohol, though, was the great yea-sayer. True, when he woke up, his hands trembled, but that was because he suffered from "peripheral neuritis," he thought. The stress of Trinidad lent itself to drinking, if not eating; he was still under

150 pounds. Trinidad cooking was rice, gravy, chicken, pigeon peas, lentils, and eggplant. Trinidadians, like Mexicans, were either slim or fat: he compared the lithe Indian boys of 17 to their pot-bellied, triple-chinned elder brothers of 27.

Spring classes ended with a month of holidays ahead. He and Henry planned a trek through the jungles of Venezuela to visit Angel Falls, the world's tallest waterfall. While Henry had been in Trinidad, he'd become something of a popular hero, labelled by the government and press as a leftist agitator. A former Catholic with an animus against the church, he gave a speech attacking its influence, especially on education: the headline the next day was BEISSEL BLASTS BIBLE. A few days before they left, Henry made a speech in which he assailed U. S. policy in Vietnam.

Landing at Maturín airport on the Venezuelan coast for passport control, they were supposed to go on to Caracas. They waited in a lounge until everyone else was processed. Finally, someone waved them through a door. Here they were swarmed by civilian-garbed, machine-gun-toting secret policemen, who whisked them into a waiting black car. They were sped away to an unknown destination, which turned out to be a windowless room with posters showing how guns could be disassembled. The officers kept asking Henry whether he'd been in Cuba, which he hadn't. They searched their suitcases: to Henry's disgust, Edward eagerly showed them everything. When they peered at tooth powder, Henry sarcastically told them it was cocaine. Edward apologized, commenting that he was high-strung.

Later that day, Edward paid the guards for their food, which Henry declined to share. They asked them to pay for their stay in jail: Edward paid, Henry didn't. Allowed into a yard, they noticed what seemed to be bullet holes in the walls. During two days of incommunicado confinement, Edward predicted that they'd soon join Latin America's *desaparecidos*. By now Henry was badly worried, and wrote what he thought might be a farewell letter to Ruth. When they were driven away, he dropped his letter out the window, hoping that it might somehow be sent on. As they passed a church, Edward, to Henry's amazement, crossed himself. Out in the country, they halted in the middle of a forest. Henry thought that his last hour had come. But it was not a bullet in the back of the head; their captors needed to take a pee. They stopped at a nice restaurant, where the *jefe* bought them daiquiris. The policemen had further treats for them. They went to an army brothel. Truly, the girls were pretty, though Edward did not avail himself of their services.

After they were returned to Maturín airport, Henry demanded that they be allowed to go on to Caracas so they could lodge a protest. Instead, they were put on a plane for Trinidad. "Don't think that it's over," Edward told Henry. He was sure a bomb was planted on board. In the aftermath, they drafted severe complaints to Venezuela authorities. Their adventure confirmed Edward's view that the country combined the worst of Latin America and Anglo-America: its citizens discourteous, domineering, and bad-tempered, ruled by a "hypocritical, student-murdering government."

On his excursions into the hilly countryside, thunderclouds gathered, and clouds of butterflies. A lake of pitch bubbled. He heard singing frogs, touched the sensitive plant that instantly closed its leaves. "Take it light!", "Take it slow!" so the Trinidadians instructed, or else said, "I don't have" for "There isn't any." The black hills softened to green and brown at daybreak, the rising sun a gong summoning the ladies to market and mass, then naps. At one o'clock, the rain would begin, then at two, the hot sun again. By the rum-shop doors, the young men "limed," idling and ogling girls. The pale rose evening curtained the mountain; darkness settled.

Inland, the high woods were near-jungles; a chain of low mountains crossed the island west to east. The poui, Trinidad's national tree, dazzled in pink and gold, air plants trembled, bowerbirds whistled. At night you heard the whirring wings of the *diablotin*, the devil-bird, beating overhead, uttering a mournful cry when disturbed. It lived in great flocks in mountain caves. Blind, these green- and red-feathered parrots ventured forth only at night to eat the fruit of the oil palm. At certain times, they flew by night hundreds of miles to Venezuela, then to Peru and Brazil, guided by some private radar so they could eat the small, sweet fruit of the oil palm. Their caves were filled with tiny etiolated palms, sprung from their excreta.

In Tunapuna, the Beissels were now a larger family. Their daughter Angelica, an only child, had begged them for a sister, "a "little girl with long hair." From an orphanage at Christmas they took in a five-year-old Indian girl, blank-eyed, covered with sores. This was Myrna, who they adopted as their second daughter. Edward saw Myrna when she arrived, a frightened little animal who hid behind doors and wouldn't speak to anyone for weeks. The orphanage had termed Myrna "retarded."

Once, Edward dropped by while a babysitter was looking after Angelica. Later, while Edward dined with the family, he said, "Oh, Angelica, show your dad what the babysitter has you do when you go to bed." Angelica knelt, folded her hands, and began to pray. The woman had taught her to *pray*! To Edward's delight, Henry was so incensed he waved his chair in the air, roaring that he would bring it down on the babysitter, or Angelica, or Edward — Angelica had no idea why her father had turned into a maniac. As Henry put it, Edward knew "exactly which button to push to get me totally destabilized." But Edward was never malicious to Myrna, the orphan: he was her defender and advocate, always.

The Beissels were leaving Trinidad, though not before Henry had extracted a promise from Edward to write a "Poetry Chronicle" for *Edge*, which was to appear in Fall 1966. He'd agreed to write the review essay, provided that the piece was bylined "Edward A. Lacey, pseudonym."

The Easter to June term had been a nightmare of red tape, committee meetings, exams to give and invigilate. The head of his division resigned. He would have liked to follow his example, and the example of another colleague, who'd not returned from Easter holidays. Just before he left for vacation in July, he encountered a handsome young Muslim bartender named Mohammed Ali. Uneducated but intelligent, he was desperate to get out of Trinidad. At times, Edward had proposed sex, but he'd always demurred. Now, depressed because his exit plans had come to nothing, he went home with him. Edward asked if he'd like to go with him to South America. Eagerly agreeing, Mohammed Ali went with him as far as Lima, where he remained, hoping to find a ship.

On the day he left Lima, Edward learned that his father had suffered a severe heart attack. He spent three hours in a phone booth, trying to make an emergency call to Canada that cost him US$15 per three minutes. Allan, 68, had recovered, but he feared that another attack would kill him. Then Alex and the family would probably expect Edward to live with her. This he could not, and would not, countenance.

Travelling through South America, he found that only alcohol stimulated his libido. He even concluded that he probably was intended by "nature" to be heterosexual, though it was too late for that now, because of the emotional dependency on men that he'd developed. He felt as if he were trapped, forced by habit to perform acts he didn't want to perform, inhibited from performing those he did want to perform. In Rio de Janeiro, disheartened at having missed a plane, he saw a boy who looked startlingly like Charles Heyden. He boy was sitting in a sidewalk café with a dozen young toughs. The boy noticed his gaze, drifted over, and struck up a conversation. They ended up spending two days together.

That August, at the University of Texas in Austin, Charles Whitman took a rifle to the top of the campus tower and, firing into the mall below, killed 17 people. He got clippings on the massacre from Mary Jane Cook. He wondered whether Dr. Nowotny was still a dean, and what he thought about it. "But he seemed so normal, an all-round American boy," Edward could hear him say. "Get the boy's Daddy on the phone." Writing to Charles, Edward wondered if it had served to make Arno feel that there might be more dangers in his world than homosexuals who campaigned for the presidency of the student body, or eccentric Canadians who took dawn sunbaths below the statue of Thomas Jefferson.

Lal had become Edward's chauffeur. He'd pick him up at the campus and take him to his place to eat, then home. When his daughter Angelica had been born in July 1966, he asked Edward to be her godfather. To support his family, Lal supplemented his taxi-driver's income by pollinating cacao flowers — a "flower fucker," Edward called him. Lal was an invaluable guide to Hindu customs like the festival of Holi, in which everybody smeared dyes on each other's hair and clothes. Edward thought that Indians were at once sly and servile, dishonest in small matters, strangely violent under the cover of torpor, pacifism, or benevolence, self-interest showing in everything they did. But, then, everything in Trinidad made him uneasy, including the vivid sense of things growing even while he walked.

Shading his porch, the red-flowered exoria shrub on spiky stems had small heart-shaped leaves, and a smoky, murky smell. One night when he'd returned from the Red Spot ("Suh, you ahh the fuhst Englishman to grace his premises with youh presence. Dranks, suh, on me") four young men hidden in the exoria's shadow burst forth. One choked him, one anally penetrated him, one pumped into his mouth, and one stripped his pockets for his house key. Did the fourth one become the first one, or the second? At some point, he may have shat upon his violator. That violation of the laws of rape was not to be brooked, especially by caste-conscious Indian boys. They left him with broken glasses in his broken doorway. Lal found him in the morning. They chopped down the exoria.

Mainly because of resignations, Edward was virtually in charge of his department. If he'd had the courage, he thought, he'd resign and precipitate a crisis. But he'd grown fond of Trinidad, after a fashion. He'd acquired a houseboy, Ali, who'd been ejected by his parents after he'd repudiated Islam, refused to behave like a good Muslim boy and marry at 17 or so a sweetheart chosen by his parents years before, and settle down to make children and money. He was drawn to Ali's slender, gracile beauty. For Edward, theirs was an easygoing relationship: he improved Ali's English, helped him to form opinions, and gave him a taste of a freer life. Ali, in turn, protected him against people who tried to exploit, blackmail, beat, or rob him. He'd always wanted someone like Ali whom he could help, train, and coddle a bit. Byron Black would understand; he'd expressed similar yearnings. Too bad Edward couldn't pass Ali on to him.

Once he was invited to a Hindu wedding. They gathered under a rain tree. In a thatched hut set apart, the bride and bridegroom sat, swathed in white. She had a frightened expression; he was sullen. He refused presents from her father—clothes, money, all heaped on the floor—until the old man desperately offered a cow. This was acceptable. Someone in a dhoti married the couple while musicians played pentatonic music on gongs, drums, and sitars. The weekend festivities could begin. They sat at a long board eating with their fingers the curried breadfruit, rice, plantain, yoghurt, and potatoes, washed down by white rum, endlessly repeated like the music. Sitting with friends next to Edward, the bride's brother was drunk. He said, "Eat youh fill, white man," adding, "Aftahwahd we boys gon take you dong by de rivah and tread you." Which they did.

When Charles Heyden's father had learned that his son was gay, he insisted that he change his name. Charles chose "Randolfe," with an "e" added for extra distinctiveness, and "Wicker," for its association with "wicked." By the mid-60s, his button shop had become a fixture in Greenwich Village: a slogan button he created, "Legalize Pot," became a great hit. Randy arrived in late January. Lal drove them past Port-of-Spain's monumental garbage dump, where Randy shot Super-8 scenes of the vultures, and taxied them all over the island. A keen student of black/white relations back home, Randy saw racism, Trinidad style: Lal's sister commented on some figure crossing the road, "Get your black ass out of here, you nigger." He took a fancy to a calypso, "No Money, No Love" and met Edward's black acquaintances like the money-lender Flash, his staff of strong-arm enforcers, and his stable of girls, as well as the violent Kelvin, whom Randy shocked by smoking dope before noon.

Writing "Rancidy" after his departure, Edward said that on balance he'd thoroughly enjoyed his visit, though it had increased his discontent. After contact for a few days with someone from "away," especially someone of drive and ambition, he found it nearly impossible to communicate with local people, even the intelligent, likeable Lal. In some ways, he was relieved that Randy reinforced his negative impressions of Trinidad; finding most expatriates reasonably enthusiastic about the place, he'd begun to wonder if he was a malcontent in paradise. He was pleased that his long vexed friendship with Randy had moved into an undemanding phase.

That year the university had instituted rigid new security arrangements, ostensibly because an air-conditioning unit had been stolen. The campus was wire-fenced, and gates were locked from 6 p.m. to 6 a.m. Now the administration had the campus road closed off with a guarded gate. Campus cops manned it, including an obese fellow termed a "sergeant," who let in a bunch of cursing drunken Jamaicans who mocked Edward at the top of their lungs. Edward wrote the authorities, accusing the sergeant of dereliction of duty and encouraging the use of profanity. The sergeant protested, "What have I done to you? What were you trying to do to me? Why, oh, Lord."

Under a new system, cars required a university sticker to enter the campus. When Lal came to pick him up, the cops said he should have a sticker on his cab. Although Edward pointed out that Lal always came in the same car at the same hour every night, sometimes they let him in, sometimes they didn't. Sometimes they let him in on foot, sometimes not. One Saturday, someone came running to say that Lal had been stopped at the gates. Edward found the fat sergeant berating him. Edward got a speech about regulations. Before students and staff, Edward declared, "I didn't care about your fucking regulations." The sergeant accused Edward of trying to assault him ("Don't touch me, sir. Don't move a step nearer. You are violating the laws of assault and battery of Trinidad and Tobago.") He accused him of being "non compos mentis" and Edward accused him of being "ultra vires." He said that he should arrest Edward for saying "fucking" in his presence. Edward wrung his hands and asked him how *dare* he use this word in the presence of a university lecturer, and that Edward should arrest *him*. At this point, the policeman moaned, "Oh, God. Oh God. I say he say fucking, and he say I fucking, and I say he non compos mentis and he say ultra vires. Oh, God, oh God."

The guards complained to the Canadian High Commission, who informed the Vice-Dean, who reported that the Pro-Vice-Chancellor, the university equivalent of Principal or President, wanted to get rid of him. But he couldn't, since the Canadian government Edward had hired him. He wrote to the Pro-Vice-Chancellor threatening to publicize the affair to local newspapers and Canadian Aid. The cops stopped bothering him, but banned Lal. Meanwhile, his colleagues elected him Deputy Vice-Dean of the College of Arts and Science, designed to enrage the administration, or possibly because no one else wanted the post, making him both an administrator and the chief administration target.

A witness to some of Edward's clashes was Lionel Kearns. Edward's aversion to Castro's Cuba, to which Lionel was well disposed, his apparent classism and racism, his homoerotic misadventures, made him seem worth avoiding. As Lionel saw it, Edward's colleagues regarded him as someone who abused his position and undermined theirs. Some grumbled about the size of his house, and his neglect of it. He did not neglect his students, though.

Edward promised to send Randy his favourite calypsos, adding sardonically, "I hope as you sit and listen to the Mighty Bomber singing about the woes of unemployment in Trinidad and Tobago, you realize how little your penny-pinching country did for Trinidad, and how zealously and earnestly Canadian Aid works to alleviate the problems of this lovely, childlike, innocent, uncorrupted people."

Lal's uncle, a muscular old man with a shaven head, was in bad shape. While going home drunk one night, he sank into a ditch, where he lay for many hours, paralyzed from the neck down because of a severed spinal cord. Lal's family got Edward to send a telegram informing a relative in Canada. The old man lapsed into a coma and died. Lal's family was grief-stricken, since he'd been like a father to them, and had given up his share of an inheritance to allow Lal's mother to build the house in which the Kaloo family lived.

Aside from consoling Lal, Edward had to prepare, invigilate, and correct exams. Exams were marked once by Edward and his colleagues, then re-marked by the department head in the main campus at Jamaica, then sent off to the External Examiner at the University of London to be marked again. Local examiners collated the marks, discussed borderline cases, and flew up to Jamaica for a meeting in late June — the trip cost $100,000, yet the administration allotted all of Humanities only $25,000 a year for library book-buying. Edward appalled his colleagues by telling students who'd asked him what marks he'd given them. They told him that he'd cause the system to collapse. He wished he could cause it to collapse, since it seemed to him a ludicrous waste of time, and greatly strained the budget, the students' nerves, and the teachers' time.

He ordered from Randy a gross of buttons emblazoned with "MORE CANADIAN AID." He wore one, distributed a few to his friends, and soon everyone was clamouring for more, not comprehending his irony. West Indians believed that the world owed them a living, he thought, that everyone loved them and was sorry for evils done to their ancestors, and that aid was natural right. Well, why shouldn't you feel that way, in a country where mangoes rotted because no one could eat them all, bread grew on trees, the sun never stopped shining, the aid never stopped coming, and there was always a white man around to beg a loan from? He scattered the buttons like confetti, careful to say that MORE should be pronounced with a pitch rise at the end of the phrase to indicate tentativeness. If you wore a button saying "Gimme a shillin nah, white man," he thought, you wouldn't even need to make the effort to ask for alms, you could just stick your chest in someone's face.

He regretted that Randy's most recent letter hadn't provided a recipe on how to prepare banana peels for their supposed psychotropic effects. Excited, his friend Flash had sent one his boys for "ah poun ah figs," bananas. Alas, Flash reported that the stuff was no good. To Edward's relief, Kelvin, another associate, was in jail: he'd been pressuring him too much for help. Kelvin had forced one of Flash's girls to perform fellatio on him after he'd caught her in a dark corner, After she complained to the police, while Kelvin was strutting in the street, telling all the boys what he'd just done, they swept down on him.

Meanwhile, Lal had been charged with speeding: the Black police—there were no Indian police—disliked Indians and, especially, taxi-drivers. Edward appeared as a witness and, on the lawyer's advice, since the prosecution was lying shamelessly, lied shamelessly as well, shocking everyone, since white people never appeared in court, and were believed not to lie. Ali overheard the chief prosecutor say, "I had a white man on de stand now, and eef you hear how dat man lying!").

Although he'd been asked to stay for another year, Edward told Canadian Aid that he'd only remain if he were transferred to Jamaica, where he had a friend in Gabriel

Couthard, the head of Spanish at the Mono campus, but he believed his Trinidad enemies found out that he'd applied and spread calumnies. Turned down, he was not particularly sorry.

Apart from Jamaica, he'd island-hopped to Guadaloupe, Martinique, Grenada, and the Dutch West Indies. From jungly, mountainous Dominica, he'd arrived in St. Lucia on a night boat—the Canadian-donated *S.S. Federal Maple*—and, once ashore, reeled from landsickness. He had also crossed on deck to Guyana, that piece of the West Indies on the mainland, with no bedding and no food except a huge roti baked by Lal's mother. After three days he arrived, red-skinned with manganese dust.

Apart from attending the occasional poetry reading with Henry, he had scant contact with local writers like Eric Roach, the Afro-Saxon Tobago poet whose most memorable line was, "I was the archipelago hope would mould into dominion." In Trinidad, the local autocrat was Dr. Eric Williams, a former university professor and an expert on slavery. He had met him once, but Williams's cold handshake, piercing eyes, and precise professorial speech impressed him. No one but Williams, he thought, could have kept such a tatterdemalion, ragtag society as Trinidad together.

Edward's "Poetry Chronicle" had appeared the previous fall, duly bylined "Edward A. Lacey, pseudonym." He also appeared on the masthead as "Edward E. Lacey, Associate Editor." Writing to Henry, he said he was using especially soft paper in order to assure him of a liberal supply of lavatory paper for at least the next month, since he knew how expensive such things were in Canada. At the moment, he was functioning, thanks to penicillin pills, Largactil, and Librium. The penicillin was to combat one of the infections to which he was susceptible, especially in this climate, in this case a large boil on his right arm, that had surfaced after his return from a weekend trip. He'd got badly sunburned on a cloudy day, forgetting about all the solar radiation still homing in. Ever since, he'd felt unwell. The Largactil was for his shattered nerves, the Librium so he could sleep.

The Forms of Loss had garnered modest praise. John Robert Colombo noted that it had "Some excellent poems and high moments. The new Walt Whitman." The dispassionate

University of Toronto Quarterly commented that the author wrote "with pity and tenderness of children and teenagers... with pity and horror of the world after the fall, a sexual world of pick-ups, blue jeans and black jackets." It was the first openly gay book of poetry to appear in Canada.

By July, Edward was not on speaking terms with almost anyone at the University of the West Indies. Leaving, he refused to pay his electricity and medical bills, instead leaving the administration with a handful of IOUs from Trinidadians, which he'd never been able to collect, telling the bursar to collect them and pay the bills with the proceeds. He stole half-a-dozen electric fans and gave them to his friends. He left unpaid a $200 long-distance phone bill and a Common Room bar bill for 57 beers, 64 rums, and 80 tins of fruit juice. He gave away his bulky portable typewriter, and bid farewell to his friends. When his boat was about to sail, Lal wept copiously.

8

THE RIVER OF JANUARY

July 1967-July 1969

Here in a strange country.
Knowing the language now, liking the people,
But not wanting to stay, not wanting to go either,
Knowing this isn't the place, knowing there isn't any place...

~ 101

When he left Trinidad he traced the arc of Central America to the Isthmus of Panama, pausing in the city of Antigua, Guatemala, to score with two shoeshine boys in the ruins of St. Francis's Monastery. After enduring days in Georgetown, Guyana, and a scary six-hour flight, he arrived in Manaus, his new passport stamped to enter Brazil.

It was October. He expected that Manaus, once a rubber boom town, would be wild-west, but found in deepest jungle a tidy little provincial city with clean paved streets, lights and water, even cars—though there were no roads to drive them on. Buying TVs as a status symbol, the *manauaras* could only gaze at snowy screens. Why do that when they could sit at marble-topped tables by the mosaic-paved sidewalks, sipping beer, cashew-juice, and white rum? His Portuguese imperfect, he made do with nasalized Spanish, interspersed with sounds like *sh* and *zh*.

For the trip down the Amazon, he caught a British boat with a Barbadian crew. He heard scripture read and grace before meals, and Sunday hymns via BBC Overseas. The Barbadians pursued him, the only passenger, with cups of tea from deck to deck morning and afternoon. The river was as wide as a sea, and he saw nothing but chattering monkeys and alligators that, he wrote Randy Wicker, "smiled at me with an expression similar to that of the head of your penis."

At the river mouth in rainy Bélem, blue-sailed catamarans put out to sea, and at a huge market, blue-winged butterflies were ashtrays, and the skins of snakes and jaguars now contained cosmetics. He spent two weeks there, and a week stranded in the island city of São Luís down the coast: the airlines kept cancelling their flights out. By now he was feeling as if he was down with malaria, yellow fever, Chagas's disease, and dyspnoea. Reading week-old copies of Rio newspapers, he saw that Che Guevara had been killed.

Along the coast, Fortaleza was the port for the drought-stricken northeast. Edward's hotel was gradually being gnawed away by the sea, its staff homeless teenagers; its guests, prostitutes. Edward cultivated the homeless boys, and learned Portuguese from the prostitutes. He watched the *jangadas,* large-sailed rafts, unstable but capable of great speeds and distances, as lean, sun-wizened fishermen departed at morning and returned at night. Sand blew down the street of glowing bars.

Afterwards, came baroque impoverished cities from Natal to Recife, most supplied with wonderful beaches and willing boys. In Recife, he patronized a bar run by a softhearted Spaniard who fed boys and let them sleep there. After two Brazilians knocked him down — taking him for one of the Americans on leave from the airbase on Ascension Island who stole local girls — a lad named Ronaldo helped him up and dusted him off. One night he found Ronaldo sitting in a plaza, crying bitterly, his foot badly swollen. Edward got him to a pharmacy, bought antibiotic ointment, and bandaged him up. From then on, Ronaldo devotedly shined his shoes free-of-charge half a dozen times a day. For Edward's purposes he was too young, though Ronaldo told him he'd already had sex in the juvenile prison to which, homeless, he'd been sent many times. He sat

on the beach with him at night and held him—and that was all
Edward wanted to do.

Then the precipitous bluffs of Bahia, once the centre of
the colonial slave trade. Black prostitutes sprawled in the gilded
doorway of the Church of São Francisco. At the beach a rainbow
of coloured bodies broke out under the coco-palms. At night, the
votaries of *macumba*, Brazilian voodoo, came dressed in white
and beat drums to sacrifice a jet-black goat or rooster to Iemanjá,
goddess of the sea, giver of life, jealous mother of waters.

At last, Rio de Janeiro, the River of January: Portuguese
explorers had mistaken Guanabara Bay for a river. The sky was
a river, too. When it cleared, there were blue and gold afternoons
in Ipanema, where surfers rode crests and young men's globed
genitals pressed like curved fruit under their swimsuits. Above
them, Christ levitated on a mountain, Corcovado. When he felt
energetic, he climbed from Copacabana through the *favela*, the
slum in the heart of the city, to the Mono da Babilônia, the Hill
of Babylon, for the heartstopping view.

At 30, as he walked the Copacabana beach, hawks, and
eagles arched and soared above him: kites that measured three
feet from wing-tip to cloth wing-tip, riding the breeze while cliff-
shadows of high rises advanced across the white sand. A scurry
of boys jumped in and out of the surf, scuffled at soccer, ogled
the girls, or ran along the beach, their kites for sale. The breeze
soon died away but if you were young and agile you could a
kite aloft for almost an afternoon, snaring the wind. Boys circled
over him, too. On a hoarding he saw written:

Enquento viveres, ame.
Não importa quem nem quando.
O importante é a chama
Que Deus him deu, e eu estou te dando.

So long as you live, desire.
No matter when, where, who.
What matters is the fire
That God gave me, and he gave you.

At nightfall, lights beckoned from a hundred beachfront
bars. He lay on the sand and stared up at the universe. At age 67,
his mother had suffered a heart attack. She'd practically never

been in hospital for anything graver than Edward's birth—though that was perhaps grave enough, he thought. His father was almost 70, retired, trying to take it easy. By living so far away, Edward reflected, he was punishing them for what he thought they'd done to him.

To escape from heat and the Carnival crowds, he set off in February for Uruguay and Argentina. Argentina lacked gay bars—the military disapproved—but in Uruguay, where he'd been two years earlier, he reconstituted his network of shoeshine boys. In Chile, his pockets were picked three times in three days in Valparaíso, and the puritanical government of Eduardo Frei cast a pall. Bars closed from 4 p.m. to 7 p.m., prostitution was illegal, the siesta abolished by law for the sake of efficiency, and no movies or TV were allowed after midnight, because "the nation that goes to bed late can't get up early."

He took a boat from Buenos Aires to Paraguay. A Paraguayan general was aboard; loudspeakers announced that, as a gesture of courtesy, passengers could skip Customs. The next day Edward went down to get an entry stamp. The officials were perplexed: "But we *never* stamp passports." He wasn't convinced, thinking that the lack of the stamp might cause him problems when he left the country, so he went to the British Embassy (there was no Canadian one). They confessed, "We really don't know who *does* stamp passports in this country." They found out it was the Department of Agriculture and Colonization, which gave him his coveted stamp—as an agricultural colonist. They would've given him free farmland, too, if he'd wanted it, where he could grow cassava and sugar cane.

How had Dr. Mengele, Auschwitz's grisly medical experimenter, managed to set up shop there? Why, *anybody*, even Hitler, could've waltzed into that country. Like a slaveless antebellum plantation, it was run by Alfredo Stroessner, who'd seized power in 1954, confirmed by elections, some less crooked than others. Women didn't have the vote. The regime was wildly corrupt, yet soldiers and police were courteous and almost invisible. Asunción, the capital, had cheap hotels, good restaurants, old mansions set in flower gardens, and clanking open-sided trolley cars. One could safely stay up all night in a bar listening to harp music, and walk home at any hour—so little traffic that after sunset the bars and restaurants set their tables in mid-street. He knew he'd have to return here often: in Brazil he had to receive remittances in cruzeiros at the official rate; here, he got them in U.S. dollars, which he could later exchange at a much higher black-market rate.

He was in Brazil, he wrote friends, because he wanted to learn Portuguese properly, and because it was silly to claim to know South America but not know its biggest country. He also liked it. Not its high prices, nor the fact that Brazilians were the world's most mathematically untalented race and constantly made mistakes in addition: half the mistakes were deliberate, and he staged nasty scenes in countless restaurants. Prices depended on whether the seller knew you, thought you could afford it, or liked your face. Mostly, he was in Brazil because of the gentle, amiable people, with a genius for confusion. Nearly half were of African descent but, unlike the West Indies, not once had he been called "white man."

Returning in April, he went to São Paulo, a metal-and-cement megalopolis. It had no parks or trees, just skyscrapers, underpasses, viaducts, and streets stretching to infinity. After clement days, a bone-chilling fog often enshrouded the city after midnight. However, even staid São Paulo had plenty of screaming queens. He enriched his Portuguese vocabulary. Homosexuals were *veados* ("deer"), "to allow oneself to be sodomized" was *dar o cú*, "to reach orgasm" was *gozar*, semen was *gala*, "testicles" were *óvos*; "to fellate" was "*chupar*." Homosexual activity was referred to, especially while propositioning, as "*fazer programa*" ("to make a program"). He rarely went to the hustlers' haunts, relying on the passing parade. But complete availability sometimes produced in him complete boredom.

Transfers from his Royal Bank account in Lindsay had stalled since March, and every attempt to withdraw funds failed. At his São Paulo bank, he tried to write a cheque, which they sent to Montréal to be verified and returned so he could be paid, but he never was. At the start of June, the branch asked Montréal to speed verification. There was no response. He soon wrote his parents and his Lindsay bank, asking for money sent directly

from his account. He learned that it had been sent, but had never
arrived. His local banker half-seriously suggested that someone
had put a curse on him and that he should be exorcised. To make
matters worse, the Canadian postal service went on strike.

Penurious, he started teaching English at night,
augmented by small cheques that the bank branch allowed him to
cash, convinced, he said, that even the most cunning kiter could
not devise so complicated a scheme for writing bad cheques.
Meanwhile, the Canadian income-taxers were trying to collect an
escalating sum toward his pension. Three years earlier, a national
pension plan had been set up, and the government had eventually
realized he existed. He'd disregarded requests sent to Trinidad to
acquire a social insurance number for it, then faced a bombardment
of demands for back payments. Letters were held up for months,
then returned to source or sent on to his parents. The government
began to write to Barbados, London, and Jamaica. To all appeals,
he replied with nasty letters, pointing out that, since he didn't
have an S.I.N., he therefore owed zilch. As for the University of
the West Indies, all it could do to revenge the unpaid bills he'd
left was to lose or delay his mail, which they thoroughly did. He
wrote Canadian Aid to ask that something be done. At once an
enormous backlog descended.

He'd been in Rio the day students demonstrated against
police brutality. Half-a-dozen people were killed, and every
downtown street-lamp for blocks was broken. Blaming everything
on the United States, protesters broke the huge, enormously
expensive windows of the main office of the First National City
Bank, and battered down its door. Edward had wildly applauded:
he only wished it had been the Royal Bank of Canada. If his cash-
flow crisis continued, he didn't know what he'd do — rob a bank,
maybe.

His school closed down for winter holidays. In Santos,
40 miles away, beach boys cavorted, flexed their muscles,
and practised *futibol*. He sat under an almond tree, drinking
beer, thinking he'd rather starve in the tropics than prosper in
a place like Canada. Admittedly, his hotel needed to know his
name, address, age, and profession, and also his father's name,
mother's name, his previous address, his proposed destination,
and whether he was vaccinated or not. All this data went to the
security police within 24 hours.

Tired of São Paulo, he sought a job in Rio, where he welcomed Randy, visiting with a boyfriend, Peter Ogden. Despite a spell of cold dripping weather, he made the hectic most of his stay. Edward witnessed "wickerishness: instant desire, instant demand, instant satisfaction and/or childish tantrum." Avoiding "queeps" — the term he and Randy had coined for homosexuals who blended queerness and creepiness — he led him to Cinelândia, a cruisers' thoroughfare named after its 1930s movie houses; the Mangue, the Mangrove Swamp, a red-light district; and the Lapa, a slum thronged with drag queens and hustlers. In a Lapa hotel, Randy had his watch stolen. Edward introduced him to harmless, toothless Silvino, a boy whom he'd had met in Santos, who slept at night in a Volkswagen van. Randy gave him an orange American polyester wash 'n' wear shirt, and white American pants. Peter, keen to go up Corcovado, found himself stuck in a cable car with an Englishman for 10 hours — a close call for Edward and Randy, who'd almost joined him.

After Randy left, his fiscal problems ended. A 12-page letter to the President of the Royal Bank, he thought, had alarmed his Canadian bankers. They telephoned their Brazilian branch to pay him. The money came in a glut, the mail strike ended, and he got a letter of apology that explained nothing. Thus ended the siege in which had figured six lost or vanished cables, innumerable temper tantrums, his demand or threat to be repatriated, and an Embassy telex to External Affairs in Ottawa.

Teaching ESL, he never saw the man who hired him. His new school, he thought, might front a smuggling operation, or the CIA financed it. In Brazil, anything was possible. He resided in the Hotel Mengo, where he befriended a Mauritius sailor who'd been abandoned by his Greek ship. Since Mauritius had just become independent, the British Embassy debated whether it was responsible for him. Edward was the only person he could speak English or French to, so, though poles apart in temperament and interests, they became close. Eventually the British sent him back to England. He wrote that during his stay Edward had been the one person who kept him sane.

With a change of weather, Rio's beach-crazy, body-worshipping playground became cold and gloomy. People snarled; feet got wet and throats sore. What angered cariocas most was a rainy weekend that spoiled their beach plans. Then the sun came out and everything changed. Writing Randy, he noted that his "nacreous and incomparable ass (which you will never have again, Chuck)" was "burning as though I'd been fucked by a squad of futebol players." But he had merely got his anus sandy from sitting on a beach, and the rubbing-together of "his two lustrous pearly pink half-apples (which you will never have again, Chuck)," had irritated it. Aiming to look like a Brazilian, he'd asked a pharmacy for a suntan lotion "*para ficar o mais nêgro possuel.*" They gave him an odd liquid called *Un Rayito de Sol*, to be applied liberally. He turned dull purple, but there was nothing he could do with "false négritude but bear the black man's burden. How I wished I had known of *Un Rayito de Sol* in Trinidad; I could have confounded everyone at the University of the West Indies."

To his dismay, the Mangue was being demolished. The Mangue had always put sex in its proper position as neither supreme source of good or evil, but a minor pleasure like eating, he wrote Randy — "a reality that one doesn't get, nowadays, with all the romanticisation & fantasisng & utilisation for consumer-good sales, of sex, except in a red-light district." He wondered whether he'd become known, not as "Canada's John Rechy" but as "the Pablo Neruda of the *zonas.*"

One night he was walking through the Mangue with a kid named Jorge. Some drag queens stood on a corner. Jorge, irritated, said that if he could, he'd do away with the *bichas*. "But Jorge, I'm a *bicha* myself," Edward said. "What, you?" Jorge said, "You're nothing of the kind." "But I certainly am. Think what I've done with you." "That doesn't matter at all. People can do anything they want to, with each other. That's their own business. You're a man, because you act like a man, not like them." Which, he realized, for all its convenient hypocrisy, was his own attitude. He liked men, he was homosexual, but he'd never been *a* homosexual.

Cinelândia, he sarcastically wrote Randy, was "full of misled young Brazilian boys, their innocence besmirched by filthy foreign lucre, their virginity sacrificed...on dark streets by sinister foreigners, doing the *trottoir*, & the homosexual vultures in the dark raincoats under movie marquees or sitting at the tables of outside bars, plotting programs. With the increasing heat, things got worse & worse, & decent family people began to protest that they could not stroll with their wives & children thro' Cinelândia without being affronted by the sight of men so cunningly disguised as women that various important people unwittingly made advances to them and were rejected." In the Mangue, "dweeps" (drag queeps) were anathema. A dweep had strayed into it one night, then, Edward wrote,

> .... a hostile crowd of us virile Brasilian men gathered around shim. While our delicate lady-friends hooted encouragement from the windows & doorways where we had been serenading them & drinking in their charms, we showered manly abuse & spittle on the degenerate. The antisocial tried to escape, but our numbers, & male indignance, grew with every moment. Finally, I picked up a stone, a relic of one of those torn-down abodes of life in O Mangue, & threw it & hit the fruit in the face. The invert looked panic-stricken, as blood began to flow from its wound & as other men began to emulate me in my manly action. The crowd, and our sweethearts, roared their throaty approval. "He hit a queep! He hit a queep!" they exultantly reiterated, & I felt the man I am."

Abandoning his *macho* parody, he added, "They should all be killed — *machos*, I mean."

When summer turned up at the end of October, he was in the U. S. Embassy's library when student-hurled sticks, stones, and bricks broke all the building's glass. On U.S. election night, Edward was again at the Embassy. Because they were several time zones east, returns were delayed and everyone stayed up all night, fuelled by free beer. Until dawn, it looked as though Hubert Humphrey might win. Only at 4:30 p.m. was it clear that Richard Nixon had become unbeatable.

Meanwhile, Silvino was in jail for vagrancy, shuffled from one jail to another. This would be his future until he got a stiffer sentence, Edward thought, or until the police shot him and dumped him in Guanabara Bay. He located him in a yard among about 1,000 blacks and their female visitors. Silvino asked him to bring a tin of insecticide powder. When he did, soldiers looking for pot tore open the packages of cigarette tobacco he'd also brought. When a soldier opened the tin, powder flew out, covering both him and Edward. The soldier tried to hand back what was left in a bag, but Edward told him he doubtless needed it more.

When Silvino got out, Edward bought him a train ticket to Santos. He knew that he would sell the ticket, avoid him for a while, then claim he'd found no work. Sure enough, he was back a week later, supposedly just in from Santos. Edward quickly broke his story down. Later he saw him at Botafogo Beach, raptly listening to a transistor radio. Though he was homeless, the transistor was what he bought with his first week's earning as a soft drink vendor. Edward told him he was "congealing" him, meaning that he'd give him no more cash. But how could one be angry with someone like Silvino? Wasn't a transistor a sensible thing for an illiterate to buy? Silvino would show up, saying that he'd had nothing to eat all day and, flashing a smile with new teeth—how did he get them?—try to sell him a nearly full tube of toothpaste. Edward always bought.

He started teaching English to employees of a U.S. bank. Running out of funds, he was startled to get a cheque from Randy, and spent weeks wondering whether to cash it, to keep it but not cash it, to tear it up, or to return it indignantly. He finally cashed it

> ...because 1) I needed the money 2) your good-
> will, or lack of designs on me have been amply
> demonstrated in our last 3 meetings, & it is both
> vain & immature & paranoid to assume that
> one is the object, with one's thirtyish, plumpish,
> body & greyish hair...of an obsession that has
> lasted nearly 10 years. So 3) I chose to accept it
> as payment for my accomplished programming
> of cheap thrills, for my main other services to
> you in the past, including all the sexual ones (at
> 1959-60 rates, you've paid, with that cheque, for
> 5 of my innumerable blow-jobs — no interest
> charged, of course), for all the trouble you've
> caused me as yr. cicerone in the lower depths of

2 or 3 different cultures, & for yr. shortchanging
me on the exchange rate of the Canadian dollar
last August.

He further decided that it "would be doing you good
& doing you a favour to indulge you in yr. life's first generous
impulse, & that such altruism was unlikely ever to recur. "

Randy had attached one string: Edward was to account
for how he spent the money. Complying, he wrote that he'd spent
two-thirds of it on dental work and then a sumptuous steakhouse
dinner for a hustler. He thought of writing up a pornographic
depiction of his dental treatment—"how the dentist drove his
hard tool into the warm soft bleeding red orifice, how he thrust
the erect gutta percha rods up the scarlet canals, how the nerve
throbbed & ached in an orgasm of pain—followed by a couple
more pages of sexy description of the meats served on the mixed
churrasco platter," such as "the crunchy luscious bull-balls, the
rubbery cow-breasts that tasted like falsies, the scrumpuous
pieces of *filet*, like slices of a god's penis." He couldn't account
for the rest of the money. As Randy liked to repeat, money was
freedom. When Edward had it, he liked to spend it freely.

When summer clouds cleared between rains, the great rocks of
the bay smoked like flints, and you could see the concrete Christ
on the hunchbacked mountain. Then a cloud formed around
Christ until the cloud got bigger, lower, and darker and spread
over half the sky, chasing the sunshine to the other side of the
bay. The *cariocas* ceased their languid rhythm and started to
unfurl their black umbrellas like a caveful of startled bats.

At Christmas, he spent three weeks in the inland state of
Minas Gerais among baroque churches and colonial monuments
dating from the days of gold and silver mines. He liked the
interior, but its people's favourite expressions were "*Sei não*"
and "*Tem não*": "I don't know" and "There isn't any." From
Ouro Prêto's steep cobbled streets, he sent Paul Weingarden a
postcard on New Year's Day showing the penis-shaped Italcomi
Hill: "You were of course expecting me to write wishing you a
long, pleasure-packed ecstatic '69, and to say that, tho' I couldn't
be with you in person for it, I'd be there in spirit, weren't you?

Well, I won't. A Happy, Holy St. Valentine's Day. And I won't even comment on what Italcolomi hill reminds me of."

With him was Dário, who'd moved from his native São Paolo to become a Cinelândia *bozinho*. Dário called him the "plofessor" (he had a funny speech defect.) Edward liked how he always defended queeps and dweeps. When Dário returned to Rio, Edward went to Quiz de Foro, which boasted a *zona* of dirty dance-hall-cum-bars, filled with diseased old women, where orchestras of one saxophone, one bass fiddle, and one accordion played sambas, tangos, and polkas. On muddy streets, he found two boys willing to program with him. But since there was no place to go except the churches, they had to program in the shrubbery behind St. Francis's church, the town's churriguerresque jewel. St. Francis had always been one of his handiest saints.

One thing the grave slow people of the interior shared with the expansive coastal dwellers was a vigorous sex drive. In Belo Horizonte's *zona* hotels, each girl had a room, cluttered with dolls, bric-à-brac, and religious statues. When not busy, the girls lay half-naked with the door open; a constant stream of johns trooped up the stairs, peered into rooms, stopped to bargain, or climbed the stairs to the next floor, or clomped down again, bound for the next hotel. He joined the somnambulistic parade. Frustrating, since he was more interested in the clients than in the girls, and there was no chance to converse. For that existed the city park, a vast ill-lit labyrinth.

While he was in Minas Gerais, a famous Rio policeman, who had a gay son, led a raid on Cinelândia, the Mangue, and the Lapa. Some 1,600 people arrested were to be incarcerated until Carnival was over. The rightwing government had upped the penalties for possessing marijuana, and drugstores would scarcely sell you an aspirin without a prescription. At Christmas, a pop singer had announced he would go to Carnival dressed as "The Royal Deer" (the deer was a symbol for "gay"). For this crime he was sent to a penal colony.

Edward was still at the Hotel Mengo. The 21-year-old Francisco, who cleaned his room, had managed to learn only to sign his name and to spell out newspaper headlines and street signs. Edward had sex with him several times, a little unsatisfactory probably because of Francisco's country-boy morality: he thought that they should go down to the Mangue and find some women. Francisco was fascinated by Edward's map of Brazil. One night, when Edward showed him his native state of Paraíba and read out the names of towns, he began to repeat them, weeping.

He'd never smoked marijuana. Edward gave him some. At first, Francisco sat stolidly, declaring that the stuff had no effect. Then his eyes glazed. He jumped up and lurched out. Edward heard the sound of distant vomiting. Francisco told him next day he'd spent the night alternating between nightmares and trips to the john. Tremendously impressed, he wanted to try dope again. Soon he was smoking every time Edward did, developing so keen a nose that by merely passing by — though Edward scattered perfume and closed the door — he could detect what was going on.

The previous fall, Edward had met a young blondish hustler from rural São Paulo State, Guilherme, who lived by programs, arranging programs for others, and trafficking pot and cocaine. If he couldn't afford a meal, stay in a cheap hotel, or get his clothes out of the laundry, Edward, his social safety net, helped. Guilherme gave him all the pot he needed. He needed a lot as an alternative to drinking. Weed increased the pleasure of sex and eating, and usually relieved depression, though it sometimes frightened him. Once he had his first daylight colour-hallucination: a green bathing suit, which a boy was wearing, turned red, zebra-striped and purple before his eyes, then returned to green.

Now, if enquirers had asked, the Hotel Mengo might have been told them that Edward had left for Bolivia in January. Actually, he had merely moved to a hotel in the Lapa. The Mengo had raised their prices, it was filled with squalling brats and with tourists who used him as a translator, and it was too far from where he worked. He had lied to the Mengo people for the same reason that he told his boss in São Paulo he had left the country: he didn't want to hurt their feelings.

Ever since he came to Brazil, he'd got melancholy news from Lal. Prices of tires and his taxi license had gone up. His wife Molly was pregnant again. "Ed, I can not forget your departure of

Trinidad. Ed, it was most heartbreaking." And at the end: "P.S. Ed, I am still crying." (Randy used to theorize that people who really liked him for himself called him "Ed" or "Eddie," whereas people who wished to use him for some purpose called him "Edward.") Lal's story was, he thought, that of any underdeveloped mind in any underdeveloped country.

Outside his windowless room, cicadas shrilled like mad burglar alarms in the oiti trees, small, laurel-like evergreens. In the mirror, Edward took stock of his towelled, sixty-kilo, 31-year-old body: bronzed skin, hairy chest, strong runner's legs, firm belly, white round buttocks. His hair turning grey, when he went to the barber's, the shearings looked like tinsel. Hustlers thought of him as an old man. His visitor's permit was 10 months overdue but he was also paying (illegal?) income tax on his illegal income, because there were two laws: one said that people without working papers should not work; the other said that people without working papers who work should pay 25 per cent income tax. At the Canadian Embassy, ostensibly to pick up mail, he leafed through old copies of the *Globe and Mail* and *Le Devoir*. He hung around the Pan Am offices on the pretext that he might want to fly back some day and if he did of course Pan Am would be his choice, but actually to read the latest copy of the *New York Times*. He didn't want to leave Brazil. He didn't want to stay, either. He deluded himself, he thought, that he was a writer (but what had he written?), a scholar (what had he published?), an intellectual (what did he read?) and a half-dozen other disguises to keep from recognizing the fact that he was getting too old to play hide-and-seek. All these years soaking up other cultures, he'd been soaking in was tequila, mescal, aguardiente, pisco, *chicha*, rum, *cachaça*, and vino.

That year the Carnival was lustreless though, at the best of times, mass gatherings made him cringe. The queens had their costume ball cancelled. Hard liquor was banned, and beer supplies gave out, so there was nothing to drink except *maté*. In any event, Brazilians were so sensual that they didn't need Carnival to enjoy themselves. Of their enthusiasm there was no doubt. They scarcely stopped dancing for four days, if you could call it dancing when the streets filled with five million people.

Edward was writing his last "Poetry Chronicle" for *Edge* and for its final issue, Summer 1969. It was the third he'd done since he'd come to Brazil. For *Edge* 8, reviewing the past horrors of Ontario liquor laws, he'd noted with mock-shock that, under Premier John Robarts, people could now stand up at the bar to drink, even drink on Sunday, and "along with their meals between 1.00 and 3.30 pm, and 5.30 and 9.30 pm, that is. Before and after those hours, and between 3.30 and 5.30 p.m., I assume one is supposed to piss, shit and praise God for Mr. Robarts." He was "just dying for a beer — or even, Heaven forbid, a cachaça or a tequila — and it happens to be a 4.30 of a Sunday afternoon in Mr. Robarts' Ontario. So maybe I'll just mosey on back to Pijijiapan, or Chichiciastenango, or Pernambucon, or even good old Tunapuna, where the literacy rate ain't so high, but I can get a drink of anything I feel like at any hour of the day or night, in any position I please, and I don't have to thank God for Mr. Robarts."

Reviewing bundles of poetry books, it seemed to him that conquered nations, like French Canadians, Irish, and Poles, might develop original, even great literatures, but colonies, never. The colonized adopted the system, values, and lifestyle of the mother country. English Canada, a former colony and current neo-colony of the United States, was doubly peripheral. For his final chronicle, he located himself in a "large tropical city," contrasting it with the "cold and dark in the city or town where you live, and the roadways are filled with drifting snow, through which only the ominous cop-cars move to and fro." His Canadians readers were "unrelated to any larger human community, forever frozen by climate and religion and upbringing into uniqueness, able with difficulty to move beyond the limits of the kingdom of self, completely unable ever to move beyond the nuclear unit of two..." He bade "farewell, till we meet again someday, back in the Canadeath."

He landed a job teaching English language, literature at IBEU, the Instituto Brasil-Estados Unidos, a binational educational and cultural centre that, in Rio, had 13,000 students. IBEU charged tuition for its language courses, but received U.S. aid. He also began to tutor Juscelino Kubitschek.

When he was told that a Dr. Kubitschek wanted him to phone, he thought that they'd got the name wrong, had him confused with someone else, or that someone was tricking him. But when he went to the Atlantic Avenue address, he was ushered up in an elevator after bodyguards frisked him, shown into a library

filled with thousands of books, display-case upon display-case of
medals and decorations, gold ashtrays, and signed photographs
of Eisenhower and Kennedy. A minute later, the famous
Juscelino entered. The mineiro boy, son of a schoolmistress
and a Czech musician, had been a seminarian, medical student,
telegraph operator, surgeon, young politician, mayor of Belo
Horizonte, governor of Minas Gerais, then President of Brazil.
During Juscelino's regime from 1956 to 1961, despite corruption
and rocketing inflation, Brazil had leapt economically. But since
he lost the presidency, everything had gone wrong. When the
army took over in December 1968, he spent two months in jail or
under house arrest.

   Edward saw him several times a week, though Juscelino
was even more disorganized than him: their 9 a.m. sessions
ended up any time in the morning. He often asked for classes at 7
a.m., and several times proposed that they have class at 6, while
he took his daily beach stroll. One day in an elevator Juscelino
said, apropos of nothing: "You're basically happy because you
have nothing and don't care about money yet; but someday
you'll begin to care about it, and the process will corrupt your
soul utterly."

   When the sky was overcast, the pastel high-rise apartments looked soiled, the sea at Copacabana grey and ruffled.
Bars had shut their doors and lowered their awnings against
the spray. Gone were the ice-cream men with their tinkling
carts and bells, the lemonade and maté salesmen bearing silver
drums of drink, the brown young surfers with bleached hair and
salt-smeared faces, the lovers under coloured parasols. Garbage
men in grey uniforms raked up yesterday's ice-cream sticks and
safes. He was feeling *saudade*, an untranslatable word forming
a nexus around "nostalgia." One part of him thought that he
should return to Canada while he still had contacts and some
chance of getting better-paid work. His friends were telling
him that the snows had melted, cocksucking was legal, Toronto
boasted its first outdoor café and Sunday drinks, Montréal had
a hotel that looked out on a court of palms. But Canadians, he
thought, would seek and take their pleasures grimly.

   Ever since he'd decided to stay in Brazil, he'd been
dreaming about his father. His letters sounded as cheerful as

ever, even when in June he entered hospital briefly for a minor operation. All during the weekend that the astronauts landed on the moon he kept thinking of his father: "Well, he's lived to be 70 and to see a man on the moon." He kept getting the impulse to phone him. It was Sunday night, July 20, that Edward finally made his call.

9

A MOTHER ALONE

July 1969-February 1970

Bring back again those snowlit streets
Untrodden by the unwhite of feet,
Bring back again the hand of cold
That touched my youth and made me old!

~ The Invocation: Lindsay

About an hour after Edward made his call on July 20, a Sunday and the day before his father's birthday, his parents were watching TV after dinner. In Rio de Janeiro, a small fine rain falling, Edward sat in a bar, drinking cinnamon tea laced with rum, one eye on the TV. A quarter-of-a-million miles away, the astronauts awaited final clearance from Houston to take a giant step for mankind.

That hot night Allan had dined well: roast beef, and raspberry pie made with the first berries of the season. He abruptly said, "I'm going to die." Alex laughed, "Oh, don't be silly." Then Allan clutched his stomach and pitched forward. Five thousand miles away, Edward was bored: who cared if men landed on the moon? Alex got Allan into bed and slipped a rosary between his fingers. She called the hospital. On a screen a blurred white shape slowly headed for a hatch, opened it, and lumbered out.

Edward asked for the bill. An ambulance, lights blinking, wailed down a quiet leafy Lindsay street. White-clad attendants carried Allan out and Alex climbed up beside him. Edward paid, and stepped outside. Allan Tasker Lacey died while Edward shivered in the cold wet Rio night.

The *Lindsay Daily Post*'s death notice listed among survivors "a son Edward in South America." It took the Canadian Embassy days to locate him with the news. He reflected that the father had been a good, well-meaning man, but he'd never been given the kind of son he wanted. Tutoring Juscelino Kubitschek, a kind of father, he corrected his English letters, articles, and speeches, and fought his desire to end all telegrams with "Embraces." He was unlikely to do much to change the linguistic habits and vocal cords of a 67-year-old, who'd only begun to speak English in 1965 during his New York exile.

Juscelino was the most easily distracted man he'd ever encountered, and one of the busiest. He often went to bed at 3 a.m., yet got up for a swim before 9. He had at least half-a-dozen phones in his office, and talked on them all at once. Two phones were always out of order, and the government tapped the others. When he wasn't phoning out, people called in. Secretaries, chauffeurs, and medicos interrupted learning sessions. Juscelino's leaky bladder forced him to get up, often in mid-sentence, and rush off. He consumed endless coffees, but habitually fell into reverie. A distant, keen look appeared on his face, his eyes seemed to cloud over, and though he was looking at you, smiling and even answering with part of his mind, he was light years away. A reference to Nelson Rockefeller might come up, and the look would appear. A minute later, he'd shout to his secretary for a 14-year-old letter he'd sent him about the Brazilian rural-aid program.

One day, Edward lost his glasses, and since it was no good using the phone — his and IBEU's phones were inoperative — he showed up to say that he couldn't work without them. Juscelino said, "You are the kind of person one meets in novels. No one loses his glasses nowadays but you," and set him to translate a document. At times, he left him sitting around, only to send a secretary to tell him he could go. He poured Edward whiskys when he had a hangover, pressed him to stay for family parties and excruciating formal dinners. He liked to reminisce. The Duke of Windsor a perfect gentleman, how well the Duchess danced.

John Foster Dulles's stubbornness; Nehru, whom Juscelino distrusted; Indira Gandhi, whom he admired. What was Castro like? "Oh, extremely intelligent. And what a talker! When he stopped at Brasília in '60 I talked to him all afternoon, and I couldn't get a word in edgewise. When he left I was exhausted, and he was still talking."

Here was the signed copy of John Gunther's *Inside South America* with flattering references to Juscelino, here was the photograph of John F. Kennedy, flashing the famous smile, shaking his hand. Juscelino once wondered whether he should have sent condolences to the Kennedy family after Robert Kennedy had been assassinated. Edward told him, "What did they do for you when the generals overthrew you?" In New York, Randy Wicker toyed with the thought that if Juscelino returned to power, Edward could become Brazil's Rasputin.

Outside the curtained windows, the yellow beach, cobalt sky, grey churning sea. Inside, Juscelino would lean back in his leather chair, dyed black hair thinning, gouty shoeless feet propped on a hassock. The pouched heavy eyelids closed as Edward droned, "For the sound of `th', doctor, tongue between teeth, and for the `r', voicing, lip rounding, tongue curled back and *no* velar friction." He was not listening. What did he care about velar friction, the one-time lord of 80-million people? They talked about politics, the past, the future. "Doctor, do you think Brasília will remain settled, or were you in agreement with some demographers who hold the interior is basically uninhabitable and the whole country is in permanent retraction to the seacoast?" Juscelino's eyes flashed and he thundered, "Don't talk of that, young man. Don't talk that nonsense. My work will never die. I BUILT BRASÍLIA!" A thousand miles away, in the dry air of the altiplano dust blew red in the hot wind. The avenues were treeless, thanks to Juscelino's lead architect Oscar Niemeyer. ("Niemeyer did *not* like trees.") In the massive office and hotel blocks of the new capital, built in less than five years, colonels and generals roamed.

Edward knew that he amused Juscelino, who recommended him as an English tutor to relatives and acquaintances. Since they were all wealthy, he could make a bit of money, but he had so overextended himself that he had barely time to attend to both them and his classes. Several times he spent the night in jail, picked up for not carrying documents, and on release found himself half an hour later with Juscelino, who, were he in power, could have fired the entire Rio police force as a favour. Once, when Edward remarked that some inane repressive political action perpetrated by the generals was going to hurt Brazil's reputation, Juscelino snorted, "Reputation? Brazil *has no* reputation!"

Though Juscelino was diabetic, Edward suspected he would live much longer. He was so innocent and so chaotic that anyone could exploit him, yet he was a shrewd businessman. The military, ransacking his records back to 1930, tried to arraign him for corruption but now were reduced to nitpicking demands that he produce receipts for lectures: Edward spent mornings telephoning New York, attempting to get data from a speakers' bureau. It was just possible that, if the military regime were deposed, he could become President again. He was constantly watched, and for a time Edward had a secret policeman of his own tailing him. After a month or so, the DOPS, the Department of Order and Public Security, called it off, weary of nightclubbing.

Wherever Juscelino went, people mobbed him for his autograph, yet it was forbidden to even mention his name in newspapers. Once, he wanted to read something in English literature that summed up for his situation. Edward gave him a choice between *The Book of Job* and *King Lear*. He taught him "Blow, blow, thou winter wind." Juscelino liked to recite it.

During July, Edward gave seminars for English teachers, and in August taught in the college-level teacher-training program. If he said something anti-American in class he joked, "Of course, I have this viewpoint because I'm not American, you know." IBEU fostered a tradition of dissent, but it had become perilous to discuss Brazilian politics. Though it was unlikely the U.S. Government would ever learn that he was, in a sense, working for them, he feared that the troubles he'd had in Texas might surface. Of course, in Brazil everyone was somewhat shady, or had been, or soon would be.

Politically, things were worse. A triumvirate of military troglodytes replaced Artur da Costa e Silva, who had wanted

a new constitution to replace the one suspended in 1968. Then
James Elbrick, the American Ambassador, was kidnapped. The
Ambassador had come over every day to IBEU for Portuguese
lessons from the supervisor, Doña Maria Muniz. A man careless
of security, he had dismissed his guards. One day, Doña Maria
was on the phone, calling the Embassy, while Edward sat outside
her office. She got the Ambassador's secretary, asking if Mr.
Elbrick would want Portuguese lessons that day. The secretary
must have replied that she thought not, since Mr. Elbrick had just
been kidnapped. He heard Doña Maria's voice rise a full octave
to a very high pitch 4 followed by double-bar juncture as she half-
whispered, half-shrieked, "Kidnapped?"

The authorities were forced to print and broadcast the
kidnappers' manifesto, and to release 15 political prisoners.
That, or risk the murder of the Ambassador, Nixon's wrath, and
possible armed intervention. The Ambassador was released,
stating that he'd been well treated. His good sense and his ability
to talk Portuguese probably saved him, but the military fumed at
his "weakness." Edward met him. He was bored by the security
now assigned to him. "I preferred the kidnappers," he said, "at
least they were young and interesting."

Nothing prevented Edward from offering group rates
to the young and interesting. They'd go off to make it in a half-
demolished building or on a wet, weed-grown lot. One special
place was a courtyard that the police called "O Mijão," The Urinal.
Raided every few hours, after 4 a.m. it was left alone to the men
in shadow. Edward could hardly stay away: the sights were so
delightful. Sometimes a man would suck half-a-dozen others in
tandem, and he saw someone thrust a rubber dildo up himself
while being fellated. Once he'd been jailed after he'd run when a
police car approached, then released for lack of evidence. The one
occasion he was caught at fellatio, he pretended to be drunk and to
speak no Portuguese. His partner whispered to give them 10,000
cruzeiros, which he did, whereupon they became so solicitous
that they took him to his room, which was full of pot and pot
smoke—also full of dirty socks, which must have been all they
smelled. They left after one of them said, "Ugh, what a stink!"

With as many young queens and army hustlers, Cinelândia
was unchanged, as was the Central do Brasil train-station. There'd
been recent robberies and brutal murders. In May, an ex-diplomat,

poet, artist, and Nipponologist whom Edward knew had been found murdered in his apartment, the walls painted in blood with Japanese characters, paintings slashed, incense filling the air. It turned out that half-a-dozen hustlers had done it after a cocaine-and-sex party. "Live freaky, die freaky," he wrote Randy.

In 1969, police had raided a Greenwich Village gay bar, the Stonewall Inn, and for the first time the queens fought back, one of them throwing a bottle. Randy spoke out against such tactics, arguing, "Rocks through windows don't open doors." With his new boyfriend, David Combs, he opened an antique lighting store, Uplift, on Hudson St., which soon resembled a holding pen for the transgendered, to whom its proprietor extended jobs and handouts. In Rio, persecutions against gays had lessened. People could even watch *Perdidos Na Noite* (*Midnight Cowboy*). Edward indulged that local cowboy, Guillerhme, in scotch or champagne. In July, Guillerhme was jailed for vagrancy. Released, he departed for São Paulo. Since then, Edward had no steady. For months, he had his eye on a boy on Flamengo beach with a beautiful physique, and one day after a chance encounter, found that he was willing to do anything. What Edward most liked to do was buy him a prostitute and watch him in action.

He befriended a Cinelândia hustler who, averring he was a Mexican of Japanese ancestry, was a Bolivian from La Paz. About four feet high, with dark good looks, and a devil of a temper, Víctor had run away from home because his parents had denied his wish to become a singer. Edward liked him, not because of their infrequent sex, but because he was so alone and such a rebel. Having lost his passport long ago, Víctor's I.D. was a karate club card written in Japanese and a suspect Chilean identity card.

Not wanting to be alone on the day he learned of his father's death, he'd asked Víctor to go drinking with him in Copacabana. Into the bar came a Dane who was working in Brazil, who struck up a conversation. Víctor and the Dane went off to a movie, saying they'd rejoin him. After they left, he noticed a little box sitting on the counter where the Dane had stood. In it, he found two gold cufflinks set with aquamarines. The bar boy said he could keep them for the Dane, but Edward doubted he would. He put the box in his pocket. After waiting a while, he headed home.

The next day, about to leave for a holiday, he heard
from Víctor that the Dane had tried to fellate him in the movie
theatre. Now the Dane was missing his cufflinks. Víctor and
Edward went to the jeweller who'd made them — his name was
on the box — who gave them a wrong address. They located his
hotel, but he wasn't in. Edward entrusted the cufflinks, which
the jeweller said were worth about $100, to Víctor. On his return
from holiday, he tracked Víctor down to a flophouse; he said
the cufflinks were taken away when he thrown in jail after a
roundup. Edward tended to believe him.

They agreed that Víctor should leave town, so he put
him on a bus to Belo Horizonte. Edward told the Dane that
he'd pay up to half the cost of the cufflinks. The Dane had an
actor friend who posed as a lawyer on occasion, and early one
morning the fake lawyer pounded on Edward's hotel door, said
he was a federal policeman, and demanded 1,500,000 cruzeiros.
Edward told him to put salt on his ass and lick it. The Dane went
to the police and accused him of theft. The police bore him off in
a Black Maria to the Copacabana station: for the next four hours
they sifted through his belongings. He and the Dane shouted at
each other, while policemen said, "Let's deport both of them!"
People at the bar swore that Edward was the jewel thief. Though
loath to bring sex into it, Edward revealed the Dane's dealings
with Víctor. Finally, they called the Canadian vice-consul, the
man who'd given him the news of his father's death, and he
remembered the Bolivian who'd been with him then.

The consul got him a lawyer, who brokered an agreement:
Edward was to pay back 50 per cent of the supposed value in
cash, and sign promissory notes, maturing over several months,
for the rest. The Dane withdrew charges, the lawyer pocketed
his fee, and it was all over except for the promissory notes.
He cabled Víctor that he could return to Rio. When the notes
began coming due, Edward balked at paying them. The Dane
threatened to turn them over to a debt-collector, and Edward
invited him to a bar to discuss the matter. The Dane paled when,
at a pre-arranged signal, Víctor and another boy strolled in.
They threatened to turn him over to the police for corruption of
minors, to have him beaten up by their friends, get him dismissed
from his job for moral turpitude, and prosecute him for libel and

slander. After that, the Dane desisted. The affair of the cufflinks had cost Edward about US$400, but the main damage was to his nerves.

Troubles with his work permit seemed unending: he had overstayed his visa by nearly a year and a half. Finally, he managed to get himself reclassified to "visiting scholar" by using influence and bribes; a "temporary permanent" visa allowed him to leave Brazil without paying taxes. Ever since his father's death he'd been getting increasingly disjointed letters from his mother begging him to come home. Yielding to her, he left in December for Trinidad via Caracas without knowing whether he'd be able to get into, or out of, the country in which he and Henry Beissel had been detained. As it happened, nothing untoward happened to him.

Over the silver mouth of the Orinoco he flew, and down to terraced green Trinidad. On arrival, attacked by colic, he rushed to a washroom festooned with Black Power slogans. A pirate cabdriver wanted to charge him $10 to take him into Port-of-Spain, but finally settled for 50 cents. His friend Flash was still living in a room with psychedelic paintings on the wall. Glad to see him, Flash gave him a joint that didn't affect him at the time. But later, as he taxied out to Curepe, he felt at one with the people of Trinidad, and heard them talking in Portuguese. As he neared Lal's house on foot, the whisky-drinking, out-of-work Indian boys offered him swigs of Black and White.

Lal's old dog came bounding up to jump on him. Molly and Lal's handsome son Pelagius was a two-and-a-half, and Nicole was a baby. Edward's goddaughter, Angelica Ann, three-and-a-half, was excited to discover she had a godfather in front of her, whose pictures she had been shown, but whose reality she doubted, especially since he was white. She couldn't leave him in peace, with her "Godfather, le' we do this" and "Godfather, le' we do that."

When Lal returned that night, he found Edward dozing on his bed. Next day they discussed Lal's many problems. Lal failed to realize, Edward thought, that the solution to his wrecked finances lay in limiting his family. Overworked, good-natured, he helped too many people. He was paying for a new, or less old, car. His father, after 40 years with the University of the

West Indies as a gardener, was retired with a small lump sum. Lal, head of the family, had to support him, too. His adolescent brothers had left school but couldn't find work. Edward coldly suggested that they shine shoes or sell rotis. Lal said, "They wouldn't, it would shame them." Edward didn't know how to help him. Cacao-flower pollinators weren't greatly needed by the world. But to Lal, Edward thought, the great "away" from which Edward arrived like a visiting god, was the world where wishes came true, and jobs were to be had for the asking. He tried to explain that, despite the problems, Lal was better off in Trinidad. Edward departed to another teary goodbye.

On his first night in Montréal he headed for the Taverne Altesse. Inside five minutes, a fellow in a lumberjack jacket was splitting open the heads of two queens who'd ogled him, and people were throwing chairs and bottles. It was only then that he noticed the large sign over the bar: "*Ici on n'est pas au Far-Ouest! Déposer vos armes à la porte d'entrée.*" In another tavern, young hoodlums knocked him to the floor after he refused to speak to them in either French or English. He made an impassioned speech in Portuguese that left them uncomprehending and apologetic, and resumed drinking beer.

When he went to Toronto, he found the city grey under its blanket of white. Why would you live in a climate like this like ants in anthills, with raging cold outside and dry desert heat inside, when it was possible to live in contact with the outdoors every day? Christmas morning, he rose in darkness to walk to the University of Toronto campus. Not a car passed as he trudged through the snow. Only an all-night hamburger stand was open, crowded with glassy-eyed, laughing American blacks. By noon he was in Lindsay.

His mother told him that someone from New York with a strange name, whose voice she did not trust, had called him up twice. Alex had not really been in her right mind since Allan died. In any case, Randy was not the sort of person whom he could or would talk about. His mother, he gathered, had told him that she didn't know where Edward was, and that he was going to Europe soon.

He and Randy began to correspond about meeting up in Colombia, Edward using envelopes from the University of

Alberta and typing on a machine that dated from the time his father started his law practice. His high school friend Larry Murphy spotted him on the street. Edward struck him as grieving little over his father's death, as if to say, "Well, this is out of the way...."

Edward was not enjoying himself: those castrating-mother feminist gals who were making such a stir had been entrenched in his extended family a half-century ago, he thought. To the bill of indictment could be added Lindsay's puritanism, sentimentality, religiosity, anti-intellectualism, isolation, and subzero weather. His mother, having lost a husband who was also a father to her—in fact, more a father than a husband—wandered after him asking questions, questions, questions, as if to luxuriate in having someone to nag and irritate. He relived the thousand unpleasant moments she had caused. His relatives constantly called him up, invited him out, sized him up, cut him down.

He escaped to Montréal, and sought a re-entry stamp for Brazil from its consulate, which gave him the same old song-and-dance about contracts, though he had brought with him a bundle of letters promising work. Some consulate: they could hardly even speak Portuguese. A few days before he and his mother left for Jamaica for the travel treat he was giving her, he talked to Randy on the phone. His mother kept breaking in. Edward was so upset that when the call ended he tore at her pajamas and slapped her to bed.

10

A CHANGE OF STATION

February 1970-August 1972

You were. You have been. You are no longer,
with all your appetite and love for life.

~ The Scales

gainst expectations, his mother enjoyed Jamaica. It was
his treat: likely, he told himself, he would never see her
again. From a luxurious hotel, surrounded by "Jamaican
flunkies and fat American geldings," he wrote Randy on the
back of a laundry form, ("Bloomers/Panties from 1/6," "Union
Suits Nightshirts 2/6"). He managed to sneak off to downtown
Kingston to drink with the rude boys. You knew where you
stood with Jamaicans' racism: they could hate your race and like
you as a person. He had never considered himself as a white
man—"Canadian" was the only label he wore abroad, since it
meant about the same as "no nationality at all." Young Jamaicans
rapped with him, a fellow longhair, gave him the peace sign,
and offered him grass. When querulous Alex was along, this
was hilarious, but she was charmed.

From Jamaica, they flew to Haiti, novel to Alex, hell to
him. Papa Doc Duvalier glowered from the currency, the flag,
and brothel walls. Edward and his mother were joined by Joe

and Alice Tangney, who snapped a picture of him coming through a hotel window to demonstrate how easily it could be done. After a few days, Joe and Alice went on to the Dominican Republic, and Alex flew home. He'd planned to go to the Dominican Republic himself, but a Dominicana plane fell into the sea, sabotage suspected. All flights were suspended, and he had to wait a week to get one with KLM to Curaçao. As it was, the plane left at 4 a.m. rather than 4 p.m. — doubtless a semantic confusion — and the airline didn't think of sending them to a hotel. He slept on the airport floor in protest, greatly amusing the Haitians ("Il fou, il fou.")

From Willemstad, KLM took him to Barranquilla. There, he happily encountered a bartender he'd bedded the last time he'd been there. He also realized that a man who followed his long strides from bar to bar was the fellow who'd once brought him home to smoke grass — so strong that he ran out of the house, took a taxi, and tossed and turned in bed for hours. He took him home again and gave him the same grass, and he had the same paranoia. But this time the man dosed him with milk and beer, and gave him the talking cure until he calmed down.

In cold rainy Bogotá, he learned that Randy might be joining him. The Hotel Torquemada, their putative meeting place, had half-a-dozen bars so he had to hop, skip, and jump among them, leaving messages with waiters and getting drunk in the process. He grew so tired of waiting for Randy and running in the rain to embassies — the Brazilian Embassy was sluggish in giving him re-entry papers — that he went on to Cali and a boy bar, where he slept with three of the six employees. He'd have liked to live in Cali, if only to go the brothel, which cost him 50 pesos, $US2.50, per boy, plus 50 pesos for the room and 85 for a quart of rum with Coca-Cola.

Having learned that Randy wasn't joining him, he flew to Santiago en route to Rio. His Avianca plane arrived just as passengers were boarding a Varig. An hour later, the Varig was hijacked to Cuba: somehow the Brazilian hijacker had managed to get a gun aboard. When officials saw Edward's passport with its Brazilian stamps, and learned that he spoke Portuguese, they found the silly gas pistol he always carried. He convinced them he was not a hijacker. By this time, Avianca had sent its passengers to hotels. A strike occurred the next day, so it was the hotel again. Still bound for Rio, he reached Buenos Aires, where he took to bed for several days—all he could do, because the money he'd arranged for hadn't arrived. He cabled IBEU that he'd be a week late returning to teach. He went to Montevideo, where the boys catered to persecuted Argentinian gays, and embarked on a three-day bus journey to Rio. Too tardy to draw a March pay cheque, he was to a poor Brazilian ridiculously wealthy; to a rich Brazilian, ridiculously poor.

To Randy, Edward urged that he help Lal get to the United States. Randy had no idea, he wrote, how dreadful it was to go around in circles on an island. In Haiti, Edward had favoured the handsomest among the ragged guides hanging around the hotels. A letter from one bore the pompous beginning that the poor tended to use in all tongues ("It is with pleasure that I take this pen in hand to have the pleasure of the circumstance of greeting you.") The boy reported that his mother had died of yellow fever. Since the mother had washed Edward's clothes, he was a little apprehensive, though he'd had yellow-fever shots. The boy hoped that Edward would put him on salary and save his life. The trouble was, he was probably right; life expectancy in Haiti was 32 years.

Rio hit the high 90s F. daily. You could hardly breathe because of factory fumes; turds floated on lovely Guanabara Bay. They were extending the Copacabana beach out into the ocean in order to build a new two-lane highway, dredging and pumping out tons of hepatitis-laden filth, carried off again by the tide. Sometimes he thought it was a plot by the military to destroy immoral Copacabana. A wall slogan frightened Edward: "*Reforma de Costumes Vem Aí*," A reform of customs is coming! His files had vanished from the police archives, possibly for reasons of "national security."

It was June. Lately, nights had become chill and humid; hoarse, coughing, he alternately sweated and shivered. To make do, he had to work up to 12 hours a day. He was always being waylaid by students or people seeking money; telephones and elevators never worked; traffic jams were such that, rushing somewhere, he spent a fortune on cabs. He was always late. Though people were still gentle and loveable, he began snapping and snarling. Since early May, he'd suffered from itching knees and lower legs. Maybe it was a vitamin deficiency, an allergy to wool trousers—or a delayed nervous reaction to his stay in Canada. He had to give a two-week course in phonetics at the U.S. Embassy until mid-July. Randy sent him a recording of the song, "Elusive Butterfly." He wanted to turn from butterfly to turtle.

For five years, his Bolivian friend Víctor had lived in Brazil illegally; at 21, he was tired of malnutrition and police persecution, nights spent on beaches, or in parked cars. Whenever the police picked him up, he chattered at them in Spanish, Aymará, or Quechua, which so confused them that they let him go, but Edward wanted him out of harm's way. At his urging, Víctor renewed contact with his La Paz family. The Bolivian Embassy gave him a new passport. Meanwhile, Edward was enmeshed in getting Brazilian resident status. While at the Ministry of Foreign Affairs with his lawyer. He learned that it would be wiser to leave the country, come back as a tourist, and start all over. This, after weeks of applications and health exams.

The episode of the aquamarine cufflinks that had plagued him the previous year was not quite over. His Danish persecutor was still around. One day, someone turned up at work with the promissory notes that Edward had signed in order to get the Dane off his back. When the stranger said that the Dane owed him a lot of money and had given him the promissory notes as part payment, Edward managed to play him back to the Dane. Meanwhile, looking about a decade younger after surgery in the United States, Juscelino had resumed his tutorials with Edward, who took a break from them with weekends at a deserted seaside resort, where young men repaired with him to the dunes and hollows of the miles-long beach.

Fleeing the joyous frenzy of football-mad Brazil's win over Italy in the World Cup final, he took Víctor across the state of Mato Grosso and into Bolivia. His passport was often confiscated, entailing battles to get it back. Surviving curfews and interrogations, he delivered Víctor safe to his grateful family, and stayed with them in their handsome house on the outskirts of La Paz. The father was a colonel in charge of military communications; an uncle and brother worked at the British Embassy; another brother was a teacher. The family, who had thought Víctor long dead, who considered Edward the parole officer who'd brought him back, couldn't do enough for him. The night before his departure in August, he took Víctor to the *zona* for recreational sex.

After he returned to Rio, Víctor wrote pathetically that he couldn't get used to living in Bolivia again, and wished he had never left Brazil. Would Edward send him postcards, so that at least he could imagine that he was there? Even better, would he send money to help him get back there? Not right away, Edward decided. Meanwhile, the wretched Haitian had written him another letter in broken French, telling him that, since he never knew his real father, Edward *was* his father.

Doubting that his correspondence with Randy was secure, he enlisted the former President of Brazil as a courier. When Juscelino went to New York in September, he took along a letter. Edward had practically composed a speech, "Brazil Today" that he was to deliver, and exhaustively coached him in pronunciation. In the event, Randy's letter never reached him. On his return, Juscelino swore that he'd given it to a friend to mail, but Edward suspected that he lost it among his mountains of personal effects. Once he had walked into Juscelino's bedroom to find him examining 80 identical pairs of black shoes. Yet all his socks had holes in them.

In an early September election, Chile had gone Communist. The Chileans were signing their death warrant, he thought. In October, Canada had also become briefly notorious after the Prime Minister had invoked the War Measures Act in the wake of two kidnappings in Québec by FLQ terrorists. He had always suspected Pierre Trudeau of wanting to be a Canadian Charles De Gaulle. Edward's heart was with the Front de Libération du Quebec.

He was suffering from carbuncles; one on his leg had so many mouths it was the size of a 50-cent piece. The other two were on opposite sides of the penis, and if *that* should get infected...! His doctor had told him he had *"antraz,"* causing him to wonder how he could have contracted a usually fatal cattle disease, until he consulted a dictionary and found that in

Portuguese *"antraz"* meant "carbuncle" and that *"carbúnculo"* meant "anthrax." The skin disease that had sapped him for six months spread upward from the ankles, red blotches breaking out. Cortisone helped, but made him nervous as a cat. Tests revealed that it wasn't an allergy; a biopsy was inconclusive. At one point, he stood like an artist's model, revolving slowly in the centre of a large room, surrounded by a score of the country's top dermatologists muttering *"Pois,* eu *acho que não pode ser a lepra," "Não, não, deve ser a doença de Dühring," "Isso é! A dermatite herpetiforme!"* They were discussing the possibility of Dühring's Disease (herpetiform dermatitis), which, consulting his beloved medical texts, he found was "a disease of no known origin and no known cure, though sometimes relieved by a change of climate. It might go on for years. His own doctor confessed, "You will excuse the pun, but we are here only on the skin of the problem! Rio de Janeiro is an anthill of unknown tropical diseases!"

He could scarcely sleep without barbiturates. He wondered if he was punishing himself by making his body undesirable: all he did was teach, visit doctors, buy medicines, and take injections. Some drugs made him vomit if he ate or drank too much. Antibiotics cured his boils and carbuncles, then they sprang up again. He was also taking something called Glauber's Salts for his liver, which turned everything to liquid in his colon. If it wasn't Dühring's, he thought, then maybe it was its deadly cousin, pemphigus, which began with similar symptoms, then developed into unhealable ulcers, and usually killed in three or four years.

For a time, he had lived in a hotel on a terraced hill in the Gloria area. Since he couldn't have people up, he took his sex on gritty beaches. Lonely for en suite companionship, he moved into a promiscuous friend's downtown apartment, small, dirty, and noisy, but you could come in with anyone and do anything. Also living there was a homeless, much jailed kid from Santos. The kid, who slept on a mattress on the floor, gave him consoling sponge baths and caressing massages. In return, Edward squired him to good restaurants and acquired falsified papers to get him into nightclubs.

As for Edward, the authorities had taken three months to locate his lost file, and he'd had to prove that he was gainfully employed. As usual, there were two laws: one said people without papers shall not work; the other said people without papers who work shall pay 30 per cent income tax. Brazilian officials first created a problem for you with some absurd draconian regulation; then they created the means for you to get around it. He also needed good-conduct certificates. Several times the police had picked him up, only to release him the next day. Still, the main police office had no record of these arrests. Though he'd been sure the U.S. authorities had informed the RCMP about him, he got clearance from the Mounties. All along, he'd had to pay a *despachante* — the fellow who did all the paperwork and paid the bribes. But he was now legal, landed immigrant No. 1055663, and could work and stay as long as he wanted.

Happily, Lal had gone to New York, and spoke of opening a West Indian restaurant. Edward was dubious about this, he wrote Randy, though the thought of Molly's rotis brought water even to his "jaded and experienced mouth." Lal even ventured north to pay a visit to Lindsay. His reports augmented what his mother's correspondence had already told him — that she wanted Edward around, and that she wanted to join his father, wherever he was — and she, of course, thought he was somewhere. Even at this distance, she still disturbed him with her demands and neuroses.

Randy and he batted travel plans back and forth. Pursuing an African option, he went to Santos, Brazil's biggest port, but abandoned the idea. Long-range travel was imperative. For one thing, he needed a change of climate: torridness alternated with chilling rain, windstorms, and cloudbursts, and he changed clothes several times a day. Yet Rio could be so lovely that it almost compensated for rain, dirt, traffic jams, the high cost of living, military dictatorship, and the police. In November, police swooped down on a clutch of his friends, arresting several. They were held at an air base, and faced up to 30 years in prison. The spate of homosexual murders spread to Cinelândia, including an American nightclub piano player, a screaming queen who dressed in red leather. Edward had often had relations with the killer.

His mother reported that she and Uncle Joe had given Lal a little financial help. Writing to Edward, Lal repeatedly noted that Canada was "so clean": Edward supposed that to somebody reared in Curepe, accustomed to pass a noisome, vulture-haunted garbage dump on the edge of Port of Spain at least a dozen times a day, cleanliness *would* be Canada's salient characteristic. Lal suggested that Molly and the children take care of Edward's mother. Poor innocent child: little did he realize, Edward thought, that the Canada would as easily let a shipment of opium poppies in the country as an unwed Black mother with three illegitimate children.

After he took a Spanish vessel to Portugal in December, Randy met him in cold Lisbon, and they took an overnight train to colder Madrid. They were happily getting drunk when a guard in black leather harassed them at the Spanish border — something about a bottle thrown from the train. Edward took off his shoes to go to sleep. About to arrive in Madrid next morning, he found that he lacked a shoe. The other travellers satirically commented on what he'd do in snowy Madrid. This lack of sympathy, aid, or simple humanity seemed to him typical of the Spanish national character. He and Randy tore their compartment apart looking for the shoe. They found that it had slid into an adjoining compartment.

They hastened south to Málaga. Since the city lacked nightlife on New Year's Eve, they hopped a bus to Torremolinos, only to get stranded after the last bus back had left. Randy insisted that they check out all the bars in his gay guidebook, though most of the addresses were wrong or wildly misspelled, and many had closed, been renamed, or reopened as straight bars. A beautiful young German passionately kissed Randy, then demanded 1,000 pesetas, to which he'd answered no, then maybe, then yes, but it turned out they'd have to travel 20 kilometres to the boy's place. He already had Randy's money and wouldn't return it — but kept kissing him. Edward let them get on with it while he played pinball in a penny arcade and ate stand-up crLpes washed down with muscatel. When the sun came up, they caught their bus.

From Algeciras, their ferry passed the Rock of Gibraltar. They arrived at dusk in Tetouan: cobbled dark streets, winter cold, brown-robed, hooded men like murderous monks shuffling silently in yellow slippers. Boys sidled up to ask, "You want hash?" "You want my sister?" "You want my brother?" "You want me?" A boy led them to a cheap hotel, and through chilly mist to get hash in the medina. Their feet echoed in the silence of endless curves, narrow streets, and hooded watching figures. Finally, a little room, the colours and grades of hash spread out for inspection, and a dark ball under which their host applied a flame, warning them to leave before he got violent. Randy refused to go to dinner without Edward; at length, they ate in a sumptuous restaurant with cushioned walls and floors. The next day, Tetouan was only a charming city in the sun.

Hot dry days and cold nights cleared up his skin ailments. The simple diet, the aggressive yet friendly people, the unavailability of alcohol and the availability of hashish and boys, the desert and mountain grandeur—all invigorated him. He recalled that André Gide had gone to North Africa. He became something of an *immoraliste* himself, dismissing the people, ideas, and complexes parasitizing him. He took it as progress that he was writing less poetry now. He didn't need to.

Travelling extensively with Edward for the first time, Randy absorbed lessons: have no fixed itinerary, stay somewhere as long as needed to learn about it, move on. One stop was Chefchaouène, a small Berber city in the Rif Mountains, a place of cool clear air and blue-white houses. In the moonlight by a hillside brook, Edward had three boys. Later a bold lad and a friend, drifting by in snow-flecked djellabas, asked if he wanted more. He said, "No. I'm tired. Tomorrow." The next day at the café, the boy and his buddy suggested they all go to a house. But Edward suspected a trap. So he said, "Thank you. Not today. Perhaps tomorrow." The third day the boy was in the market. He slyly smiled at Edward, his eyes blacker than olives, his cheeks brighter than tangerines. The last day they saw each other in the souk. The boy repeated softly, "Come to my house with me. We'll be together," staring him down with laughing bright eyes. Only then did he realize that the boy wanted *him*, not money. But the bus was due to leave in half an hour. The boy laughed, and said, "What a joke. Forget the bus. There'll be other buses, but the time you'll had with me you'll never find again." But

Edward hated to waste tickets already paid for. So he said, "No, some other time." The boy urged, "You've half an hour. In half an hour we could still do something that would be fun." But running for buses at the last moment did his heart no good.

"It just can't be," Edward said. "Goodbye. I'll be back."

"No, you won't," the boy answered.

Edward walked downhill to the bus stop where Randy was waiting for him with 10 bags full of trinkets, 20 complaints, and 50 demands and questions.

After Meknès in central Morocco, built by a seventeenth-century sultan, he and Randy spent part of a raw day in Fez in the tanners' district, stinking of leather and blood, the pits half-filled with icy water in which the tanners stood or sat half the day and worked hides with their feet. When Randy greeted them, the shouting tanners angrily flashed their genitals.

Marrakech was rustic yet touristic. In teeming Djemaa El Fna Square, men played the crowd with trained doves and handlers made Barbary apes do handstands. In brasseries, American hippies drank beer and talked English, as though they were back in Oshkosh, Wisconsin. The medina was full of rude greedy merchants. Randy departed for New York with a trove of trinkets.

Alone in Casablanca, in a hotel kitty-corner from the bus station, Edward waited days for money to reach him. The city, whose central plazas were ringed by concentric, circular avenues from which streets radiated, was hellishly hard to navigate. He drank in cafés under white colonnades, drinking wine and pastis, nibbling free *ful* beans seasoned with the Morocco mixture of salt and sage. Bars had signs forbidding Muslims and women to drink in them, under pain of having their heads shaved and 30 days imprisonment. In big Lyaultey Park, even by day, soldiers cruised among bushes and side paths. One morning he passed, but did not pass up, a gardener raking the grounds.

In the southern Morocco town of Zagora, near the ill-defined Algerian border, he saw a sign that said "Tombouctou — 1000 kms." Told that Timbuktu was just more adobe misery, he did briefly visit Mali and Bamako, its capital, and took a Niger boat-and-dusty jeep trip to the Dogon cliff villages. His tour of the Sahel wasteland had begun in the Spanish Sahara, encompassed

Mauritania, and ended on the Atlantic coast at Bathurst, capital of the Gambia. On the way, he arrived in Dakar in Senegal amid a cholera epidemic. Not venturing even ice water, he slaked his thirst with imported orange soda. He noted the market women's magnificent costumes, and an island-prison off the coast, where the slave trade to America had its start. To his disgust, he was the most visible of minorities. Everyone touched him for good luck.

One could only travel very expensively or very cheaply: the former, by staying in one of the few luxury hotels, the latter, by staying with the natives, which meant cultivating their friendship, something he found dangerous and difficult. Foreigners weren't allowed to travel steerage or deck class with the natives on the Niger steamers, only first class. Since all those countries had bad relations with each other, cross-border travel and roads were either impossible or fraught with delays.

In late February, he was back in Tetouan, sitting with a boy where a café spilled chairs and tables into the plaza, and old men, dressed like Franciscans in coarse brown djellabas, took the sun. His tea was perfumed with orange blossoms. Honey bees were buzzing and crawling everywhere, around their ears, on the table, on the rims of the tall green glasses, falling in, falling out of the liquid, mysteriously not drowning. One of them stung him.

By March he was in Rio, coordinating language and linguistics courses for IBEU's teacher training section. He wrote Randy that he had "become embroiled in an exciting controversy with my colleagues." The rest of the letter was filled with a thousand words of linguistic bafflegab and mad pedantry concerning the phonemic status of vowel nasalization in Brazilian Portuguese.

He learned that his mother had suffered a stroke in February. Although she had improved by the end of April, her vision and brain were permanently impaired. He wrote Randy sardonically:

> She is like a white pure candle, slowly flickering
> away and guttering and he greatly fears she may
> soon leave this vale of tears and pass on to a better

life. At all events, I should like to gaze upon the
face of the poor darling once more before she
passes away and to revisit this once again the
scenes of his childhood, the little Canadian town
where he prayed and prattled innocently and
lived so purely and happily. Then too, it is time
for me to think of settling down, marrying etc.,
and though these Brazilian girls are attractive
and have kept me busy in the last few years, I of
course should never think of making a marital
union, of selecting as his life companion and
helpmate, any but a good pure Canadian girl to
bear my progeny and perpetuate the name of
Lacey.

Despite the facetiousness, he was upset, especially when
his aunts wrote that if he wanted to visit he had better do it
soon. After two months in the hospital, Alex required round-
the-clock care. In June, he came home, arrayed in a garish blue
silk sweater, hung over and unshaven. His staring mother said,
"*Who* are *you*?" Then she collapsed in his arms. She retained a
good memory, a keen appetite, and still enjoyed a stiff drink,
though she usually spilt part of it. She tended to fall asleep
toward the end of a meal. She saw only out of the right side of
each eye. But one day she was in the backyard, when a pair of
blue jays alighted on the grass to the right of her. Delightedly,
half-distrusting her luck, she exclaimed, "Oh, look! Blue jays! I
can really see them."

She couldn't tell the time anymore. She said, "Now,
the big hand is at six and the little hand is at ten; now, what
time is it?" He said, "10:30, mother." Nearly an hour later the
housekeeper came in, and his mother said triumphantly, "It's
10:30, Fran." Before Edward could intervene, she told Alex
that no, it was 11:20. Her eyes filled with tears. She said, "Now
yesterday was August 4th. What day is today?" and believed it
was August 5th for the rest of the week. When her false teeth
were in, she wanted them out. When they were out, she wanted
them in. She had to take digitalis, blood-thinners, Librium, and
a diuretic that was supposed to ease the burden on her heart but
made her wet the bed or stumble to the bathroom. Her world

had shrunk to the block on which she'd been born and lived on
most of her life. Although Allan had left her well provided for,
she fretted incessantly. Where were her stocks and bonds and
bankbooks and GICs? Why did the trust company never send
her anything? Were her own sisters stealing from her?

Yet she told him, "Now that you're here, I *will* get better.
I don't want you to think you had a madwoman for a mother. I
won't be foolish again. I was wrong. I'll refuse to worry about
things. Oh, it could have been so lovely if I hadn't caved in. Your
father would be so ashamed of me. But I'll get better. I must get
going again, and have some parties for you, and try on his new
dresses and see what you think of them. Now, the big hand is at
five and the little hand is at four: what time is it? Let me guess,
now – 9 o'clock?"

She became obsessed with Brazil. She wanted to see the
Amazon and the jungle and Brasília. She wanted to sail into
Guanabara Bay and see the Christ statue and Sugar Loaf and the
blue sky and the beaches, and the brown people swimming. She
wanted to go back with him. He told her she wasn't well enough
to travel, but they should plan for her to visit him next winter.
She smiled her lopsided smile. Next afternoon he came in and
found her crying. She had dropped and broken a plate. She said,
"Now I know I'll never go to Brazil."

He got power of attorney and sold a foothill from the
mountains of Victorian antiques that Allan had collected. Alex
dusted and polished the ones that remained. The day he left for
Brazil, she tottered onto the veranda, just as she used to when he
left for college after weekends at home. He ran back to kiss her,
and she said, "I'll never forget you in that blue silk sweater." He
darted to the waiting taxi.

At the end of August, his mother had a second set of
strokes. She called the housekeeper's dog "a goddamned
Protestant dog," lay down on the kitchen floor and wouldn't
get up. After a few months' wait, during which he managed to
convince his aunts that he'd never live in Lindsay, they sold the
house. His mother knew none of this. Admitted to the nursing
home in September, she was bed-ridden and half-paralyzed. She
planned bridge games, parties, and picnics that included her
father, mother, and husband, all dead, the nurses, and of course

Edward. He wrote long monthly letters that her sisters read to her. One day, she said she wished Edward would marry because she'd like to see a grandchild. She still talked about travelling. One day, trying to get out of her chair, she fell and broke her hip. The bone was slow to knit. She developed a yen for cantaloupe and strawberries, but she no longer recognized the seasons.

In Rio, it seemed to Edward that his mother had lived, in her terms, a good life, but to him it was—like that of all those who never felt all that they could feel, nor see all they could see, nor taste all that they could taste—a wasted life. She'd had little tragedy, and much simple happiness. But she'd had to go through life with a lip deformity, and if she hadn't found his father—a timid man who could love only someone maimed physically, as he was psychically—she would had found no one, and Edward would never had been.

He was now 33, and felt immensely old, which didn't mean that life had no pleasures. He had money enough for his needs, few responsibilities, and good health, though tricks he brought home robbed, tried to beat him up, or attempted to blackmail him (the usual techniques: suicide attempt, wrists slit with a razor blade, "I'm a minor.") Since the Argentine peso hit an all-time low, he enjoyed himself with the boys in Buenos Aires, puffing pot, popping pills, drinking elaborate cocktails that cost 40 cents, eating superb meals for a dollar. Arriving in Santiago, Chile after backbreaking train rides, he headed straight to a Turkish bath for a massage. Feeling raunchy, he hoped to pick a boy up. But fathers and sons surrounded him, and young men cutting each other's hair, naked without coyness. Watching the camaraderie, he realized that he could call one of the young men aside, pay him a dollar or two, go into a shower room or get a cheap hotel room. Instead, he wanted to say, "Take me out with you and your friends, and I'll pay for a couple of bottles of wine and we'll get to know each other."

At Viña del Mar, he smoked grass on the beach with hippies, and met the usual middle-aged female schoolteachers who latched onto him because they were lonely, too. Under the Marxist regime of Salvador Allende, Santiago lacked razor blades and Valdiva, the southern provincial capital, lacked cigarettes. In the desert north, Antofagasta had no soft drinks.

The United States had strangled foreign credits and inflation was so bad no one heeded printed menus. Workers, students, and peasants seized and occupied everything and produced nothing. Trains only ran sometimes. With twinkling eyes and tired smile, Allende lectured his citizens that too much wine produced impotence. Edward did not obey: he went to the wine festival of Mendoza.

Puerto Montt, 700 miles south of Santiago at the end of the Pan-American Highway, was so far south that it became north: pines, poplars, chicory, and dandelions. The small wooden town lay between hill pastures and pebble beach, with an island-dotted aquamarine bay and a cone of snow-covered volcano. From a hotel near the flower-crowded plaza, he caught a rowboat across to an island and walked along its mud beaches. He nibbled lustrous blackberries growing in jungly tangles from hilltop to water's edge. A boy showed him a shortcut through farms, over stiles, and along narrow lanes dark with blackberry bushes to a hillside restaurant, where he got mildly drunk on strong yellow cider.

Rowed back to the mainland, he saw at the fish market chains of shellfish meat hung up to dry. The vendor split the green spiny shell of sea urchins, tugged away the orange, starfish-like membrane, tossed aside the purple guts, the empty shell, and popped into his mouth, alive and kicking, a tiny parasitical crustacean that lived inside. "The best part of the animal. Pure iodine. Good for the pecker." Indian women sold ponchos whose colours gleamed in the twilight; he bought a hand-knitted wool sweater. He chanced on a street of bars and dance halls and, hearing faint sounds, entered a barnlike back room to find dark faces of the Mapuche, marvelous knitters and weavers; pale German faces, descendants of settlers; brown mestizo faces. Eyes glared, then flashed welcome, glasses of white wine and papaya, or pisco and ginger ale, were thrust at him; in the air was the sweet heavy perfume of pot. At midnight, he followed two boys, who followed two girls. Block after block they went, hunters and quarry. A fine cold rain fell. When he screwed up courage to make allusive vague opening remarks, one replied, "Sir, we already know." Suddenly they were at his hotel. He wished them luck and said goodnight. Next day, the night-girl woke him up with a beautiful smile. Laden with baggage, he faced the cold shock of morning. The bay was stormy, loons bobbing on the water, gulls flung like spray.

After he returned to Rio, panhandling, drug-taking, or hitchhiking backpackers slept at his place, eating his food and making off with shirts and socks. Sometimes he threw them out until he grew lonely and invited a new bunch in. When he set off for the interior during the mid-semester break, he thought he'd left his place securely locked. Returning, he discovered that his friends had made copies of his apartment key, not only living in his place, but also inviting in their friends, and the friends of their friends. The squatters partied, smoked pot, and left taps open during the water-rationing cut-offs until neighbours called the police, who broke down the door. But everyone had gone, taking the drugs they had with them, so all the police found was an empty apartment with all the taps running. His friends hadn't stolen much, but it took him a week of cleaning out the mess they'd created.

In exchanges with the Beissels, he learned that Ruth was beset by arthritis, Henry by an avalanche of term papers. Although it had been about six years since he'd seen them— they kept missing each other during his visits to Canada—he thought often of Angelica and Myrna. Children on the verge of adolescence were at a peak of perfection, he thought, perfect little adults, so wise, so knowing, above all so much in control that it seemed tragic for puberty to come along and shatter with hammer blows that sense of a meaningful small world. Soon would come incomprehensible changes of the voice, sexual urges, growth of the body, appearance of hair, bloody emissions. What was happening to me? Was I becoming a monster? How tall would I grow? Angelica and Myrna would soon experience, he thought, the secret terrible fears of adolescence.

His mother suffered another stroke. In late April, she rallied a little, then relapsed. Sometimes she could see, sometimes she couldn't. Sometimes she could eat, mostly she couldn't. She was so thin, wrote an aunt, that you could span her thighs with a fist. Edward no longer wanted her to live, but he didn't want her to die either. On a Tuesday in May, his aunts cabled, "Mother low. Might last three days." When he telephoned, he learned that she had regained a little ground. Grace, the beloved *Tante* of his youth, was dying of liver cancer. He might have gone to Lindsay then but May was a blue-and-gold month in Rio. He cabled that he couldn't return.

From the welter of Cinelândia, Paulinho's smooth brown body and green eyes surfaced. The bow of lips, the smooth cupped jawbone, round cheeks, the deep pools of eyes, the flare of nostrils. Over time, he pieced together the shards of his past. Paulinho had seen his alcoholic father savagely beat his mother; at 6, he'd seen her die in childbirth. He was raped at age 10. Abandoned, he'd subsisted as a peanut peddler in the streets; his father had refused to recognize or to register him as his — or anyone's — child, so he had no legal identity, no protection against the police, and could neither go to school nor legally hold a job.

They moved in together. The Copacabana morning brought the swish of traffic beyond the windows, the whirring air-conditioner in the cool gloom of the bedroom, sunlight through the Venetian blind. Paulinho lay beside him, one leg sprawled across his; his ribcage rose and fell. Edward kissed the flat brow, and the eyes of a frightened animal opened ("Where am I, Eduardo?") then closed again. He kissed his eyelids; lips curved into the faintest of smiles as his tongue touched them and he whispered endearments.

He padded away to shave, put on swimsuit and sandals, descended to the already crowded street, sunlight gold among the oití trees. It was hot and cloudless; he was already sweating. He stopped for a codfish ball and a mango juice at the Portuguese corner bar. Three blocks further, the beach was starting to fill up with mothers and maids with children, teenagers skipping school, bronzed young men and women under parasols. Miles of beach spread out on a dazzling arc. The blinding sun glittered on the moving water. He strode through the thickening crowds along flat intertidal sands, the waves laving his feet, effacing his footprints. Children tossed soccer balls, sliced through breakers. On Mono da Babilônia, tiny black men and women moved in and out of tin huts, up and down trails. Sunbathers at the other end of the arc were only a blur of colour, though each pointillist dot stirred with life. He sank into cold, still water, sweat washing from his skin. Salt dried on his skin on the homeward walk.

He dragged a wet bill from the secret pocket of his swim trunks and bought the *Jornal do Brasil*. At the beachfront bar, he sipped golden draft beer in a stein, cold and metallic. News of the day: the Death Squad, censorship, Nixon, Vietnam. Back through the market. Time to buy tangerines — one cent each. He bought four dozen. Walked back to the boy in his darkened room. He slid off his swim trunks, showered, slipped into bed. Paulinho woke to the touch of Edward's wet skin. Warm fingers massaged him, and the catlike tongue moved over his body, licked each part.

Noon whistle. The sound of construction drills and hammers stopped. Paulinho showered, fussed, listened to the Bee Gees, and chose his wardrobe for the day. Should it be his purple pants and his red Air Force t-shirt? Or his orange pants and the blue-striped sailor shirt? Shoes or high-heeled clogs? Did his hair look right? And was he *really* handsome? At 16, Edward told him, everyone's handsome. Edward put on a black T-shirt and black trousers and sat reading a linguistics article. Feigning indifference, impatience.

"Hurry up, Paulinho. I'll be late."

"Eduardo, I need 25 cruzeiros."

"Here's 20. Find the rest yourself."

They hailed a taxi. A glimpse of the beach, the crowded streets, the open sea, then into the tunnel. Through them, and out to Botafogo beach, and blue Guanabara Bay. Sugar Loaf to the right, the Christ statue to the left in the distance on its sheer green-and-white hill as they circled into Flamengo, whirled past more beach and bathers. Downtown, and out of the taxi at the corner stand where he bought a tuna-fish sandwich, and for Paulinho a submarine. They shook hands, Edward's slick with sweat.

In his cubicle office, the air-conditioning wasn't working. There was mail to answer, a stencil to prepare, a drill to work up. The secretary was sick. The mimeograph machine was out of order. He suddenly remembered he had to go to the Royal Bank before two o'clock to cash a draft. Into narrow winding lanes of the financial district, brushing elbows with maybe a hundred thousand people. At the bank, air-conditioning revived him, waiting for the manager's signature as they discussed politics, inflation, the rate of the Canadian dollar.

Students filed in. The ceiling fan stirred sluggishly. "Today we were going to compare and contrast the English and Portuguese fricatives." An hour and a half of fricatives, fricatives, fricatives. Thirty minutes for sweet black *cafèzinho*, and a staff meeting. What about next semester's registrations? Everyone's workload? Another class. Another hour and a half, this time about stress and intonation. The ceiling fan was out of order. Thirty minutes for more *cafèzinho*, another conference. Someone had complained about the quality of the mimeographs. Somebody else had missed too many classes. Tomorrow the director of courses would come to inspect. There were rumours that the Secret Police had infiltrated their American History classes. The sun was setting, the city darkening. Another hour and a half — of Thoreau, Emerson, and Transcendentalism.

It was 7:30 p.m. Still hot. He had no more sweat to sweat. Down in the taking-forever elevator, a goodnight to the porter. A taxi to an empty building where Soares awaited in an office, a grey Buddha with hooded eyes. "You look tired, Eddy. How are you feeling? How is your family? Now let's get down to business. I have received a letter from a Herr Werner Schulz in Düsseldorf who's interested in importing passion-fruit juice and conserves. And another from an American company, enquiring about homeopathic medicines. These must be answered at once. "Then it was 10 p.m. They had a beer and a sandwich in the last restaurant left open. Soares drove him to Cinelândia.

The hustlers camped on park benches or preened beneath movie marquees. For Edward, two lemon batidas in a stand-up bar, and talk with the counter boy, who would like to study English, and earned 10 dollars a week. Now Dário found him, invited himself to a batida, and whispered, "Professor. I need 10 cruzeiros for a place to sleep. Or can I crash with you?" No, he couldn't. He went to the corner café where all the world passed by. Dário got his money, shook hands, left him. Maria, the madwoman, passed, dressed tonight in white. A kleptomaniac who possessed the city's amplest wardrobe, she bathed in the park fountain and flashed her pudenda at female tourists. A deaf-mute begged, selling a sign-language chart. When Edward said no, he got the fuck-you sign. The snake-charming woman went by, boa constrictor draped around her neck. A five-year-old girl sold roasted peanuts. No. Someone hawked *O Dia*, the midnight paper. No. A one-armed man begged. Again no. Abelardo came up.

"Remember me, professor?"

Yes, Edward remembered him. Last time, Abelardo had robbed him of 50 cruzeiros when he thought he wasn't looking.

"I went with you two months ago. Now I need money badly. I'm hungry…"

And truly his aspect was lamentable.

"Do you want to go with me again?"

No, he didn't. He gave him five cruzeiros.

He strolled among the promenading drag queens and stopped for a draught beer and a slice of pizza. Sérgio came up, shook hands, introducing two of his fellow soldiers. "They're game. If you want we can go with you tonight. We all need money." Good boys, no doubt, but he was drained of money and desire. "Bus fare, then, professor. " They couldn't get back to barracks without it.

In the velvet night, the lights of skyscrapers around the bay twinkled as his taxi returned him. It was nearly midnight. On the corner, the sea breeze revived him a little, the sea quaking in the moonless night, waves crashing above dying traffic noises. In a bar, a tired Portuguese said, "You and me, we are strangers here. What brought you to this wild country? What brought me?"

Then Paulinho next to him in the darkened room. The down on his cinnamon legs was silver, his rump shone. He nibbled Edward's ears, licked, and stroked him from softness into hardness. Kisses, nuzzling. Gave him his hand. Held him.

On May 20, 1971, as the priest was anointing her, Edward's mother diéd. On the same day and hour, Edward's *tante* Grace also died. After requiem mass, Alex was interred in St. Mary's Cemetery. She was, the *Lindsay Daily Post* said, the "Dear mother of Edward of South America." She had "Entered into rest."

Edward had to leave Brazil. He had an estate to settle.

11

AN ESTATE TO BE SETTLED

August 1972-June 1974

My mother the sun and my father the moon
gave me to eat with a silver spoon.

I threw the spoon into a wishing-well,
reached for it, followed it, that's how I fell.

~ Downward Mobility

To settle an estate is not the same as to settle accounts. Some accounts, like the one that Edward jointly held with his parents, could never be resolved. At the beginning of 1973 in Lindsay, Ontario, in the backwash of his mother's death, he did what he could.

He'd ended teaching at IBEU the previous August. Though a sizeable inheritance was now his, he prudently obtained a letter of recommendation from Susan Fitzgerald, the director of courses. She called him "a brilliant teacher, temperamental often and excitable, but with the ability to inspire tremendous enthusiasm among his students." By November he finished his tag ends of teaching at other schools and his private classes, including those with Juscelino Kubitschek, and left Paulinho behind.

As if to postpone the unpleasant task that lay ahead, he wound his way slowly through Bolivia, Ecuador, Colombia, and Central America. In Managua, he saw such familiar sights as the legislative assembly — not that the assembly was needed, because Anastasio Samoza was in charge — and a bar with chilled steins of beer and a checkerboard of sunlight through lattices. A fat old lady at the dawn market sold a mixture of steamed rice, beans, and bananas that she called "Marriage." Flying out, he watched the city lights spill beneath the plane as it shuddered and lifted. Then on December 23, 1972, only a few hours after he'd left, the earthquake hit. The city was levelled, 10,000 were killed, and dead fish lined the shores of the blue lake. All the clocks stopped.

In Guatemala, he accumulated gifts for his family and the Beissels, and entered Mexico at midnight. With the power out, surly officers poked by candlelight and flashlight into his luggage, looking for the coke they *knew* he was exporting from Colombia, then charged him for after-hours inspection. The only taxi into Tapacula passed palm-tree silhouettes riddled by heat lightning. Tapacula had a mosoaicked plaza with a gothic-aspiring cathedral and an ornamental fountain. All the restaurants were closed, the hotels had locked doors or no vacant rooms, and there were no buses until tomorrow. Nothing to do but sit at the southern tip of Mexico, under the shade of the guanacaste trees that dropped fan-shaped, lacquered seedpods. Down a side street a flickering neon sign announced, *Agencía Fúnebre — día y noche.* The smiling little proprietor, plainly hoping that he might have a mangled wife, lover, or mother-in-law to bring him, showed him mahogany silk-lined orchid-coloured caskets for the local gentry; modest purple-lined ones for the decent poor; tiny magenta candy boxes or silk-lined cradles for departed children. Which just went to show, Edward thought, that in the tropics you could arrive in town too late to eat, or drink, or even sleep in a hotel room. But you were never too late to buy a coffin.

In Montréal, the Beissels put him up at their foursquare brick house on quiet treelined Oxford Avenue, where he ate lentil soup and succulent sauerbraten. After returning from a sanatorium in Germany, Ruth was out of sorts. A surprise party was arranged to cheer her up. Edward, the perfect host, greeted guests and fetched them nibbles. His hosting was not always so well received. One morning Henry found two pairs of unrecognizable shoes in the front hallway. Edward surfaced, alcohol-reeking, explaining that he had brought home two men he had met and felt sorry for. One of them, he said, had an eye "removed" by a police officer. The Beissels laid down the law: no more overnight guests. Once, when Henry was away, he came home so drunk that he couldn't get up the stairs. "Crawl up! Crawl up!" Ruth and the girls ordered.

Among his Christmas gifts was a 1959 Olympia portable typewriter that had long served Ruth's family. When he got to Lindsay, it came in handy to type up a long, dull, technical translation that he had to finish. Much of Alan and Alex's lifetime hoard had to be sold or given away. His favourite cousin Marg Wansbrough got a handsome carved monk's armchair to join a tall dark heavy medicine cabinet she'd received from Allan's estate. The lepidopteral collection box of his childhood, like the grey convent of his childhood, had vanished.

He stayed with his Aunt Marion, a former nun and teacher at Fordham University, in a house his father had owned. Marion was fond of him, but maddened by his untidiness. Most of his time, he reported to Randy Wicker, was spent "sitting around on my arse doing nothing in dreary Lindsay, while the trust company executing my mother's will dawdled & the lawyers wrote letters & the Ontario & federal govts. demanded interminable quantities of money in succession duties, gift taxes, etc.)." He began to feel that either the estate would not be released to him, or there would be nothing to release. Suspense and indecision beset him. He was conversing with too many talkative relatives and family friends, too many *old people*.

In Peruvian hat and poncho, he materialized at the green verandahed house that his cousin Don Blanchard and his wife Sharon were moving into shortly after their marriage. Bestowing gifts from the outer reaches of Latin America, unkempt in greasy hair and thick glasses, he visited Marg and her family on their farm, and dispensed nature lore to the now-married Susan Wilford. To Randy he wrote that he spent too much time in "grey, grimy, pseudo-mod, pseudo-liberated WASP Toronto, sitting for hours in seedy Graham Greeneish homosexual beer parlours talking to misfits, sadists, and failures. " On one visit he saw his old mentor Barker Fairley, hale and still painting.

Letters from previous lives trailed him: gossipy notes about academic politics in Rio, and a series concerning Paulinho. Delegates were looking after Paulinho's interests in Rio, but they were poor, too, and needed "loans." Sometimes the illiterate Paulinho dictated notes, and he asked for money, too. Lal Kaloo, back in Trinidad, wanted him to help his 19-year-old sister Tarrah when she came to Toronto; she was "very handy in the kitchen especially with her fry rice and chow mein a chinese dish...." But Edward was in no mood to help anyone. Looking for him, Tarrah made herself known to his Uncle Joe Tangney. But by now it was April, and Edward had left for Mexico.

After many years' absence, he returned to Veracruz to heat, sea, winds, stinks, sensual torpor, avenues of palms, boys who thrice weekly polished his shoes. It reminded him of Rio. Sidewalk cafés were awash with the sounds of mariachis and marimbas. Mildly bewildered tourists thronged the beaches, trying to enjoy themselves and not quite succeeding, pale Northern fish cast up flopping on some tropical strand, wondering how they have got so far from home and into such an alien environment, and what to do about it. At night along the promenade, boys went looking for girls and girls waited for boys. Further off, men looked for boys and boys waited for men, languidly playing with themselves.

Ruth Beissel joined him, the first time they'd travelled together. They saw the huge Archeological Museum in Mexico City, but never got beyond the first floor. They crisscrossed Southern Mexico by bus and taxi, staying in first- and fifth-class hotels. Spending freely, a perfect gentleman, Edward treated her, Ruth thought, like a princess. Everywhere they travelled, men stared hungrily at her blondness. Once, after she admired a young man's beauty, he offered to bring them together: "You can have him!" He was impressed by Ruth's amusing, even desperate, attempts to communicate across the language barrier, even to learn something about the life of a lout of a taxi driver who borrowed money from her and never returned it.

Their journeys abruptly ended in Tehuantepec in southern Oaxaca state, where North America narrowed and Central America began, a shabby, straggling jungle-town on a river bend, with unlighted streets through which pigs wandered. The town's tiny plaza was crowded with buses, peasants, hippies, and stalls. At the stalls, the Zapotec women, big, bossy, and garbed like gypsies in long dresses and flowered velvet blouses, sold fruit drinks in unnatural shades as well as melting ice cream cones with embedded deceased flies. All the men seemed drunk — maybe with the heat — but there was no bar except an ancient beer hall, frequented by ancients. At windless nightfall, whistling crows from leagues around converged, seeking perches in the bearded fig trees, scolding and jostling one another, drowning out lovers' conversations, defecating on passers-by. It was just a local custom like the Sunday-night boy-and-girl strolls around the plaza. In his hotel room the air conditioning didn't work and the doorknob fell off in his hand.

The town's sinister atmosphere disrupted his amicable relations with Ruth. Agitated, he urged that they go to Guatemala: "Let's get out of here." Then, after a stranger pestered them, he told him details of their travel plans. Ruth, furious, said, "He wants to rob us!" She decided to return to Montréal. After she departed from Veracruz, he lingered. One day, sitting in the plaza, a piercing pain in his jaw told him that a crab shell fragment had cracked a molar. Capping it with gold took a few days, varied by visits to fishing villages on coast and lagoon.

A through bus took him to Tuxtla Gutiérez, capital of Chiapas, anomalous with its clean, well-lighted streets and a refreshing breeze. From there it was only three hours to San Christóbal de las Casa. It hadn't changed much since he'd been there a decade earlier. Under the spell of Leary or Lawrence, he supposed that visitors on an LSD or time trip expected plumed serpents, human sacrifices, bandits, orgiastic rites, or magic mushrooms. None were present. The town was named after the now desanctified St. Christopher, patron of travellers, and a priest, Fray Bartolomé de las Casas who, more than 400 years earlier, dared to assert that Indians were human beings. Now the Indians were colourful cultural artifacts, available to be photographed, anthropologized, socialized, phonemicized, and psychoanalyzed.

He strolled, sat in the hotel garden, and read, or went to Casa Blom, where the anthropologist Franz Blom had lived. There he saw a film on Greenland made by a Danish guest who'd spent a year of military training in Thule, the world's northernmost town. The film consisted of nothing but snow and ice, and views of an unimpressive mountain, the only object that broke the white monotony. After it was over, an old lady turned to him and whispered, "I'm so old, and there are so many places in the world I still haven't seen and want to see before I die. I'm so glad I can cross Greenland off my list now."

The countryside was dotted with Mayan villages. Thank God, he thought, here was somewhere the human male had the prettier plumage. The Maya came in hiking or in the back of trucks to buy and sell at the morning market, thereafter to munch peanuts, lick ice cream cones, and down endless small bottles of rum. By local custom, they had to be out of town by sundown. If they couldn't walk, their women came and plucked them out of gutters. During their nominally Catholic fiestas the Maya sang, danced, and worshipped nature deities in the guise of saints' statues, with which they held long, angry conversations before falling down drunk. He gazed at their veinless hands, aquiline noses, and muscular hairless legs.

Out at Zinacantan, a church, its floor strewn with pine needles, writhed with drunken, chanting Indians here for the feast of the True Cross. They tried to push him out of a side chapel until he made a donation to St. Michael — why St. Michael, he had no idea. They passed him little cups of 180-proof alcohol. After dressing the Christ, they chanted to him in Tzotzil, then did a little dance to harp music. After this, a procession, led by local authorities in black tunics and red headgear, set out for another church half a mile away, where everyone danced and drank to flute music. They wouldn't let him in, so he crossed a mountain to the village of San Juan Chamula. The Chamula, even drunker, mournfully followed him around. Most of the worshippers in the huge church had passed out.

He left for Comitán near the Guatemalan border, arriving on a Sunday night as hundreds of girls strolled on the plaza in one direction, hundreds of boys in the other. By taxi, he went to Mayan ruins with a pyramid, from the top of which you could three lakes. The next day he reached the border. Ferrying grass he'd bought in San Cristóbal, he was a little nervous, especially when it turned out that a bus companion was a French girl who had just come from Cuba. The Guatemalans confiscated her books. She thought Cuba a terrible place because of the regimentation and police grillings; in fact, she told the customs people, it reminded her greatly of Guatemala. It was a wonder, he thought, that she wasn't shot, either there or here.

In Huehuetenango, home of the Mam tribe, it poured for two days straight; dressed in red and white, the Mam dashed through the drenched market. He bussed to Quetzaltenango, all narrow curving streets and red-tiled houses. Depressed by the ever-dripping rain, he took an excursion to the village of San Martin Sacatapéquez, where all the inhabitants wore long white togas. God, how he hated rain! Heat and cold just irritated him, but rain made him suicidal.

On Sunday, he left for the country's most famous market town, Chichicastenango, where all night raw alcohol made him vomit up everything he had drunk or eaten for days. He took a five-hour walk in the hills, but still had what Angelica used to call "the twitches." The local men dressed in black breeches, black coats, and red headdresses; inside the church, worshippers lit candles and incense and murmured to their saints. They did the same to a set of idols on a hill up behind the village.

In the few days he'd been in Guatemala, newspapers had reported the deaths of peasants and soldiers in a shootout over disputed lands, the murder of a member of parliament; the slaughter of Communist guerillas by army troops; the murder of a resident American philanthropist; the evacuation of villages threatened by lava from eruptions of the Fire Volcano. A miles-long fissure had appeared in the same region where the peasants and soldiers were shooting each other up; and an earthquake jolted all Guatemala, including him, out of its sleep at midnight.

Remembering that it was the tenth anniversary of the death of Pope John XXIII, he speculated about devoting his fortune to founding a religious order (all members must be fat, wine-drinkers, and over 80 years of age.) He wrote dozens of postcards and caught buses down to Panajachel on deep Lake Atitlán, where many Indians spoke better English than Spanish.

The next day he developed anxiety attacks connected to fear of a heart attack. He countered them with the only remedy he knew that worked: alcohol.

Based in Panajachel, he boated to weavers' villages around the lake. Every house seemed to have a handloom. Men wore blazing checked shirts, red sashes, knee-length purple and white striped trousers. Or they might be decked out in pajama-like red and white striped trousers, patched with embroidery and pieces from worn-out shirts and pants, a little apron or kilt of brown and white checked wool, and a leather windbreaker with a batwing design on the back. Or bright red-striped shirts with embroidered cuffs and collars under a black sheepskin jacket, and a black-and-white wool kilt with a pink sash under it, or checkered plaid shirts and knee-length striped trousers. He couldn't resist buying. Result: he now had a huge rope-bag full of clothes, and walked around with it like Santa Claus.

Amid the sounds of clipping and planting in the gardens and of the geese and ducks that lived there, he wandered into a bar run by four little boys, cousins of the owner who appeared to tend his place (and drink his own liquor) only late at night. The area had a colony of gringos, and, truly, he could wish for no more beautiful, primitive, yet comfortable place to which to retire. An expatriate American, a former banker, took him home to meet his wife as well as Lola, a 93-year-old macaw: she might have been even older, since no one knew how old she was when caught in the jungle. Lola had been thought to be male, but at the age of 80 had laid an egg.

In the boy-run bar, a German said the Indians were all carbon copies; in his view, the U.S. should have bombed them, not Vietnam. Edward retorted that the U.S. should have bomb Germany. He met an American poet, a poor little rich boy with his money tied up in trusts, parents dead, manic-depressive, with an alcohol problem, fond of travelling, lost in the world. They became great friends, especially since Edward was the only person around who had grass.

At a market at Nahualá, he was the only tourist. The parish priest, an American, was going back to the U.S. the next day and was saying goodbye in terrible Spanish, followed by a Quiché translation, all this broadcast by loudspeaker, and the church was crowded with weeping Indians. Afterwards, everyone started saying *"Buenas tardes, padre"* to Edward, thinking he was the replacement.

Through pine forests he went to Tecpán, whose churches often had no altars, or very tiny ones, but rows of wooden statues with crudely Indian features. The Indians knelt and chanted to them, drank to their health, and left offerings of food and little clay animals. It was bitterly cold. A large police dog strolled into his room: there were no locks, and no water, in this, the town's only hotel. But what did he expect for a dollar a night?

After a stop for the beaches of Tela in Honduras, and the less-idyllic Coxen's Hole, capital of the English-speaking Bay Islands of Honduras, where he had to sleep next to a generator for three nights, he returned to Mexico via British Honduras. In steamy, Caribbean-side Belize City the streets were muddy and the market squatted by a sewage-reeking canal. A day-trip took him over roiling turquoise sea to the glassy surfaces around the tiny mangrove islets of the coral reef chain. On a lagoon, semi-permanent hippies and lobster fishermen from the Yucatán populated white-sand Key Caulker. Pelicans and kites circled. In palm-thatched huts, he drank iced beer and ate lobster salad, and stayed at a cheap hotel run by an English beachcomber. It was an idyll, though one night he awoke to find a young man trying to climb into his bed: whether to rape him or to rob him he never found out.

He was back in Canada by August. For some time, he and Ian Young had been writing each other. A poet who had emigrated to Canada from England some years before, Ian had been involved in a Toronto graduate-student literary magazine called *Catalyst*, and turned it into a small publisher of gay poetry and fiction: he had taken three poems for a gay poetry anthology called *The Male Muse*. A letter from Juscelino Kubitschek had revealed that his tutoring had not been in vain: "the mornings in Copacabana beach are truly wonderful. I would like very much to have you here again. I was accustomed to your opinions especially about international policy." He advised him to "Improve your experience and come back to talk with us having yet on your feet the dust of all the roads of the universe."

By November he was in Montréal, using the Beissels' home as a return address, but living in an apartment on St-Hubert in the east end, communicating with Ruth by tavern telephone. Through the fall he'd been plagued by postcards from Angel, a boy he'd spoken to briefly in a Mexico City bar. It proved that one could not be too careful about whom one talked to. Paulinho, too, had dictating pathetic letters, telling him of his daily battles. Now that he was financially able, Edward resolved to help him now when he needed help, and was still young, educable, and malleable. This would be helping himself as well, he thought, because he had no one else to live for.

The Québécois were an odd people, both Latin and Nordic. Though the felt more at home with them than with WASPs, he thought them a crude, narrow-minded breed. But they ate and drank well. About sex and drugs, the younger ones were surprisingly liberated of church and curés. As the blazing autumn ended, he wore a stiff heavy Chilean poncho, taking crisscross snow paths to *tavernes*. A drunken Mohawk woke him up by pressing so many times on his buzzer at 3 a.m. that he had to let him in. Well, that was all right. He was not made for sleeping alone and, rather than toss and turn, he'd rather have somebody, anybody.

He frequented PJ's Cabaret, where he joked with the shemales and drank *crème de cacao avec du lait*. He met a Peruvian named Arturo, who soon owed him money. The pub he most favoured was the Taverne Montréal on the Main, St-Laurent Blvd., the traditional dividing line between French East and English West. There, someone spiked his drink with something tasteless while he was in the washroom, giving him panic attacks and hallucinations. After he had dragged himself home, he was out of commission for 36 hours. Concluding that the Mickey Finn had been phencyclidine, he carried around a card in his wallet warning of its dangers.

When he passed through Toronto en route to Lindsay in mid-December, Ruth Colombo had asked him whether he felt "Canadian" or "Latin American," at which point John interjected: "The problem with Edward, I think, is that he doesn't feel *human*." This rang a chord. The world was strange to him, and everywhere he was a stranger. His main themes, he always maintained, were exile and alienation, "the pervasive sense of not belonging *any*where, to *any*thing..." John remarked that Edward's poems were filled with an explosion of sensory details, but, in the attempt to prove his humanity, it was "the mind willing the body to be sensory and sensual, not the instinctive sensuality of the body."

Elsewhere, Henry Beissel had met Arlette Francière, a translator and *français de France*, and was now with her in Formentera in the Balearics. Edward spent Christmas with the female Beissels, devouring rum-filled chocolates. He dragged a tree home from a lot one bitterly cold day. A snowstorm blocked the city for days, and on Christmas Day the family presented him with socks and jockey shorts — or whatever the indecent things were called.

His current apartment guest was Michel, an 18-year-old who had "*Vivre*" tattooed on his chest. The part Native adopted child of a farming family in Drummondville, a reform school graduate, he had long lustrous black hair, a mocking smile, a pale and urgent penis. "*Je suis aux hommes*," he told Edward. Alone, Edward went to the downstairs part of the black nightclub Rockhead's Paradise to play on the jukebox Gladys Knight's cover of "Help Me Through the Night."

Early in 1972, the Beissels had tipped me off to Edward's existence, and I'd written him while he was still in Rio de Janeiro. That year I published three of his poems in *Northern Journey,* a magazine I edited. I met him. Slim, wearing dark glasses, he reached across, as tentative as some feral creature, to give me a dead-fish handshake. It was a kind of calling card. I liked him at once, and saw him as often as our erratic schedules allowed. That winter, the poet Al Purdy, temporarily absent from his lakeside A-frame in Ameliasburgh, Ontario, was staying in a flat on Côte St. Luc lent him by a fellow poet Ron Everson, a place with a conservatory and a largesse of stark Jean-Paul Lemieux paintings. Getting him and Edward together was like trying to establish diplomatic relations between the United States and China. Al said that Edward was to bring along advance copies of his book with long dedications to himself and me. At last, I was able to introduce the unlikely pair: Edward, wary, diffident, yet self-assertive; Al, all rangy rough edges, at the extreme other end of the homo-hetero spectrum, a hater of Canada meeting a lover of Canada. But they got on well, and on leaving, Edward told him that he was a "damn good poet."

For his part, Edward introduced me to Michel. One night, as the three of us drank, Michel initiated me into the matey custom of blowing hashish smoke down a friend's throat. In Edmonton, Edward had not met a Beissel friend, a Frenchwoman named Monique de Gaye, who lived there with her piano-teaching Swiss husband and their three small children. Now she was in Montréal, and I was living with her. Edward sampled my beef vegetable soup, and I took him to hear Dutch Mason, a white bluesman from Dartmouth, Nova Scotia: he sat in a swoon through the limber guitar licks, rumbles, and growls. Once, when we both happened to be in Toronto, I brought him together with my friend Terry Kelly, then beginning his novel-writing career as M. T. Kelly. We set off for the Colonial Tavern to hear the Bobby Bland Blues Band. On the way there, we were riding the subway when we heard the sounds of an altercation at the far end of the car. Head down, intent, Edward beetled toward it but by the time we got there whatever had been going on had subsided. After hearing B. B. King's colleague, Bobby Bland, who wasn't, I asked him why he thought the bluesman was so good. "Oh, it's that lost quality," he said.

He had at last settled the Lindsay estate, though his aunts, Marie-Camille and Marion, with an uncertain grasp of commercial values, had sold 10 Mill Street at a rummage-sale price. Still, he was financially independent. Pooling information, Randy Wicker and Byron Black reckoned that he might have inherited about $250,000 from the house sale and from investments, which included two mortgages he held through a trust company. At the end of 1973, he declared to the Department of National Revenue that he had received $9,028.13 in interest for the year. With some prudence it was enough to give a single man a modest competence.

For Michel, who smoked a lot of dope and dropped a little acid, he laid on steak and seafood dinners. Always avid for new cultural experiences, Ruth asked Edward to take her to a gay bar. When they got there, someone asked him, "Are you straight?" "No," Edward replied, "but she is." The Beissel family got to know Michel, perhaps a little too well. At various points, he propositioned Ruth and attempted to pick up Myrna.

Before Edward left Canada again, he wanted to publish a collection of poems, and had money to do it. Henry suggested a bilingual title, *Si tu vois mons pays / God Save the Queen*, but Edward dismissed the idea as frivolous. By February, Henry had put him in contact with the poet and teacher Louis Dudek, who had long been active in small-press publishing. Dudek didn't want to handle the work, "alleging ill-health and pressure of work," as Edward put it to the Colombos, but he suspected it was because Dudek didn't like it; he had told Edward it represented something "intermediate between poetry & prose." This amused Edward, because it was what he'd have said about Dudek's work. Dudek suggested his printer, a Hungarian named Robert Feher, who had also done Henry's magazine *Edge*. He proved to be a slim grey quiet man in black overcoat with a shop in Old Montréal. Edward liked him, found his price tolerable, and was soon correcting proofs. There remained a dilemma: how to get the book distributed.

This problem was solved when he finally met Ian Young, as well as his friends Ed Jackson and John Forbes, during a March visit to Toronto. When John gave him a treasured copy of *Forms of Loss* to autograph, Edward wrote, "Every author, however obscure, needs a biographer." To his admirers, Edward seemed spiky and patronizing, very down on Canada, very up on South America, which made John feel like asking what South America had done in the way of gay liberation. Further to their meeting, Edward wrote Ian that he regretted they'd talked more about business than literature, or about life. Montréal, he regarded as "a very free, open place, not perhaps any longer (or ever) so wide-open as Toronto in respect of baths, massage parlours, whorehouses, political activities etc. but definitely less guilt-ridden & sick than Anglo-Canada..." Amid snowstorms and cold snaps, he was growing keen to leave the country, in the meantime surviving on "hope, mandrax & valium." *Path of Snow*'s typesetters, he said, also did half the tabloids in Montréal. It would be delightful if they got a few pages mixed up.

In the spring he left Michel, who was costing him too much money and causing many problems. As well, his feet stank disgracefully and he had got tired of his penis, just as, he noted, he grew tired of everything. He now lived in an apartment above the tracks on a street between St-Matthieu and St-Marc on which his building was the only house and number, and he heard shuffling, bumping locomotives in the night. Oppressed by the cold grey Montréal April, he managed to slip across the border by train to visit Randy in New York. It was his first time he'd been in the United States in more than 15 years.

He opted for a hotel rather than stay in Brooklyn with Randy and the volatile David Combs. Randy, he found, was a matchless guide to the outré. He pocketed a membership form for the Eulenspiegel Society, "the world's only S&M Liberation group," which included slots to check off: "basically top," "basically bottom," "switchable," "Heterosexual," "Homosexual," Bisexual." The Society, which met for discussions at the Church of the Beloved Disciple, or at the Spike Bar. Randy conducted him to a bar specializing in dwarves and fatties—not that Edward had ever been a chubby chaser. Under the sway of Randy's gay activism, he joined demonstrators in front of Cardinal Newman's palace, chanting:

Cardinal Newman, Cardinal Newman,
Where are you? Where are you?
Hiding in your closet, hiding in your closet,
Shame on you! Shame on you!

At one such gathering, he spotted a bearded demonstrator in a skirt and thought, "Ah, Fraser's finally come out!"

At Randy's urging, he made a flying journey to Puerto Rico, staying at the Limon Guest House in Mayaguez. Surrounded by jungled hills, it had a stable of boys and seemingly every male student in Mayaguez on tap. The proprietor played wild piano all night long. Edward wondered whether Randy had known someone named Tomás because, written on a lamp in his room, was the inscription "Tomás y Randy."

The U.S. trip snapped his lengthy depression. Canada was itself a depression, just as the United States was a disease. In retrospect, he felt unaccustomedly grateful to Randy and even to the disliked David Combs. Everything in New York and Puerto Rico renewed him: the greening, flowering landscape and parks, the weather, the foreign foods and ambience, the gay scene. Another therapeutic factor was the 133-page book waiting for him on his return, 250 hardcovers priced at $10,

650 softcovers at $3.95. Edward knew it wouldn't sell. But he wanted to get these poems out of his life. He identified his self-publishing venture as Ahasuerus Press. The Wandering Jew. A white diagonal slash across the cover represented the path of snow, bordered by blue and yellow. One epigraph was from the nineteenth-century writer Antoine Gérin-Lajoie's "*Un Canadien Errant.*" The Canadian banished to exile says:

> Si tu vois mon pays,
> Mon pays malheureux,
> Vis, dis à ses amis
> Que je me souviens d'eux

Like a vade mecum atlas, the poems tracked Edward from his Lindsay boyhood through his Latin American travels. Value-added were notes often longer than the poems they referred to, and several pages of passport stamps and photograph-booth snapshots of his boyfriends.

Writing to me, he commented on a review essay about *Path of Snow* that I had written for the journal *Canadian Literature*:

> The real theme is alienation, the pervasive sense of not belonging *any*where, to *any*thing...of not being able to communicate with *anyone*, in *any* language (hence the linguistic interests) — & homosexuality, like criminality ("Laws"), racial discrimination (the West Indian poems), exile from childhood & my past (the "*je me souviens*" theme, as you call it) and, above all, expatriation, both physical and mental (*passim*) is simply one of the forms this alienation takes.

Among the complimentary copies he sent, Susan Wilford's was inscribed, "in memory of a childhood spent together." He sent a copy to his University College friend Bruce Trigger with no return address. Having noticed that Edward had thanked Louis Dudek for help with editing, Bruce asked Louis if he had Ed's address. Louis turned bright red and asked, "How did you ever know that person?" adding that Edward "was the most degenerate person I've ever encountered."

That year I had commissioned him to write a long review essay for *Northern Journey*, "Canadian Bards and South American

Reviewers," in the style of the "Poetry Chronicles" that he had written for Henry Beissel's *Edge*. The Canadian poets hardly knew what hit them: he subjected batches of current books to a daunting wealth of quotations from their work and the kind of rigorous close reading they'd never encountered.

When he revisited Toronto, the horse chestnut trees were just coming into bloom, with their associations of final exams and the beginning of summer. On the May 24 weekend, he suddenly turned up at the home of Roslyn Paleff, his college schoolmate. Though her letters were seldom reciprocated, now and then a postcard would arrive, every corner of it filled, just as cobweb calligraphy unspooled across marglinless pages in epic letters to other friends, her Russian mother served him glasses of tea with lemon and lump sugar. He was going to walk uphill from the Paleffs north to where the Colombos lived. Roslyn's mother pointed out that it was an awfully long trudge. No, said Edward, he was going to walk it. Roslyn accompanied him to the corner. Three blocks on, he turned and waved. She watched him disappear from sight.

With Ian Young, he worked out details for *Path of Snow*'s distribution. Over the phone, the voice of Robert Finch was as velvety as ever. At 74, Finch was preparing his memoirs, which, unlike Edward's confessional work, would doubtless be less than revealing. Finch told Edward that, like him, he had always lived for the moment, and Edward told him that he thought Finch was the best Canadian poet. Meanwhile, he had got wind that Ian MacDonald who, as Dean of Men at University College, had expelled Edward from the student residence, was about to be named President of York University. Evincing a sudden interest in university administration, he wrote to the York authorities declaring that MacDonald was manifestly unfit for such a position.

Henry Beissel, who'd been setting up Ayorama Cottage, a new home across the Québec border, was visiting Toronto, too. He took Edward to the hamlet of Kleinberg to see Group of Seven paintings at the McMichael Museum, exposing him to inhuman, non-human, pre-human landscapes. He thought the paintings did precisely what they set out to do: paint the picture of an empty country. But that was not the country he'd like to live in. Art was not life, but it *was* about people, and that was what Canada was *not* about. With them was Arlette Francière, to whom Edward gave his deadfish handshake. Henry had warned her that Edward could be nasty but she found him gentle and charming. She seemed to be a "nice" person, he wrote Ruth, in the way in which he considered people "nice" who had not yet done anything to hurt him.

On a bright afternoon he joined in celebrating Barker Fairley's eighty-seventh birthday. Barker sat on his verandah in his cane chair while the wind sprinkled white chestnut blossoms on the grass and steps of his home. The birthday boy sipped whisky, enjoying the attention of friends flowing in with presents and best wishes. He was affectionate, abnormally so, considering the general if superficial crustiness that had always daunted Edward. His eyes blazed under the craggy brow and his jaw trembled as he talked in his precise Yorkshire accent about art, life, letters, painting and politics. He said, "I don't want to die. I want to live." When Edward pointed out that the house next door was No. 88, a good number to aim at, Barker said that he was aiming at nothing less than 90 now — his own house number. He'd long coveted the portrait Barker had done of him. Learning from Henry that Barker only got a negligible pension from the University of Toronto, he realized that buying it might help him a little. Giving instructions for Henry to pick it up, he put it on permanent loan to Ruth.

Back in Montréal, he had left something else with Ruth: a massive Chilean poncho. It was extra baggage.

12

THE REDISCOVERED CONTINENT

June 1974-June 1975

I take my time to go where I am going.
No one is waiting for me.
I am a leaf on the stream.

~ The Message

The Guadalajara to which he'd flown was a midnight-curfewed remnant of the vibrant tawdry city he'd fondly remembered. To bed early, he dreamt that Queen Victoria bequeathed him a garnet crucifix, an amethyst rosary, and a *Book of Common Prayer* dated 1837. In Ruth Beissel's garden he listed his five favourite flowers, realized he'd forgotten the lilac, then he looked up, and one was blooming near the garage. He called out, delighted, "Oh, look, Ruth, the lilac is in bloom," and began to scratch out "cinquefoil" in his list and put down "lilac." A booming voice said, "I know," adding, "Will you ever go back to your own country, now that the lilac is in bloom?"

When he ordered a beer in Torreón after a decade's absence, his usual barman looked at him calmly and said, "It's been some time since you came in here for a drink. What's the matter? Did we do something to offend you?" Everyone assumed he had taken up his old teaching post after an extended vacation. Though Doña Aurelia, his old landlady, had died, her house was unchanged. The cantinas, renamed a dozen times, had the same waiters dispensing the same free lunches. The same prostitutes, or their daughters, sat in the doorways of the same red-light districts. He wished he could stop time as thoroughly as a dozy provincial city could. Leobardo, who still worked in a bar, lived with a former domestic in a mud hut with their three children, and spent his money on booze and amphetamines. Naturally he and Edward went to bed together, and naturally Edward helped him financially.

The girls who'd been his students were married, locked away by their husbands. Meeting his former male students, he tried coming on as a liberated gay, but they were baffled, took it as an eccentric's joke, or as an invitation to have sex with him ("Well, come on, let me fuck you, then"), but he didn't want sex with people he'd taught. Leobardo had worked for a while in a gay bar, but left because he hadn't liked working among "faggots." This, despite the fact that he'd sex with Edward many times, and in all positions. Former students scornfully told him that two of their number had become "screaming queens." They were shocked when he pointed out that he did exactly what queens did.

In the tri-city area of Torreón, Gómez Palacio, and Lerdo he revisited little country towns with rustic red-light districts, and states like Zacatecas, where bullet holes in bars dated back to the days when Pancho Villa ruled. In this season the mountain towns were at their best; even black Zacatecas was green. In Guanajuato, he sent a postcard showing mummies in a cemetery crypt to John Colombo, pointing out that it was "in no way an attempt to represent the Colombo Family in group portrait with me."

In Coahuila, a former student, now a dentist trainee, extracted two teeth and filled several others. The first molar took two hours and the efforts of at least six students to get it out. He hoped they'd left his teeth in good shape for the next decade. Monterrey was bawdier than the last time he'd been there, but Mazatlán wasn't even worth visiting for turtle eggs downed with tequila, lemon, salt and a dash of sweet red wine: the little port city he'd liked was full of crass Californians, the prices sky-high.

By August, a mountain of mail awaited him in Mexico City. His Aunt Marion, the ex-nun, had recovered from what he suspected was a mild stroke, combined with the effects of malnutrition—she'd eaten practically nothing for years. He'd dispatched copies of *Path of Snow* to cousins, and was surprised that they'd taken the book calmly. Some seemed even to have enjoyed it. He'd thought the nasty references to Lindsay might have upset them and the more sexually explicit poems would have shocked them. But nobody, he reflected, took poetry seriously.

As the Beissels' marriage unravelled, he wrote Ruth and Henry on each other's behalf, assuring Ruth that she was attractive enough to have an affair. He wrote that he'd looked in the mirror and decided that his hair was prematurely grey so he had his hair dyed medium brown: being grey just wasn't gay. He felt a decade younger, and people again called him *"joven"* instead of *"señor."* But a woman was always desirable; as the gay world unpleasantly said, "You can't compete against a cunt."

Each day had a different timetable. If one day he went to bed at 6 p.m., then the next he retired at 3 a.m. and slept till 6 p.m. What routine his life possessed— a morning read of the newspapers, an afternoon walk, an evening meal—disappeared when he was in transit. If it wasn't vomiting, it was diarrhea, and if it wasn't diarrhea it was a hangover, and if it wasn't a hangover, it was a panic attack, and if it wasn't a panic attack, it was insomnia. What he regretted most about drinking was the time it wasted. But there was no remedy for that except to stop, and the remedy was worse than the disease. Scratch 90 per cent of heavy drinkers, he thought, and you'd find a homosexual or someone sexually repressed —hence the Irish. He'd settle down with a book in a bar, self-absorption punctuated by flashes of aggression and sexual outreach as his inhibitions slackened — or spasms of altruism. Once he tailed an inebriate for hours in a taxi because he feared he'd have a driving accident. When he saw him home, he had a long, pleasant chat with his mother.

Call it anomie, alienation, or cosmic loneliness, he felt it in Mexico City, which was sinking under the weight of its 11-million inhabitants. In Mexico itself, six decades after its Revolution, the poor were poorer, the rich, richer. For homosexuals, the capital held campy, self-satisfied cliques of actors, fashion designers, and hairdressers, but only about three gay bars and a few filthy baths. The prevalence of fems and drag queens, he thought, mirrored a society's degree of sexual sickness. Repression against gays ensured that the only way pariahs could gain social approval was by confirming to the stereotype the macho mind made of them.

Fleeing the capital, he returned to Torreón for a week of goodbyes. The gay brothel had been closed down after other bars complained that it was a moral peril — actually, it took too much business from them. The police beat up and threw the dancing couples in jail, shaved and sheared them, fined them, and put their names in newspapers. Most of the kids fled to the border town of Ciudad Juárez. A former student had him examine a 34-year-old who had the misfortune to possess a vestigial penis and only one descended testicle. He promised that he'd write to Randy to enquire about medical treatment in the United States, though he thought cure was hopeless. But precisely because it was hopeless, he thought, one must try to give such a person hope.

Returning to Mexico City, he turned south. Cacahua-milpa, on the road to Taxco, could stand for many little towns. A snot-nosed girl begged money from passengers. A child had an iguana to sell. A barefoot man hawked lemon ices. Two brown dogs, rear ends locked together, rotated slowly, a miniature merry-go-round, their faces wearing the pained, foolish expression dogs always wore when copulating ("How did we ever get into this mess anyhow?") In a basketball court, a dozen sweating teenage boys shouted and cursed. The angelus rang. On the steps of the looming baroque church a priest stood, black cassock billowing. The sun set, the hills darkened. Passing men murmured of weather or crops, their sandals stirring dust. A fitful night-wind shook fragrance and blossoms from a chinaberry tree. *Ranchera* music leaked from a jukebox in a corner bar that sent a golden band of light across the blue roadway.

Through Oaxaca to the highlands of Chiapas, he encountered peasants who fought duels with live roosters in their hands, and worshipped pig deities called *teponaztles*. During fiestas. The pigs were beribboned: if not properly honoured, they might run off to visit their fellow *teponaztles* in other towns, cause bad luck, and have to be lured back with gifts and festivities. In Irraínzar, the Indians were all so drunk for the feast of San Miguel that they chose Edward, the only one sober, to light off the firecrackers, which terrified him, but which he had to keep doing almost all night. He'd gladly give southern Mexico back to the iguanas. Feeling in need of a mother's — or somebody's — care, he slept in damp *pensiones* and, slimming to a little over 60 kilos, ate nothing but beans, rice, and avocado. He'd been in Mexico four months, much longer than he intended. But, now that inherited money permitted it, he was determined to travel at his own rhythm and rate of speed, however long he took.

Rain pursuing him, he crossed into Guatemala, and up the 3,500 metres of the Cuchumatanes, its villages tucked in mountain folds. Suffering from "a toothache, which make me lucid, and dysentery, which makes me loose," he wrote to me from Guatemala City one rainy night, touching on literary matters. He'd donated a copy of *Northern Journey*, the literary magazine I edited, to the Canadian Embassy's library in Mexico City but the people there didn't sound properly grateful so he hid it on a shelf and walked out. He speculated that an early Canadian winter might push up sales of *Path of Snow* since people would take it for a manual on snow shovelling.

He learned of the death of Gabriel Couthard, a Latin American expert at the University of the West Indies in Jamaica who'd always shown him a good time. Like Lowry, he had killed himself by drinking, dying of a heart attack in his fifties. He also got a letter from Susanne Forster in London, England, happy with her new baby. They hadn't communicated in at least eight years, but it was just as though she and he had been talking yesterday in Edmonton, Alberta. She wished that Edward would "come around a windy corner of this city and we could go and drink undiluted gin and talk."

Rain poured, and three volcanoes decided to erupt. Torrents of lava and ash brightened the sky at night and darkened the day. Inches of atmospheric dust lowered the temperature to nearly freezing. The glowering, spitting Fire Volcano looked

like an astronomical phenomenon or a forest inferno, its growls
heard a hundred miles away. He'd eaten so much dust that he
had no appetite for anything solid. He got a bad cold, and began
to be concerned about his heart. He went to a clinic for three
days of examinations; tachycardia was diagnosed. The smiling
specialist told him not to worry. His heart consistently beat 100
times a minute, one-third too fast. He should cut down on coffee
and alcohol, not smoke, and take his Valiums. He recalled that
pulse rate was linked to lifespan. A shrew's heart beat 1,000
times a minute; a shrew lived two years. An elephant's beat 25;
an elephant lived 100 years. Edward's beat 100; he was in his
thirty-sixth year.

With friends, he climbed the Pacaya volcano, the road to
it knee-deep in ash. Every half-hour, a roar came and rocks and
lava shot up. Since there were no buses back, they spent the night
on the slopes, hugging each other to keep warm. In weavers'
villages he bought trousers and a sash for Henry Beissel, for Ruth
and the girls blouses with red-and-gold embroidered sunbursts.
He wrote that he was highly offended to learn that they had not
yet hung Barker Fairley's portrait of him "to remind them of
my imperial presence"; if they kept up the neglect, he would
disinherit them and give it to the German Department of the
University of Alberta. He reminded Ruth and Henry that Aunt
Marie-Camille was praying for them — maybe that was what
was driving them apart; he'd have to request her to ask God to
separate them. Aunt Marion's mind was as keen and sarcastic as
ever, her letters advising that he should live his life, and avoid
the trap of Lindsay. Hah, as though he were likely to fall into
that!

He dreamed that he'd gone to visit the National Palace.
A rotunda was fronted by little bar-restaurants with names like
"*Mi Casa.*" After reclining on a room's unmade bed, he stood in
red underwear in a red-and-gold reception hall of the Guatemala
legislature, where they were trying to decide what to do about
him. In rage, he ran out, then discovered he was naked, and tried
to cover himself with a record of parliamentary debates. But the
president made a conciliatory speech saying that, like Nixon,
Edward had paid for his crime. He rushed back to the bedroom
and found his clothes. At that, a bevy of teenage girls joked that

this was the most interesting thing that had ever happened in the legislature. Next, he was running out into snow or sleet, dodging the big green oranges that were dropping to the street.

In Guatemala City, he sated himself with half the boys along Sexta Avenida. Nice boys, gentle, honest, grateful. Still, even if the boys did it for the pleasure of it, *you* paid, because you were the rich tourist. Anything else, he wrote Randy, was what "fags recount in gay bars to impress other fags: `I got it for free', `He begged me to let him fuck me'...." He had no erotic contact with the Mayans, a moral, monogamous people, though they were mouth-watering with their smooth, muscular, perfectly proportioned legs in short knee-breeches or kilts, slim bodies, and noble, severe faces. They did not *know* what sex with men even meant: when he described the specifics, they thought it was not just funny, but physically impossible.

By the end of October he was in El Salvador. The country was still reeling from a disastrous war with Honduras five years earlier. By day, San Salvador was hot, humid, and stinking; by night it was cold and humid. The first night two drunks told him to leave the country and slapped his face. In a bar called El Faro, he asked some 15-year-olds what age they had started their sexual activities: almost all of them told him "10," and one said, "Not much may be going on here, but we fuck like rabbits...."Which was probably how El Salvador, the smallest country in the Americas, was also the most overpopulated.

By night, he walked down the middle of the badly lit streets, since hoodlums waited outside bars and on street corners. Policemen didn't dare to patrol: *they* went around in cars. He soon began to take taxis to go a couple of blocks. He planned to stay three days at most, but about 5 a.m. on his second day, a trio whom he'd met in El Faro choked him and stole his wallet. He felt for his passport, and it wasn't there. Without it, he couldn't change traveller's cheques, leave the country, get a visa, or confirm his identity. He couldn't even change his hotel, a dump that he'd taken because it was handily located halfway between the two red-light districts.

November 2, the Day of the Dead, was a public holiday, and everything was closed. He tried complaining to the police, but they said he was drunk. On Sunday, he went back, but they told him to go to his embassy. On Monday he went to the British Embassy, which represented Canada. At his expense, they called the Canadian embassy in San José, Costa Rica. After asking multiple questions and scolding him for his carelessness, a lackey said that the British embassy would have to issue him a safe-conduct to Costa Rica, where he could get a temporary passport. In order to get the safe-conduct, he had to go to Immigration and get a proof of entry into the country. This took all one day. Then he had to go to the police and register his complaint. He found someone to listen to him, and was told to buy stamped legal paper and come back the next day to make an official statement. That night on the street, a boy with whom he'd just had sex sneaked up behind him with two friends to pinion and rob him.

When he saw the police again, it was another public holiday, and no one was there. Returning the next day, he told to come back on Friday. On Friday, they told him nothing could be done till Monday. He went to the British Embassy and complained of police obstruction. They phoned, and sent him back. He got a slip of paper, proof that he had complained about his passport loss, and ran back to the Embassy with a set of passport photos. He got a large, stamp-covered sheet stating that "The government of Her Britannic Majesty sends its compliments to El Salvador, Honduras, Nicaragua, and Costa Rica, and asks on behalf of the Canadian citizen, Edward A. Lacey, etc." He was to take this to Immigration to get an exit visa, then to the embassies of Honduras, Nicaragua, and Costa Rica, to get their entry visas, permitting him to get to San José, where he could get a temporary passport. By now the embassies were closed, so all he could do was to go to Immigration to extend his stay in El Salvador for another 90 days—how he welcomed that! They gave him his exit visa with no trouble, and said, oh, by the way, they had his passport.

He looked up the priest who'd turned it in, a Spaniard who'd spent years as a missionary in Peru and Brazil. On November 2, after early morning mass, three "suspicious-looking characters" had handed it to him, saying they had found it on the street. The priest took Edward for a colleague—it took him time to convince him he was wrong. He could understand why he was taken for a priest; the passport photo was sacerdotal-looking. Everywhere in Latin America, people started up discussions on religion with him, asked him to say mass, or to give his blessing, and stood up in buses to insist that the padre sit down. He supposed it must be his grave mien, or his habit of talking to himself that made people think he was praying. A decade of this had begun to annoy him — especially when he was trying to seduce some boy who called him "Father."

His joy at recovering his passport soon abated. He realized that his visa for Nicaragua had expired. No, said the bus company, it could not be extended at the border, and no, they could not let him travel without it. Another weekend in San Salvador. He withdrew his police complaint: more stamped legal paper. On Monday, besides getting his Nicaraguan visa extended, he returned to the British Embassy and gave them back their safe-conduct. When he tried to buy a ticket for Nicaragua, the solitary bus company said they were booked up; he'd have to wait till tomorrow. Which he did. Then he found that extending the visa could have been done at the border after all.

At last in Nicaragua, he went to Léon, a city with an immense grimy cathedral, where beneath a monument the poet Rubén Darío was buried, crowned by a weeping lion pawing a broken lyre. The main street was named after him; his house where he died in 1916 was preserved with the bed he died on, and a frightening photo of his death agony. A few miles east, in the little Pacific resort of Poneloya, a tree grew in the middle of a seaside road. The silence was total except for surf, buzzing cicadas, and squeaking bats, which flew in and out of his room all night, and hung from the ceiling during the day. He was the only guest in a huge hotel that could have been lifted from *The Great Gatsby*, all pillars, arches, fretted balconies of late-Victorian gingerbread, rocking chairs, and a big empty dance-floor. He wore the Guatemalan shirts that Randy and his boyfriend David had fought over so much that he'd repossessed them in order to calm them down. He reported to Randy, who was worried about cholesterol counts, that he'd just had a satisfying breakfast of a half-litre of milk and a dozen turtle eggs, and noted that semen was supposed to be rather rich in cholesterol. Randy would die when the right time came. He himself had taken a test that appeared in a magazine, and came out dead at a little past 50.

He'd remembered Managua as a bustling town. Now huge faults traversed fields of grass where rows of shops had stood. About half the former residents had returned. Makeshift hotels, banks, bus terminals, restaurants, now at vast distances from one another, were wooden-walled and zinc-roofed. No one knew where anything was.

He headed for the Mosquito Coast, named after the Mosquito tribe, whose king had allowed the British logging rights. The British brought in Jamaican slaves to cut the mahogany and rosewood. After the United States forced England to give back the coast, West Indians remained, more arriving when the big fruit companies set up banana plantations. A further wave came to help build the Panama Canal, and then scattered all the way from Belize to Panama, and you could still find English-Creole blacks and stilt houses, Protestant churches, tinned milk, and reggae. He took a seven-hour bus to Rama, an outpost where only half the inhabitants and the parrots spoke Spanish—four bars, a whorehouse, and no electricity after 10 p.m.—and took a riverboat (60 miles, six hours) down to Bluefields, where Baptist and Moravian missionaries had set up schools. The Chinese controlled the groceries and restaurants, though they made nothing but "Choc sui" and "chay min"; Arabs and Jews owned the shops. Bluefields was "the home of rain"; it poured about 300 days a year. Besides marinating himself in rum, listening to reggae, and watching the shrimp boats come and go, he toured the cemetery where ornate mausoleums of Spanish-speaking Catholics loomed next to wooden crosses and headstones of the Protestant West Indians, with touching inscriptions and verses from hymns ("Sleep, sleep, sleep" — this on a tomb for three little children), ideograms on the Chinese tombs, odd names like Abdulkader Benoît, and gravestones for people born in Montmagny, Québec and St. John's, Newfoundland.

On the cargo flight to Great Corn Island, a fellow passenger said, "What luck! We'll have a safe flight, with a priest aboard" and began to discourse on the beauties of the Catholic church in Bluefields, asking him if he wouldn't like to be stationed there. Shaped like corn kernels, Great and Little Corn Island were peopled by friendly, white-skinned, fair-haired descendants of Cayman Islands pirates who lived on

three-by-two miles of white sand, palms, and palms. They lived
by shrimping and gathering coconuts and copra. Walking under
palms in the wild wind he feared for his safety: someone got
beaned by a flying coconut practically every year. He thought
that a lovely addition to his Bluefields tomb would be: "E.A.
Lacey, killed by a flying coconut on Great Corn Island, in the
36th year of his age. `He is not dead, he only sleeps!'"

The only tourist at his hotel, he found the U.S.-leased
island ringed with soft white coral-sand beaches, and clear, clear
blue water. A couple of nightspots with jukeboxes, and dancing;
starchy meals on little plates. At lunch, he met an American
woman who planned never to leave. Walking with her to her
place on the other side of the island he met her stepson, with
whom he spent the afternoon smoking and arguing; he was a
logical positivist and worshipped Ayn Rand. Edward wasn't,
and didn't.

The howling wind blew with intermittent rain for two
days. No plane could land or leave. When he did get to Costa
Rica, he spent a week in the muggy torpor of Puerto Limón, a
decaying banana port. By New Year's Day, he was in San José,
where everything stopped dead from December 24 to January
6. He waited it out, calculating that he had spent each of the
last 16 Christmases in a different place. Still in a statistical
mode, he reckoned that he had slept in 72 different hotels or
pensions during the past year, not counting ones used for
quickie sex. He wandered the sunny empty streets and found
a solitary barbershop open, where he got a shave and massage.
He needed to communicate with, be touched by, some other
human being—even if it was only a barber. He kept delaying his
return to Rio because he was afraid of what he'd find there. In a
few more months, once the summer heat had receded and Rio
was livable, he'd find out that, as he suspected, Paulinho had
changed beyond possibility of contact or recognition.

On January 20, the Feast of San Sebastian, patron saint
of Rio de Janeiro and of masochists, he was robbed of the
passport and traveller's cheques that he left in his hotel room.
His portable typewriter was gone too. The 20-odd poems he had
written since leaving Canada were tucked inside the case, but he
managed to recreate all of them. He was also mugged. Though

Costa Rica was said to be a safe literate democratic little country
it turned out that, in the absence of an army, the National Guard
spied on everyone, everywhere, as did the secret police, the DIC
that, he estimated, committed or abetted most of the country's
crime. Another banana republic beneath the peel. He was being
blackmailed into acting as a decoy-informer against U.S. cocaine
smugglers when he fled, vowing never to return.

After a stop at the English-speaking free-port island of
San Andrés, Colombia, he regained the mainland. As always,
Colombia was inexpensive, thievish, and thoroughly enjoyable,
"the liveliest country in South America, and nearly the cheapest,
a crazy-quilt resembling, in its different zones, every country
on earth," he wrote me. Everyone and everything was buyable
and if you committed, were caught in, or framed into, some
infraction, he wrote me, a bribe was always welcome. Larcenous
Colombia had the world's highest percentage of its population
in jail.

Barranquilla was a hot, scummy, dangerous port that
everyone hated and he loved, the quintessence of tropical
South America's rapacity, sensuality, and misery. He took in
the carnival and its Battle of the Flowers, which should have
been called the Battle of the Flours. Everybody threw flour on
everyone else for four days, though a few men covered in black
grease threatened to paint him black if he didn't contribute
money. In Santa Marta, two hours east, was the hacienda where
Bolivar died, saying, "I have ploughed the sea." Out of season, it
was dull. Four hours west, Cartagena was better, the poet Luis
López's city "full of rancid disarray," "*ciudad triste, ayer reina de
la mar,*" the sad city, former queen of the sea, which he famously
compared to the fondness one had for a pair of battered shoes.
After seeing the "*Monumento a los zaptatos viejos,*" he wrote to Ian
Young to wonder "what monument Lindsay will raise to me. A
snow-sculpture of a penis?"

In Colombia, the hotel maids still maintained their coffee-
or-juice-at-6 a.m.-routine, thundering on your door at dawn,
screaming "*Su tinto! Su tinto! No quiere su tinto?*" Newspapers
read like García Márquez *One Hundred Years of Solitude*. All the
things in García Márquez could, and did, occur here, including
invasions of yellow butterflies, 10-year-long rains, massacres of

banana workers, and brothels with swimming pools swarming with alligators. *Everyone* broke the law: they smuggled out cocaine, dope, emeralds, sugar, beef, and petroleum. They smuggled in cigarettes, whisky, wine, perfumes, canned luxury foods, electrodomestic items. Typically, soldiers stopped buses 10 times in as many hours for customs inspection. The customs people roused him to fury by poking holes in his baggage with sabres. If the government put a stop to smuggling, millions would starve.

In Tunja, an old, cold mountain town 100 miles from Bogotá, men wore poncho-like *ruanas*, and black-garbed women wore bowler hats. After stumbling in the dark over drunken Indians, he wrote me that, Montréal having witnessed some gangland discothèque murders, I should, passing the Taverne Montréal, tell "the lovely people inside," probably including Michel, that he would be "back someday to greet and repay them (with a submachine gun.)" Meanwhile, he noted that too many things had happened to him to make sense. Life didn't imitate art, but rather movies or melodrama, and surrealism was the most real of the isms.

He'd begun to think of his recent book, *Path of Snow* as *Path of Snot* or *Pathology of Snow*. I'd been kidding him that people might suppose he was my bumboy. "Why should people call *me your* bumboy," he replied, "when everybody's quite aware (because of that air of virility and manly self-reliance I so marvellously, sweatily and Laytonesquely project—my balls are indeed irresistible) that *you're mine?*" He couldn't sleep because a chilly rooster was disconsolately crowing, and his water closet was melancholically dripping, which reminded him of me and of *Northern Journey*.

Two years earlier, one of my fellow editors, Wil Wigle, had published a short story, "Slow Burn," in which the writer Margaret Atwood appeared under her own name. She gives a public reading at a university and is honoured at a party. The narrator, who is with his girlfriend Marlena, senses that Atwood "seemed just a little uncomfortable with her role as the reigning queen of Canadian literature." Marlena joins Atwood for an extended conversation. Accepting Marlena's offer to drop her off at her hotel, "Ms. Atwood sits up front. She says she was satisfied with the reading but not as pleased as she was in Montréal when John Glassco had paid her a grand compliment. After her performance there, he had come up to tell her that she had given him `a great big erection.'"

Those who knew Atwood and Glassco—the frail, white-moustached author of *Memoirs of Montparnasse*, a poet, translator, and pornographer specializing in sadomasochism—found the passage amusing. Atwood did not. Her lawyer Rosalie Abella, purporting to represent both her and Glassco, threatened a lawsuit for libel. We refused to withdraw the issue or apologize. The brouhaha reached newspaper pages and radio airwaves. Atwood's legal case collapsed when Glassco refused to join it. In the same issue of *Northern Journey* in which we cited an open letter from Glassco in which he dissociated himself from any "gestures of outrage or pressure," we published "Canadian Bards and South American Reviewers," Edward's long review essay about current Canadian poetry. Although Atwood once had been, in a small way, one of Edward's benefactors, he had no trouble picking sides. Some months earlier he had written me to say that, seeking to perpetuate the uproar, he wanted to send *Northern Journey* a letter defending Atwood's honour against a satyr's impulses. To Ian Young he echoed Glassco's words: the affair was "an erection in a teapot."

Colombia's capital was drab, cold, rainy, but cosmopolitan: they said that in Bogotá even the shoeshine boys read Proust. Cockfights were legal in Colombia. Homosexuality, technically, was not. In any case, Bogotá's half-dozen gay bars were excruciatingly dull. Everyone wore a dark coat, dark trousers, dark shoes, a dark tie, and a white shirt, so exquisitely polite so it took about six hours to proposition or be propositioned. Homeless boys slept in doorways, throwaway children. On a clear day, if such existed in Bogotá, you could take a funicular trip to the top of Monserrate, one of the green hills that relieved the city's drabness. You had to watch your belongings in hotels, though, and Bogotá was dangerous. One night he was stopped seven times and asked for his I.D. tourist card by the police or DAS, the secret police. Finally, he pretended to know no Spanish: the only English word the police captain knew was the one he used: "Go."

He was almost about to leave Colombia in late February when a telegram at the Canadian Embassy told him Randy was about to arrive in Barranquilla. Edward hastened there. At the airport, Randy glimpsed a distant stalking form: a quasi-military flip of the arm confirmed that it was Edward.

In a Barranquilla café, Randy was offered a dazzling exchange rate on $50. When they returned to their hotel, he found he'd received a handful of pesos wrapped around a clump of newspaper clippings. "I knew it would happen," Edward said. "I just wanted to see how they would do it." Randy was so upset about the sleight-of hand that Edward made up the difference. It had been worth it just to see legerdemain performed.

In Cartagena, their rhythm established itself. Randy documented the trip with camera and tape recorder, Edward booked hotels and buses, ordered meals, translated, and pimped. Randy bought so much artisanry that Edward thought it was a wonder he didn't try to buy the Cartagena walls. Going up the Magdalena River to Bogotá, a long bus trip took them to Magangué, where they transferred to a speed launch that took an hour-long tour upriver to a point where they were met by a *collectivo* jeep that took them to Mompós, where all the houses were white and colonial, there were no roads to anywhere, people all had the same surnames, and the locals made gold jewelry and rocking chairs.

After Randy had bought a passel of "gold" earrings, they took boats and jeeps to Tamalameque, where a bus took them to Bucaramanga, six hours away, an industrial city with a wild red-light zone. The Venezuela border was only three hours distant but Edward vetoed it. Randy bought horn boxes and a horn coat rack, and shot home-movies, whose footage included shots of "Jenny," the queen that he'd picked up and then, in Edward's opinion, jilted. Jenny, a charming doomed 17-year-old, was in his view much more grateful and helpful than Randy's crew of zombie associates back in New York.

After a six-hour bus ride to Tunja, Randy filmed Edward's caressing the hair of a waiter under a restaurant canopy. Down a side road through mountainous countryside was Villa de Leyva, with low, tile-roofed Andalucian houses and cobblestone streets. In the towering mountains were millions of ammonites,

shell-like fossil sea-animals, so common that the locals used
them to pave driveways and stud their homes. Nearby was
Chiquinquirá, where they intricately carved tagua, vegetable
ivory, into miniatures that Edward, the devil in him, made Randy
buy. He suspected that the multiple sets of miniature cups and
saucers of dung-coloured clay that Randy also acquired would
long grace his kitchen cabinet. Stuff began to fill hotel rooms and
they needed more and more little boys to help carry it.

In Bogotá, a few hours away, they checked out the arts-
and-crafts centre to get an idea of where carved wood carbuncles
could be found, and which penal colonies made horn ornaments.
By now several hundredweight of items had to get back to
Greenwich Village. One good and one bad thing happened to
Randy in Bogotá. He was walking beside Edward one minute;
the next, he was six feet deep down an open manhole. The
good thing involved their meeting a middle-class young man
from Pereira named Harry Horácio, who became their travel
companion. The trio went to Cali and, at the end of Holy Week,
to Buenaventura, four hours away. When they arrived at the
port, it was like the last hours of the Saigon evacuation. Houses,
bars, hotels, and people stood in three feet of muddy water, and
hundreds on the dock fought to get on a boat. "I just wanted to
go to a resort, and you take me to this!" Randy raged. Then they
discovered that the floodwater was merely high tide. People
were leaving because the holiday was over. Later, when Randy
and the tides had calmed, they found a hotel hut, and a room
with a hole in the floor, which they used for pissing. They ate at
stalls, ogled boys, and had such a good time that Randy didn't
want to leave.

Their next notable stop was in Manizales, Colombia's
most Catholic and conservative town, perched on the saddle of
a snow-capped mountain. But despite the city's staidness and
enormous, Québécois-looking cathedral, they found a male
brothel where the boys laughed and kept on dancing when the
police came to check I.D.s and ages, and *three* red-light districts.
One, downtown, swarmed with drunks; one, uptown, swarmed
with queens and included a transvestites' bar: the regulars must
have been taking growth hormone because they were all about
nine feet tall. The third, in the lower depths, was thronged with

criminals. They also found criminals in the Rokasol Hotel. They had left travellers' cheques in their room and the maid helped herself to a few. When they complained to the manager, he said that it was their fault and *"lo que le dé la puta gana,"* they could do whatever they fucking well liked about it. This incited them to protest so volubly at the front desk that other guests checked out on the spot. They complained to the Tourist Department, which chastised the hotelier and told him it would blacklist him; to the DAS, the not-so-secret police, which fined him; and to the newspaper, which printed a story on the robbery. But they didn't get their money back.

Pasto, eight hours by a bad road, was another city that looked dull but wasn't. Shops lined the streets offering handmade furniture, burnt-wood items, and carvings covered with red-and-black or white-and-black "Pasto varnish." Randy bought a set of miniature tables, and paid $13.30 for a human skull. Two hours south, tremendous rises and falls along the way, the ugly border city of Ipiales pointed the way to Ecuador. Once there, they paused in Otavalo, home of the otavaleños, great textile-makers and travelers, whose Saturday dawn market drew thousands in white trousers and blue ponchos. Randy acquired a trove of glazed figures a fat lady had baked out of dough.

Oil wealth was changing Ecuador, but it remained poor. Quito was still one of the loveliest cities in Latin America, and one of the dreariest, miles long, with streets winding up and down and around hills. The city was filled with plazas and the plazas with statuary. In the cold rainy capital, altitude sickness went away in a day or so. But while it lasted, it brought chills and fever, splitting headache, and shortness of breath. Edward had found that a sleeping pill like Mandrax, a Quaaludes brand name, was the best thing for it. In Randy's opinion, his use of sopors would do him in long before his own use of poppers. By midnight, the city was a tomb. There were no gay bars. There were no brothels. In the old sector highlands Indians trotted around in red ponchos like busy little bishops.

Three hours by bus plunged them into the slovenly town of Santo Domingo de los Colorados. The few remaining members of the Colorado tribe came into town on Sundays, ostensibly for the market, actually to get drunk from the bad beer in big bottles.

The Colorados shaped their hair into helmets and dyed it with a mixture of annatto, cold cream, and kerosene until it formed a stiff red peak, painted black rings on their bodies and dressed in bath towels. They also listened to transistors, read newspapers, and went to the movies.

In Quito, he put Randy on the bus to the border. He arrived back in the United States with $10 in his pocket and, thanks to Edward, imperishable mental images: a photograph of himself and Edward in too-short trousers, between them a boy seated on a donkey; a filmed shot of Harry's delectable buttocks taken in a Bogotá hotel room in Bogotá; and the memory of that bar in which, when he and Edward entered, a man greeted them with the words, "Tell us who you are, where you come from, and where you're going."

On the Guayaquil *malecón* river-walk, he contemplated chunks of island floating to the sea. It rained every day. Hotel fleas tormented him and his ankles were raw with mosquito-bites. There were lots of discothèques, but nobody in them. The *zona* had pools of scummy green water, and scummy brown women. He counted 269 rooms there, and since two or more women often shared a room, there must have been at least 500 women in residence. Ecuador law forbade all homosexual acts, with a penalty of four to eight years in jail for *both* parties. As Randy had predicted, he found himself wandering into shops asking out of habit about, say, a wicker rocking chair, "*Cuánto es?*"

While returning to Quito, where he would await Randy's repayment of a loan to arrive, his bus skirted the snow line and he bought postcards captioned, "childrens of the region complete the landscape." On April 24, he sent a postcard of a Colorado to Susan Wilford in Lindsay, suggesting that her husband and children should ask her to try out the Colorados' hairdressing formula. He sent one to me of Tulcán cypress topiary: "I am torn between being buried in this cemetery, and being converted at my death into one of the mummies of Guanajuato." Tulcán, he wrote, had "a slight aesthetic edge."

In Peru, a nationalist, socialist military government had stripped the ruling families of power and broke up landed estates. In some ways far to the left of Allende in Chile, it recessed Congress, banned political parties, nationalized foreign concerns, seized newspapers that, handed them over to peasants, workers, and teachers, became noisy unreadable organs of anti-U.S. virulence. This had been going on for seven years.

The Peruvian coast was mainly a cold desert of sand dunes, bare mountains, and bright blue sea. He took side trips far inland to see the ruins of Chan Chan, once the capital of the Machíca-Chími empire until ca. 1400 A.D., when it was conquered by the Inca, then looted and destroyed by the Spanish. The natives left behind erotic pottery: penis-shaped drinking vessels, and men trying—and almost succeeding at—auto-fellatio. He ventured to the Callejón de Huaylas, an area hard-hit in an earthquake five years earlier. In the town of Yungay, 25,000 people had been buried by a *huaico*, an avalanche of ice, stone, and mud amounting to millions of tons, with a forward speed of 100 miles an hour. The fields were bright with crosses and tombstones, mementoes of the May Sunday that had killed the town. Three miles away, behind a hill, New Yungay was a-building.

In Lima, he devoted himself to getting drunk and reading letters, not necessarily in that order. He had received communications from his Lindsay trust company confirming that, as he suspected, he was $1,500 "DVPs (devalued Canadian piastres)" richer than he thought—or they thought, or they thought he thought. Aunt Marie-Camille the nun still prayed, and Aunt Marion, the ex-nun, got names mixed up, and wrote him letters on a day she thought was her birthday, but was actually a month later. Her last letter had said, "Why do we *have* to go on?"

Among the letters were ones from me. Planning a trip to Colombia, I'd hoped that Edward could be a guide. He wrote back that I would not be so demanding as Randy, with whom he had just spent seven weeks, he wrote, since I was not a "paranoid schizophrenic aging downwardly mobile homosexual activist." But he begged off, instead sending densely detailed pages of travel tips, "excerpts from *The Paranoid Schizophrenic Continent.*" Before I left Montréal, I was to give my regards to people at his favourite waterholes, among them "that Peruvian bastard

Arturo, who owes me 300$ and to whom I've been sending threatening postcards for the last year." He advised me to warn everyone I met not to stay at the Rokasol Hotel in Manizales.

Suffering from a bad hangover, he felt like Sidney Carton. What a life, he reflected: half of it drunk, the other half hung over. He summarized the year of travel: he'd lost his passport twice, been robbed about a dozen times, arrested about the same number, had slept in 125 different hotels and visited about double that number of towns and cities. He was worn out with sleeping in a different bed every night, a promiscuity in itself, and living in a different town every day and empathizing and eating meals and having orgasms. If people thought travel was pleasure, they didn't know the Third World: "Let's hear how you feel after two months in Colombia," he wrote me. "*I* feel like Kafka's travelling corpse."

Lima's coolness and unending mizzling pizzle came from the Humboldt Current, named after that exuberant titled German who, at the close of the eighteenth and the beginning of the nineteenth century, botanized, mountain-climbed, wined, dined, and buggered his way around South America. In Lima were raisin-faced pedlars from Huancaya, pushing intricately carved gourds and filigree silver earrings; bowler-hatted woman from Lake Titicaca, sitting against the street-wall, with outstretched hand; silent, homeless fruit-cart men; sweaty fried-tripe salesgirls; desperate-faced vendors of pornographic playing-cards.

The previous night he'd passed four drunk young men pissing on the sidewalk. In Lima, pissing was a public art. That chorus line of brown men with their brown peckers before them in the street beside a hotel was neither a prostatitics' convention nor the invitation to an orgy, but merely papa, uncle, and three or four sons relieving themselves after a night of beer-drinking at some Chinese restaurant. The highlands women who wore seven superimposed petticoats practised a simpler method: squatting on a street corner and pouring away, and no one would see anything but the slowly forming pool. Lima smelled of ammonia.

In a weeklong alcohol-and-drug binge, he lost hours and days. One night in his hotel room, shaking uncontrollably with dry heaves and muscle spasms, he heard two young men chatting out in the hallway. He begged them to come in; they were joined by a third. In their early 20s, they came from the jungle interior. One, Lucho, brought him hot milk and gave him a massage: marvellous to feel caring hands touching him. He had survived, he thought, thanks to those young men. Lucho was religious, also a heavy drug-user: grass, coke, and yagé, which last apparently made you vomit and unable to move for hours. Reading passages from the Bible and St. Francis, Lucho calmed his spirit; sleep and a day off alcohol and drugs calmed his body. When he talked to the trio, it was like breaking through the sound barrier or recovering the use of language. They told him he was "consuming" himself, and must stop.

His hands still trembled when he wrote Randy that he'd dropped his copy of the *South American Handbook* in the toilet. His trouser leg was torn. He couldn't find the cheque Randy had sent him; he might have torn it up while drunk. He had masturbated five times thinking of a boy. He was sure, he wrote, that his nervous crisis had been a message from God and from his mother, whom he had asked recently for a "sign." He was not leading a proper life, or properly employing his talents or money. He'd give up drink and pay more attention to sex, that was what he'd do. The world was filled with delicious fruit juices; he'd had 15 years of alcohol and that was enough. He still was attractive to people, he still had a good body — he just had so many hang-ups.

Sleep brought nightmares involving his parents. A year ago he had left Canada. And three years and two days ago his mother died. He had suffered for the way he neglected her in the last years of her life. If he went on this way, he would pay with his life. The only thing that could save him was Paulinho: needing him, being needed by him, educating him, loving him, turning him into a complete person. Yet the nearer he got to Brazil, the more he feared returning to the beautiful, affectionate child who'd been given to him. He had abandoned him, as he abandoned his mother. Perhaps Paulinho *was* his mother: her spirit giving him another chance.

The Peruvian trio swapped cocaine paste for Colombian grass via the jungle frontier near Leticia. The grass was sold

in Peru and the coke exported to the North America. They'd
been born near where the borders of Peru, Colombia, Brazil,
and Ecuador virtually touched, schooled by French Canadian
missionaries. Peruvians by birth and citizenship but amply
provided with false documents, they were sitting on 40 kilos of
grass that they couldn't sell because a buyer had been arrested.
Róger, a student, supervised sales. Róbert tried to wean Lucho
from his emotional dependence on nuns into the healthier
channels of drug trafficking.

Róbert fed him coca-leaf tea and hot milk. He said he'd
never had homosexual relations, but you could always tell if
a man was enjoying sex, and Róbert enjoyed it very much. He
had just got out of jail in Colombia. He had chiselled features,
a muscular, hairless golden body. Moreover, he was a real
man, embodying machismo and a hard penis, yes, but also
a combination of toughness, tenderness, an ability to take a
beating and rise again. Though only 23, Róbert seemed like a
sympathetic older brother. Aware of the risks he was taking, he
said that he wanted some day to be rich or dead. He seemed at
times to be many people in one: some Edward feared, some he
trusted implicitly.

Broke, the trio had to get out of town. The trio had saved
him; he saved them. Eluding the Lima police, they traveled to
a briny port, to snow-capped mountains and pre-Inca ruins,
and south to Lake Titicaca and Cuzco. The relation between
Edward and Róbert was exclusive. "One doesn't meet someone
like you every day or every year," he said. They spent long
affectionate hours discussing whether they could live together.
He paid Róbert's expenses, but these were picayune, compared
with the pleasure, protection, and fun he got. He half-seriously
considered investing in the drug trade. But they agreed it would
be better for them to live separate lives but meet—every now
and then.

13

THE BOY IN RIO

June 1975-December 1976

a few more days
time will divide
bodies now joined in the bed of night...

~ A Few More Days

When he got to Brazil, the worst cold wave in a half-century had turned green to white. In Rio, he took to wearing his poncho-like Franciscan-brown *ruana* from Colombia in and out of bed, nursing an inflamed jaw and the cough he'd caught in Lima. He'd returned by way of Bolivia, where he'd eaten roast guinea pig and dehydrated black potatoes at 13,000 feet. Apart from a few respites, he'd been chilly ever since Bogotá.

Through his window poured the tolling of church bells and from the next-door apartment the sounds of rising, farting, washing, and children. Rio was as infantile and unruly as ever. It was strange to return: a life had been lived here once, lived by someone who both was yourself and who was not. Not so much that you couldn't go home again, as you couldn't go anywhere again. He flowed through time: people quickly, places slowly.

He was looking for someone, but hadn't found him yet. What he did find, miraculously, was the passport someone had stolen from him. The police recovered it from a gutter, marvellously watermarked. Prices had more than doubled in three years, and he awaited a transfer from his Canadian bank, thinking of how much publishing *Path of Snow* had cost, and that copies of it sat unbrowsed in a dim corner of a downtown Montréal bookshop.

While he searched for the boy, he mused that all relationships were partial. Friends used friends, relatives used relatives. So long as both used and user consented to their roles, and sometimes even reversed them, what harm was done? Human relationships were based on need. What was wrong with cont(r) acts for sexual use alone? In Rio, he was pleased that of the street kids he'd known one gave him a free shoeshine, another stood him to a drink. Of course he "used" them, and they "used" him, but each respected the other, he thought. One former pick-up he met was Dário, who'd been living in São Paulo, where he had pulled a couple of robberies and, he explained, needed to pay off the police monthly to avoid going to jail. They spent the night together, and Edward gave him, or the São Paolo police, 200 cruzeiros.

Dário's was not the body he sought. But he found it, and it was Paulinho's. After years of dreaming it, effacing it with others, substituting it with his own, here it was in the flesh, the smooth brown body, the tangled tawny hair, the grave eyes under fringed lids, the curved lips curling in a child's smile. Paulinho had big problems. For the past two years, he had been in and out of the State Mental Hospital for Indigents, and in between had to return to the slum hovel of his bestial father, who'd died earlier that year. Edward got him into a program of pills and psychiatry.

Reviews of *Path of Snow* straggled in. Gerald Hannon in the *Body Politic* said it "does some unfashionable things; and by surviving the risk of being un-modish, presents us with the truly fashioned." He was not up to preparing another collection. Maybe he should write a novel. He'd long felt like trying out the theme of a government official in some third-world country who was devoted to socialism and to law-and-the-new-order, yet was homosexual: destroyed by the fact that homosexuality was intrinsically subversive, individualistic, anti-family, anti-regimentation. He'd call it *Corruptions of Minors* and outrage both moralists and gay activists. Yet life seemed to him flux and chaos, and he resented novelists' architectonic structures and strictures, bolted-on plots, and narrative devices. He cared nothing for place-setting or for character development, his dialogue was weak. So what did that leave?

He got a much-delayed letter from his Peruvian friend Róbert, who was in West Virginia, where he'd married an American missionary-linguist's teenage daughter. He'd left her three days after the wedding after discovering she'd "betrayed" him before they married. Alluding to "everything that happened that only you and I know," he implored Edward to go to the United States and take him back to South America. Edward didn't know how to answer: he didn't want to break up a marriage, even an unhappy one. Yet he felt Róbert was his, somehow. How wonderful it had been to have a good-looking, well-dressed, intelligent young man interested in him! He sent an equivocating reply, suggesting they meet in Buenos Aires.

Meanwhile, letters from Henry Beissel had virtually accused him, he thought, of being a gossip, mischief-maker, and meddler. Henry had asked him not to discuss his marital breakup with me. Edward replied that our references to him were few and far between, and, since we both knew him and Ruth, it was inevitable that we should mention them. No one should be afraid of gossip, especially literary gossip: it indicated mockery, but also interest, not indifference. He had always maintained that I was malicious and a gossip; he was merely malicious.

He spent two weeks in Paraguay, cashing in on its happy exchange rate, though banks opened at 7 a.m. and closed at 10. In country towns, he sipped sugarcane juice, and heard mass said in Guaraní. He sent as Christmas gifts some of the tablecloths, bedspreads, and wall hangings women made from spider-web lace. Opposite Asunción, a tribe of jungle Indians lived in palm huts on an island, where the men hunted with bow and arrow, or fished for the giant piraçu. Both sexes painted themselves in red and blue, adorning themselves in macaw feathers. Whatever their earlier idea of the holy, they now worshipped General Stroessner.

Only Graham Greene could have done the foreign colony justice. A Frenchman who was wanted by France for extortion ran Edward's hotel. Among guests were an Irish meteorologist and his wife ("Lacey? Ah, yes, the Laceys have been in Cork and Waterford for a long time, since Henry II sent them over. Why did you ever change your name from DeLacey?"), both about 80, and a U.S. river engineer who was trying to plot the course of the Pilcomayo River. Plus a American pilot who was pretending to open a trading company and had just got out of jail in Angola, where he'd helped run the Portuguese airlift. When he was arrested, Edward translated. He was released.

He slept long siestas and ate sausage under grape arbours in leafy patios in the hot afternoons, drank sparkling cider in the warm evenings. On a postcard blazing with macaws, he reported to Susan Wilford's children that macaws looked like parrots, but could not be taught to speak: they only shrieked "Macaw" all day. In the south, he visited mansions built by Jesuits who, before being expelled in 1767, had organized the Indians into huge missions to protect them against marauding bands of Brazilian slavers. Maybe that had preserved the Guaraní and their language; maybe, like French Canadians, Guraní were just stubborn.

Rejoining Paulinho, he took him in January to the inland state of Minas Gerais. They viewed the work of the late-eighteenth-century sculptor and leper, António Francisco Lisbôa, "Aleijadinho," "the little cripple" who, having lost fingers, toes, and the use of his lower limbs, tied hammer and chisel to wrists in order to carve soapstone. He found Paulinho in São Jono del Rei's stone angel in an archway niche: the baroque, faintly Indian angel, grave yet light-hearted, sexless yet sexed, a cherub yet a human being. He sent me a postcard: "Since you already know Michel (intimately?—I hope not) and have received a postcard from Leobardo, I thought I should continue your collection. Unfortunately, Iguaracy (Paulinho to you) cannot write, but he can sign his name and will do so; I am the mere transcriber of this earnest of his affection and concern for the Canlit. scene."

In São Francisco Church in Ouro Prêto, two hours southeast of Belo Horizonte, guides sat in aniline pants and hot shirts, talking of money, sports, and copulation. In Santa

Efigênia's church, the saint was painted black, with frizzled hair, a church held in her arms. Legends said that, ablaze with love for God, she ran into a burning church to save God's white body, and died in the fire. The flame within her and the flame outside burned her black. In the Church of Nossa Senhora Do Ó in Sabará, Our Lady's lips framed a small O of pain as she writhed in labour: the most baroque of acts, he thought, next to that of conception.

Returning to Rio, they drank for old times' sake in the one bar still standing in the Mangue. In recent months, the houses in the doomed red-light district stayed open day and night. As the *zona* shrank, the bedlam increased and the women became more numerous and brazen, the streets were filled with babble, stinks, and thieves' market vendors. Now the tarts were vacating their rooms in panic, having been given until the evening to get out, the wreckers standing by.

Paulinho was almost as happy as when he had lived with Edward as a 15-and-16-year-old. He was taking his medication and went to a psychiatrist weekly. Later that month he would begin to learn to read and write which was something, Edward stressed, that he must do on his own.

At the start of March he left on a solo trip. In largely gaucho southern Brazil, Germans had settled among mountains. Palms, bananas, and bamboo groves flourished among pines and hollyhocks. The bus to Blumenau took him past massive barns washed in soft blues and greens, blonde blue-eyed women in long dresses and men in overalls got on and off at every stop, children played with ducks in muddy yards. The annual beer fest in Blumenau took place in a huge tin-roofed arena with free beer and about a dozen oompa-oompa bands. A rainstorm set the roof drumming. As lights short-circuited or a transformer blew, the polka dancers bumped into each other, and the band halted in mid-phrase ("*Ja, das ist die Liehtensteiner Polka, mein Schatz, Polka mein Scha – .*")

Before leaving Brazil, he enjoyed the carnival in staid provincial Pelotas, where about 15,000 young men dressed up as women vamped from noon Saturday till the sun rose on Sunday.

Costumed boys kissed each other and strolled around hand in hand. But it was only a parody, and the police did no policing. Respectable families applauded heartily as the boys paraded. If there had been more burlesque and the breast padding, lipstick, and rouge had been less artful, he'd have been less baffled.

In Argentina, with 600 per cent inflation, bank notes were printed so hastily they sometimes were blank on one side: handy for scribbling poems or propositioning people in cafés. Everyone was a millionaire — on paper. A lady in a luggage shop urged him to buy a suitcase of unborn-calf skin because next week it would cost double, and after that there would be no more. Then she wailed, "What will become of us? Please buy my suitcase."

In Brazil, a pair of shorts, a sweatshirt, and sandals sufficed for daily wear. Here, a tailor seriously suggested "Why shouldn't you take six suits back to Brazil? The merest bank employee here has at least six suits!" Edward believed him. He rarely saw an Argentine wearing the same clothes twice. The shoeshine boys wore coats and ties. He visited remote Argentine cousins, and bought two tweed jackets at "Lacey and Sons." Argentinians were so status-conscious he couldn't pick one up unless he was better- or as well-dressed. But he refused to wear ties, which throttled his large Adam's apple, and disdained underwear.

Was Buenos Aires, the "capital of nostalgia" in Latin America at all? On majestic avenues lined with plane trees, he half-expected to see the whole Paris gang—Ernest Hemingway, Scott Fitzgerald, Morley Callaghan, and even John Glassco—burst around the corner to sit down at the Jockey Club Café at 9 de Julio, the world's widest avenue, to quaff a champagne cocktail, served with hors d'oeuvres of escargots, quails' eggs, potato salad, sausages, pickled vegetables, shrimp, octopus, squid, and ham-stuffed croissants for 60 U.S. cents. If you ordered only a main course, or preferred anything other than beef, waiters asked you "Are you not feeling well?"

An all-night bus took him south to Lake Epecuén, in the midst of the pampas, where he arrived at a spa. He strolled down to the glassy lake. Six old bent men, stumbling one after another, gathered salt crystals in big bottles to take back to Buenos Aires. Later in the day, all sizes, shapes, and races walked in the shallow water, some wearing shirts and sweaters, even shirts and ties. People sat on the pier, caked with white salt or wearing mud masks. He got used to water burning his skin, and tasted the pleasures of floating, something he'd never been able to do. He realized his dream of reading a newspaper as he floated like an unsinkable toy boat. When he tried to stand up, he nearly upended. Salt made him and the shoreline white as frost. Only salt cedars and the eucalyptus could grow: the latter could probably grow on Mars. Only one living creature inhabited the lake, the tiny "iodine bug," which, if crushed, left a red stain. Even the tap water was brackish: they said the locals, when travelling, added a bit of salt to water to make it palatable.

In a thermal bath, heated lake water pumped into large stone tubs, every ache and pain eased. His blood pressure — they took it before and after each bath — went down and stayed down. He found, or was found by, two fortyish sisters of Argentine-French descent, whose husbands couldn't leave Buenos Aires because of the financial crisis. Bored, they were happy for him to squire them to the one nightclub and one dance hall. The region's administrator took him on drives. Ruth, he wrote, should come here. His hotel, for which he thought he was paying 1,800 pesos, $6 — a bit too much, even for a double with private bath — turned out to cost a tenth as much.

Meanwhile, Isabel Perón — a country girl from la Rioja, one-time cabaret dancer, in Panama an ex-president's mistress — was *La Presidenta* on borrowed time. The night they overthrew her, he was in Bahía Blanca, a nondescript naval port 200 miles further south. He got up in the dawn cold to stroll in his brown poncho to the bus terminal, the only thing open. He was suddenly encircled by soldiers with machine guns, telling him to stand against the wall, his hands raised, and not move "while we see what's under that *ponchito*." His buses were apt to be stopped at checkpoints, where jittery young soldiers ordered passengers out at gunpoint, and lined them against the sides of the bus for frisking.

Leaving the fertile pampas, he headed for the plains of Patagonia, an arid expanse of tumbleweed and millions of grazing sheep that held only 0.005 per cent of the country's population. In Puerto Madryn, nearly the latitude of Montréal, people still spoke the Welsh of its nineteenth-century settlers. Nearby were colonies of sea elephants, sea lions, and Magellan penguins. Writing of the sea elephants to Randy Wicker, he asked, "Wouldn't you just love to thrust your hard, firm, throbbing ___ into their warm, pliant, enveloping ____ and pump away until you ___ explosively in jets of hot, white, gushing ___? And then club them to death & skin them, dying, for their pelts & blubber?"

The sea elephants, up to 20 feet long, weighed tons. If you irritated them enough, they tried to run after you, but could never manage it. Sea lions were fractious and dangerous, only to be observed from behind a fence. However, he could walk through the penguins, numbering in the millions, taking care not to step in one of the honeycombed underground nests lest they peck his legs with scissor-like beaks. If provoked they'd attack, waving their wings and braying like a donkey. He enjoyed provoking them, discovering that they became nervous if you circled them, and huddled until a defender emerged. They constantly wagged their heads, with a malicious look that seemed to say, "All right, you're bigger, but never trust me. My safety is in numbers." They were monogamous for life, but male and female looked so alike that they had trouble telling each other apart, and made many exploratory mistakes. Their homing instinct was so exact that they returned, year after year, to exactly the same nesting spot. With all the virtues of this exemplary bird — its eggs made fine omelettes, its lanolin-rich skin splendid ponchos — he wondered why the Canadian government hadn't stymied invasion of the North by filling it with penguins. They'd daunt any trespasser; they frightened *him* with their sheer numbers and clone-like identicalism.

But they were preferable to soldiers. Coming back one evening from the beach, clad in his swimming trunks, he encountered a patrol that demanded documents. He pointed out that swimmers could hardly carry passports, but was taken in handcuffs to a military checkpoint where a sergeant spoke breathlessly into a telephone about an alleged foreign suspect wearing an alleged swimming suit, allegedly claiming to be Canadian. A call to his hotel resolved the problem. The same truck and same soldiers that had brought him to the checkpoint took him to the hotel, slapped him on the back, and joked about their mistake. He wondered with what jocosity they'd have tortured or killed him.

Comodoro Rivadavia, Patagonia's biggest city, was filled with lonely soldiers and sailors from big army and naval bases. The place looked about to be buried by a sand dune, actually a sand-covered mountain of iron. The long nights falling early, the young men sat in chill dreary taverns, composing letters to faraway families and sweethearts. Sex was out: there were no trees or shrubs to go behind. Even the pleasures of the tavern and table were denied him: his liver was trying to save him from himself. When he lunched on asparagus soup, crab salad, flounder in cream sauce, fruit salad, Roquefort cheese, and a half-litre of wine with soda he had to go into the washroom and vomit it all up. The Roquefort, he wrote me, "looked pretty coming out — all those blending pinks and greens with nuances of cream."

The petrified forest of 70-million year-old trees near Colonia Sarmiento, an agricultural oasis inland, looked "much more interesting than Lindsay, Ontario, and much better preserved, and, since their inhabitants are all araucaria pines, much more sympathetic." Every knot and notch in the tree-trunks showed. No collecting was allowed — "as if anyone could stow away 30-foot-long stone logs." In the dearth of company, his dreams were impoverished and obsessive. He dreamed about Switzerland, a land he never hoped to visit. Made desperate by insomnia, he read or reread the *Obras Completas* of Jorge Luis Borges. He thought that Borges's posturing remote prose was of one who chose to know, not to live, in fact the kind of writer *he* might have been — if not for certain events in Texas, if not for his sexual inclinations.

After a long bus trip, he made it to Lago Argentino, where a green-blue glacier cut the lake into two arms. He saw snapped trees and scraped rocks as the glacier ploughed on and sent off little icebergs with a terrible roar. After two days of trying to land and turning back, his plane managed to set down in Tierra del Fuego. In the wet, almost sunless climate, even potatoes wouldn't ripen, though beech trees flamed red, creating the Land of Fire. Beavers and muskrats had been imported from Canada and were now pests. The mountains were snow-carpeted: he had forgotten how thrilling red forest and blue-white snow could be. At 55° S, Ushuaia, pop. 7,000, only about 100 miles from Cape Horn, was sided by sharp-peaked mountains; from one a glacier hung, looking as though it might slip at any moment. Ushuaia was a naval base; the world's southernmost refinery was located outside town, only a stone's throw from the world's southernmost brothel, where he paid the world's southernmost exorbitant prices for the world's southernmost drinks for the world's southernmost whores. At exactly the latitude of Edmonton, Alberta, only south, the night was 18 hours long. Aided by Mandrax, he lucidly dreamed about his parents, about witches and monsters, about writing or reading a Victorian novel in Portuguese, about travelling with Paulinho.

A few late flowers bloomed, but it had snowed a little; the channel was dark and foam-lashed. On Good Friday, he sent me a postcard ("Dear Freezer") to say, "to everything there was an end—the last sheep farm, the last farmer, the last sheep." Ushuaia was the last town: "ne plus ultra, Ultima Dim Thule, the end of my path of snow.... Below here and beyond, there are only penguins, meteorologists and other crypto-Canadians." What to do here? Hike in the mountains, visit the lakes, bays, and beech woods, try the king crab. Across the bleak island of Tierra del Fuego on the Chilean side was Punta Arenas, a port-of-call for ships passing through the Straits of Magellan. At 43° South, it was the world's southernmost city, as distinct from Ushuaia, the world's southernmost town, a busy little place midway between the Atlantic and Pacific. Bewilderingly, many descendants of Yugoslavs and Scots lived here. The cemetery, which he saw during a snowstorm, showed how people born in far corners of the world came to repose under cypress trees and a jungle of brambles.

With its many restaurants and bars, Punta Arenas must have been lively once, but now there was a curfew. Besides, everyone was broke. He had a passionate encounter with a young man from Valparaíso who'd been a guard in an internment camp where Allende's ministers had been forced to dig ditches. He'd have liked to take a boat through the Fueguian fjords but one couldn't do everything. What a strange liberty. He felt the need for stability, for roots, for support and anchors in the form of friends, lovers, institutions, job, yet the need to uproot himself, and strike out for new places, people, sensations. But why, if he knew that all places, people, sensations were the same place, person, sensation?

He spent the May Day weekend in Puerto Natales on the Argentine border, writing letters by a fire in a little hotel with warm beds and plentiful quilts while outside snow, rain, and wind rattled and roared. Ruth's mother had died, and he sent his condolences. His own older relatives continued their slow decline; Aunt Marie-Camille went on praying for Ruth and Henry, and Aunt Marion sank further into misanthropic ill health. He went walking in a flurry of big soft wet lumpy flakes that melted as they touched the ground. Everything was closed, but he had company: a humorous Australian hippie; an ex-Canadian hippie born in Holland and now living in California, who knew about gurus, ashrams, Tantric sex, and other unappealing topics; a young U.S. draft dodger who had recently become a Canadian citizen.

About 150 kilometres away was Payne National Park, a work in progress. When the park was completed it would be binational, though how Argentina and Chile could cooperate on anything he didn't know. The park was home to the Patagonian ice-sheet some 500 miles long, dating from the last Ice Age, descending on both sides of the Andes to lakes it carved out and filled. Glaciers, tongues of the ice-sheet, left a moraine behind on which a young forest had sprung up. He slumbered under four piled ponchos in a refuge near the glacier, and next day climbed trails, listening to creaks, groans, roars, and crashes as pieces, some as large as city blocks, fell off into the lake's milky green waters. Signs warned, "Beware. The glacier is in constant motion."

Within Payne, refuges were being built, roads graded, footpaths traced, fences pulled up, farmers, cattle, and sheep expelled. The head ranger took him on his rounds. Patagonians were embarrassingly generous: you need never want for a meal, or a bed for the night. Back in Punta Arenas, he boarded a plane to revisit much milder, very wet Puerto Montt. Gorging its abundant seafood, he felt so iodinized after a few days that he suspected he'd turn purple. But Chile was disheartening. Under Augusto Pinochet, inflation was still fierce, wages were frozen, half the population was un- or underemployed. Tales of torture, firings, jailings, the exiled or vanished, depressed him. Hammered by Salvador Allende's fiscal errors, the Chilean economy had shattered. Instantly freeing up the economy, Pinochet was, in Edward's view, not a monster. He was something more dangerous: a fanatic.

Since their journey a year earlier, Randy had reported that he'd managed to make a little money from the trip, though it hadn't matched what he would have gotten from the same funds invested at New Jersey flea markets. He'd sold a human skull for $85, but still had a surplus of miniature black pyrite furniture and ammonites. Edward suggested that he might give the latter to customers he disliked. Randy said that the Yorkshire terriers he bred — to him "lovable little dogs," to Edward disgusting tarantulas — were doing well. Edward invited him to Rio de Janeiro. Of course, he'd have to share house with Paulinho, who was, Edward said, "like most catatonics, very easy to get along with — it's like living with a statue."

He returned to Argentina in early June via a chain of lakes, a ski resort, and Mendoza. Though he still could drink chilled cider in chalices and eat opulent canapés, Buenos Aires had changed since late March. Once thronged at 4 a.m., the streets were deserted. In his chosen cruising spot, Retiro train station, he picked up half-a-dozen soldiers and sailors — though not all at once — taking them to cheap hotels. Everywhere, plainclothesmen demanded to see documents; soldiers with submachine guns stopped and searched; police cars howled. He was arrested for the crime of waiting around without a passport and with too much money on him: "How do we know you aren't a terrorist who's just robbed a bank?" They also robbed him of the dollars in his wallet: "confiscation of foreign currency for investigation."

During his days in jail, he kept company with an old gambler, a gaucho, an epileptic, a schizophrenic, a consumptive, and, briefly, a corpse. The gambler taught him card tricks and how to beat casinos. The gaucho farted incessantly from leftover gruel with gravy. When the epileptic had a seizure they held him down and stuffed cloth in his mouth. The schizophrenic didn't know his own name, and slept beside Edward on the stone floor of the unheated cell, shivering and holding his hand. No sex was involved: Edward was simply wearing a heavy sweater, a tweed jacket, and overcoat. He claimed that Edward was the only person who understood him which, he thought, was probably true. The tuberculous man coughed and vigorously spat. Indignant, he'd been on leave from a san when he was picked up. "I'll infect you all, you scum, and the police in this station to boot." Edward believed him. The corpse was thrown in one night for want of anywhere else to put him. Fiftyish, well-dressed, he'd died of a heart attack. Edward declined the chance of necrophilia.

None of the cell-dwellers knew why they were there, or when they would be let out. A lieutenant called the roll each morning and left them alone to hear periodic bursts of machine-gun fire, distant shouts and screams. The gambler worried about deportation to Uruguay. The gaucho chafed to get back to the pampas. The epileptic feared he'd lose his job. The schizophrenic couldn't recall his name. The tuberculous man coughed and spat. The corpse got greyer, though he was the first to get out. Twice while Edward was in an office, explaining why he hadn't carried documents, bells starting ringing. His interrogator grabbed a machine gun and sprinted off. For an hour he sat hour looking at secret reports until the officer returned, saying, "What are *you* doing here?" Since he couldn't shave, his beard grew; since he couldn't bathe, he began to stink and itch. The gambler was deported to Uruguay, and the gaucho released. Witnessing a seizure, the officer let the epileptic go. On the fifth day while he called the roll, an officer barked at Edward, "What is your nationality?" He proudly replied, "Canadian." The man clapped his hand to his head and said, "That's terrible. We can't have tourists in places like this. Come with me." In moments he was eating pizza and chatting about politics and literature. In a few more minutes he was free, told, "These are trying times. But I'm sure you understand." Though exhausted, he spent several hours taxiing around the city, chasing down the address the schizophrenic had given. But nobody had ever heard of him.

He changed clothes, shaved his beard, and dyed his hair jet-black. That day, Juan José Torres, ex-president of Bolivia, was found dead in a ditch. Why not a Canadian poet added to the identifiable and unidentifiable corpses — likely Lorca thought it could never happen to him — especially since he'd met underground Marxist gay libbers. At best, the police harassed and entrapped them, using the legally ambiguous age of consent however it suited them. The *Frente de Liberación Homosexual* dared not publish anything, or hold any meetings. They gave him their publications, which he dispatched to Toronto's *Body Politic* magazine.

The embassies were filled with political refugees who'd sought shelter in Argentina, and now sought refuge anywhere else. Rightwing goons, operating from Ford Falcons lacking license plates, had abducted some U.N.-sponsored refugees, mostly Chilean or Uruguayan, tortured them, and gave them a day to get out of the country. The police chief was blown up in his bed by a time bomb allegedly placed by his daughter's 19-year-old best girlfriend. In revenge, about 20 young people were slaughtered, their bodies bobbing in the River Plata. Two weeks after that, the captain who'd befriended Edward was blown up with his colleagues by a bomb planted in the police canteen.

He travelled to La Plata, and northwest to the Sierras de Córdoba. Despite the perils of Buenos Aires, he'd procrastinated about returning to Rio, the reluctance centring on Paulinho. He wrote Randy that he could not

> ... find anything but temporary physical peace & happiness with a person who, even if educable, even if, after long years, educated, comes from, lives in a world so alien to mine — not lower, nor less worthy, nor less noble in the sight of God...but simply, so different. I do not love him (maybe) but I am *very* fond of him & I miss him when not with him. Sexually we are perfectly compatible & temperamentally as well. He is even useful in moderating my drinking, fits of melancholia, rages, etc. But culturally — my God, the difference.

He didn't want to hurt Paulinho again by helping him and then going away, but he was not so dependent as he'd been: he now called him his *amigno*, not *pai*, "pa." Still, Edward was the most important person in his life, even though he'd said "You went away, and I can never forgive you for that. If you'd really loved me, you wouldn't have" — which was unanswerable. He'd tried to prepare him for the fact that he'd leave. "But it is so hard with a person who is almost pure feeling & no intellect."

In a hill resort, he tried to combat insomnia with hot showers, Valium, and masturbation, but the most he achieved was a hypnogogia in which a series of butch teenagers took their pleasure in his mouth. But just as each was about to stiffen and come, each dissolved and faded into the next. Maybe the insomnia came from something he ate, say, a typical day's ration of hot chocolate with sweet rolls, artichoke hearts in olive oil, chicken cannelloni in cream sauce, and a baba au rhum, all with wine, a strawberry champagne cocktail and a little plate of canapés that they always gave you with cocktails (which you had to nibble at otherwise you hurt their feelings), and for dinner at 11 p.m., the usual hour, marinated vizcacha, a rabbit-like local animal; *locro,* a stew of wheat, corn, and beans with herbs and meat, and charlotte russe.

No, he wrote Randy, he was *not* going to write a book on food. One *ate* food. He was not going to write a book on his experiences, sexual or otherwise. One *lived* life. He was not going to write anything, in fact, except poetry and endless letters like this one. In letters one communicated, or tried to communicate, with a specific human being. He'd only write books for three reasons: 1) if he thought he had anything unique to say, or anything that he felt greatly needed saying 2) to become rich 3) to become famous. None of these motives were operative.

By mid-July, he'd got to tropical Tucumén, where matched pairs of soldiers with submachine guns manned every street corner. He went on to Cuzco in Bolivia and, finally back in Brazil, crossed the Mato Grossó, a Wild West of Indians, squatters, and itinerant miners, which the ranching interests were trying to turn into a cattle spread. He'd bussed to Cuîabá, its small hot capital: a boulder in a park marked the geographical centre of South America. He arrived back in Rio via São Paulo. Then he

saw the headline: on August 22, Dr. Juscelino Kubitschek had
been killed in a road accident. Up to that point, Juscelino had
seemed as well as any 73-year-old could hope to be. He rose
early, attended numerous social functions, rarely went to bed
before midnight.

Juscelino had entered his life just before his father
died, an older man whose advice he asked for and heeded,
someone whom he could always appeal to for a loan, a letter
of recommendation, a timely phone call. With exasperated
fondness, he had told Edward, "What I like about you is that,
when I need you, you are never there. And when I don't need
you, you appear. *Espèce de miracle.*" He didn't have time for
cruelty, malice, or revenge. The worst he would say about an
enemy, or a friend who had failed him, was that he was "*burro,*"
stupid. He didn't even malign the military for having stripped
him of honours, denied him the right to vote, stand for office,
or speak in public, forced him into exile for three years, put
him under house arrest, threatened to lay corruption charges.
Every time he needed an exit visa to leave Brazil he was called
in and cross-examined. From him, Edward had learned that a
politician could also be a good man: His regime had been free of
censorship, martial law, tortured political prisoners, and death
squads.

The body was brought to Rio, where thousands flowed
past it. By the time Edward got there, an enormous crowd was
about to set off on foot for the airport, from where the body
was to be flown to Brasília for burial. When the plane landed,
people marched with the coffin for hours to the cathedral and
then for miles along the treeless avenues for burial at midnight,
in the presence of half a million people, practically the city's
population. Only then did the government declare three days
of national mourning. Now they were taking advantage of his
popularity, busily naming streets, parks, and stadiums after the
man they'd disgraced.

Writing to Ian Young, he reported that a subway, begun seven
years earlier, still hadn't a line in service; downtown was
filled with ditches, craters, mounds, and broken water mains.

Cinelândia had been wrecked in order to lay the subway line. The Mangue was now a muddy field. The girls had moved to a nearby avenue but they'd have to leave there, too, because the Carnival parades were to march through it, and foreign visitors were not to see prostitutes, brothels, or pimps. So it went: hilltops lopped, landfill heaped in the bay, extending Copacabana Beach. The febrile rhythm of Rio made him feverish, too. The Amarelinho, the old bar and sidewalk café in Cinelândia that was *the* spot for boy-watching, was to be torn down soon; the 12-storey yellow Victorian building it was housed in would become 42 storeys of glass and concrete. Rio, he thought, would become a São Paulo with beaches.

That fall he saw again the film version of *The Boys in the Band*, just released after six years' gathering dust in the Censorship Department, since it faintly suggested that homosexuals were human beings and hinted that there *might* be such a thing as durable gay relationships. Drag queens, transvestites, and limp-wristed stage comedians, as well as screaming unhappy hairdressers, interior decorators, and fashion designers, were barely tolerated by the gorillocracy, but *never* happy homosexuals. It was useful, Edward wrote Ian Young, to see the film again. Though he was probably no happier than when he'd first seen it, he thought he was more at one with himself. He gave some credit to gay lib for the improvement. Or was it an improvement? Development, perhaps.

To Randy, he wrote after being awakened from a self-aware dream. He was flying, as he often did in dreams, through streets of unknown cities, looking for two boyfriends from his adolescence. Surely the dream would guide him to them. He peered at the face of every person he passed, and every one was an attractive young man. Until he suddenly remembered that his boyfriends would no longer be young men. He woke up to find himself in bed on a hot and windless night in Rio de Janeiro, Paulinho breathing peacefully at his side.

He was paying too much for a small, scantily furnished living room plus bedroom plus tiny kitchen, tiny bath, and minuscule servant's room, servant's bath, and laundry near the Copacabana beach. He also had to pay for Paulinho's visits to a psychiatrist, and for his clothes, food, cigarettes, and movies.

When he had money cabled, he lost more than 40 per cent on each transaction. Inflation was at nearly 50 per cent per annum. He had never trusted the Brazilian economic miracle. "Riches aren't a contagious disease," said the Brazilians, "but, ah, poverty is."

It was so hot and humid that sex was unthinkable. Ditto for eating, his other favourite activity. Paulinho loved, he wrote Ruth, the swimsuit she'd sent him the previous Christmas. At the moment, the boy was washing shirts, singing snatches of melody that he made up on the spot. Some people sang while they took showers; Brazilians sang while they washed clothes. While writing his letter, he ate purple sour-sweet grapelike fruits called *jaboticabas*, which you had to suck the pulp out of, spit the skin into your hand, and then spit the seed. Brazilians had the process down to an art. Like the French, they were absurd about such things: they peeled the skin of apples — for him the best part — radishes, and grapes, looked aghast when he ate shrimps, shell and all. The fridge's freezer compartment was piled with fruits: he liked to eat them frozen, like sherbet.

While Edward had been away, Paulinho had stopped taking medication, quit school, and avoided the psychiatrist. But he had not relapsed into catatonia, and he could now write his name. He faithfully attended his new school two hours every day, and did his homework and the extra exercises Edward set him. Slowly, he was learning to decipher street signs, restaurant names, and billboards: Edward often saw him stop and mouth the letters silently. He was beginning to socialize more with other students and old friends from his days as a Copacabana *boyzinho,* and to depend less on Edward. He took his pills. The psychiatrist was satisfied with his slow progress, convinced that he was "the victim of a psychosis, of childhood trauma, and of a sort of mental retardation produced by the environment" — in short, Edward thought, like any poor black slum kid in the United States.

Paulinho had just turned 20, struggling to get documents in a country where the police could murder someone and the crime wasn't even registered because he had never existed. It took Edward months to get him all the papers. In many ways, the current problems of Myrna Beissel, spells of running away and scrapes with the law, were those of an "abandoned child,"

which was what she'd been for her first five years. You could try
to save a Paulinho, or a Myrna, he wrote Ruth, but how difficult
it was, and how mixed the results! Myrna was an adolescent,
and adolescence was a disease, a mental disorder from which
most recovered, but to which a more-or-less fixed percentage
succumbed. If Myrna now chose to live like a Trinidadian, what
was wrong with that? Trinidad had formed her. Paulinho's
reactions were similar; he desperately needed, and all his life
had sought, a "home," a "family."

Angelica, working at a bookstore, was doing well: some
poet would probably seduce her there, he wrote, alluding to
how Ruth had first met Henry. His Aunt Marie-Camille prayed
for both Ruth and Paulinho. She was well, though his Aunt Alice
had suffered a stroke earlier that year. He was glad that Ruth,
whose vocation always had been helping people, was working
in a pain-control clinic. The doctor was lucky to have her, the
patients even more so. She had fought a good fight to save her
marriage, he wrote, but she had lost, and so had Henry.

One day he walked four miles along the beach, picking
up seashells, little tombstones to the dead animals that made
them. He liked to imagine what creatures lived in each, and
asked Job's supreme idiot question: "Why?" As he walked, he
saw a handsome man in his 20s unwrap a package of a dozen
red roses. He found the right wave to throw the roses into it,
an offering to Iemanjá, the goddess of the sea, mother of life
and death, and watched a while to see if she accepted his gift.
Satisfied, he went away.

He'd been amused to hear, he wrote Randy, that Fire
Island had been in the path of a hurricane that had hit New
York: "An island of screaming faggots battling a tidal wave and
a hurricane—what a plot for a play to outdo even *The Boys in
the Band*." He was startled to learn that his Trinidad friend Lal
Kalloo and his family had recently been in New York. Lal had
embarked on an ambitious quest to grow a fingernail so long it
would figure in the *Guinness Book of Records*.

At the end of October, Paulinho lost all his documents,
so they had to set about replacing them. When they had gathered
nearly all, the originals miraculously turned up. Needing
documents himself in order to leave the country, Edward was

vexed at having to obtain 10 different ones: a good conduct certificate, a residence certificate, an income-tax payment certificate for the last five years, and seven different criminal and civil court certificates. Otherwise, he'd have to deposit US$1,000 for a period of one year with the government, at zero interest, every time he wished to leave the country. That was unconstitutional, of course, because he wasn't a Brazilian, but who cared about constitutions?

He was leaving soon, and Paulinho would not be going with him. After he finished his literacy course, he would look for a job and enroll in primary school at night. Edward would leave him with enough money for his needs. He realized that he could have Paulinho for the rest of his life: he satisfied his needs for sex and companionship — Paulinho would massage him and he'd fall asleep like a baby, and then how wonderful to wake up and feel his body there beside him — but he had other needs that Paulinho could not satisfy, and hungers that he could never sate.

Edward would leave the alluvial strip on the south shore of Guanabara Bay between sea and rocky islands, the breathless view of city and bay he got when he climbed through the *favela* from Copacabana Beach. Yet, he told himself, wherever he travelled he would take Rio with him. He would walk its streets, sit for a moment in the shade of its almond trees, hear the rustling palms. Whenever he smelled the sea, or sat at a sidewalk café to watch the passing crowd, Rio would be there. Whenever he kissed a boy, the boy would turn in his arms and become Paulinho.

14

ADRIFT IN THE SEASONS

December 1976-September 1978

She braids her dark hair with a single jasmine star.
She will hear this poem.
She will sing this song.
But she will never know me.

~ Wanderers Nachtlied: III

The Amazon had guided him into Brazil. He left it the same way. From Manaus, his entry point nine years earlier, he reported to his college friend Paul Weingarden that he was "being doped-up on pain-killers & antibiotics, & my face wrapped in bandages, as a result of an interesting river-front scuffle I had in an interesting river-front tavern with some interesting Amazonian riff-raff."

His farewell had taken him through hill towns of Minas Gerais that had palms and pines. That was what he loved: palms *and* pines. He'd bussed to Cuîabá, then three nights and two days of a dirt road took him through savannah and slashed-and-burned jungle to the inaptly named Pôrto Vélho, where a new grid of mud streets and houseless avenues straggled over hillocks, hollows, and culverts. The new asphalt road to Manaus crossed six rivers.

From Manaus, he took a *gaiola* upriver to Leticia, rocked and lulled in a deck hammock. Aboard the steam launch were three cabin-occupying *grandes dames* with their army-captain husbands. The *grandes dames* quarrelled bitterly with their husbands about what to wear on shore as the bank-hugging boat stopped at towns with paved main streets but no cars. On New Year's Day, they paused at Coari while punts paddled the milk-blue water to peddle oranges and palm fruit. One punt was filled by a *pirarucú*, a 10-foot-long fish. A car, just brought in, roared up and down the town's few blocks, giving rides to the kids. When he walked out of town, dozens of ebony vultures stretched their white-tipped wings to dry.

After nine days of *pirarucú* on their dinner plates, they reached a dirt town named Benjamin Constant. Some day, he thought, he would found a town and call it Ruth Heydrasch, after Ruth Beissel's maiden name. A Peruvian island — three countries met here — lay only yards away. A boat whisked him upriver to Leticia, Colombia's only Amazon port, a few blocks long and wide, whose plaza was filled with screaming parakeets at dawn. Through Leticia passed coca paste to be refined into cocaine in Colombia. Yet no one checked his luggage or documents: all the aggravating paperwork he'd undertaken proved unneeded.

He wrote Ruth that his alcoholic, 74-year-old Aunt Marion had recovered from internal ailments. For the benefit of Randy Wicker and myself, his postcards depicted a priest and another man grappling with a boa constrictor. In this "wonderful allegorical fotograf," Randy might find something of Edward "in the priest's tight-lipped smile, and more than a gleam of yourself in the serpent's eye." But I could recognize him in "the priest, the serpent or maybe the tree-trunk in the background." He recommended sleeping in a hammock aboard a riverboat: "My God! What I've missed all these years! How can I ever confine myself to the strait-jacket/winding-sheet of a bed again! And you ent had sex till you've had it in a hammock..."

He'd intended to fly to Bogotá, but it turned out just as cheap to fly to Iquitos, the Peruvian capital of Amazonia. Two thousand miles from the Amazon's mouth, it was the world's farthest inland seaport. Oil tankers docked, and the town was filled with blue-and-white garbed sailors from the nearby naval base. The waterfront walk of stone belvederes and balustrades had been so eaten away he often had to walk through people's houses to continue a stroll. Whether or not because he did, he left town with stitches on his upper lip after a fight in which his lip had split open nearly up to the nose.

In Lima, inflation was nearly 50 per cent a year, the sol devalued by half. Lima was dense with uprooted peasants, perhaps a fifth of the city's five million people. Because of a trigger-happy curfew, restaurants and bars closed early. It was like a city in wartime. It was a relief to take the world's highest train-trip through the world's highest railway tunnel, then a collective taxi past reed-and-bird-filled Lake Junín and adobe villages.

When he reached Cerro de Pasco, people were running around dodging hail. After the storm, market women in stovepipe hats and bright petticoats wielded brooms to knock sleet off their stalls. It seemed so comically Canadian, yet weirdly foreign. The sod roofs, grass and mosses growing on them, were snow-covered, as were the hill meadows where singing children led flocks of sheep in the thin sunlight. Everyone had brilliant red cheeks in brown faces. Everyone spoke Quechua. Quarried for centuries, the open-pit mines so honeycombed with tunnels dating back to Inca times that whenever a heavy truck passed the town trembled. Snaking cobbled streets and hilltop-stuck churches perched between two toxic lagoons. His hotel's water was ice-cold, and he forsook washing or shaving. It was like a brief visit to a planet called Winter.

From here, a stony road dropped and then rose over an Andean ridge, then down, down to a tiny tropical town on a rushing river set among tumbling jungled mountains. Here, narcotics agents and coca traffickers posed as tourists. Nearby, a cave, extending for miles, housed the *guacharos*, the blind shrieking oilbirds he remembered from Trinidad. A terrible road and wonderful waterfalls, tunnels, and bridges led him to hot humid Pucallpa, which had no paving, public lighting, drainage, or sewage. They were building a floating sawmill and plywood factory nearly as wide as the big river. Half an hour away, linguists studied and alphabetized local languages, and he chatted with them about phonemes and allophones. Well-intentioned people, he thought, but Protestant Bible-pushers.

Here the drug traffickers he'd met in Lima prospered. Róbert, 25, owned a bar-restaurant-nightclub, a lumber business, and three cars. He was still raging about the young wife who had "betrayed" him, and hoped to murder his rival: Edward was the only one he could talk to about it. Róbert wanted to jump into bed with him practically on his arrival, but Edward turned him away. Róbert was offended: a queer rejecting a macho! He took a plane back to Lima, and then set out for Ecuador.

A Peruvian peasant named Bruno
Said "There is one thing I do know.
Sheep are quite tight,
And pigs are all right,
But the llama is numero uno.

"That's the way it is with great poetry," he wrote to Ian Young from Quito, "it never dies."

Randy Wicker had spoken of joining him but, after a Bogotá phone call costing $76, he learned that it wouldn't happen. He looked up Harry Horácio, their young companion of two years earlier. He consoled Harry, who couldn't get Randy out of his mind, with filet mignon dinners and hotel-bar cocktails. He was fed up with sweatbath discos until the night he met a 16-year-old hustler. He concluded that there was nothing—no poem, piece of music, flower, or baroque church—so alive, beautiful, and satisfying as an adolescent boy. The "Locombians" restored his *joie de vivre*. But in Cali one drunken night a young man named Reinaldo broke his glasses.

He reached the Caribbean. In Costa Rica, he took a room with people he'd met on a bus to Quepos. When he returned one night, he found both them and his traveller's cheques gone. He told the police that the hotel had allowed men to enter with the consent of those he'd brought there, but not with *his* consent. By mid-June he was in Antigua, Guatemala, dispatching a baker's dozen of postcards, mainly to Colombian adolescents. "Some day Death will call me, I'm sure," he wrote Randy, "while I'm in the midst of writing postcards." Reinaldo wrote that breaking the glasses had been the fault of drink. He plaintively begged for forgiveness. Edward did not bestow it.

In Guatemala, the capital still stood despite a recent earthquake, though one could not say the same thing about

Managua in Nicaragua. He had trouble getting across the El Salvador border, where they thought he was a liberation-theology priest. They allowed him only five days in the country: quite enough. In San Salvador, the green volcano looming, a fat dark girl sold him a pair of brown fur slippers, hair intact. The bustling dirty city was not as bad as he'd remembered it. Several times he merely *almost* got robbed.

He returned to Guatemala City via the Caribbean coast and Honduras, passing through the port of San Pedro Sula, where he dined on banana daiquiris, iguana soup, and street boys. One stifling night in a bar-brothel, a barefoot ragamuffin dashed in with the morning paper, shouting hoarsely, "¡ *Murió Elvis Presley! El rey está muerto!*" He thought, "There goes my youth!" Next year he would be 40. He spent nearly three months in Guatemala, part of the time trying to avoid a patron-seeking boy named Carlos. The bus taking him to México broke down in Orange Walk Town, British Honduras. Becalmed, he sent me a postcard showing a booby bird: "The booby bird is Nature's best analogue to the poet — it is so trusting it allows its eggs (poems) to be stolen from under it...."

In Mexico, he lingered on Cozumel's larger island and on Isla Mujeres, where among the reefs vivid fish swam between his legs. He made it with a handsome fisherman, a sailor, and two hotel boys. In the main square of Mérida, marble tables stood under portals and arcades, a church bell tolled, and restive youths ogled girls in the laurels' shade. In the infernal heat, he found a gay bar thronged with luscious teenage hustlers and impecunious students. Alas, he was short of funds. He slowly made his way north to Mexico City, and then to Guadalajara. At the bus station, lugging heavy suitcases, he was jostled, losing his wallet, tourist visa, and passport. In the Torreón house in which he'd lived, the fig tree on the back patio was gone, vines and flowers uprooted. He remembered Doña Aurelía, the ugly old woman who had tried to protect him from himself.

Although he lacked a passport, Canadian Customs grudgingly admitted him on the strength of a birth certificate. From Montréal, he wrote Ian Young that "certain freedoms" were "just as important as freedom of the press, religion, etc., that people never seem to talk about—the freedom to go out and have a drink in a bar at 4 a.m. if one wants to, the freedom to get drunk and fall down and sleep in the street, the freedom to frequent prostitutes in a red-light district, etc. " If one "were to tell a Brazilian or Guatemaian the number of things a Canadian *cannot* do, he'd come to the conclusion that we're indeed a dictatorship."

December Montréal was stark with white snow and dark buildings. He took a cockroach-rife apartment near the Canadian Pacific Railway tracks, where the sound of trains shunting below proved that the cold had not killed all life. He joined Ruth and the girls for Christmas. They gave him a present of flaming-red briefs. Since he never wore underpants, he was not so much annoyed as puzzled. He tried them on, putting both legs through the wrong hole. He fell on the ice so much he was a mass of bruises and bought an ice-gripping pair of boots. Atop Mount Royal, the mid-city mound Montrealers called "The Mountain," he hired a ride, shrouded and muffled in buffalo robes in a bell-tinkling horse-and-cutter. The horses laboured through drifts while fresh snow blew in his face.

In January, he bussed himself to St. Catharines, Ontario, to the nursing home of his father's sister, Helen Eicheldinger. His old aunt was ecstatic to see him. In Toronto, he met Ian Young, and talked long one evening with the Colombos. He told John that he'd thought of using the title of the rock song "Drift Away" as the title for the poetry collection he planned. "Yes, because that sums up the story of your life, Edward," John said. When Ruth asked him whether he felt he was a "Canadian" or a "Latin American," John interjected, "The problem for Edward, I think, is not whether he feels he's Canadian, but to define for himself whether he's really human at all."

Late that month, Randy turned up from New York at midnight, only to find his friend absent. When he rolled in at 5 a.m., his Barbadian neighbour advised him that "you have a friend waiting for you and he sure look miserable! I try to invite him in, but he too 'fraid to come." At his door, Randy thought that the building resembled a charming rooming house. Edward indignantly snorted that two people had just been murdered in it. Noticing a tea towel that Carlos in Guatemala had hand-stitched with hearts and *Mi amor* mottos, Randy wondered why anyone could walk away from such devotion.

Once a letter from Aunt Marie-Camille had advised him, "I still think you should get a good little wife to take care of you and you could easily find one! You're handsome. You're clever and talented!!!.... My other advice is to bring *God* into your life." In Lindsay, Marie-Camille was found unconscious while at prayer alone in the chapel, and died a few days later. Father Bud, her brother, said mass for her soul. Aunt Marion was dogged by grief. After she had returned to Lindsay from Fordham University, where she'd taught, she started drinking heavily and starving herself. Marie-Camille made her eat and went everywhere with her. They had shrunk to the same size looking, Edward had thought, like a little old Muslim man and wife.

During a Montréal visit, I looked up Edward, taking him to a personal haunt, the Blue Angel Café on Drummond St. for the Monday session of the Old Time Country and Western Music Club of Canada. We heard the immortal "It Wasn't God Who Made Honky-Tonk Angels" and "Don't Forget to Give My Love to Rose." The goateed, straw-hatted M.C., "Country Bob" Fuller, garnished his giant overalls with a giant safety pin, and introduced his pickers and singers, including a petite middle-aged blonde still cute-as-a-button and a cadaverous banjo-player. An aged factotum sold chewing gum, toothpaste, and combs at the washroom door, and we got free hot dogs at midnight. Edward later sent me a newspaper clipping headed "Slower the music, the faster the drinking: study."

For the new poetry collection, to be published by Catalyst Press, Ian Young calculated that a 100-pager would cost about $2,000. Edward agreed to pay half at once and the balance when printing started. Settling on the title *Later*, he had thought to reverse the title of his first book and call it *The Loss of Form*. The Montréal printer of *Path of Snow* was still warehousing unsold copies, and Edward asked if Ian could distribute them. His publishing plans, he said, could be called "self-assertion, or self-affirmation, the effort to prove — even tho merely to myself — that I still exist..."

He'd been corresponding with Winston Leyland, an English immigrant who published *Gay Sunshine* magazine in San Francisco. To it, he donated money and contributed work. Despite the public outrage caused by Gerald Hannon's piece, "Men Loving Boys Loving Men," in *The Body Politic*, he thought it was simply good reporting. Though he himself was not a "pedophile," he was "definitely a pederast; boys and young men in the age range of 13-14 to 24-25, and esp. between 15 and 19, are my passion, and I can't live without them, not just for sex, but because I love their company, their vitality and enthusiasm and undefinedness." He asked how responsible pederasts like himself, "who wd never dream of forcing a boy to do anything against his will, much more of doing him violence," could defend themselves against Hannon's attackers. Although he wrote Randy that he thought children should execute parents who *forced* sexual relations on them, underage sex was "the line straights will not give up without a terrible battle, because here the family is most directly threatened."

In early March, lacking hot water, he couldn't bathe for three days. However, the drought defeated a rash that he'd developed: perhaps, he wondered, he was allergic to the soap he was using, or, like Bathless Groggins, to water itself. He got a new passport, and saw much of the Beissels. Although Ruth and Henry were tensely discussing divorce terms, they held hands when the three of them attended a play together. That was the night of Myrna's seventeenth birthday, celebrated with a hotel buffet at which Henry and Ruth had fought over who would pay the bill. Never get married, he advised me.

A reunion with Michel, his hoodlum friend of four years earlier, was a mixed blessing. Michel sneakily tried to appropriate his hash, but he managed to recover it. Michel had spent two years in Bordeaux Prison for armed robbery, and was out on three years' probation. He would soon face a charge of possessing hash. Yet he worked as a carpenter and shared an apartment with his *blonde*, whom Edward thought looked and behaved like a transvestite. Michel, he realized, viewed him as a meal ticket, but it was fun to nightclub with him in the city of many solitudes, even if he was prone to smoke or swallow every kind of pill and powder. Michel gave him all the sex he wanted, and left notes for him like "My friend is Mr. Edouard Lacey it a good friend for me. There he is; when I need him Es mui buonito amigo mike the tattoo man," signing them "OK Bye my friend Take car Michel (the tattoo)."

Other young people seemed to him the coldest of cold-fish Canadians. One day, he picked up a passionate 16-year-old Colombian from Medellín. Such a pleasant change. Randy sent him picture postcards to remind him — well aware that he needed no reminding — that he wasn't getting any younger. One showed a harp seal pup on the Labrador coast ("Here is a souvenir of your cuddly Canadians — a memento of your love life winter 1977-78!)," another of a Colombian boy holding up a string of fish: "The fish are running in the Magdalena right now as you sit in slushy Canada..." The half-Irish Edward gladly reminded the half-Irish Randy that snow flurries had ruined New York's St. Patrick's Day parade.

An ice storm glazed the streets, tree branches crashed, and falling icicles nearly impaled him. After an absence, Michel resurfaced, tearfully relating that he was debt-laden, had fought with his *blonde*, and felt like committing suicide. Offering escape, Edward bought him a train ticket to New York, where he could stay with Randy. Michel, he wrote Randy, would avenge all the trouble Randy had caused him ("We'll see if you *really* are my friend....") But he reassured him that Michel wouldn't steal anything because he'd have nowhere else to stay and wouldn't know how to dispose of the loot. But, come departure time, Michel didn't show up. He next gave him money for a Mexican trip. Instead, Michel chose to spend the money his way.

He had grown weary of his smelly, cockroach-infested building, and his apartment replete with wizened apples, sprouting potatoes and onions, empty fruit juice bottles, and mountains of periodicals. After a drinking bout and battering, Angelica said to her mother, "Edward is really destroying himself with drink, isn't he?" To which Ruth replied, "Yes, but he knows what he's doing."

Bent on visiting Randy, he was blocked from crossing the border. He told Customs that he thought the long-ago marijuana incident at the Texas-Mexico border was forgotten. The rebuff put him in a foul mood. When I visited Montréal, staying with

Monique de Gaye, he was annoyed that we'd learned of his border defeat, and brusquely declined a dinner invitation. On a subsequent visit, I found a mystifying paper slip with only the name "Aubrey Devere" and phone number on it in a wooden barrel in The Word Bookshop, where the proprietor kept mail for me. This, of course, was Edward, but I failed to recognize him. The night before I left, he went to the Blue Angel in search of me, but the manager wouldn't let him in because he wore blue jeans. When he said that blue jeans were a perfectly appropriate mode of dress for a place specializing in country and western music, the manager began screaming about René Lévesque, the Québec Premier, and how people were being forbidden to speak English. Ergo, if Lévesque could do that, *they* could establish an anti-blue jeans policy.

He donated to its defence fund for *Body Politic*, which had been contesting a raid the police had made in search of the obscene. From Guatemala City, his fellow translator Erskine Lane thanked him for a letter that had related "treks through the Petén jungle, spectacle-snatching in Mexico City, the assault on your pharnyx and larynx in Guadalajara," and said he enjoyed a "claim to direct contact with the legendary, elusive E. Lacey — much like those people who have actually seen a quetzal in the wilds or a horned guan."

On a brief visit to Lindsay, the bus whirled him past rows of remembered houses, and he registered at the Benson Hotel, which his great-grandfather had built. He had an erotic encounter with a Bajan in its washroom. Strolling, he saw the old mill was idled, the lift-locks still in service; on the wide main street his uncle's furniture store. In sight were longhaired hunky boys from a forestry college; absent were the boys that he had loved in secret. Gone were his high school, gone the hobo jungle by the iron bridge, gone the WASP first families and St. Joseph's Convent. His father's friends? Old men recovering from strokes in nursing homes. His mother's friends, the socialites? Crones who wept and received his visit as greedily as a sparrow might crumbs.

He took sandwiches and sherry in Mrs. Wilford's kitchen, from which Susan's mother used to call out "Yoohoo, Alex!" She asked him to guess her age, and he said, "Well, I know your approximate age, Mrs. Wilford, but you *look* like a woman of about

60." She smiled and preened, "Not bad for an old girl of 78, eh?" While he was there, Susan dropped in, and they reminisced in their old, slightly ironical, sparring way. Her mother exclaimed, "Here we all are together again; why, it's just like old times, isn't it?"

He was on the move. In Montréal, he boarded a train to the Maritime Provinces, passing through New Brunswick's evergreen forests and manicured farms. He hated dinky little Fredericton, and disliked unpainted, falling-apart Saint John. In Halifax, he patronized black pubs in its twin city, Dartmouth. He didn't visit me in Pictou County, 100 miles north. He'd tried to phone me, but discovered that the directory consisted of practically nothing but Sutherlands, and he didn't have the patience to call them all. Nor did he get off the bus when it passed through nearby New Glasgow. He had never liked his friends to meet his family — nor did he particularly want to meet theirs.

In Cape Breton, he boarded the overnight ferry to Port-aux-Basques in Newfoundland, en route to the French islands of St. Pierre and Miquelon. Once aboard a coastal steamer for St. Pierre, stymied by a stevedores' slowdown, he spent several hours in a stuffy lounge, enduring Sunday TV programs of every religion going. Beginning to move, they came to a misty outport where wood stilt houses were painted in harmonized bands of colour like outdoor wallpaper, a great relief from mid-Canadian drabness. A little way into a deep, rock-walled fjord was a cove whose tiny collection of church and houses sprawled over stony hillocks. He was revisiting, he realized, a primitive insular existence like that of the villages he'd touched in river trips on the Amazon.

By twilight they reached Burgeo, which had cars but nowhere to go in them. Teenagers with dark hair and apple cheeks invaded the boat, milled around the TV lounge, turned cartwheels in the corridors, shouted and ran up and down the gangway, stormed from room to room in quest of a drink. Down the coast in Ramea, built on a rocky island, they anchored overnight. When they left, Burgeo adolescents threw stones and spat at the Rameans on the dock below, as the Rameans had done to Burgeons back in Burgeo.

Among passengers was a M. Girardin, who spoke slow strange French. Originally from St. Pierre, he'd spent most of his life in Manitoba. From 55 years ago, he remembered the taste of cod, the sand beaches of Miquelon, the Labrador retriever that pulled him around the island in a cart. Now he was going back. At dawn, they saw Grey River, a shack cluster set deep in a fjord with a river tumbling from the mountaintop. After the provincial government had shipped communities to more accessible areas, the south shore was strewn with ghost towns. From Fortune, they swung out to sea and found what the Vicomte de Chateaubriand called "*l'affreux rocher de St-Pierre*." A village appeared in the mist, with signs like *Tabac et Alcools* and *Crédit Lyonnais*. An impeccable gendarme, courteous but ironic, came aboard to stamp their passports. Soon M. Girardin had gone to the *mairie* and *gendarmerie* to check on his family, found his old home, and rediscovered multiple cousins. Edward left him wearing a new beret, happily meeting friends each noon in the *bistrot*.

By day the "frightful rock," three miles long by two miles wide, was the dampest, foggiest place he had ever encountered and St. Pierre the coldest and windiest. He tried to navigate the tangled moss, shrubs, and thickets of dwarf spruce trees crisscrossed by ponds and streams but the peat bog was like walking on foam rubber. Even if it was dry, you sank, or you bounced. Miquelon, where he went with the mail boat one day, was narrow and long, with wild horses and a sand dune studded with remnants of wrecked ships. In this *département d'outremer*, people drove madly through narrow streets, and people held 4 a.m. discussions under his hotel window. Good food, good drink, good talk, but also stinginess, snobbery, xenophobia. They did *not* like Canada, which had declared a 200-mile limit for fishing. The foreign ships that used to buy provisions now bought them in St. John's. People blamed him for this, and he nearly got into fistfights over it.

When he left, the coasts were thick with pack ice, though the pussy willows were out, and flowers bloomed. The only passenger aboard the M/V Taverner, he thought he would leave the ship when it anchored in Argentia, but the minibus to take him to St. John's would only come next morning. Thinking of

Ruth, taking treatment at a spa in Germany, he thought that ships were like spas: the same reposeful, sometimes boring sense of suspended time and space, like Newfoundland itself with its eternal enclosing mists, its outports, its face of stone and sea.

The minibus landed him in St. John's. From Signal Hill, you saw the coastline down to Cape Spear, the easternmost point of North America, and the spot, a few yards distant, where, in 1901, Marconi received the first transoceanic wireless message. St. John's had a shacks-and-dories ambiance, houses garishly painted and crazily atilt. His first hotel tried to overcharge him for a room with no bath, a window that wouldn't open, no hot water, and a non-functioning elevator. He complained to the Tourist Bureau, and got his money back. But he liked St. John's. With their unassuming kindness and curiosity, Newfoundlanders seemed un-Canadian. From strangers eager to help the lost or confused, or just to strike up a conversation, he heard, "What's ye be lookin' for, me lad?," "An' where d'ye belang now, me b'y?" ("Where are you from?"). He wrote Randy that Newfoundland speakers could be reduced to those who pronounced "fucker" as "fooker" (in the west) and those who pronounced it as "focker" (east).

He chatted with cod fishermen in a late-closing row of bars and clubs. Bars had open front doors, children, shoeshine boys, and vendors wandering in and out—the official unemployment stood at 18 per cent, the worst in Canada. In one doorway, a guy slandered the paternity or maternity of everyone who passed, including Edward, which was why he went in: to show he wasn't afraid of him. The place must have been a feminist hangout. Within an hour he saw one girl throw a glass of rum-and-Coke, glass and all, at a pimp, another attacked him with a billiard cue, and a third slapped his face.

Next day, a CN Marine coastal vessel was to sail from Lewisporte, 300 miles away by cross-island bus. Edward's bus climbed to a tundra of bogs, rock, and stunted shrubs, then down into dwarf spruce and fir, passed over a narrow land-bridge—all that kept the indented Avalon Peninsula from being an island—plunged into forests, and traversed a nature reserve with sights of cape and cove. From Gander, the usual drab big airport, a taxi took him to Lewisporte, where M/V Hopedale was waiting. With three hours to kill, he bought a five-pound lobster at $1 a pound A quayside restaurant prepared the monster with vegetables and potato. He had just time to get back to the boat, then learned it was to sail eight hours later. In a vile mood, he gained the town's only bar, where he sat till closing with a half-Inuit chap, listening to country 'n western. When they staggered back to the ship, the purser had a cabin for him.

He woke up at the base of the Great Northern Peninsula, where icebergs were pure white, others eerie phosphorescent green or electric blue, and a few ferried seabirds. Drifting south, some had caverns eaten into them; some calved off smaller icebergs. Some drifted into coves and sat stranded like beached whales. Ahead, a big one was splitting apart. When they reached it, only floes and ice patches remained. They steered clear of floating islands of pack ice. They slipped into a deep bay, which narrowed into a fjord, then opened into a smaller bay, surrounded by forested mountains, on the shores of which lay a little town with the impossibly romantic name of Great Harbour Deep, stretching around the bends of a bog. He and another passenger followed a stream to a whirlpool, rapids, and waterfall. They dined at a church supper, and dropped in on a billiard parlour and a teenage dance while tons of provisions were unloaded into wheelbarrows and carts.

At dawn they sailed past cliffs into the Strait of Belle Isle. Along the island-dotted coast on the Labrador side only dwarf firs in hollows grew. From tumbledown shacks they took on fishermen, wives, and noisy brats, and dropped them off. His congenial cabin-mate, a half-breed, was going back to help with the fishing. At Black Tickle, teenagers boarded to peddle beaded headbands and to cadge drinks. The waterfront stirred as the year's first ship unloaded, and he heard Inuktitut from welfare alcoholics. The soil was rich, black peat, but the houses stilted against the permafrost, straggling over hill and hollow. A wood-enclosed tube that conveyed water and disposed of sewage snaked from house to house, and you had to crawl under it or climb over it. A stink of raw sewage hung heavy. Ice or soggy snow still lay around, fleshing the black hills. Like exhibits of ice sculpture, mini-icebergs and floes littered the harbour. He felt as if he'd stumbled into a polar expedition.

Further on, the boat dropped off his cabin-mate. It reached Cartwright, a town so well laid-out and clean that he went back to the boat to sleep. When he woke up, they were in a long inlet narrowing between evergreen hills and snow-flecked mountains. He sunbathed. An ice field had crept in close to shore like a moving white wall. Beautiful in the dying light of the year's longest day, it worried the captain, who spent about two hours steering through it. Most of a morning, they unloaded at an Inuit village, which had shortages of almost everything, including milk, flour, and meat. Teenagers, handsome as Bolivians, came aboard to experience the Coke machine.

How much satisfying reading you could do if you eliminated urban poisons! Neither bored nor lonely, he had to do nothing and had nothing to do. Sometimes he wished the trip would never end, but it did, at Goose Bay. He flew to Sept-Isles, Québec, following the Côte Nord, the north shore of the St. Lawrence. Tall dark pines, like Nordic prophets or Viking kings, marched in sharp-profiled lines amid the pallid birch, poplar, and willow. Black waves broke over black rocks and on the brown sand were the broken shells of mussels and clam, wild-strawberry blossoms, whitened sea-grasses. Sugar snow lingered. Inhuman things: the cry of gulls, the crash of wave on rocks. He proceeded to Chicoutimi, cruised for 10 hours the majestic fjord of the Saguenay, but merely glanced at picturesque Quebec City. Then he was back in Montréal.

That spring, Ruth's friend and houseguest Renate Jürgensen, a 28-year-old with long brown wavy hair and a sturdy chin, had fallen in love with him. It was an unwelcome development. Long ago, Edward had determined that he didn't like being mothered by women, he didn't like being dominated by them, and he didn't like dominating them. They were a world apart: you never know what they were thinking, feeling, or wanting. They were like cats; they both clung and clawed. He liked what he could understand: men who had the same emotions and with whom he could empathize, who sought the same physical pleasures as he, felt the same orgasm.

In early April, he and Monique de Gaye had hatched a scheme to send Ruth to a German spa, planning to pay her airfare; Henry agreed to cover medical expenses. He and Renate were to supervise the girls while Ruth was overseas. This would no hardship for him, nor for them. Edward had always paid them the greatest compliment an adult could pay children: he took them seriously, once to the extent of sitting with them through six hours of *Pink Panther* movies. He moved into Ruth's house on Oxford Avenue. He had been annoyed that Renate had gone to the Maritimes — to track him down, he suspected — because she was supposed to stay in Montréal until he returned. However, the girls had managed well on their own. Now he slept in the guest bedroom, Renate in a room off the kitchen. By mail, he reassured Ruth that all was well. One "breach of the peace" had occurred, though, on account of Renate's "stormy bosom," which heaved on the other side of his barricaded bedroom door. While he was asleep, she would slide *billets doux* under it, or scratch on it for admittance, moping and pouting, he said, when he could not be with her every waking hour.

As work toward *Later*'s publication advanced, Ian Young pointed Anthony Reid in his direction. Reid, a wealthy English collector of limited-edition books, broadsheets, and printed ephemera of gay writers, wanted handwritten poems and inscribed copies of future books. When Edward replied, Reid wrote that he was gloating over "the manuscript poem; improved, for me, by its deletions and corrections...by its exotic hotel notepaper, and by its being in your own writing and signed. " For one boy-poem, Reid had "immediately made one of my superior slip-cases of green card and white cloth, titled and bookplated, to keep letter, envelope, manuscript poem and photograph in perfect condition...."

In a letter, I accused Edward of having described me as a "literary vulture." He pled not guilty, adding, "People are not at all literary material for me, or if they so turn out, it's only in retrospect. I have enuf material in myself for my limited purposes. I am the most unBalzacian of men." He said, "one of my few virtues is a predisposition to accept without question precisely the image of himself that everyone wishes to present to me and the version of life, or events, that he wishes to have propagated." This didn't mean that he believed it, but that he was merely amiable and incurious: "I accept seeing people as they wish to be seen... everyone is a completely incorrigible liar about himself, esp. to himself." Humans were "merely a series of masks one under another, progressively pretending to reveal themselves, with growing intimacy, as the `real me', until, after we reach the last mask, we find nothing is what is hiding under it in the end."

Aside from the begging letters of impoverished boys, he got a circumstantial account about Paulinho. On April 25, a mutual friend wrote that Paulinho was sleeping in the street; he'd refused to attend a psychiatric clinic. Paulinho talked about him all the time. Edward may have abandoned Paulinho, and his own relationships may have been transient, but he liked to see his friends stay together. This was true of Ruth and Henry, and it was true of Monique and me. One evening, Monique and he got drunk together and wept together at the perfidy of young men.

Ruth had returned, and what with "Renatechen" and "Ruthilein" he found himself immersed in German. Ruth thought that he was gentle and patient with Renate. As for Renate, she thought that Ruth encouraged their relationship. At any rate, Renate believed that if one didn't give "reliable love" to anyone one would always stay lonely. Having urged Renate to travel, he went with her to Toronto on the first leg of a transcontinental trip. While he lodged at a hotel, she stayed with a friend of a friend. After they arrived, they walked to Chinatown, and the fishmongers, fruit stalls, and junk shops of adjacent Kensington Market. They sipped passion fruit juice, and crossed to the campus of his alma mater. The next day they saw the fake rococo castle of Casa Loma, and strolled the grassy expanse of High Park. The city lights were going on when they took up the elevator up the CN Tower, the world's tallest self-supporting structure. Back at street level, Renate insisted on knowing what Edward thought about her.

To him, she seemed obsessed with a self-analysis and analysis of others and analysis of others' analysis of her and analysis of her own analysis of others and of her own self-analysis. He would never think of asking anyone else what he or she really thought of him; he knew the answer would not be truthful; and if it happened to be, he'd be afraid of the truth. It was an intolerably impudent question, he thought. If he spent his life in a futile attempt to understand himself and his own inhibitions, blocks, and motives, how could he ever understand Renate? A saint was someone who thought about himself only 95 per cent of the time.

Late next morning, they took in Group of Seven landscapes and Henry Moore sculpture at the Art Gallery of Ontario, and ferried to the Toronto islands, where they saw a pair of Canada geese take flight, exactly parallel as they rose. When they dined that night, Edward said that he saw Toronto through different eyes with her; she trembled with emotion. A Portuguese feast, happy people with their children, was going on; inside a church, chrysanthemums and roses flanked the altar. He was to see her off on the train to Vancouver. Before she left, she had trouble with her host's escapee cats. One, she persuaded back into the house, but the other one ran away.

Replying on August 12 to her letters and postcards – she'd also phoned from San Antonio, Texas – he said that both of them had parental problems, tended to lethargy or despair, were self-punishing and guilt-ridden, had low opinions of their abilities and qualities, and were liable to choose the most "unreciprocating objects" for their devotion. When he sought not to make her feel rejected, she had misinterpreted his motives and misread his actions. She must "realize by now that there cd be no romantic and/or sexual attachment between us. My sexual inclinations lie, have always lain and will always lie, in a completely different direction, and I have *no* desire to change that situation. I am quite happy to be homosexual and find my fulfilment, physical and emotional, in relationships with men." He would not be in Montréal when she returned; he asked that she not try to find him. When she read his letter after her return, she was angry that he had fled without giving them a chance to talk. He had pretended, she thought, that nothing had happened between them.

Renate believed that he'd left Canada, but he was in Toronto, hiding out. He reported to me that she'd been snooping through his effects stored in Ruth's basement, demanding to know why he'd left so much clothing behind, and expecting to find him cached away in Monique's apartment. At Ruth's, he had left behind his Colombian *ruana*. Renate appropriated it as a relic.

Back in Montréal, Renate gone, he sought restorative sex with two Québécois teenagers: they were indelibly impressed when he took them to a Polynesian restaurant for birthday drinks, and the waiter served cocktails smoking with dry ice. Since he didn't have a car or apartment, they had to find a "tourist home" on St. Catherine Est. But later, he stood them up, fearing police entrapment, and spent the next few days in an alcoholic semi-stupor, at night returning to Ruth's. He bought traveller's cheques in a drunken fog. He was going to Morocco.

He had tickets to buy, letters to write, packing to do. Henry called Ruth to ask if she wanted to attend a poetry reading that night. To Henry's surprise, he said that he'd like to attend, too. At the event, he thought that the poet, Steve McCaffery, was a poseur and *farceur*; worse, he took his ideas seriously. The poet's appropriation of linguistics and his remark that "no one's very much interested in semantic meaning anymore," enraged him. What were these people trying to do to language? You couldn't extend its boundaries forever — that had all been tried before *ad nauseum* — you could only work within them.

He begged off the post-reading party, opting for gay bars. He had once taken Ruth to one called The Quest, the right name for a gay bar: the impossible search for the perfect partner, endlessly frustrated, endlessly reiterated. As Ruth had put it: "It's fascinating: all these people standing around, and all of them waiting for something to happen. For someone to come and completely change their lives. And afraid that might just happen, guarding themselves against it, at the same moment.'"

He went upstairs to The Hollywood, which had nude go-go-boys, and a screen showing flickering blurry ever-repeated fuck movies. The crowd pressed near to watch guys going down on other men. His penis hardened as he rubbed against the buttocks of the man beside him, he felt a cock hardening. Men masturbated, one eye on the screen, the other on the one or two fellators inside a crush of craning necks.

On his penultimate day in Montréal, running errands for Ruth, he passed an apartment building whose garden held huge-leafed castor-bean plants. An old lady sat by the door in the sun; he asked her how the plants could survive in this climate. How did he know the castor-bean plant? He'd lived in Brazil, he said.

"Oh, and I've lived in Guatemala," she said. For an hour they reminisced. She invited him to her apartment ("I can't give you lunch, but I can give you a nice, brown, hard-boiled egg") but he declined the tempting offer. A wonderful human specimen: a pity he would never see her again.

A florist sold him a potted fuchsia like a floral fountain. He told of a Trinidad relative who was scandalized: "Jake, you chargin' $30 for that plant grow wild like weed in Trinidad!"). They had a lively chat about calypsos and carnivals. He could hardly get the fuchsia through the door. After a duck dinner prepared by Myrna, he went back to the Hollywood. He crouched and gave head to every penis that offered itself. Some came – a silent white explosion within him – some didn't. His office was to serve their hardness. He didn't lift his head once to see who owned it. He felt at one with every man in that great amoebic blob. Finally he stood up, and jacked off into the blob himself, not caring whom or what he ejaculated on. They were all the same flesh.

Sunday, fuzzy after his oceanic experience, he crammed two suitcases, and called a taxi. The driver, a Jew, chattered so much about Israel, Arabs, the Canadian dollar, and the United States that he couldn't concentrate on taking a last glimpse of the city. The airport bus took him into the countryside, the leaves turning red. He buried himself in the pages of *La Presse* to desensitize himself. At Mirabel airport, he phoned Ruth for a long second goodbye, and drank his fourth beer of the afternoon. After being seated in what seemed to be the longest, narrowest jet he had ever travelled in, they lifted off. The autumn woods flared below them.

15

SOULS IN A CELL

September 1978-January 1979

... red as the pomegranate,
disquietude, the fear
falling with night like dew,
the fruit long eaten now, the sense
of something coming due..

~ Some Seeds from the Pomegranate

He updated his diary in Essaouira on November 2, All Souls' Day, when you were supposed to pray for the dead in Purgatory. Later, after giving his young friend Abdelfateh a thumbnail of hashish, they bought pomegranates, which they ate in an earth-floored café. Tea came in an immense pot while hooded men sat by the wall and night settled. Abdelfateh rolled hash and tobacco, sharing it with the locals. When Abdelfateh heard "*pulis*," he boasted that he wasn't afraid of police.

To return to their hotel they had to pass the white-painted, iron-grilled French colonial *Hôtel de Police*. An inner voice said, "All very well, but some day you'll be walking by a police station and they'll come out and arrest you." Then he felt a hand on the nape of his neck, saw another hand on Abdelfateh's. A voice said, "*C'est la police, messieurs. Ayez la gentillesse de m'accompagner là-dedans.*

Some weeks earlier, he'd been told to stay put during Royal Air Maroc's New York stop. Anxious to bid farewell to Randy Wicker, he fomented such a row that the crew let him go, escorted, to a pay phone. Once over the Atlantic, *Black Orpheus* played in-flight; the headphone's trilingual soundtrack kept switching tongues on him. He sighed for Rio and, arriving in Casablanca, saw Mexico from the window of the bus into town in mesquite, donkeys, ground sheets mounded with prickly pears.

In a city of three million, he wondered dazed the broad spokes of avenues and rabbit-warren medinas. He sought the long *allées* and dark shrubbery of Lyaultey Park, a shadow among shadows. Until Morocco, there'd always been a sporting element in his pursuit of boys. Now the hunter had become the hunted. Staring back at the staring young, there flowered "*Vous cherchez quelque chose, m'sieur?*," the "*Oui, oui*" and "*Ça va? Ça va!*" alternating with nods, smiles, and emphatic Arabic. They whistled at him, chased him, shouting "*Voulez-vous du hashisch?* Shoeshine boys grabbed his foot, others pursued him on bicycles. When he took off his glasses, he was told, "*Sans lunettes, tu es si joli!*" With a "*Fikel-fikel dans les cabines. Entrez-y*" they tried to lure him into mosque washrooms. A suit-and-tie *employé* of the Syndicat de Tourisme said, "*Vous êtes si beau*" and suggested mint tea and a sleepover. Never, the *Spartacus* gay travel guide said, be afraid to approach a Moroccan. Be afraid, he'd say.

One night in Lyaultey, he was orally and anally penetrated: "this double pleasure, the daydream of many a closet homosexual was one for masochists," he wrote, "since actually there were not many positions in which the human anus can be penetrated without causing considerable pain, especially when you have an anus as tight and small as mine is, and in such primitive, danger-fraught circumstances." Later that night, a soldier, as drunk as he, pulled him under a palm tree. He woke at first light. "Someone," (one of his alternate personalities, he thought, who took over in such circumstances) "must have had a glorious time." The soldier shouted "*Paie-moi!*", knocked off his glasses, and stomped off. But another evening, when he asked directions of a *gendarme royal* standing guard over a columned palace, the Berber took him up to the portico, where, on cold marble in the moonlight, they embraced. His fine sharp features crinkling as he smiled, the "very romantic & democratic policeman" courteously apologized for his slow orgasms.

By day, Edward's cockroach-ridden hotel room was unbearably bright. Wailing muezzins woke him: they began about five minutes after the other, a discordant duet like rival rock bands. A million mopeds whizzed. He tried to distract himself from an agonizing tooth by "a last spurt of sexual hysteria." He did someone on a park bench, then *soixante-neufed* with another. He started with one young man when another emerged from the shrubbery. Sitting between the pair, he fellated them. The first masturbated him; the second, standing, pumped his mouth. Edward asked him to urinate. When piss poured into his mouth, he came explosively.

After a dentist yanked the tooth, he swore off booze and bussed to a rocky promontory where men in blue-and-gold djellabas and black turbans swam fully clothed in cold booming surf and broken-walled swimming pools pulsed with pushing, diving boys. On a tongue of land, women busied themselves over braziers, thick scented smoke rising. In a rock cleft, a crouching woman moved a smoky brazier over a recumbent black-robed man. A blue-robed man slit a squawking black rooster's throat and passed it across someone else's body. He asked the exorcist if he might enter the nearby shrine. Of course, he said, giving him a candle, but take off your shoes. Filling the small dark space, people parted a curtain. In the reddish gloom he thought that, in this churchlike atmosphere, he should do something suitable. He began to murmur the "Our Father" and the "Hail Mary." This also seemed wrong. A woman asked why he, a Frenchman, came here. He piously noted that saints were universal.

In the medina, a woman went by, one side of her face a cockscomb of wattles and folds, uttering inhuman cackles and grunts: he thought of his mother. In Lyautey, he made "a formal adieu to an old theatre," trembling to think of what he'd done there. He packed, paid, and got a shoeshine boy to take his bags to the bus terminal. He had thrown Canada over like a dirty garment. In decolonized Morocco, French was no longer enough to get around with. But, still, he got around.

Bearded fig trees and whitewashed houses lined El Jadida's square. Skidding on dates dropped from palms on a promenade crackling with fronds also underfoot, he was much accosted. When final-year *lycéens*, high school students, bombarded him with questions about study abroad, and his opinion of Morocco, this give-and-take, not sex, was what he wanted. He thought he could fall in love with the handsomest, Jamal (*"Ça veut dire `Chameau', mais je ne suis pas chameau."*) The next day they all went to the thick-walled fort in the old Portuguese enclave. When he returned alone, a trio of swimsuited teenagers trailed him. He serviced them, then, tired of their jabbers, shouts, and sallies, said, *"Bezeff,"* enough. A ragtag of voyeuristic urchins trailed him into town, pathetically mumbling, *"C'est grosse, m'sieur."* He explained to *lycéens* that he liked boys, but that there was more to human contact than sex. After they parted, he repeatedly coupled in the municipal gardens. Yet that night he thought of Jamal.

The next day in nearby Azemmour, he saw from town walls the river pass into a gorge, surf breaking at its mouth. When he descended, the wind flung stinging dust. In a café, barefoot men sat cross-legged on straw mats, playing cards for beans as a stake. A student named Abdalhakim led him down a hill to a walled-in field where stalls were setting up for tomorrow's souk. After sharing his kif pipe, Abdalhakim had to return to class. Crossing a field, they met schoolmates. *"Its feront des bêtises,"* Abdalhakim warned, amid an uproar of sexual allusions. To friendly girls outside the *lycée* gate, he meant to say he found Azemmour *"coquette,"* charming, but instead it came out *"cocotte,"* a tart. Boys followed him when he left, making witty remarks like *"Vous aimez le pénis, m'sieur ou madame?"*

In the souk next day, water sellers wore bronze drinking cups ringing their bodies, skinned sheep hung on hooks, and Biblical bearded men sat sideways on donkeys, lashing sticks. Storytellers, snake charmers, and vendors spieled. While Abdelhakim retrieved books at his place, his aunt came out with a staring naked infant covered with flies: Abdelhakim's brother. At a cousin's place, they took tea, while the cousin scrabbled to find a map of Canada. He gave Edward a photo of himself, and Edward gave him a ballpoint pen from Montréal. In a nook of the kitchen, a baaing sheep fattened.

In close-by M'heula, a self-appointed guide took him to a viaduct, where Edward stared at a donkey that was staring at him while the youth lounged in an irrigation channel. He had met a Frenchman, who'd given him money to build a house, which he showed off to Edward. As they sat on the bed, the young man closed the shutters, clearly ready for sex. But Edward was not auditioning to be another Frenchman. Later, *lycéens* at the bus stop asked if it wasn't true he'd given a pen to someone: everyone knew *everything* about *everybody* and *everyone* watched the tourist. One hash-smoking boy's great dark eyes taunted and dared and they had an eyeball-to-eyeball staring contest. Though mightily attracted to him, he rushed for the bus. On an El Jadida boulevard, three strangers asked if he'd enjoyed the Azemmour market.

The next morning one of the fort's voyeurs trailed him, noting, "*Beaucoup de tourists font l'amour avec les petits garçons....*" He ignored him, except for the occasional "*Non, mon fils.*" The boy muttered, "*Je ne suis pas ton fils.*" Teenagers approached him with friendly remarks like "*Vous voulez un pénis dans la bouche, m'sieur? Ou dans le cul?*" A boy named Muhammed shared hash. Friends named Hakim and Abdul joined them. Near the market, Abdul quarrelled with a soldier. The soldier left, vowing retribution. Soon police bore Abdul off to jail, but the next day Edward encountered him, drunk, stoned, or both. When Muhammed went with him to his hotel, the owner's son denounced him as a "*type très dangereux, qui enmerde les touristes.*" After talk of "*pulis,*" "*contrôle,*" "*carte d'identité*" he left them alone. Muhammed announced that he'd make love to him: would Edward give him a souvenir, and could he get him a passport? Edward resisted his sliding hands. As though he'd made a terrible mistake, Muhammed kept repeating "*Alors, vous n'êtes pas pas homosexuel?*" The owner's son now demanded that he leave. He did, taking Edward's sweater, and could now boast of owning a Chilean sweater knitted of uncarded wool by a Mapuche woman. Following St. Edward's Day, Friday the Thirteenth, he met Abdul and friends, including Muhammed in his sweater. With clashing cymbals and beating drums, a wedding procession passed, then an open-sided hearse and casket. Knowing that Edward was leaving, the boys shook his hand endlessly. He felt sad saying "*à tout à l'heure.*"

During a few days in the sardine port of Safi, he thought he might buy up quantities of glazed pottery and send it to everyone he knew. Waiting for a bus to Marrakech, he drank in a bar, arguing about Arabization. One man said Arabic was the language with which God had talked to Mohammed. Edward replied that if He had, Mohammed wouldn't have understood Him.

The bus swung away from the coast. The Atlas Mountains, purple with distance, grew bigger, bluer, harder in the clear air. Palms began to appear. The bus entered the *Palmeraie,* whose millions of date palms were owned by the king. Casablanca was the White City, Marrakech the Red City, the burnt dusty red of mud brick or stucco. They ended up in Djemaa El Fna, "Dead Man's Square," noisy crowds and a meandering line of food stalls in the heat and gathering dust. For days he had not showered.

The next morning, he traced the thick city walls, passing mosques with green-tiled roofs; a huge stork's nest perched on a minaret. *Lycéens* in a park threw rocks at date palms to knock down the tasselled fruit. An avenue linked the old city with the Guélez's wide, tree-lined streets, big hotels, and French restaurants. Marrakech was like something extraterrestrials might concoct to fool earthlings.

A boy in a dirty gandora—hoodless, unlike a djellaba— stopped him. They sipped tea, while Allal babbled about the prices of gandoras and djellabas. En route to the medina, he prattled about kif and hashish. Edward told him he shouldn't talk so openly. A djellaba'd shill followed them. When he told him he was capable of choosing for himself, the shill began to abuse him. Pricing silver tea services, he explained he was merely looking. An angry owner snarled, "*Au revoir, au revoir.*" He informed several vendors that under *no* circumstances would he buy *anything* in such a rude city.

Next day, Allal helped him find another hotel, where the rooftop terrace café was crammed with fat packaged French and German tourists. They looked faintly uncomfortable but grimly determined, a touching mixture of temerity and timidity, personal humility and patronizing chauvinism, superior amusement and longing for "real life." The drama of poverty and suffering around them was a tableau. These curious natives with their charming snakes, Berber dances, and gorgeous, outlandish foods! How authentic! How charming! And how *unhygienic*!

They had their photographs taken safely on the terrace. Herded by their guide, they went like sheep to the medina where, Edward hoped, they'd find hospitable merchants.

In the square thronged with comedians, storytellers, peddlers of aphrodisiacs and magical oils, how far away Ruth Beissel and her herbal remedies seemed! (The folk remedy for arthritis here was a distilled Jewish-made liquor made from figs. It tasted vile, as horrid as Ruth's Devils Claw remedy. Maybe it *was* Devil's Claw.) Hucksters hid objects under little poufs in slight-of-hand games. Drumming Berber troupes in flounced black trousers and cowrie shells sewn on their caps leapt and capered. Barbary apes did handstands. Snake charmers showed off fat rattlesnakes and beady-eyed cobras whose wavering, tapering, shining bodies rose like dark flames.

In a corner of the Guélez, elderly French tourists did jigs to an accordion. Moroccans applauded and laughed. A mixed emotion of sadness and joy seized him. Here in a strange land these old people tried to recapture their youth and the approving Moroccans urged them on. A moment of oneness. The evening paper brought news of a new pope, the first non-Italian in four-and-a-half centuries. That night he had an examination dream. You were confronted by an exam in a subject that you knew nothing about, or you didn't have time to finish it, or you could get nothing down on paper, or it was the night before, and you couldn't possibly learn everything now, your mind was a blank and you were going to disappoint people who believed in you. The kitchen fan had vibrated all night and, before dawn, men shouted, clanged metal curtains in the café, and banged chairs until he roared at them.

He fell into a Paul Bowles mood: "What *are* these people doing, engaged in their innumerable activities, and what am *I* doing in the midst of them all? Is it just sheer Brownian movement?" In a bank he discovered that the U.S. dollar was down, and the Canadian *désastre-piastre* even more. If it kept tumbling, he'd be ruined. Where there was money, Randy had said, there was anxiety.

With a new companion, he consumed four bottles of wine in as many bars. Moustafá was a Berber due for plastic surgery on his thickened upper lip who took Valium and Artane every day. Edward wondered why the Artane: it was used to control Parkinson's disease. One time when Edward took it, he saw double for three days, even with one eye closed — of course, he *had* taken eight pills after drinking a bottle of champagne. Moustafá got so drunk he vomited over the table and himself, which didn't seem to bother anyone unduly.

Moustafá and he took a three-hour calèche tour of the Palmeraie. On the way back, a woman with tiny stumps for legs crawled along the highway. Edward made the driver give her a lift. He moved to yet another hotel, and discovered that he'd left his Spartacus guide behind. God damn! Everything about Morocco — Moustafá, the sun, the heat, the cold, the noise, the language, the music — had begun to grate. He thought he could manage his drinking by sticking to wine, but found himself downing up to four bottles a day. At one point, stoned and drunk, he let sex happen with Moustafá. The crouch-style toilets were messy; he hadn't shat since the previous week. What pleasure, he asked himself, did he get from sitting for hours in dull bars reading foreign newspapers, listening to people chatter and quarrel in an outlandish language, subjected to toneless, tuneless love wails from a radio or jukebox, downing rotgut wine?

The hash Moustafá pestered him to buy sent Edward reeling, causing him to drink more to control the high. To escape him, he retreated to the other side of town. After wine, vodka, cognac, and rum he returned to sleep, only to have Moustafá wake him. They went out. Moustafá ordered scotch and Coke: none but the best for Lacey and his friends! Always Moustafá's doe-eyed presence, his never-terminating laments, which he was supposed to terminate. The boy's policeman father wanted his lazy son to leave home. The Deutschmarks he was expecting from a German friend hadn't arrived. He needed an injection. No one loved him. No one understood him. He asked for *"l'argent de l'amour."* Edward pointed out that he'd paid, and given him a pair of blue jeans. Oh, yes, but that was yesterday, he stammered, with many a *"M'sieur Édouard, mais, M'sieur Édouard...."*

Endless nightmares, dreams of Paulinho in Brazil, and *timor mortis*. He didn't want to die, but he wished he was dead. One night, he masturbated four times. He wondered about the neurological connection between hangovers and erotic excitability. He bought a newspaper — the dollar was falling to new lows — drank tea, went to the pharmacy for a tranquillizer. Guides and touts pressed their services, teenagers leered and pointed. He wished he had just *one* wise, sympathetic friend in this cutthroat country. A friendly-looking student came up. Edward began to tell him his troubles. Soothingly, Saïd observed that it was natural people should be preoccupied with money in a poor country. But he didn't need to fall into the hands of hustlers and, criminals, since any young man would be happy to have sexual relations. Afterwards, you paid, but you paid what you wanted to.

At his hotel, he suffered consecutive bad dreams: of his parents and home. Of travel, a plane trip with someone who at times seemed to be Ruth, to a place like an amalgam of Mexico and Brazil. Then he was in a Rio *favela* in a filthy, lowlife beer hall with sawdust strewn on a wood-board floor. A river of run-off and sewage poured tumbling from a rock into a narrow street beside the bar and became the water supply for a big toilet.

In the morning, the 800-year-old Koutoubia Tower, elegant among palms, was refreshed by rain. He strolled alleys of olive and palm astir with birdsong. No one was about except gardeners, who sat cross-legged in yellow skullcaps and blue smocks, taking tea. He resolved that he would not drink. He would not patronize bars. He would not read newspapers. He would eat sensibly and regularly. He would think positively. He would close his eyes to poverty, he would take guiltless advantage of sexual opportunities, and would give no thought to those missed. He would talk only with people who attracted him. He would not allow himself to be exploited.

He saw again a flower, the lantana; its oval, furry, scalloped leaves smelt faintly of verbena, the flowers in small spirea-like bunches, the inner colour yellow, the outer orange or red, or the inner white and the outer rose or blue. The colour changed as the flowers pushed farther from the cluster's centre. It occurred to him that he might die and never discover the scientific reason for this little mystery, like so many others that idly teased him in life, but that he was too inert or busy to seek out the answer for. He took a hot shower, late for a rendezvous with

Saïd. On the way, he met Moustafá, looking unwell. Moustafá's father came by on a motor scooter and drove off with him.

One form of hell, he thought, would be an endless medina maze. Passing through one, Saïd and a friend took him to a house where, after the inevitable mint tea, they coupled, Saïd sitting on the bed, giving instructions, while women outside chattered and cooked and children played. Impassive, Saïd's friend sat on a chair against the door. Sex to these boys wasn't even a game: almost no touching, no caresses, no embraces afterward: Saïd went off for Koranic ablutions.

A cycling boy, with open fly, hotly pursued him, saying, "*C'est belle, m'sieur.*" He threw a stone at him. In the park, a boy with a scarred, badly broken leg hobbled after him on crutches, called that he needed money to reset his leg. The boy's French was tenseless, and the memorized formulas came out with stunning circularity, but that did not subtract from the kid's desperation. When he suggested sex ("*Tous les touristes le font ici*"), Edward kissed him and gave him his loose change. The boy remarked contemptuously that a French friend had given more.

In the Guélez, he had a screaming match with a news vendor who claimed not to know the difference between French francs and Moroccan dirhams. Then it turned out the man was only standing in for the vendor. Edward would neither accept the newspaper nor his money back. The man threw the money into the street, where urchins snatched it up. Later in Djemaa El Fna, someone proposed sex in a public toilet. What pleasure could be possible in a Moroccan public toilet? An unending row of nut stands. Why not just one big nut stand for the city, instead of this cursed initiative and competition? Reduce, simplify, unmultiply! The thought of an infinite universe made him reel with horror: another image of hell. At one time, he had wanted to contain everything: objects, places, people. Now he wanted to expel and reject it.

He considered the artistry that went into shop displays: the lowliest Moroccan decorators surpassed North America's best-paid window-dressers. The work that went into the setting up stalls and shops, the hopes, fears, and aspirations they embodied, the need of earning a meal and a place to sleep every day! Someone once called him the only serious Canadian he'd ever met. This he considered a great compliment, and it was nearly true. He wished he could see it all as a *National Geographic* spread, dripping local colour. But it was the similarity of sufferings that haunted him. That night he dreamed of endless bus and boat trips, planes just missed, linguistic conferences at which he was supposed to meet his college friend Mary Jane Cook. Of late, his subconscious didn't like what he was doing to it.

In torrential rain, people took on a wintry look in heavy djellabas and poncho-like blankets. He lunched on coquille St-Jacques and rabbit, dined on *potage*, frogs' legs, pigeon with almonds. An impressive range of his fellow animals had to die that he might eat well that day, he thought. If only one could eat well, drink well, read and write with no guilty conscience and no desires all the days of one's life! To friends, he composed mystifying postcards with Muslim-calendar dates and Arabic messages. The next day he tracked earthen crenellated ramparts to an olive grove. The olive, with its silver-sided leaves and knotted trunks, at a distance resembled the willow, thousands of trees stretching to infinity in equidistant, nearly identical rows. The olives hung down, black and luscious-looking.

The twelfth-century Agdal Gardens were nearly deserted. A blue-smocked workman, unblocking a drainage ditch, grinned wolfishly and licked his lips. In a crumbling irrigation basin, waterfowl swam in turbid reedy waters. From the roof of a half-ruined pavilion, he saw red turrets and green-tiled minarets; millions of olives, citrus, and palm trees; the red bare plains around; to the east, barren red ribbed foothills, rising to the Atlas. West were the piled red-and-blue shapes of the Anti-Atlas. From the eastern wall, he saw a barren plain where sheep grazed, nibbling stones.

At ground level, a handsome kid on a bicycle stopped him. "*Vous prenez les vitamines? Vous faisent l'amour avec les garçons?*" He liked the "*vitamines*" line. Yes, but where? The Agdal Gardens. In a ruined adobe palace they made it. The boy was explicit: "*Plus vite! Plus vite! Plus lent! Presses plus! Fermez plus!*"

Strolling, he met two little boys, who pressed him to come home with them. They gave him their names and addresses and took down his. No request for money or a gift. It was good to forget sex and money and experience friendship for a moment, even with little kids. He went into a small treeless plaza and bought a pomegranate. Mohammed, who manned a bread stall, showed him how to eat it. You pried it in half, split the halves into quarters with pressure of your hands, used your fingers to scoop the ruby grains out into the cupped palm of the right hand—never, never the left hand!—then lifted the hand to mouth.

In a lane that night, he witnessed a tussle between two lads, more serious than the usual quarrel in which it seemed people would come to blows, but were merely debating, say, the price of milk. A boy with broken teeth smiled at him, and said, "*N'ai pas peur. Ce n'est rien.*" He was a country boy named Abdelfateh: *fateh*, "The Open Door," one of the 99 names of God. He slept in a friend's tailor shop; if the shop closed before he got back, he slept on a café table. Sent to a *lycée*, he'd had a falling-out with a math teacher, who failed him. He'd spent six months in a hospital. (Edward ruefully reflected, that he could pick 'em, or maybe they could pick him.) He told Edward that he loved him and needed 10 dirhams. Next day, they went to see marble tombs and cedar-lined pavilions. The guide roughly told Abdelfateh to wait outside. After a spiel in bad rote French, the guide expected 10 dirhams. Edward gave him five, along with a lecture on the right of Moroccans to see their own national monuments.

Although the heat and flies, the racket from touts, vendors, mopeds, cars, and calèches irritated him, he thought that Marrakech was what medieval cities must have been like: dirty, noisy, crowded, dangerous, mingled rich and poor, a barter economy in which artisans supplied the merchant class that in turn supplied the public. What had repelled now charmed him. The rest of the world could vanish tomorrow and Marrakech, indeed, Morocco, would go on.

He resisted the blandishments of a snake-charmer, who also boasted a trained scorpion, and of Berber women who dangled jewelry in his face. He gave coins to a self-appointed guide, who demanded much more. Edward told him to fuck off, adding a peroration on Moroccans' greed, commercialism, and exploitation. The man threatened him until, seeing soldiers approach, he slunk up an alley.

He went off to meet Mohammed, the bread-stall proprietor. Mohammed's next-stall neighbour was a Jew, who said that Marrakech had six synagogues; at one time there'd been 30. Jews had been here long before they and the Moors had been expelled from Spain. Edward made Mohammed take him to a Guélez bar where you could order kosher food. A young man drunkenly offered to take him to visit the Jewish Home for the Aged. King Hassan had provided jail penalties for anyone who even insulted a Jew without cause. But the moment that Mohammed was absent, the Jews whispered to him: *"Pas de confiance avec les Mussulmans. Pas de confiance."*

When a noisy trio of Casablancais clumped down at their table in another bar, he shoved one over to make space, causing an uproar. He put the incoherent Mohammed in a taxi, and returned to the bar, where he rejoined the joint-rolling son of the owner of a hotel on Djemaa El Fna, who was astounded to learn that his hotel figured in the *Spartacus* travel guide. Come headachy morning, he restored himself with beers in a corner bar. In the square, Abdelfateh awaited him. He pondered an economy in which a man could keep another waiting four hours. Aboard a bus making endless stops, they ate pomegranates and necked. Abdelfateh let the head of his penis jut up between his shirt and pants. None of the other passengers seemed to mind.

On a fortified hill in Demnate, they sat on an earthen floor and drank mint tea—the room needed only bars to make it a prison cell—then set off by cab for the Moulay-Youssef dam. They strolled through a valley green with palms and eucalyptus; for a pittance a truck gave them a lift to the dam where, hedged by low mountains, lay a deep blue lake. It was getting late. A young French couple, teachers in a Marrakech *lycée*, gave them a ride. Reaching the highway, Abdelfateh was itching to say something, and it finally came out. Wouldn't they like to go and visit his family?

A bumpy track led to the *duar*: adobe houses with a little mosque and a couple of shops. Abdelfateh, the eldest of eight, kissed a timid teenage brother, then approached his father, tall and dignified in white turban and blue-grey djellaba. The family— brothers, uncles, aunts, and cousins—lived on the second floor of the house, the kitchen and stables below.

His mother, his father's first wife, was away, but the other wife, whom he called "*la marie de mon père*" or "*mon autre mère*," was home. Edward didn't find out which children belonged to what wife. The shy little girls and boys solemnly kissed his hand, then put their hands to their heart.

After they'd seen the dozen cows and sheep, they were ushered into a long, high-ceilinged room with reed mats, in the corner a pile of pillows and rugs woven by Abdelfateh's sisters. They sat cross-legged. From the open window a plain stretched toward purple mountains. Pot luck was a tajine of sundried lamb with onion with homemade bread and spring water. Before and after, Abdelfateh brought a cylindrical, perforated metal receptacle and a kettle of cold water. He poured water over their hands, dried off with a towel. The uncle poured tea, apologizing that it was not mint, but contraband "*thé de Tantan*," Chinese tea. It was getting dark. Outside, they had to bid farewell to everyone separately, and to say goodbye to the animals, who played a concerto grosso of bleats, moos, and gobbles: the sheep in the fold; the turkeys on their roost; the two camels, small and large, in their pen. Abdelfateh took his father aside for a long, serious conversation.

God, Abdelfateh said later, had rewarded his devout father. Edward asked him why, with such a fine home and loving family, he wanted to live down and out in Marrakech. Abdelfateh said that he didn't want neighbours to say, "He used to be a student, but now he does nothing: he lives off his father." The *autre mère* had collected eggs and given them to the French girl, who tried to pass them along to Edward. But what was *he* going to do with eight eggs in his hotel room? Make an omelet, Abdelfateh suggested. That night he had a vivid nightmare of sharing his bedroom with a big black-and-yellow cobra.

He resolved to take Abdelfateh south to Essaouira. He left his heavier suitcase at the hotel, which would entail returning to Marrakech, but it was worth it not to have to drag it around. Abdelfateh in tow, he tangled with a ticket-taker who insisted on the suitcase's going on the express bus's roof for a fee. He opted for a series of local buses. In darkness, they reached the white cubist buildings and gap-toothed ramparts of Essaouira, a town with umbrella pines and a jumble of streets, alleys, and flat-roofed adobe houses set on a sea-battered peninsula.

Abdelfateh had his first taste of wine, brought clandestinely from a shop. They strolled the long wide beach as breakers crashed. In a beachside café, Leonard Cohen's "Suzanne" played. Strange, manifold, variegated world! That night he slept badly. It was odd how, when lonely, you thought another body beside you was what you most wanted and needed. When that wish was granted, the other body turned out to be discommoding. A dozen times he woke up, either wondering why Abdelfateh was there, or fearing that he had left with his money.

In the morning, he walked along a platform lined with cannons: war booty now covered with a green bloom. From the tower he looked out on medina, town, coast, and rocky islands. A small slip was full of fishing vessels, vendors of grilled sardines at open-air stalls, and spinning, yacking gulls. You could walk along the cement breakwaters; a small lighthouse looked across a strait to a rock-pile wasteland with the ruins of a prison. Southward the beach swept in an elongated crescent, and dunes stretched back to low broom-covered mountains.

When Abdelfateh got up, they found the beach swarming: the tide was low, the sun warm. Lunching outside last night's café, waves crashing against the wall, he ate sea urchins, served in the shell, with guts, juice, pebbles and all. Later, he was fascinated by a pump that sucked up sardines from the hold of the fishing boats, spewed them onto a conveyer belt, then dropped them, like a moving river of silver into the back of a waiting truck. So many fishy lives into the human maw! The sunset was beautiful, but there were sundogs, presaging colder weather. It was good, he thought, that they'd be going further south. He felt absurdly happy.

Back at the hotel, they talked about sex. A boy had once told Edward that his sexual conquests had begun at age 12. When Edward doubted this, he vehemently declared that Moroccan boys of nine or 10 were capable of having sex with men or women. Edward wondered what North American child-abuse handwringers would say to that? Abdelfateh had begun to have women at age 10, he said. Like other country boys, he had practiced bestiality — "*avec une jeune ânesse.*" Of his own species, Edward asked, which did he prefer — the male anus or the female vagina? The former, infinitely, he replied. Which did most men prefer?

The former. Then why did they have relations with women at all?
"*Pour avoir les fils.*"

He stared at the smiling, badly shaven *inspecteur* in striped djellaba,
and said "*Ah, oui?*" The man said, "*Oui, la police, messieurs.*" By
then, they were up the steps. In a moment, Hamou, *l'inspecteur*,
found the hash in Abdelfateh's wallet. He cuffed him, demanding
to know where the rest was. Weeping, Abdelfateh kept pointing to
Edward, who appealed, reasoned, placated, baffled by a recurrent
Third World dilemma: how and when did you offer a bribe — and
how much? Hamou whipped off Edward's money belt, declaring
it was illegal in Morocco. About midnight, their money, papers,
belts, and shoelaces were taken away, and Edward's glasses. With
a morose peasant and two blanket-grabbing drunks, they shared
the floor of a cold damp cell. Next day, the hash was weighed:
less than two grams. They signed statements in Arabic, which
he couldn't read and Abdelfateh wasn't allowed to. Hamou,
now more amiable, said that they'd be let off with fines. He took
Edward to his hotel room, and let him pick up his belongings. A
diligent old madman made 15 sets of Edward's fingerprints.
They were transferred across the square. On the upper
floors lived police and army officers with their families. Children
bounced balls and women slammed doors. A wedding was on,
and Moroccan weddings lasted three or four days. The first night,
Koranic chanting, then a choir of maidens yodelled, ending in
a bloodcurdling howl of "U-yu-yu-yu-yu-yu," like a party of
scalping Indians. The second night a serenade of bagpipes, brass,
string, and accordion came at midnight, like Wagner gone mad or
A Night on Bald Mountain. The third night, the same music, more
scalping yodels. A band of dancers swept out of the building
at 4 a.m., and returned, yodelling, at 6. Two Big-Ben-type bells
counted off every hour and quarter, one about half-a-minute
behind the other. He recited poetry, tried to recall every hotel
he'd ever slept in, all the students he'd ever taught. Abdelfateh
alternated between hysteria and hypochondria. His head! He was
dying! Call the guards! Call the doctor! After five days of water
and unchewable bread, Edward's passport was seized, "till this
affair is settled."

A patrol wagon hauled them to a prison outside the city walls. Here were several hundred *condamnés*, convicted men; *prévenus* like them awaited trial. The *condamnés* had jobs but the *prévenus* had nothing to do but peel *ful*, broad beans, later transmuted into a thick, yellow potage like French Canadian pea soup. Shelling the beans, Edward saw that each harboured, deep in Cnossian labyrinths, at least two small white lively grubs. He couldn't see the grubs in the soup, but he knew that they were there. Afflicted by diarrhea, he couldn't find the small foul toilet in the dark.

Sharing a room with 40 others, he was sure they'd be unable to breathe, let alone fit. But they did. Each cell had a *chef de chambre*, and the *chef* arranged each person in a place. They slept with feet on each other's heads and heads on each other's feet. The room half nearest the corridor was privileged, rising to an apex of superiority around the *chef*. This side spoke Arabic, often French, and was urban. The other, djellaba-clad side was the Berber-speaking peasantry. Edward got the prestigious side, Abdelfateh next to him. Later, they moved up beside the *chef* himself. The lice likely came from the Berber side, but knew no boundaries.

The prisoners shared baskets of food from their families. Abdelfateh told him to accept because, "for a Muslim, it is an honour and a duty to give." "*N'ai pas peur*," he had told him. *Mukktub*, it was written. *Inchallah*, they'd get out. They were packed off to court amid an uproarious crowd; half the population of Essaouira seemed to attend. As soon as he saw the judge— foppish, cold, and inquisitorial—he expected little mercy. The trials were in Arabic, and Edward was given a French translator, whom Abdelfateh said didn't render half of what was said. The judge's questions were few. Laconic, Edward said that he was solely accountable. Judgment was due in a week.

On the day before Aid-El-Kibr, the first feast that Abdelfateh had spent away from home, the frail prison *directeur* awkwardly slit the throats of eight sheep, and they had shish kebab for the next few days. A week later, the guards read out the pardons accorded by King Hassan, a feature of important holidays. But for them the judge pronounced "*deux mois fermés et 4000 dirhams d'amende de la Régie des Tabacs*." The fine was based on the fiction that, since kif and hash were about 20 per cent black tobacco, it contained contraband. Meanwhile, he smuggled out a letter to the Canadian Embassy in Rabat, explaining that he couldn't pay the fine because he couldn't cash his traveller's cheques. If he couldn't, he had no idea how long he'd have to stay in jail.

After lights-out, people boiled tea in tin-can kettles over makeshift braziers, played cards with improvised packs, read books. Someone always performed a belly dance; a storyteller told endless folk tales: Edward often fell asleep to the lulling expressive rise-and-fall. He woke up long before anyone else. The call of the muezzin came. As they lined up, an army of beggars, trustees called the roll: "*Debout! Deux à deux! Chef de chambre! L'inspection! L'appel!*" You'd think they were about to march on Europe. They eventually allowed him his French-Arabic phrasebooks, but considered subversive the *Journal du Prisonnier* that Monique de Gaye had given him. He was afraid that they'd find his explicit dairy, a ridiculous fear, he realized, since they wouldn't have time, patience, or eyesight to be translate 80 pages of microscopic handwritten prose.

The *chef de chambre*, who romantically favoured him, was in prison for having drunk in a private house with an unmarried woman. He was acquitted, replaced as *chef* by an *ex-gardien*, imprisoned for drunkenness. His brother had come to bail him out, but had in turn been arrested for insolen ce. Someone had struck a live-in girlfriend; she complained and he was given a year in jail. She, too, was arrested and got four months for immorality. A Spanish-speaking black *condamné* from Sidi Ifni was serving seven years for pimping, drunkenness, and beating up a policeman. He washed Edward's clothes and brought him tea and candies. A young waiter, who had accidentally killed an abusive customer, was in for four years. A man was anonymously accused of possessing an illegal weapon. Though no weapon had been found, he was in jail, and so was his slanderer.

Many cases involved peasants in complex land disputes between robed, bearded, Biblical-looking protagonists. One case had been going on for over a quarter-century, the parties still pursuing their clashing goals. A farmer, whom Edward thought of as "*l'ancien combatant*," had fought for the French in Algeria, the Congo, and Cambodia. Age 70, he was imprisoned because of a property quarrel. Asked about his soldiering days, he merely answered, "*La guerre, elle n'est pas bonne, m'sieu, non, non, elle n'est pas bonne.*" A white-bearded man always hailed Edward with "*Allahu akbar,*" pointing up to heaven. When he'd pulled out real estate documents from his djellabah to show to the police, his money fell out, and he was charged with attempted bribery. Eventually acquitted, he was last seen grinning and pointing upward, having proven that *Allah* was *akbar*. Sometimes whole families were jailed. Edward thought that eventually the entire population of Morocco would do jail time, with such laws, and such law enforcement.

The only time he saw the guards violent was when Abdelfateh demanded a receipt for Edward's money: they slapped him around. One night, a prisoner kicked someone in his sleep and knocked out his front tooth. The *chef* settled the uproar by cuffing everybody concerned and assessing a fine, never paid, as indemnity for the tooth. A prisoner vomited over his neighbours and caused a midnight ruckus. Once Edward sat up all night because his floor mates were shoving and hitting him, or complaining that he was shoving and hitting them. Another time, he refused to sleep in an allocated row because it gave him claustrophobia, and demanded to be removed to an isolation cell. He was almost taken seriously.

Resourceful Abdelfateh swapped shoes and the blue shirt he was wearing for privileges and treats. The wandering eyes of country people, who had never seen a foreigner up close, followed Edward's every act, surprised perhaps to find that, in prison, a foreigner had the same small problems and small pleasures as they. On November 29, they were shipped to a rural police station, where they slept on piles of old tires, except for Edward, who spent the night reading. Next morning they were shipped to the prison in Marrakech. The guard who anally probed for concealed drugs offered sexual favours. Put in an empty cell, Edward panicked, thinking he was being punished for resisting the guard's overtures. But a little later he was joined by three young foulmouthed Basques, caught with one and a half kilos of hash and hash oil, and an immensely fat man, a kingpin in the kif trade.

With enough space to stretch out, he slept soundly. The food was better. Mornings the *prévenus* filed out to a courtyard, where he shuffled around in his El Salvadoran fur slippers. A *fakir* came to read the Koran; the Christians sat under the olive trees. The prisoners whiled away the time reading, and even the kingpin took to poring over songbooks and religious texts. He got to know a crushed Koranic scholar, jailed because, contrary to Islam, he'd unwittingly married someone before the hundredth day after she'd divorced her previous husband. The woman was also in jail, for false witness, and her father as well, because he'd permitted the marriage. The *petits prisonniers*, as young as 8, mostly pickpockets from Djemaa el Fna Square, said *"Bonjour"* and *"Bonsoir"* to him as he passed. He took up smoking. It relieved the nerves.

Personal hygiene seemed pointless. Pouring great drums of water from the prison roof flushed the toilet, a big hole in the yard. This splashed feces and urine over half the courtyard, and the marchers had to splash through it. This never failed to enrage Edward; he fantasized throwing the guards down the toilet. He nicknamed one guard "Pinochet." Pinochet at first enforced the marches rigorously, then wearied of the struggle, since it was impossible to keep a thousand men marching forever in strict lines. They straggled around and around, or sat in the sun.

Loath though he was to accept aid from a priest, he was glad to see Père Joël, a Franciscan who for several decades had served in Marrakech's only church. He brought books and food baskets. When Edward first met him in the director's office, Père Joël said he'd contacted the Canadian Embassy, who confirmed that they'd received Edward's letter. They'd sent someone to Essaouira to see him, but by then he'd been transferred. When he explained that he couldn't cash his traveller's cheques, Père Joël said that he'd pay the fine.

Things were looking up. The suitcase he'd left in his hotel was returned. The *directeur* apologized for the circumstances in which they had met, and they discussed what English textbooks would be best for his sons. By mid-month, the Canadian consul turned up, a polite young Québécois who might have expected to find a hippie, but was confronted by a tweedy scholarly gent with greying hair. He agreed that the embassy could negotiate the fine with the *Régie*. He would try to locate his passport.

The next day he and Abdelfateh appeared before an appeal judge. Judgement rendered after a suspenseful week, Abdelfateh's sentence was confirmed, but the fine was cancelled. Edward's prison sentence was suspended, though he had served virtually all of it, but the fine was confirmed. He was to be deported after a few days at a hotel under house arrest. The next day Père Joël paid the fine. But the case had to go back to Essaouira, whose court was to pronounce his *mise en liberté*. Meanwhile, Christmas was coming, though few prisoners even knew what day it was. The priest brought a basket of delicacies, including ham: Edward gave it to Abdelfateh so he could be thrilled by trying forbidden meat.

When a week went by, he learned that his release order had been signed by the Essaouira *procureur*, but had been mistakenly sent to an appeal court by mail rather than to the prison by telegram. No one could find it, so Edward stayed where he was. With only a few days left to serve, Abdelfateh was being transferred to another prison. He refused to believe that Edward would have to leave Morocco. He made plans for them to meet at the family farm.

Just when Edward was about to go on hunger strike, the order arrived. He said his farewells but, outside, waiting for him, was the Marrakech *sûreté nationale*, who shipped him to the main police post, where he signed an incomprehensible document, and then to the Djemaa El Fna station's *caves*, underground cells. Since King Hassan was in town, the police had arrested several hundred, who now huddled in the *caves*. The police used whips liberally. Prisoners flared into fist fights. The police had no idea why Edward was there. It seemed he might be tried over again. He got bronchitis. After two days, a detective took him back to Essaouira by bus: he'd been looking all over Marrakech for him.

In Essaouira, he was reunited with his old friend Hamou and spent New Year's Eve and Day in an office, watching drunks brought in and beaten up, jailed, fined, or freed. Sans blanket, he lay on the floor amid his clothing, suitcase, and books. He got his passport back. The next day they put him on a bus for Casablanca, handcuffed to a policeman. He'd been promised that he could see Embassy people at Rabat and repay Père Joël, but after a few hours in the Casablanca police station he and the same policeman boarded an overnight bus for Tangier. In

Tangier, after a stay in *caves* as grim as Marrakech's, they took him down to the docks, where he was caged, given his passport, and told to buy a ticket for Málaga. They escorted him to the boat. It was January 4, some two months after All Souls' Day.

16

THE RAIN IN SPAIN

January-August 1979

He is not the one. I am not the one.
And this is not the time or the place, and rain —
will merely worsen my cough or give me rheumatism...

~ Meditation One

When he left Morocco, they put a simple *"Départ"* on his passport. During his first days in Málaga, he took a bath, slept 18 hours at a time, and deloused his clothing. He threw the last into a bathtub of scalding water, left it or four days, then washed it. Whether this drowned the lice, he wasn't sure.

Another task was to repay a debt of honour: he gave the Canadian consulate money to forward to Rabat. He was now in a city just south of winter. Under craggy shielding mountains, avocado, sugar cane, and custard apple grew; hibiscus and flowering shrubs were everywhere, and the city's main promenade was fringed with palms. For a few days, the temperature rose for a couple of hours, children skipped school to play in parks, European pensioners crept out to sidewalk cafés, the Nordic young sunned on the beaches and even swam. Mostly, it was a bit too cool for all that. At night, he bar-hopped and ate tapas in dark, barrel-filled bodegas: a Spanish custom he approved of, but it had become an expensive one. "Town of a thousand bodegas and one bookstore," people said.

At nearby Nerja, he had his picture taken descending a stair in a cave among stalagmites: hunched, in dark glasses, dark tweed jacket, dark shirt, dark trousers, striped socks, and slippers. For a friend's benefit, he wrote on the back, "The poor old fellow looks half-blind, doesn't he?" The coast from Nerja to Marbella was one long pan-European conurbation; even the smallest fishing village had an English pub. The mountains, sea, and coves were spectacular: *that* couldn't be spoiled. The previous summer he'd sent Renate Jürgensen a postcard to Germany, and half-promised to be her Morocco guide. Now, knowing that she was vacationing in the vicinity, he feared that, if he met her, her infatuation might flare up anew.

At the foot of the snow-topped Sierra Nevada, Granada's lower town was a shapeless mass of apartment blocks and office buildings. Winter-flowering shrubs grew in the Alhambra gardens, but it was hard to imagine what dalliances, intrigues, and passions could have occurred there when it was now cold, and rained most of the time. When the rain let up, he wondered how the human mind could conceive and execute such intricacy of calligraphy, geometrical form, and stylized abstraction, all in fantastic complication, order, and sense of proportion.

In Córdoba, it rained, rained, rained. Like Granadans, Cordobans were withdrawn; as a book warned him, the city "was *not* light, festive and noisy, but severe, mystic and retiring." The mosque, dating from the Caliphate, occupied a city block, with multiple keyhole entrances; inside, a forest of stone and marble columns, the arches alternating red and white, the pillars gleaming blue and green in the half-light, fantastic mosaics of golds, blues, and greens. Outside again, soaked and shivering, he viewed winding Arab alleys and flowered patios behind curtains of rain. He dashed from bar to bar in scarf, heavy wool Ecuadorian jacket, and Peruvian tuque. If anyone ever mentioned "Sunny Spain" again, he'd punch him in the nose. His hard-to-shake bronchitis made him sound, he thought, like Marlene Dietrich. The British seemed happy with the fog, mist, and rain, though, and treasured the hour or two of tardy sun, stretching out on deck-chairs or camped at sidewalk cafés, saying, "Oh, but it's so much better than, such a relief after, *home*." It made him wonder what "home" must have been like.

He found it impossible to befriend Spaniards, though it was possible to argue with them. They seemed never so pleased as when they were putting down someone. If they were taciturn like Canadians, he could resign himself, but they conversed, jested, and opinionated among themselves, and he felt intolerably excluded. Writing to Ian Young, he fiddled with his portable typewriter, trying to figure out why a small, delicately notched wheel let the carriage move backwards but not forwards. The wheel turned out to be a Canadian dime. Moral: Never travel with Canadian coins; they messed up everything.

Little orange trees lined the streets in Seville, their fruits glowing like light bulbs against dark leaves. After so much rain, the cathedral was flooded, the city practically an island. Like Córdoba, it was on the banks of the wide Guadalquivir; unlike Córdoba, it was near the river-mouth. The city was the great port of departure for Latin America, so maybe this was why it was friendlier. In the Giralda mosque, he got inside a minaret, and discovered how muezzins could climb it so rapidly; there were no steps, but an easy sloping ramp.

He'd wearied of massive cathedrals and baroque churches glinting with gold, a-squirm with cherubs, but lighted like mausoleums. And museums, cemeteries, aqueducts, Roman bridges. He'd scream if he saw yet another notice from the Board of Tourism inviting him to visit at least 50 important monuments, which entailed getting lost at every corner. Europe had too much of the past. The New World, especially Canada, had too little. Everything in this land was freighted with time and bloodshed, yet Spain had become a modern country, with soldiers in buses reading porno magazines beside little old ladies in black rebozos. A blaring TV in every living room, a car in every garage, a video game in every bar.

One night in a bar he spotted two hash-smoking sailors. Striking up a conversation to talk about his Moroccan adventures, he asked if he might buy a little hash. They took him to an abandoned spot near a picturesque Arab mill by the river, at which point they stripped him naked, robbed him, and raped him at knifepoint.

Ferrying across the river to Portugal, he got a ride to Faro in the Algarve. I had married the previous October. On St. Blaise's Day, February 2, he posted a postcard to my wife Alison, who he did not "have the honour and pleasure of knowing personally, but of whose beauty, virtue and sagacity I am more than assured, knowing well, as I do, the lofty ideals, impeccable taste and elevated stands of the gentleman who had chosen to bestow on her the supreme accolade of his sterling manhood. May you both be happy, and may life treat you gently. Sweet Guadalquiver, flow softly, till I end my song...." St. Blaise's Day, or Portugal, was infecting his style, because a postcard to me, including belated Christmas greetings, characterized me as his "chum, buddy, bosom pal of my boyhood ecstasies and puerperal torments, adolescent anguishes and first hectic flushes..."

The Portuguese were a rural people still. How pleasant, after the nervous tapas bars and clamouring bodegas, were leisurely restaurants, cafés where you could linger for hours. How nice to meet again people who took a minute out to show a bit of interest in the passing stranger. How pleasant, after Spain, were little baroque churches and chapels, bright with gold woodwork and *azulejos*, coloured tiles, on the walls.

Via Faro, where mango trees were abloom in the plazas, he went to Albufeira, a fishing village of flat-roofed white houses set on a cliff above beaches reachable by tunnels and staircases. The vacationers and retirees, mostly English, were less abrasive and ostentatious than those on the Costa del Sol. It was still too cold and windy for swimming, but fine for walking, so he trudged along the beach, returning along the cliff-tops. The rains were now tapering off. At Cape St. Vincent, the southwesternmost point of Europe, three capes jutted in different directions, and the wind could blow you away. On Sagres Cape, the half-English prince, Henry the Navigator, had built his fort and set up his school for the study of navigation and exploration, and spent years there, outfitting expeditions. During his lifetime—he died in 1460—his labours led only in the discovery of Madeira and the Azores. But in the next few decades, Christopher Columbus, who'd studied at Sagres, sighted America, Pedro Avares lit on Brazil, and Vasco da Gama rounded the Cape to Asia.

In Lisbon, there was money at the bank and mail at the Embassy. Refugees from civil wars and socialist regimes in Angola and Mozambique gave the city a raffish multicultural air. He housed himself in a penny-pinching hotel, where he paid exorbitantly to get enough heat for comfort and water hotter than lukewarm, and enough water to take a brief shower. Since the hotel had not see fit to supply him with either chair or table, he wrote Ian Young on a bathroom stool, typing on an extension of the bed the same size as the typewriter. Ian had been dividing his time between Toronto and New York, where he had sometime-employment rewiring lamps in Randy Wicker's shop. He enclosed a cheque for $1,340 *"désastres"* — his name for "the Canadian *piastre*, or should one call it the `Cando', or the `dodo', or the `dildo.'" It was the balance due for the printing of *Later*.

Seeking warmth, he boarded a banana boat to Madeira. Discovered uninhabited in 1420, Madeira was nearly all mountain, but everything flourished in the volcanic soil. Crazy with flowers from every continent and climate, Funchal was afloat with bougainvillea grown on trellises over brooklets and drainage ditches; orchids, anthuriums, and the bird-of-paradise filled the flower market. Like a happy woman, Madeira had no history. He sent the vegetarian Monique de Gaye a postcard that mentioned the "Société pour la Canonisation de St-Édouard Lacey," an organization they'd once joked about. The postcard showed, amid racks of barbecuing meat, a man showing off a laden skewer to an impressed female.

Madeira lacked beaches, and the only way to get out into the country was one of the undependable, infrequent, and unlocatable local buses, or a tourist excursion narrated in five languages, on which everyone else was over 70. The island was a little self-contained continent. Nothing was lacking, only the heat of the real tropics. Only the boys of the tropics.

Finding unsuspected mechanical attributes in himself, he determined that a further typewriter problem was caused by a loose screw in the part below the carriage that controlled capitals. He temporarily replaced it with a shoelace, before seeking repairs in a shop. Repairs took about 15 minutes, involved a lever that he'd never heard about or noticed in the machine, wasn't mentioned in the instruction book, and cost $1.25, including a new, all-black ribbon. The man said the machine was a "*mequina muito boa*," and would give many years of service. This was why he liked to live in countries where people still know how to repair things.

He used his rejuvenated machine to write Ruth Beissel. Her divorce to Henry had come through, and she was selling their house. He'd phoned her from Spain, but he could hardly talk with his bronchitis, or hear her. He constantly thought of his friends—Ruth, Henry, the girls, Monique—the last someone, he thought, whose peculiar calm was extracted from deepest inner turmoil, darkness, and despair. He missed all of them.

He noted that the Beissels were now in their birthday season, Myrna first, then Henry, Angelica, Ruth. Angelica was now 18; it seemed to him she'd been an adult, and done the things adults did, for years now. But any birthday could be celebrated for managing to survive one more year of this life, in this world. And Henry would be 50! Fifty was an age he could not associate with him. He'd always be a man in his mid-30's, because, he supposed, that was the age he was when Edward knew him best. When they conversed, he'd always called Edward "my boy." Yet he always felt that Henry was his own age, or perhaps even, in his buoyant energy, younger. A half-century of being Henry Beissel!

Having heard that the sulphur dioxide in wine destroyed almost all the body's thiamine, he popped thiamine pills. Human contact? Unlikely. Sexual contact, even more unlikely, unless someone unaccountably struck up a conversation. It happened about as often as lightning struck church towers. A useless, meaningless, meandering river of a life. He could go to a disco but he intensely disliked the racket. Anyway, what was a single, unaccompanied, middle-aged man going to do there, when he didn't even try to dance?

He'd learned that, in January, Renate had been in Marbella, near Málaga. He'd even gone there one day, and sent a postcard to her from Torremolinos. He got a cable from Randy, proposing to join him in Madeira in April. Edward phoned to say that he wouldn't be there. Anyhow, Randy would go crazy in Madeira, where there was little to do but admire the landscape. He sent a postcard depicting "Wicker handicraft of Madeira."

Given the happy coincidence of the names, he wrote, "you would have bought up the entire contents of this shop... esp. the wicker deer (esp. when you learned the deer is the symbol of homosexuals in Portugal). Maybe the more-than-lifesize Wicker mastiff in his Wicker kennel would have tempted you beyond reason...." He boarded a boat back to Lisbon, among the passengers a neurotic family planning to inter their 25-year-old daughter in a psychiatric institution. Their doctor accompanied them, sharing a cabin with Edward.

Spring came early and suddenly. He had never seen such a country for gardens, wildflowers, florists, bouquets, and window flowerpots. He sent Henry and Ruth birthday greetings. He warned Ian Young to pay little attention to anything Randy might say about him: "With him as with everybody, I lie and wear a mask." Commenting on *Gay Sunshine* magazine's Brazilian issue, he said that the "gay lit" movement had gone about as far as it could. Though the movement had been necessary, it was now time for gay poets to move on. He was so tired of the "cock-'n'-cum" school of poetry that he swore that his next book of poetry would be called *Poems Asexual.* He met an ex-legionnaire in a waterfront bar, who spoke French and Spanish, had been in North Africa, showed him the slits on his wrists from a suicide attempt, and needed money to get to Geneva and try to enroll as a mercenary. Likely everything was a lie, but they roamed Lisbon together, and enjoyed each other in bed.

May turned chilly when he went, along with about a million other people, to Fátima on the anniversary of the Virgin's appearance before three shepherd children. He thought that something strange might have happened there. The place gave off odd vibrations; there was little of the singing and gaiety of other religious feasts. Amid the pilgrims' hunger and exhaustion was meditative quiet and awe. The temperature suddenly rose for the two days to 35° C, causing hundreds of sunstrokes. Like many others, he spent the night in a pine grove, and sent Randy a postcard depicting the huge crowd. He said he hoped that the sheer number of heterosexuals would impress on Randy how many more there *still* were of *them*, and always would be, outside San Francisco and Greenwich Village.

From the interior, he set off for Extremadura in western Spain, birthplace of *conquistadores* like Herando Cortés and Francisco Pizarro. He had to stay up all night in Badajoz, since the hotels were filled. Falling asleep on the train to Mérida, he outshot his destination. In a little transportless town, he had to wait all day in an empty train station, strolling into town in an ankle-length brown fustian shepherd's cloak with a fur collar and two capes. He took a night train back.

Disagreeable things always happened to him in Spain. Banks wouldn't accept his traveller's cheques, after letting him sign them. He had to quit his room because it was needed for Holy Week tourists. Further on, every hotel in Cáceres was full of Holy Weekers and the relatives of soldiers who were to swear allegiance to the flag. He walked around little Plasencia's monumental cathedral, feeling as though he were pregnant with a stone baby. Before he lost count inside, he tallied 26 cherubs — or cupids, as he preferred to call them — on each side altar. Curious how a religion that scorned and punished the flesh as much as Roman Catholicism should have such a taste for naked males: Christ, St. Sebastian, St. Stephen, *ad nauseum*. He might do a study of this, he thought; then, again, maybe he wouldn't.

His room exposed him to all-night traffic pulling in and out of a next-door service station, and to the antics of Holy Weekers. Were he the government, he'd declare strict mourning, curfew, and domiciliary detention for all Spaniards in Holy Week. A barking dog on the hill kept up all night. He couldn't understand how dogs could keep up their infernal noise for hours on end without ruining their vocal cords, though he supposed it was no more mysterious than the interminable noise called speech that human beings produced, especially the Spanish, who bit their words and barked.

His dreams featured his parents: he wished they would leave him in peace. In the morning, he woke to sun shining on the town set below in a valley, and on snow-covered peaks. The Sunday-deserted town had a hillside *Parque del Generalísimo*. Most of Franco's statues and portraits were gone, but there were still too many around for his liking. In the afternoon came the drenching Spanish rain. Caught downtown, she struggled morosely through crowds under the plaza's porticos, darting down bar-filled lanes for glasses of wine or beer, elbowed by Spaniards indulging their zest for noise, confusion, and haste. He thought the children in the bars should be kept away unless they were vendors, or had dropped in to call father home. Children reminded patrons of their families, which most men were trying to forget. But men were so unpleasant that he supposed he should be thankful for any civilizing element.

A pitcher of sangría improved his mood. As he was typing a letter in his room, the phone rang. It was the night man, who said *"Estacione su máquina"* peremptorily. No prelude, no "please," no suggestion that he was being asked to do anything: he was being told to. A neighbour had complained, but why didn't he knock on the wall, or come to his door? But no, a Spaniard would never do anything so reasonable. He told the night man that he'd *estacioner* his *máquina* when the night man had *estacionado* the barking dog next door and the noise of all-night traffic in the *estación de gasolina*. And hung up. Result? The dog was silenced and he had a good night's sleep.

The landscape brightened with white and yellow bloom. Seen from every corner in Guadalupe, the emerald mountains variously reminded him of Mexico, Colombia, Ecuador, or Guatemala. Sheep, cows, horses, and donkeys strolled the cobblestones, and an infinity of footpaths wound out of town. He took half-day walks into the countryside, with his cape to protect him from the intermittent rain. He met a shepherd out looking for a lost lamb and told him he hadn't seen it on the stretch he was about to cover. When he met him in town after that, the shepherd introduced him as "the man who helped me find my lamb." He suspected that his robe made him look like the Good Shepherd.

He stayed at a private home, since the tourist hotel was filled with fat pilgrims from Madrid. The easy-going landlady and her family farmed, and gave him fresh milk for breakfast. When he put such a high value on isolated country towns and a simple rural way of life, he realized that he condemned others (and himself: he, of course, would be the village schoolmaster and queer) to poverty, disease, and blinkered ignorance. But these were preferable to twentieth-century alienation, massification, and materialism. Despite the fact that it produced most of

Spain's cork, olives, and chestnuts, Extramadura was poor. Was that why its people seemed nicer?

Back in Lisbon, he went to the beach resort of Nazaré, whose people supposedly descended from Phoenicians, the men in plaid trousers and shirts with black caps, the women in seven skirts, covered with black shawls. He visited nearby Leiria and Óbidos with their castles, the Norman cathedral of Batalha, the Templars' church at Tomar with its Manueline façade of coral, anchors, squids, and artichokes. In Alcobaça was a tracery of Gothic towers, a river, fresh trout, and cherry wine. The university town of Coimbra, the combination of ancient architecture and youthful students, the spring itself, revived him.

Porto just meant "the port" and gave its name to Portugal. It straggled over hills on both sides of the River Douro. Its dark seedy narrow streets were full of prostitutes, thieves, fishwives, children. Washing hung out over streets. It had hideous late baroque and Victorian architecture; and much more low life and night life than in Lisbon. Porto was damp and chilly in the morning and at night; hot and damp in the afternoons. On the other side of the river were the port-wine houses. After visiting six vintners' bodegas, sweet red and dry white ports began to look and taste the same.

He nostalgically viewed a porno movie called *Jungle Blue*, filmed in the jungles of Colombia and Peru around Leticia and Iquitos, and found an 18-year-old who'd been raised in Spain but had lived with abusive Portuguese relatives. He'd run away to live on the streets. Edward took him on a train with just one coach, in which they were the only passengers, to the little inland town of Amarante. The townspeople baked phallus-shaped cakes for the June feast of the saint of marriages, São Gonçalo, the same saint who, according to a Brazilian legend, once danced all night with the whores in a Minas Gerais town, in order to avert fornication.

They washed down local cherries and strawberries with green wine, and paddled a rented rowboat on the river. The boy wanted to go with him to Spain, but he paid for his ticket to Lisbon. All he wanted, Edward reflected, was to help people, be helped by them, learn a little of what life was for them, have their companionship, and, if they consented, enjoy their bodies.

It seemed little to ask. Tucked into his luggage was a fragmentary sex diary, parts of it inside a paperback of Katherine Anne Porter's *The Leaning Tower*, organized by country, with names, ages of sexual partners, and cryptic notes in French or Portuguese about the nature of the encounters. There were hundreds of names.

The *portenses* were celebrating the night of St. John, or Midsummer Night's Eve — as were the Montréalais, he recalled, on St-Jean Baptiste Day. At 3 a.m. the feast gave no sign of ending. Young men jumped over bonfires, and children launched fire-balloons, which looked beautiful in the sky but could set roofs ablaze. The, besides dancing, singing, and shouting, ran around hitting each other with plastic hammers, making fearful click-clack sounds. They also hit each other with leeks. They ate enormous corn, rye, and wheat breads and gooey, egg-filled candies. He was not out enjoying all this because he had a sore cavity in his jaw. For some time, he'd hated a lower front tooth that jutted out, caused him to bite his lip, and gave him, he thought, a bulldog-like look. The previous week, after grimacing in the mirror for the millionth time, he found a dentist. The tooth gone, he'd only been able to take liquids.

Sleepless, he wrote letters. Since Ruth Beissel was selling her house, he supposed his books, papers, and winter clothing in her basement could be moved into storage. His unforwarded correspondence mouldered in a postal box. His Aunt Marion was now in a Peterborough, Ontario nursing home, and his Uncle Joe Tangney had died. His schoolmates were lost, too. Twenty years earlier his classmates at the University of Toronto had pledged they'd have a reunion this year. If and when they did, they'd recognize each other not just by face but by the reputations they'd made. It was not a reunion he would attend.

Angelica was troubled by a boyfriend, but they'd sort it out, he was sure. Myrna was troubled, too, and was now in Toronto. If only Myrna realized, he wrote Ruth, that she had a lovely personality, that she was Indian, not black, and that skin colour counted with Canadian bigots, but not with as beautiful as she. Her feeling of worthlessness was what made her so malleable, so easily influenced by others, he thought. Myrna was not as irresponsible as she seemed. Maybe she should go and live with Randy. Randy's complaints about his friend David were practically identical to Ruth's about Myrna. Maybe *Ruth* should go and live with Randy.

Northward, county seats combined piety and oenology. In Barcelos, they made cheerful red-and-black clay roosters. Braga, the "Rome of Portugal," was clotted with baroque churches, including a cathedral with mummified saints and bishops. He saw the monastery of Tibnes, a huge rambling rural structure falling to pieces, divided between two proprietors, an old lady who lived with her servant in the dozens of rooms on one side; and a peasant family in the dozens on the other. The two were enemies, and if you visited one's side you could not visit the other; they'd refuse to show it to you. He chose the old lady's side, since it contained the chapel, also disintegrating. Portugal had more ex-churches than Rome or the government knew what to do with; he'd seen them housing movie theatres and even a dance hall, though not a nightclub in a former funeral home, as in Montréal.

In a postcard to Monique de Gaye, he graphically described a porno film he'd seen. In innocent, backward Portugal, the filthiest movies, featuring rape, group sex, and bestiality, now played. Once an aged, formally dressed, exquisitely mannered usher escorted him to a numbered seat in a velvet-and-gilt neoclassical emporium, which formerly echoed opera and classical tragedy, to watch a film about a woman copulating with a pig. No doubt, he thought, there was pleasure to be derived from sex with a pig, and one could even make an art film about it; but these films treated sex as ugly, crude, and violently sadistic. They treated sex—and the body, and therefore the human being—as a mechanistic joke. People, he thought, should discover sex for themselves. He'd ban porn and TV: both jaded and coarsened the sensibilities and impoverished the fancy. Sex should be underground and hard-to-get. Then it could perform again its proper liberation. But he still attended porno films whenever he could.

He crossed into Galicia in northwest Spain, green farming country, its dialect close to Portuguese. Restaurants offered huge portions of fresh produce and seafood. Galicians were beefy peasants, friendly but rather avaricious and stupid, he thought. Vigo, a great port, had a lot of sailors and nightlife, and no damn churches to visit. La Coruña, another port with fine beaches, had the world's oldest functioning lighthouse. Here was the grave of Sir John Moore, killed in 1809 in defence of the city against Napoleon's troops in the Peninsular War. Charles Wolfe had written a romantic poem about his burial, now engraved on Moore's tomb:

> Slowly and sadly we laid him down
> From the field of his fame fresh and gory;
> We said not a word and we carved not a stone
> But left him alone with his glory.

The pilgrimage cathedral in Santiago de Compostela gave him a fierce headache and neck ache from staring up at domes, ceilings, and arches. Santiago was a lively university town, though the monstrous cathedral dwarfed everything. In Vigo, he'd met a Portuguese and a Spaniard teenager. He wrote Randy, "…you *know* how tender I am in some areas: I've scarcely been able to sit (or shit) since." But he didn't regret it: it was a good birthday present. He'd grown older, but not wiser, he considered, and though he attracted people least suitable for him and who least appreciated him, this had immensely broadened his world-view.

Asturias was another green, hilly, coastal province, famous for its apple cider, which he amply sampled. Across rugged mountains was Léon, from which he headed straight for Madrid. Grey, grimy, frenetically noisy Madrid was an oven, his hotel inner room a black, unventilated hole. Terrorist bombs exploded in the subway, at the airport, and at the main railway stations, policemen and generals were murdered. The city was tense. He changed hotels thrice, drank gallons of sangría and gazpacho, grabbed on the run tapas of seafood and garlic mushrooms.

His hand shaking so badly on the Feast of the Apostle, St. James, patron of Spain, that he could hardly manage a pen, he complimented Ian Young on *Later*, copies of which he'd received. On the cover was Barker Fairley's portrait of him. He hoped that the 40 people on the list he'd provided were getting their complimentary copies. He was cheered by a nice letter from Monique de Gaye, who'd been undismayed by the explicit postcard he sent her from Braga. In Toledo, despite the splendour of the cathedral, the paintings by El Greco repelled him, and the barren sunbaked town was infested with tourists. But he liked Segovia with its airy Alcázar and Mexican-provincial air, and Avila with its marvellous walls, its blessedly cool climate, and reminders of that gifted neurotic, St. Teresa.

But Madrid was a mad cathouse, or a catty madhouse. The theatres and nightclubs offered revues called "Penis-tration" and "Collective Coitus"; you could drink in the Clitoris Club. Kiosks sold corny porn novels. Gay bars were everywhere, though homosexuality was still technically illegal, potentially subject to severe punishment, and sternly disapproved of by the average Spaniard. He practised his Arabic with penniless Iraqi boys, mostly Kurd, who had fled Saddam Hussein. Madrid had become a mecca of refugees: blacks from its former African colony, Equatorial Guinea, and Arabs in blue robes from the ex-Spanish Sahara. He got close to Latin Americans, political refugees, smugglers, criminals, artists, and singers, who agreeably contrasted with the locals.

Later that year, *Gay Sunshine* magazine was going to publish his 23,000-word review essay on *Now the Volcano: An Anthology of Latin American Gay Literature*, most of which Erskine Lane had translated. "Latin America: Myths and Realities" was an epic introduction to a culture that, starting with Mexico, embraced Central America and part of the West Indies, and all of South America, including Brazil, a continent unto itself. He concluded that for gringo visitors the society, the macho code, and a Latin lover "will ensure that any psychological masochist gets his full quota of satisfaction in Latin America."

He fell in with some Portuguese boys, who fed him drugs and sex, then robbed him. Had they been just commercial contacts, he'd have considered it just another rip-off. But he'd liked them. What was it someone wrote on the Consul's house in *Under the Volcano*? "*No se puede vivir sin amor.*" But no more friendships with young men, he swore; they jeered at, despised, and exploited him, not because he was homosexual, but because he was such a dupe, an idiot, an old man trying to be young. Let the young come to him now: he wouldn't go to them.

17

A FLOWER IN THE ROCK

August 1979-May 1980

Now your pale scentless blossoms
are not for me, acacia,
I have seen
other colours
other countries
other flowers.

~ Acacia

Heading south to Alicante, he boarded a ferry for Oran, and next morning saw the coastline of Algeria. Customs poked into his suitcase's crannies, leafed through every book, searched each crevice of his person until at last he was permitted to enter the *République Algérienne Démocratique et Populaire.*

He soon found what travel was going to cost him in the democratic popular republic. A taxi charged US$10 to take him a few blocks to a modest hotel in which rooms were an immodest $40 a day. Almost everything was closed. During the Ramadan fast, the women, sheeted phantoms, directed one reproachful eye when he bought a soft drink. After sunset came the muzzein's calls: it seemed to him that only men with the most unpleasant, unmusical voices were selected as muezzins. Sex, even embraces or kisses, were permitted only at night, and had to be followed by a Leviticus-style purification. After a predawn meal, workers slept in, then went listlessly to jobs, breaking for siestas during the hot hours. This went on until the new moon gladdened the sky, and the feast of Aid El Kbir began, two days of unconstrained eating, visiting relatives, buying gifts for children. Westerners tended to think of Islam as puritanically joyless but, he thought, it had its festive side.

A cheaper hotel came with cockroaches and filthy crouch toilets. Water arrived an erratic couple of hours a day. If he didn't make it to a restaurant and grab a table by noon he might have to wait until 7. Most stalls offered unspiced, saltless messes, and restaurants bad expensive fake-French dishes under elaborate mendacious names. Taxis were scarce, and buses were booked up days ahead, or you could not get to the ticket window — if one knew *which* ticket-window. Algeria wasn't a police state; it was more a state of chaos.

The only French newspaper irreconcilably spouted pro-government propaganda, Islamic pieties, and pro-Communist, anti-imperialist jargon. After long years of French rule, Arabization was in full spate. The big estates were broken up, but the young were abandoning the land. Feverish to immigrate, young Algerians showered him with questions about life abroad. They sometimes had $5,000 in savings from their oil or mining jobs but no way to spend it; they could only buy a car, cassettes, or clothes, or drink in the few dismal bars, where whisky cost up to $200 a bottle.

Hot, muggy Oran had been *the* French city: they still called their café-lined main street, all of two blocks long, the Champs Elysées. A pickpocket lifted his passport in a shoving crowd at the bus terminal, having mistaken its leather case for a wallet. He went to the police. Amazingly, by the next day they handed the passport back to him. Having exhausted the attractions of a palm-lined waterfront drive and a Spanish castle on a mountain amid piney woods, he found diversion in two days in a nearby village with a handsome 35-year-old. The man loved him solely for his body, he thought. At least that was something.

In Tlemcen, a mountain city near the Moroccan border, a man gave up his room at the Turkish bath so that Edward could have a bed: the hotels were crammed with Brazilian oil workers. He had never seen a town with so many maples and poplars, except maybe Lindsay, Ontario. Lindsay never had such weddings, though. There were 15 of them that weekend. Dressed up like an idol, the bride was paraded, showing, for the last time, her face. Honking cars drove around, the back seats occupied by sheeted female relatives. Blaring Berber orchestras also, drove around. Processions wended back and forth from bride's house to groom's house. The horseback groom and best man pranced through town while their friends tried to unseat them. All night, he heard bloodcurdling yodels from women. They called it "youyouing."

He sought the desert, which began barely 200 kilometres from the coast. In a country the size of France, the Sahara took up eight-tenths of the land. On the 14-hour bus-trip he crossed dry rolling steppes, river valleys, and the desert itself, at first stone and scrub, then sand and lunar mountains. Next were the black tents of nomadic shepherds and mud-brick buildings, date palms, tamarisk trees, the willow and the eucalyptus. Just after nightfall, they pulled into Ghardaia, a ramparted oasis near oilfields. In the shadow of a mosque, the medina was thronged with white- and blue-robed men retailing Berber rugs and blankets, ornamented copper and bronze, jewelry, amulets in tin or silver with turquoise, and edible lizards called skinks. People slept out under the colonnades of a long, sand-drifted street under the immense starry sky.

As he travelled south, blue increasingly became the colour of robes, the dazzling whitewash of houses tinged with it. The dune-carpeted desert ended in El Golea, an oasis hidden among millions of palms, which he might have enjoyed more if it had not been for the millions of flies. It was a further 1,200 kilometres to Tamanrasset, just below the Tropic of Cancer, as far as he could go by bus. Avoiding the heat, the bus left at 10 p.m and arrived in predawn Ain Salah, where they spent a fly-haunted day; even the market was deep in sand. Back aboard, he could make out in moonlight the jagged looming Hoggar Mountains as they neared Tamanrasset.

The town had a long history, though it was hard to tell why. A few palm and olive groves, and a long main street lined with tamarisks and salt cedars that sighed in the all-day wind. A garrison town, it was the last one before the Niger border: bored restless soldiers picked fights in his hotel's café; the only recreation was the much-patronized brothel. Young, bearded, and blonde German and French tourists made the trans-Sahara trek in car or jeep, though some tried to hitchhike, only to have the police turn them back. The townspeople's muffled shrouded faces menaced, while merchants traded with the "*hommes bleus*," the tall, stately Touaregs who ranged the desert with their herds. A Tourareg struck him after he accidentally stepped on his foot.

He took a plane east to Ouargla, the oil capital. When he entered a flophouse, he found himself glared at by dozens of men on mattresses. But they were just ordinary, harmless, uprooted folk from all over, lured here by high wages. He found a hotel. Ah, air-conditioning, a warm shower, running water, a swimming pool, sit-down toilets. The market was filled with the local "*roses des sables*." They were gypsum, which crystallized around sand grains in forms that often resembled flowers, though not roses. The locals said if you watered them, they'd grow. Every morning the merchants hosed down their roses religiously.

On the eastward road to El Oued, nearly in Tunisia, stalls appeared out of nowhere, and spires of domed mudbrick buildings. Surrounded by mountainous dunes, El Oued meant "the river," but the water was underground, and the sand-piled date palm groves had to be dug out every night. The one tavern exactly resembled a Canadian beer parlour: no comfort, no entertainment, no food, just beer: evil-smelling, dirty, and noisy. From the dunes, the city looked like a forest of mosques. The translucent, honeyed dates sold here were called the "finger of light."

He backtracked through the desert—if you half-closed your eyes, it was a Canadian snowscape—and entrained north to Biskra through date-palm oases and along a dried salt lake in whose shimmering air mountain mirages loomed. In Biskra, André Gide, Oscar Wilde, and Lord Alfred Douglas cultivated *petits arabes* in the 1890s in the first Saharan oasis the railway had opened up to the European tourist. Gide had stayed at Edward's Hotel du Sahara. Biskra, once a spa, had a great past, but not much of a present. A hailstorm had smashed all its roof tiles and half its windows; plaster sifted onto his bed. Water only occasionally trickled out of the nineteenth-century English faucets. He hoped for adventure with *petites arabes*, but they now wore Western clothes, went to *lycée*, and scorned you if you didn't have a big car.

He entrained to Batna through the cool highlands, then through a terrifying gorge. Among green and purple mountains, the Hotel d'Angleterre et d'Orient had good French cooking, though the toilets were flushed by buckets of water lugged inside. Accessible were dozens of Roman temples and baths, ruins of Timgad, *ca.* the second century A.D. He spent the night there in a hotel festooned with vines and flowers, and saw the ruins in the setting and, even better, in the rising sun. It was wonderful to see the shattered stone columns rearing up to the blue sky.

He bussed through desert and mountain to Algiers. The French had left the city indelibly colonial. The huge, ship-filled bay curved in a crescent, the city rising almost in tiers in blue, green, and gold. From a balcony in the hard-to-find Che Guevara Hotel, on Che Guevara Blvd., where at times there was even water, he watched the bustling port. Despite six weeks of reading newspapers on Algiers crime, he felt safe even in the kasbah, the narrow, winding streets that wound up to a ruined hilltop fort. Among three million hemmed-in people, the few he talked to were either Francophiles who adored everything French, or Arab nationalists who abhorred everything non-Muslim.

The train to Tunis passed through Constantine, its streets honeycombing the sides of the great rock on which it perched. The trip was supposed to take 18 hours: it took 24. At noon, he repeatedly had to show documents at the border to Algerian policemen, answer why he'd stayed, and hand over all money-exchange receipts, which they closely compared to what he'd declared when he entered the country. Maybe it was a police state after all.

He reached Tunis in a chaos of baggage-carriers, touts, taxi-drivers, and peasants. At his hotel, birds in a laurel tree opposite his window woke him early. He was at least spared a plague of muezzins. He'd had disquieting dreams of his family, people he'd known, places he'd been. From his Aunt Phyllis in Lindsay, he'd heard that Mrs. Wilford, the elderly mother of his friend Susan, had entered hospital. Affectionately writing to Susan about their childhood, he noted that in more than a year he'd seen no one he knew, and gone weeks without uttering a word to anyone except waiters and hotel clerks.

Writing to Ruth Beissel, he reported that he'd killed half-a-dozen buzzing flies: he enjoyed squashing their pulpy little yellow bellies, their glossy blue-black bodies. There were millions more where they came from. If flies would just stay still for a little, he could abide them. But that constant movement and buzzing! Only the tropical mosquito, which was not content with biting you once, but must return often to make a proper meal, was more exasperating. One of his culture heroes was the Roman emperor Domitian, concerning whom Suetonius related that whenever he was not to be found, his manservant would reply: "In his chambers, pulling the wings off flies." He added, "Thank God I'm not a cow. "

Five letters from Renate Jürgensen caught up with him, one calling him "an old fool." He could accept either epithet separately, but together they were too much: he could admit that he was a fool, but seemed at least, if only to himself, still young. If he were old, she should give him the benefit of *some* acquired wisdom. To the sensitive Renate, he related that he'd seen at Carthage the pit-sanctuary where firstborn children were sacrificed to the Phoenician deities Baal and Moloch. Their throats were slit, they were cremated, and their ashes placed in urns and tombs occupying half an acre. Sheep baahed from rooftops, in yards, in apartment buildings. When sheep were slaughtered, they just stood there and let the blood pour out from their slit throats until they were too weak to stand.

He thought that Renate should welcome the teaching job she'd got. For him, once he had seen the world as meaningless, it was hard to accept a routine, or even going to work at all. If she should ever see him again, she should be prepared to find him depressed and depressing. To travel, you had to have a place to travel to and from: otherwise you "wandered lonely as a cloud" — a rain cloud.

While he was in Tunisia, there was hostage-taking in Iran and burnings of U. S. Embassies in Pakistan and Libya, though a guerilla attack on the Great Mosque at Mecca made more impact in the Muslim world. The people he discussed these events with mostly listened to him respectfully. Every night, boys passed with baskets of nosegays; young men bought flowers and stuck them, along with spare cigarettes, behind their right ears, sniffing them romantically from time to time. The plentifully available boys were likely to tell you how much they enjoyed sex, to want seconds, to whisper endearments. They were free from complexes, at least about their brand of active, male-role sex, naturally. They were, however, a little rough, though he was getting used to that.

A gang preyed on him in the coastal town, Gabès, and he lost two pairs of glasses, but that often happened to him. He adored nearby Sidi Bou Said (Gide had been here, too) a whitewashed village on a seaside cliff. The Roman and Punic ruins had shattered palaces and pillars. Always, the same small sweet alyssum and dandelion blooming out of rubble and hillocks. The same snails clinging to stone and stem. The same brown children, hopelessly proferring statuettes, oil lamps, and *real* Roman coins. Always, the guide in a rough cloak, dropping down beside him like a mountain goat from some crag. Old or young, he spoke six languages badly and was the sole support of a family of 12. Edward was the only tourist today, he'd say, shyly, slyly fondling an eager, growing bulge under a Biblical robe. Guides offered ritual visits to villas paved with still bright mosaics of fishermen in cockleshell boats and of cupids sporting on dolphins' backs; gladiators battling animals in arenas; lions pouncing on gazelles; the eagle raping Ganymede; drunken Silenus; Orpheus charming wild beasts. Finally the broken stelae; the violated sarcophagi in the necropolis; the imperial public shithouse; the stone cock and balls pointing to the brothel.

Christmas Day he was in Ghoumrassen, a cliffside Berber village under the blue of sea and sky, and the deeper blue of a mountain. At the year's turn, he was in Djerba, a subtropical Berber island, the days warm and sunny, the windless nights cold and starry, the sea mirror-calm. Most locals belonged to the Kharijite sect of Islam, but there were also Jews, who wore as a yarmulka a little red wool cap. They claimed to possess the world's oldest extant synagogue. He'd been in Tunisia three months. When he left, they didn't even look at his passport.

After 30 seasick hours to Marseille, he resolved never to take a floating parking lot of a car-ferry again. No entertainment, no bar, only a self-service restaurant that was open for about two hours—not that anyone could eat—with stratospheric prices. The mistral blew against them all the way. When they arrived at night, no immigration officials accosted him: he could have brought in half-a-dozen Tunisians and a ton of hashish. He found a small hotel near the ornate old railway station, reached by going up about 100 marble steps. *So* convenient: the French thought of everything.

In Marseille, his alter ego, Rimbaud, his leg amputated, had died. The city had always loomed large in police chronicles, but it was just a dreary provincial town, though unexplained murders, bar shoot-ups, and police raids enlivened it. While he sipped a *café-cognac* in a little Arab bar, policemen bore down on him because of his Tunisian robe. They phoned headquarters twice to see if they had anything on him. At the mouth of the old port, a castle had once headquartered the Foreign Legion. Cold and rain alternated with cold and sun, and the mistral wailed. He drank in Arab bars, saw porno movies, read newspapers. Nearby Toulon had a district of little neon bars full of bargirls, at night swarming with sailors crowned by red pompoms.

He set off for Seillans, the inland village where Henry Beissel was spending an academic sabbatical with his wife Arlette and their daughter Klara. The Provence *arrière-pays* held stony villages marked by gnarled plane trees. Seillans was sited on a hilltop, its impossibly narrow Grande Rue curving from a lower to an upper plaza where people strolled and played *boules*. In his Portuguese shepherd's cloak, he greeted his old friend at the door of a rented house only a few metres across: five floors, two rooms on each. Despite the insane house-plan and the dangerous spiral staircase, the couple seemed happy.

He had seldom seen Henry so relaxed. Though Arlette seemed less adoring toward Henry than Ruth had been, she typed for him and translated his poetry and plays into French. Ruth might accuse him of disloyalty in paying them a visit. But if one cut all one's friends because one disapproved of their conduct, he thought, one would have few friends left. Henry had said there might be a teaching post for him at Concordia University in Montréal. But what could he teach? How to become an *artiste manqué*? Or graphology?

Seillans would have been the quietest place on earth, except for Klara. Arlette seemed a bit pale and run-down, but who wouldn't be, with Klara? Too bad that a new pill couldn't render children catatonic when you wanted to talk. In his view, the stubborn wilful precocious Klara needed to be spanked at least half-a-dozen times a day by someone who ignored her tears, which she could turn off and on like a veteran actress. She should be told, he thought, what his elders had oft repeated to him as a kid: "Children are to be seen and not heard." Henry huffed and puffed, but totally indulged her. Edward would have taken a cat o'-nine-tails to her.

Of course, the poor kid had been raised as an "onliest" child in the Ontario countryside. When she had begun to collect friends, she was whisked away. She pounced upon Edward as a long-lost brother and followed him everywhere, prattling pathetically about her imaginary friends, happy to have *him* as a new playmate, like King Kong's bride or the girl who loved the Frankenstein monster. Only the loneliness of the adolescent or the very old could be compared, he thought, to that of the only child. What she needed were peers to help her avoid, by their rough democracy, the singleton's solitude and egotism.

Henry took an afternoon off to sadistically take him into the foothills to see snow. He took a day trip alone to the Fragonard factory at Grasse, where essences for perfumes were extracted by soaking violets in cold lard. Workers sprayed and anointed him so much that he came back smelling like Solomon's bride. Around Seillans, where palm, olive, citrus, almond and fig mingled with and gave over to pine, lavender grew everywhere. He crushed handfuls of it to inhale the fragrance.

One day, Arlette was making an apple tart. He diffidently asked her if she needed the peels. No, she said. He eagerly dumped half a pound of salt on and devoured them. He endeavoured to put his stern parenting theories into practice by offering to babysit Klara while her parents went off for a dinner to celebrate the anniversary of their first meeting. They returned from their romantic evening to find Klara hysterical. In the interim she had accidentally smashed a lightbulb, and Edward had threatened to call the police. Her doting father was outraged at him. As an aftermath, she began to hemorrhage from the mouth: it turned out to be grape juice.

He ventured to Cannes, whose curving bay, coastal islands, backdrop mountains, and a long, palm-lined street reminded him of Rio. But the Côte d'Azur was just a pallid imitation of it, or of any Brazilian town with a beach. Even the beaches were artificial, made of trucked-in sand. But he ended up staying twice as long as he intended because he met a French beach-boy who wanted them to go to Venice: to bankrupt him, he supposed. The boy had always dreamed of going there. Though they slept in cheap rooming houses, Marc was costly, though he kindly shaved him when his hand shook. All right, Edward said, we'll go to Venice. They made a date to meet the following Tuesday at the train station.

Cannes had put Edward in bad shape, his hosts noted. As for Edward, he feared that he might have overstayed his welcome. One morning he heard quiet breathing as he crept downstairs in the darkness. When Henry and Arlette got up, they found him absent. They thought he'd gone out to buy a newspaper.

He didn't meet Marc. In Nîmes, one of his Provence halts, he noticed that through buses went to Barcelona. It was a city in his private mythology, the homosexual and intellectual capital of Spain. Jean Genet had thieved and sold his body there; writers he admired like Gabriel García Marquez and Mario Vargas Llosa lived there in exile. He boarded a bus. En route, he met an Andalusian Gypsy (vide Lorca), who flirted with him. Arriving, he meant to let Henry and Arlette know where he was. Instead, he wandered the Barrio Chino and drank muscatel in a bodega with soot-blackened walls.

From Barcelona—pushing, diverse, enormous—he took in the beach resorts of Sitges and Lloret del Mar, and Montserrat, which might have been Wagner's inspiration for *Parsifal*. He gazed at Antonio Gaudí's Sagrada Família with its crested, spiked towers, and façade like melting candles: maybe in a couple of centuries it would be completed. One night, he attended a mass conducted in Catalán. He could understand it perfectly, but couldn't say a word in it, even though he bought a marvellous phrasebook called *Catalán in Two Weeks*, which translated "Oh, I have stepped on a rusty nail" and "I have not had my period for three months now. What shall I do?" Five years earlier, Catalán had been forbidden; now it was as conspicuous as Gaudí's tilted angles and dripping façades.

He distrusted the bright playful colours in the Joan Miró museum: all art had to be representational for him. By night, the Barrio Chino of bars and clubs was a sinister labyrinth of streets and impasses. The Barrio was off the surging Ramblas, the wide, tree-lined pedestrian walk between two narrow lanes of motor traffic. Along it, you could buy newspapers, books, blatant pornography, flowers, and cage birds. Across the Ramblas, the Gothic Quarter was full of sing-along places and louche bars. The nearer you descended to the port the more dangerous the streets became, and the cheaper the prostitutes and pensions.

Felipe, an unemployed fellow who wrote verse about lonely vagabonds, Bohemians, and broken hearts, took him to Badalona across the river. Hustlers and druggies fed Edward hash and kif. But he managed to elude their larcenies, usually by feigning drunkenness. The hash must have been drug-laced, or maybe his body was stockpiling it. He kept getting higher and higher, till he needed to start drinking in the morning to bring himself down.

With France expelling people and tightening up entry requirements, North Africans had discovered Spain. Anyone penniless could enter as a "tourist" and stay forever. With the new freedom, the once-feared Guardia Civil arrested nobody. He encountered someone he'd met in Marrakech, who introduced him to "safe" Arabs for sexual purposes, and looked after him when he got drunk. The man was in love with Elizabeth, a lesbian prostitute. Looking as if she could be Edward's sister, she came from Perpignan, and in love with Alma, a withered, toothless Uruguyan whore who always gave Edward her flaccid cheeks to kiss. Mohammed couldn't understand why Elizabeth didn't want to go to bed with him, and it took Edward weeks to explain what a lesbian was. As Edward understood it, the situation was thus: his Marrakech friend slept with him for money, but he loved Elizabeth, who loved Alma, who loved Edward because he knew Uruguay, and Edward loved Abdelkader from Algeria.

With Abdelkader, he trysted in windowless rooms, the best sex, he thought, he'd ever had in a life of one-night stands and pickups. When Edward required his body, he groaned, turned from sleep, and kissed him. Abdelkader and Mohammed introduced him to the jobless and homeless, like a handsome genteel Algerian boy, Abdelwahad. He paid for everyone, and they "borrowed" from him. Yet they didn't victimize him. He thought it was simply redistribution of income, though he realized that if he kept this up he'd have no income left to redistribute.

High from morning to night, he didn't bother to shave, change clothes, or bathe. He let his hair grow long, roamed the Barrio Chino in his shepherd's cloak like a demented monk, drawing stares from everyone except the Arabs, who by now all knew him. He decided it was time to pull out. On Sunday, in a bar where he and his friends met, he said he was going to a barber, which he did. But he didn't return. Intending to take the afternoon train, he made a last round of the Barrio Chino, where he encountered Abdelwahad, who persuaded him to share his bed. In some respects it was worth it.

Next day, he was on a slow afternoon train that changed over in Port-Bou. At the border, he was nervous, sweating, and hung over. The customs guards decided he must be a drug trafficker. They sifted through his baggage, stripped him, and probed him anally. He told the fools this was useless. They discovered two cancelled passports, which came in handy if he lost his current one. Not a smuggler: an international spy! After they compared the passports, and concluded that they all referred to him, they noticed that his current passport had also expired. It hadn't: he'd got it in March 1978 to replace one he'd lost the previous year. Canada gave it to him for six months, then extended it to 1983. But they didn't change the expiry date on page 2, but wrote it in on the extension, page 8. On page 4, where it was mentioned that the passport was valid only until September 1978, they'd stamped "Annulé," leading the French to think the passport as a whole had been cancelled. So the police wrote "Annulé" on his entry stamp to France as well. By turns enraged and distraught, he pointed out that on page 8 the passport had been extended. After endless discussion, the police abdicated. They gave him a new entry stamp: *ils ont annulé l'annulation.*

He rushed for the Marseille train, which pulled out just before he could catch it, and had to wait till midnight for another. Reaching Marseille, he found heaped mail waiting at the Canadian consulate, including hundreds of pages of Brazilian Portuguese and Spanish Mexican prose from Winston Leyland for reading, comment, and possible translation. He related his passport troubles to the consul, who supplied a letter stating that his passport had *not* been cancelled, and peppered his passport with little notices reading "*Voir page 8* See Page 8," and "*Ce passeport n'est pas annulé.*"

When he arrived at Seillans, the pussy willows and yellow shamrocks were out, mimosa bursting into bloom. But he did not see the Beissels, who had departed for Munich the night before. He got the house key left at the *épicerie* and picked up the typewriter and crammed bag he'd left behind.

In a Draguignan pension, he rinsed his incomparably dirty trousers and hung them to dry over the radiator, so that his room was as humid as Trinidad. He wrote to Ian Young on stationery from the Westminster Hotel, 240 Jarvis St, Toronto, "Home of the Fabulous Town and Country Buffet," selected from a store of varied stationery housed in his typewriter case. He noted that he was "trying to create a persona or series of personae," admittedly closely related to his own life, "the poet as an aging gay wandering Jew, the semi-closeted gay who cannot communicate or avoids communication; the Canadian as quintessential avoidance of experience and communication." He was trying to deal "with what growing old means for gay and for people in general, what it's like to be a Canadian, a permanent exile, an outsider, using the material of his own life. His poetry was "*not* an autobiography, more a biography, a novel or series of short stories...."

In Nice, bitterly cold in mid-March, he spent a weekend strolling the promenade fronting the black-pebble beach. Visiting museums filled the void of afternoons. The museum of malacology housed more than 15,000 types of seashells. The study of molluscs was like his childhood butterfly collecting. People like him, he thought, used classification and taxonomy as an excuse for indulging their love of beauty and variety.

Writing Ruth Beissel, he said that in his pattern of alternating opposites and polarities (north-south, city-country, desert-jungle) he sought to prevent *cafard*, that boredom that lay at the bottom of all experience, all relationships. Debriefing her about his Seillans visit ("That child, my dear Ruth, is your revenge"), he observed that she and Henry had wisely forestalled the perils of only-child isolation by adopting Myrna as Angelica's sister.

Ruth had been in Europe earlier that year, and they'd discussed meeting. He now had to explain why they hadn't. She should remember that he'd said, "I promise nothing." When he'd arrived in Seillans, he learned that Ruth was in Berlin. He'd tried to phone her, but learned that she'd flown to Montréal the night before he'd arrived. Anyhow, they hadn't met. "Anyhow" was his favourite word; it implied his attitude toward life: a shrug of the shoulders. Or maybe the word was *Maktub*: "It is written." That was the great thing about Islam. You need blame yourself for nothing, so long as you followed its precepts. Everything else was in God's hands. This reminded him of how he missed his aunt the nun, who was always praying for him. Even if he didn't believe in *her* god, the thought that someone *did* believe in the efficacy of prayer gave him strength.

Following the coast, he stopped in the sliver of Monaco. In the drugstore, slot machines whirred non-stop. He saw a ballet-like aquarium of tropical fish squired by gruesome lamprey and moray eels, and those other aquariums, the sumptuous lobbies of luxury hotels. Along the Riviera coastline to Genoa, resorts, sea, and mountain were a sun-sparkling succession. The white masses of the Alps neared, snowstorms swirling around their crests. Pisa was a university city swarming with merry students. With trepidation, he climbed the famous tower: though he really didn't care what happened to him, he didn't want to fall off the leaning tower of Pisa. He went on to Florence, which made him wonder whether the Médicis were governing, a gang of kings, queens, popes, and hangers-on, actors in a great drama of family, culture, and city-state. The lira was tumbling, which was good, as was the ice cream. Who needed to eat anything else?

By Easter Sunday he was in Rome, having come from Siena. He reported to Randy that in a sleazy bar near Roma Termini station he'd been mugged by Arabs, lost his birth certificate, and incurred a broken nose but not broken glasses: a variation on Tunisia, where boys had robbed him and stole his glasses but left his body intact. Rome was "a sophisticated horror, half supermetropole, half-convent." The Eternal City rubbed his nerves raw with its million tourists and omnipresent images of John Paul II, who he thought "a rancid reactionary demagogue." Mad traffic, pollution-raddled monuments, seedy accommodations that boasted cold water and cold rooms. After two weeks he left "the Eternal Wreck."

Once a fever port, Naples had funiculars and fumaroles, tumbledown mansions, outdoor markets, churches with mummified saints. Giant rats and cockroaches swarmed his hotel room at night to caress him, he wrote, "with a touch lighter than a lover's," He visited the Pompeii and Herculaneum ruins and climbed Vesuvius, dispatching sprightly postcards. One to me showed a statue of "Drunken Hercules" from Herculaneum, toying with his penis. Out in the bay, Capri was all rocky heights and blooming flowers. He visited the villa of Jacques Adelswerd-Fersen, a French Oscar Wilde, a minor poet who, involved in a scandal, retired to live there until his suicide in 1924. The villa had fake Greek finery and gilt falling into ruin, but above the entrance, the legend *Amori et Dolori Sanctum*: "Sacred to Love and Sorrow."

In chilly rain, he took the boat to the mainland, a train across the peninsula to Brindisi, and a ferry to Corfu. The boat was jammed with scruffy backpackers who, though they came from everywhere, looked, talked, thought, dressed, and acted identically. Corfu seemed to him curiously un-Greek, with Venetian and French architecture, and Sunday cricket; Prince Philip had come from there. About 3,000 British sailors on the scene did not improve his mood. Long, lush, mountainous Corfu had everything to please, but he was drinking hard, and was not to be pleased.

But Ioannina in Epirus, a cruise through the Ionian isles, and hitchhiking around the Peloponnesus restored him. All the flowers of the Greek spring rose from the rain-sponged ground. In the Mani peninsula, the asphodel with its pale spikes.

Elsewhere, the flowering Judas, a round-leafed tree whose small red pea-like flowers grew from the trunk and branches. The wild poppy, and the scarlet anemone or windflower, eight tongues of fire around a dark eye. Oleanders grew like weeds in meadows and dry riverbeds, lining the streets of the small whitewashed towns with clusters of cream-coloured or rosy blooms. With its fragrance, paleness, and briefness, the wisteria was the root of wistfulness. The acacia's lobed leaves, massed small white flowers like pea-blossoms: Canada's locust tree. Scentless white blossoms, tumbling in gutters, wind-shaped like snowdrifts, blowing unseen away like yesterday's snow and yesterday's country.

Greek ruins were very ruined. All that remained of Megalópolis, once a great city, were tiers of the theatre that had echoed to Euripides's words. All that it echoed now was the caw of crows. In the plaza of Andrítsena, he watched the strolling boys circle arm in arm, eyeing girls who waited and watched, watched themselves by old women in black. The village elders—grey-moustached, black-capped, fondling worry beads—sipped ouzo, played dominoes, drank coffee. In the warmth, leaves were growing; the fingers of grape and mulberry, the hands of the fig groped larger every day; even the scaly plane trees wore small green hearts.

The boys were green and growing, too: they circled around and around, wrestled one another, challenged and boasted and laughed, voices breaking, resembling no Greek statue ever sculpted and yet resembling all. They ogled and circled him, but he did not know the language yet. He had never felt so verbally frustrated: he could satisfy the basic needs—hotel, bus, food, drink—except the really important one. Then Athens. It was warm, the city was small enough to easily get around, the monuments superb, the people often kind. The boys were approachable. Who knew? Maybe this might be *the* place.

18

A PATCH OF ICE

May 1980-February 1981

*I shook your hand, wished you well, watched you leave, alone
like all the homeless wanderers I've known.*

~ José

Athens was his base camp. He dined on retsina and tripe
soup at three a.m. in the market bar, as workers— part-
Slav, part-Turk, part-Arab, maybe even part-Greek—
lugged in slimy squid, bleeding slabs of lamb, and glowing
tangerines. He tramped odorous sage on the hills of Aegina, the
nearest island. Then he chanced upon Latin Americans trying to
get work in Piraeus, Athens's port. He'd take the subway there
to meet new rash, drunk, always impecunious friends in the
sailor bars. With them, he felt happy, though, he wrote Renate
Jürgensen, "Happiness is like orgasm, which is said to occupy a
full 2 hours in the life of a man." One job seeker was the stocky
30-year-old José, from San Pedro Sula, Honduras, who'd worked
in a bank until he tired of being a paper-pusher. Now he was in
Piraeus. They became friends.

With sound reasons to return, he set off for the Cyclades.
It was hot dry summer, the islands buffeted by wind. From
Mykonos, he sent a postcard to Randy, depicting the "utterly

divine temple of Dionysus, on the neighbouring island of Deles (where that luscious butch stud Apollo was born) and its just too delicious phalli." For the first time, he could stroll a long beach naked, except for the civilized touch of shoes and socks. However, straights were invading paradise: crass charter tourists with box lunches, appalling accents, and narrow minds. Kids crowded in, lugging backpacks, stumbling along like pack animals. They rushed on and off every island boat, slept on every beach and street, filled every bar and café, till he thought of stealing around at night to slice off their backpack straps. They were a new generation, he thought, of massified, standard-issue zombies, wearing the clothes and long hair of 60s hippies, but without their convictions.

Big, green Naxos, where he spent Bastille Day, was a mountainous hinterland of villages, miles of beach, and a capital with alleys, byways, and dazzling white houses. Santorini was what remained of a volcano's rim but with brightly striated cliffs, villages atop them. Hydra was international, pretty, and arid. Crete was huge, a country, and he spent nearly two weeks crisscrossing it. Swimming much, he wrote Randy that under the sun he'd "turned black *all over.*"

He also ventured into the central mainland, and to northern Greece. By September, he was in Ioannnina in Epirus, Greek Macedonia, by a deep blue lake among dark hills near the Albanian border. He had his photograph taken inside a cave, standing in bell-bottoms and a light short-sleeved shirt with his hands behind his back, like someone about to be shot among the stalagmites. He sent Henry Beissel a postcard of Lord Byron touching down at Missolonghi, and to Ruth an equally hideous one of the beautiful Euphrosyme and her 16 innocent companions in the process of being drowned in the lake "under the orders of the depraved potentate Ali Pasha (she wdn't go to bed with him, tho' she was his eldest son's mistress: the 16 companions seem to have been drowned from spite & the pangs of unrequited love." In Salonika, a city of half a million, Alexander the Great's hometown, he saw that the boys were much taller and handsomer than further south.

He'd once thought travel was a time machine, allowing you to pack many years into one; now he thought that it was paid for in solitude and disappointment, which could make you old fast. Alcohol, he thought, didn't age him: it did damage his nerves. Moreover, he was having more frequent coma-like blackouts. More and more, he found himself waking up in hospitals or first-aid stations with contusions and injuries, unaware of how they'd happened. When he'd given up drinking that summer, the depressions and bilious hangovers vanished, he was even able to sleep well. He was not, he proved to himself, an alcoholic, but a "problem drinker." Ninety per cent of the time he could drink socially or not drink at all, the other 10 per cent he binged. Sobriety was good, except that he got bored.

He'd go on, he thought, until he self-destructed, or until his money ran out. As it would: what seemed like a lot in 1971 seemed much less in 1980, especially when it had been badly managed. From 1975, the bonds his trust company had committed him yielded little, and he'd been paying 25 per cent in non-resident tax to the Canadian government, while the devalued currency was only worth three-quarters of what it had been. He was now Winston Leyland's translation workhorse for Gay Sunshine Press, beset by manuscripts for appraisal or translation. So long as he worked hard he was able to stay off booze.

He was thinking of eastward travel but there'd been a military coup in Turkey, and Iran and Iraq were trying to annihilate each other. On impulse, he chose Yugoslavia, taking a train to Macedonia and its capital, Skopje, practically destroyed by a 1963 earthquake and rebuilt in *Scheisshaus* style. He liked Yugoslavia at once, though, with its two alphabets and five hopscotch languages, he never knew what was, or was about to be, spoken. *Ćevapčici*, meatballs, were the only thing he could recognize on a menu.

He entered the Albanian "autonomous district" of Kosovo to visit the old cities of Priština, Prizren, and Peć. Men dressed in fezes, skullcaps, and turbans, women in a weird mixture of Turkish trousers, veils and ankle-length black dresses, alternating with bright skirts, embroidered blouses, and headdresses. After a brief detour to Bulgaria, he took in Montenegro, whose terrain showed why it was called "Black Mountain." From Cetinje, its tiny inland capital, he traced the

Adriatic from Kōtor northward: the coast had the beauty and subtropical climate of the Côte d'Azur, without the prices or tourism. Massive-walled Dubrovnik, which had never been Turkish, but an independent maritime republic under the sway of Venice, was the right size to explore the sensibly laid out streets.

He ferried to Italy. From Loreto, with its Holy House (where Christ lived in as a child, transported by angels from Nazareth to Loreto when infidels took over Palestine.... sure, sure) he found his way to San Marino, a republic measuring all of 63 square kilometres, with some 25,000 inhabitants on a vertiginous mountaintop covered with castles that you approached up and up and up. No wonder that it had always been independent: no one in his right mind could or would invade it. At the peak, he watched the world's oldest, smallest republic fall away in rings and ridges.

He saw Ravenna's Byzantine mosaics, Bologna's marble tomb of St. Dominic, Padua's frescoes. But cultural tourism wearied him. Italians were the antithesis of the ancient Roman virtues. Nor was Italy peopled with figures from Shakespeare, though he could talk to them, eavesdrop on their conversations, engage in the small linguistic investigations that were the stuff of life for him. Venice arranged for him a south wind, a full moon, high tides, and rain funnelling the highest waters of the year. He left the railroad station to find rowboats in the streets; the owners of hotels, cafés, and shops stood in doorways, hip-deep in water; boys took tourists around in vegetable carts. It took him three hours to find a "dry" route to St. Mark's, where the plaza was deep in water. He thoroughly enjoyed the flood.

Venice was one place that lived up to its billing: a museum-city of a museum-country. Though he abhorred the gold mosaics of St. Mark's — he'd paint them all black, and see how many tourists would come to admire them! — he trod interlaced alleys, the Bridge of Sighs, the prisons of the Doges' Palace, the islands of the lagoon. He could have spent a lifetime here, and it would pass like a week. It was a stage set, and the most exquisite of cities, even with the polluting smokestacks from Mestre across the bay. Yet he found himself bored, irritable, and hermetic. Since he was near Vienna, he thought that he "should"—always these Germanic moral imperatives—take it in. For the first time, his knowledge of German proved useful. But Vienna chilled him from the start: a scurrying, bourgeois city of restaurants, cafés, and endless castles, museums, and art galleries. The frosty city was dead, though to say so would have been impolite, and everyone here was *so* polite.

Vienna, he wrote Randy, had palaces, palaces, palaces. Randy, he said ironically, would enjoy going with him to tearooms and coffee houses while old ladies and gentlemen whiled their days away reading free newspapers in a dozen languages. He toured the Hofburg, Schönbrunn, the Belvedere, and their innumerable, interminable annexes. He strolled the woods, saw the Danube and the Prater park, drank the new wine of the Grinzing. Nothing pleased him. Besides waiters, the only people who smiled at him were Turkish boys who shivered as they sold hot chestnuts.

Prague beckoned, since times were interesting in the Soviet bloc, unrest stirring in Poland. Vienna had chilled him; Prague froze him. At the start of November, the temperature dived. The country, city, and people immobilized him in an atmosphere of hopeless northern greyness. The Czechs understood German, but disliked it. Then again, Czechs seemed to dislike everything and everybody. He felt himself spied upon in an atmospheric prison, symbolized by a monstrous castle that dwarfed everything else from any vista, with churches and sub-castles tucked inside, squiggling medieval alleys leading everywhere and nowhere. The baroque churches, open but empty, dust covering the gilt; the crazy town-hall clock with its procession of saints' statues and three different timepieces; the Jewish cemetery with its tottering tombstones. Pro-Russian propaganda abounded in preparation for November 7: Solidarity Day.

He disliked Prague as much as one could dislike a city. The people seemed crushed and dismal: no wonder they drank so heavily. Life was so boring, service so bad, so many shortages of everything, so many queues, so much red tape. The hotels were full, the shops were empty, restaurants had depleted menus: he lived practically on dumplings. Thanks to the black market, he had plenty of money, but there was nothing to buy.

He vainly searched for a pair of gloves, and finally found a pair, abandoned on a café table. Was it worth coming so far to see a gross of old statues, some gorgeous baroque churches, and that rococo doll called the Infant of Prague?

With the smallness, meanness, closeness of everything was the overhanging, overpowering Castle, which taught you better than any seminar why Franz Kafka wrote as he had. What could he do? Drink. In a tavern late one afternoon, he got into a row with Palestinian students: there were hundreds of them in Prague. He told them that they and the Jews must live together, and Jerusalem must become an international city. They waited for him outside and karate-chopped him. He toppled across a patch of ice, breaking two ribs.

He didn't feel like going to the police. He did seek medical help, which Czechoslovakia offered free. The doctors were gloomy — one had a bandaged head, so Edward supposed he had reason to be — and predicted a three-month convalescence. They were amazed that he could walk and wanted him to go "home to Canada — where you have a family and friends and more comfort." Ha! They spoke of complications, and told him, "You are going to suffer much pain whatever medicine we give you. You must be like a soldier..." What a people! How could that optimist of Brazil, Juscelino Kubitschek, have had Czech forbears?

The pain at first was delirious; the nights, torture. He could only sleep with six pillows under him. All he could do was creep from his hotel and drink to kill the agony. After two weeks, he could take the train to Budapest. There, the weather turned almost warm. Rooms and food were cheap. The people were more chic, livelier, the city more animated, there were more goods for sale. In one big hotel, he could even buy subversive publications like *Time* and the *International Herald Tribune*. He thought he was staying in Pest, not Buda, but it was confusing the way the Danube twisted and cut around. He looked off from a mountain that could as easily be Montréal's, and saw the pseudo-Gothic parliament buildings like the ones in the Canadian capital, "Nottawa." The Hapsburgs had endowed this part of their polyglot empire with museums but, after Italy, even thinking about art depressed him. He had been in Europe nearly a year now. Among Latin Americans and Arabs, you could meet more people in one day, and more intimately, and profoundly, than in a year here. Too many churches, sculptures, and paintings: even two world wars hadn't appreciably reduced the charnel weight of the past.

Xenophobic, slightly sinister, the Hungarians insisted on speaking only their own language instead of one of the handful that he had. He stared at menus, realizing he could only understand *boeuf tartare*. He remembered the revolt of 1956 when, that winter, 50,000 of them came to Canada: how silly his *crise de nerfs* then seemed now. When not trying to heal himself in thermal baths, he wrote postcards, using a pen as lousy as the restaurant and hotel service. It was enough to convert him to the glories of free enterprise.

One night he got drunk in a café, and woke up in a hospital. He'd blacked out and lost his glasses, rendering him nearly blind. Meanwhile, he must have re-broken a rib, because the pain grew more intense. The optometrists told him that it would take two weeks to get new glasses, so he set off for Belgrade. In the Yugoslav capital, people were helpful to a blind semi-cripple who could hardly even carry his own baggage or see where he was going. With the help of the Canadian Embassy and the tourist bureau, he got new glasses in a couple of days.

Venturing out from his icy boarding house, he visited the War Museum, which outlined the city's history from Roman times—everybody seemed to have passed through Belgrade, beginning with the tribes from the East that poured into what was now Yugoslavia. History was recorded insanity, he thought, and the best thing you could do with it was ignore it. All the deportations and uprootings of this century, which people thought were something new, had been going on since the dawn of time.

He began his way back to Athens, pausing in Sarajevo. He wrote Randy that he was glad to be among mosques, minarets, muezzins, and Islamic law, which suited him, since he had become a celibate teetotaler: "such fun, it *saves you oodles of money*, it solves all yr. social & communicational problems... if the flesh is a bit weak sometimes, there's always dear loyal old Manuel Palma, most faithful of girlfriends to give one relief."

In Sarajevo, everything, from coffee houses to the old market, took Muslim form: a provincial Austrian administrative city had been built around a core of medersas, mosques, hammams, and bazaars. A unique city, it was the most curious blend of East and West possible, it had the largest mosque in Europe — if this *was* Europe.

After a slow journey, made slower by a train strike, he arrived in Athens, glad to be alive and in one slightly reassembled piece. He wondered why he had ever left. Admittedly, Athens was having troubles. A two-week strike cut telephone service connections in December, and an endless series of riots commenced. The taxis, mails, trains, shops, high schools — all had been or were on strike. The inflation rate was 25 per cent. The two biggest largest department stores were firebombed. It was an original way to celebrate Christmas. It reminded him of Brazil in 1968. *Viva la muerte! Viva la anarquía!"*

Dealing with neglected correspondence, he wrote Renate that suffering from unrequited love was a horrible thing: "next to having a hangover, I guess." The Weavers used to sing:

And it's hard, and it's hard, and it's hard, good Lord,
To love one who never will be true,
And it's hard, and it's hard, ain't it, good Lord,
To love one who never will love you?

He regretted, he wrote, that he had not at least offered her his body, though it was "nothing much, and I'm a lousy, egotistical lover, who thinks only of his own pleasure." These days he didn't want his friends, "even people like Ruth, who has been almost a mother to me, and Randy, who I love like a brother (because we are so different, but share the same sense of humour; anything sexual between us is 20 years in the past) to witness my degradation, my falling-apart." Fearing greyness more than baldness, he'd dyed his hair with Miss Clairol Raven Black.

On December 12, the Feast of Saint Spyridon, patron of Greece, and of the Virgin of Guadalupe, patroness of Mexico, he wrote to Ruth. She had reported that Michel, his former companion in Montréal, was faring well, though he didn't believe a word of it. Tempering hurtfully laudatory comments he'd made about Henry's new ménage, he said that there'd been something special, exciting, "right," in the couple Ruth and Henry had made. Apart, both of them seemed incomplete. As for the marriage break-up, he blamed Henry. Though he liked him just as well as before—perhaps more, knowing him fallible—he could not take him seriously. Before, he had trusted him, feeling, "Well, Henry Beissel, even if he exaggerates, even if he blusters, even if he pontificates, will have, will adopt, the morally correct attitude in this—whatever it might be—and in any other case." Now, he didn't feel that.

He also wrote Randy. Knowing that it would annoy him, he took issue with his friend's atheism. "I'm a Catholic, and believe man is a fallen, weak, wretched, evil creature, and our society and mankind are both doomed from the start. Only God could provide an illumination and meaning in such a theology, and unfortunately he is not present in mine, or does not reveal himself very easily." He'd never considered himself a "lapsed" Catholic, but simply a non-believing, non-practising one. He was socially and psychologically a Catholic and could never be anything else.

He noted that he'd never lived in the gay subculture, and didn't find gay people more interesting than straights. Or less interesting. He'd seen the movie *Cruising*, and it had not seemed to be unfair or unsympathetic to gays; leather bars *were* like that and, though their atmosphere stimulated him, he agreed with Randy that they were limiting and limited places, though he had nothing against sadomasochism as such, only this stylized, rigidified, stereotyped form. People "should be out making interpersonal contacts," he said, not indulging in "bizarre metalinguistic codes..." His own dress code drew puzzled stares from the Athenians when he went about in his Franciscan-brown cloak.

Randy had better visit soon, because refreshingly relaxed Greece would vanish when, in a couple of weeks, it joined the "devilish" EEC, the European Economic Community. Already, bars and taverns closed early, which used to remain crowded all night, ostensibly to conserve energy but really to train an undisciplined, nocturnal people to the bit-and-bridle of industrial life. Though Greeks were slow, sloppy, and slovenly, he liked them. They were kindhearted and, despite so much tourism, scrupulously honest: he could leave his belongings anywhere, for any length of time. This didn't mean that they weren't ready to exploit the tourist, or overcharge. It meant that they did not steal. He loved their bearded, black-robed priests; every time he saw one he wanted to confess all his sins to him.

Taking breaks from correspondence, he'd go out. Walks in the cold made him welcome his warm room, and his belongings gave the illusion of order and permanence, even if the bars on the window reminded him of jail. He amused himself by sending my wife Alison a postcard of a prancing, massively erectile Selenus, telling her that it represented her "revered husband, so proudly and prominently displaying his noblest attribute."

One night, as he was leaving his Latin American bar in Piraeus, someone hit him on the head with a blunt object. Badly hurting, he went to a hospital emergency, blood staining his neo-black hair. He'd been robbed of $300, which he shouldn't have carried, but you couldn't always be wise. He vowed never to drink again, or at least not for a couple of months. At this point, Randy advised him that he was coming to Athens. He rushed to check connections and consult maps.

Despite recent mishaps, he'd been feeling more human. One night in a porno theatre, he witnessed 30 seminal outpourings: he counted. He enjoyed straight pornography probably more than gay: it was merely male orgasm and cocks he enjoyed. Male orgasm was a kind of sacrament. Recently, he'd been bedding a 20-year-old soldier, honest and affectionate, but with a small penis. However, he was not a size queen; he found that most cocks swelled up quite satisfactorily. Greeks were touchingly proud of their equipment, and grateful when you praised it. On the way back from a late-night hotel tryst, he passed a guy who looked at him, and he looked back to see if he had looked back to see, and the moon was full and the Acropolis white in the moonlight and its grass was their bed.

On Christmas Eve he was in Skyros in the Northern Sporades, named, he wrote me, after Sporos, whom Nero had castrated, and then married: "poor guy — no more spores from Sporus." The translations he was doing kept his mind limber.

One of them was of *Adonis García: A Picturesque Novel*, the adventures of a Mexico City hustler, by a young writer, Luis Zapata. Zapata disdained capitals and spurned commas, semicolons, or periods in favour of spatial punctuation, so his tab key got a strenuous workout, as did his typewriter ribbons fading to grey. He was also toying with another poetry collection, he wrote Randy, "which of course will be a stunning popular success, like its predecessors *The Hair That Grows On Ears*, *The Harlish Goop*, and *Masturbating Statue*."

Skyros in winter had all the charms of Saint-Pierre and Miquelon: sleet, rain, wind, cold, and rock. On a sunny day, he walked seven hours through pinewoods. Since the restaurants weren't open at noon, he could only have one meal a day, a choice between chicken at the chicken place, or souvlaki at the souvlaki place. Resisting temptation, all he drank was sage tea. Even if he was in the up phase of his manic-depressive curve, Christmas was not particularly cheering. He'd come here to avoid everything connected with it.

He was travelling in the Peloponnesus when a freak snowstorm hit. It was startling to see the shining orange and tangerine groves deep in snow, though tragic for the farmers, the split, fallen olive trees, and the high mountains around Sparta growing white. Meanwhile, he heaped suggestions on Randy for their tour of Greece, now expanded to include Turkey and Egypt. He couldn't wait for him to arrive.

19

THE DONKEYS OF CAIRO

February-August 1981

You set it on a shelf
until some Judgment Day.
The gift you would not take
was all I had to give.

~ The Gift

When Randy arrived in Athens, Edward was foiled in his hopes to show off Greece and the Greeks. In the rain and cold, Randy wanted to quickly move on to Turkey.

Edward's reading of regional history had made him a Greek partisan. Nor did the Turkish present turn out to be inviting. After the long bus ride to Istanbul, they were let out on a blacked-out hillside: he expected Dracula to rise from one of the tombstones adorned with sculpted fezes and turbans. Eventually, they found a crummy hotel. Nightlife in drizzly, smoggy Istanbul was dim; the sombre Turks wore dark secondhand clothes; practically bankrupt, the country even imported Turkish coffee. Turkish tourism was reeling from the bad publicity generated by *Midnight Express*, a movie about brutality inside the country's prisons. An energy crisis made for frequent blackouts, and curfews lasted midnight to dawn. The unpaved streets were muddy; a chilly wind blew off the

Bosphorus, and their room was scarcely warmer. They swam in the tiled subaqueous atmosphere of the Blue Mosque and, to Randy's delight, and his disgust, paced the vast columned reception rooms of the Dolmabahçe Palace, the sultans' all-marble monument to bad taste, where the clocks were stopped at 9:05 a.m., the moment Kemal Atatürk had died in 1938. By this time Edward was fantasizing that the palace's 4.5-ton crystal chandelier might providentially drop on his friend's head.

Under less strained circumstances, Randy josh him out of his black moods. But Randy got on his nerves with incessant comments on his drinking, eating, weight, salting of his food, clothing, dark glasses, hair style or colour, his battered luggage. Edward refused advice on what to do with his life or money, and ignored chatter about America. He wearied of jibes about "the heir," an allusion to his private income. Taking instant dislikes, making split-second decisions, Randy dragged him into unwilling conversations with everybody. They were each other's punching bags, Randy's speedbag to Edward's heavy bag. Randy thrived on debate and polemic, but Edward wondered why every matter, from their taste in sexual partners to what he did with his money to the politics of Africa to his choice of razors have to be thrashed out. Naturally, his own habits, tics, and preoccupations also irritated Randy. If Randy envied his private income, Edward envied his work ethic and sense of purpose. He wished he had them. They were each what the other could not be.

They followed the Aegean coast to Marmaris, a little fishing port in the extreme southwest, set in a deep fjord at the angle where the Aegean met the Mediterranean. Rhodes was two hours distant by boat, but relations between Greece and Turkey were as bad as ever. Yet Greeks and Turks ate much the same food, drank the same drinks, made the same music, danced the same dances, frequented the same kind of cafés.

Crossing the Taurus Range, *Guide Bleu* in hand, they went to snowbound mountain villages. In one, they saw women offering socks and dolls for sale as the snow began to fall. The only place with warmth and light was a café and women weren't allowed in it. Thinking the saleswomen should display their wares in comfort, they took them through a snowstorm to a café and banged on the door. The men grudgingly admitted them. Striking a blow for the Women's Movement was a rare Turkish moment when they worked in concert.

In Cappadocia, they saw churches hewn out of cliffs and crags, and cone-shaped pinnacles, castles, and needles of tufa, compressed volcanic ash, perforating the soft rock. In Anatolia, Randy took pictures and recorded home movies, though saw little point in Edward's making a pilgrimage to visit the column of Julian the Apostate. Anatolia was cold. What was it they'd heard an Englishwoman say to her children in that Lisbon restaurant? "The Anateowlian plateow is vedy keowld in wintah!'"

They flew to Egypt. Cairo's size, noise, and congestion did not improve their relations. Nor did the weather help. On the second day descended the dust storm called the *khámsin*, "50," because it was supposed to last 50 days. It was like hot snow: you couldn't see anything, and it got in your eyes, your food, your hair. Quarrelling, they separated for a day. Both were almost ready to leave Egypt. Amid the heat and chaos, Randy met a university student named Ali. A romance ensued, and soon Randy thought of bringing him to New York that summer.

The train up the Nile Valley took them past a sameness of palm groves, fields, and irrigation channels in the habitable four per cent of Egypt. The *pièce de resistance* at dirty Luxor was the temple in the town's centre. Across the river was the Valley of the Tombs of the Kings and the funerary temple of Queen Hatchepsout, the usurper-queen who insisted that images of her should be male. In villages, boys had been unimpressed by Randy's poppers because tobacco smoked in a waterpipe gave a stronger rush: Edward would stagger down the street after smoking one. Randy and the available boys took mutual advantage of each other while Edward grew drunk and abusive. Why? The heat and oppression of seeing too many ruins? Because Randy was always with his boys and he had no one. Because of apprehensions for him. Because there was a bottle in his room.

At Aswan, the rising water of the Russian-built dams had altered the climate, increasing humidity, insects, and diseases. Below the dam, the Nile no longer brought its precious freight of fertilizing silt; the Mediterranean was eating away the siltless Delta. The driver of the collective taxi that took them back from the Red Sea coast to Cairo not only smoked hashish but drove at speeds more than 100 miles an hour. This pleased Edward but terrified Randy. The driver also tried to hit birds with the car. When he succeeded, he'd stop, get out of the car, and bite the bird's head off and keep it, presumably for dinner.

Back in Cairo, they gave each other parting gifts. From Randy, a big towel; from Edward, an alabaster egg; a net bag that he'd bought in Guatemala; and a tent-like bedspread. When he said farewell at Cairo airport, he felt so alone that, rather than watch the bus take his friend across the tarmac, he went to a bar and wept. During his first week alone at their hotel, he wanted to talk to someone, and that someone was Randy. Two months had been a long time to share nights and days, he thought. They'd crossed Greece by bus, and nearly 5,000 kilometres of Turkey, 2,000 or more of Egypt. To celebrate Randy's departure, or to mourn it, he went on a three-day binge. Then he stayed put and slept. He had another pressing reason for self-confinement. In the past few years he'd found it difficult to write poems. Now he wrote them day and night. He couldn't seem to stop.

The donkey belonged with the butterfly, macaw, iguana, and turtle as his favorite animal. He even liked its Arabic name, *hmaar*, suggesting an ancient Egyptian deity on the order of Thoth, Khnoum, or Ptah. In the oldest temple carvings and tomb paintings, blue-grey donkeys plodded to fields, carrying corn and cane. Mary rode on a donkey. A donkey carried Jesus into Jerusalem. In Arabic, the word meant "stupid" or "stubborn." Its bray was an unexpected, unexplained, dragged out lament, a mounting, suddenly stilled cry against the pain of living. He had an idea for a film to be titled *The Donkeys of Cairo*. The documentary would show them trotting along from early morn, when they brought the produce to the markets, till long after midnight, still collecting garbage or carrying their weary garbage-collectors home. It would show them in all their moods, sometimes trotting gaily, sometimes sore-covered, more dead than alive.

At work, it trotted or stood with those sad eyes, the bowed, bent neck but with long, soft, silky ears pricked to attention, an odd grimace or half-stupor on its face. He saw donkey carts, driven by three flyblown children sitting on piles of ordure, applying switches, shouting commands to three tired donkeys. One was usually grey, one white, and one brown, with whitish nostrils. The outer two always seemed to be male, and the middle female. Work was all that donkeys did, work till they died of malnutrition, cardiac arrest, or maltreatment. One day he saw a cart with four dead donkeys on the way to the glue factory, pulled by a living one. The dead looked tranquil, the living screwed up its grim, sarcastic face in reproof, and plodded on. On the muddy Nile and its green canals dead donkeys floated downstream, bright red wounds crawling with flies and worms, bellies shining in the sun.

The donkey seldom got gratitude, love, or even friendship. Edward liked to see it uncharacteristically stamp its feet, or kick backward: it was whipped until it slogged again. It had the simple pleasures of grass, shrubs, and sometimes garden flowers. It drank the water of stream or well with unslakeable thirst. It enjoyed scratching its backside against walls. It endlessly flicked flies away with its tail, and leaned its heavy head on walls. In its few moments loose in a field, it would lie down and roll over. But that was rare. He would have liked to own a farm where freed donkeys roamed fields and rolled, kicking delicate hooves up to the sky. If you stroked its nostrils, neck, or ears, it would close its eyes in pleasure. When the carts were stopped, he'd go up and stroke their ears and murmur endearments to them, and they lay their big soft heads against him in a moment of affection and understanding. The Egyptians laughed at him, calling him "*hmar.*"

Cairo was long and narrow, bisected by the Nile, which flowed smooth as dark blue or milky brown glass from marsh or mountain through half a continent. On the east, it was ringed by cemeteries in whose house-like mausoleums thousands of homeless families lived, ate, and did laundry. Cairo's stretched for miles. Wide-awake at 3 a.m., the khámsin blowing, he rose and walked by the Nile. The hot breath of the Sahara began at the city's sepulchral limits. The khámsin might blow for 50 days, 50 years, or 50 centuries.

After he had typed his poems, drained, he wrote a letter to Ruth in dim light, his typewriter ribbon fading fast. Nothing could halt his self-destruction. Who'd wounded him? He blamed family, church, society, himself, and nobody. He'd thought of suggesting marriage to Ruth now that she was divorced. But Ruth needed protection that he could not give her, and the protection he needed she could give only in part. He had sought protection from tough young men. Double their age, he'd felt younger than they and sought their advice and comfort, and they almost always referred to him by a diminutive, like Ruth's "Edwardlein"... Eduardito, Eduardín, Eduardinho.

He had constant diarrhea, and all his stomach could take was juices or expensive Perrier with ice. He told his woes to a bar waiter, a pianist married to an English girl but unable to join her in England because he lacked funds. Edward offered to lend him the money so he could go. The pianist thought this was a seduction ploy, and offered his sexual services.

He avoided returning stares, and blinkered himself against amputees on skateboard carts wheeling through the streets, the beggar women clutching children. In the streets, perpetually torn up to repair the ever-bursting water mains, cars honked from dawn till midnight—he thought by contrast of the Beissels' home on Oxford Avenue in snow-muffled Montréal. He avenged himself on drivers by shouting insults in English and Arabic into open car windows: it seemed to work. But one night a passing car clipped him on the chin, opening up an old knife-cut. He sometimes had to visit fearful Tahrir Square, on the other side of which was the Mugaaba with its dozens of floors and hundreds of rooms, which he had to visit to get his visa renewed. The bureaucrats' workplace could have served as the model for the Ministry of Missing Persons in *Black Orpheus*.

One night he was standing in the centre of another terrifying square, El Ataba, mildly drunk, mildly high on hashish, when a boy came up, looked at him, wordlessly took out his penis, and put it in his hand. For the next few seconds, Edward pondered what to do. Then a man in his 20s approached on the other side, and did the same thing for his other hand: he went with them. You could take a *felukka* sailboat ride on the Nile, romantic and pleasant, but when you got some distance out, the boatman would expose himself. If you found a boy, one of the ineffably creepy, sullen, and omnipresent black-uniformed policemen would turn up, wanting a bribe. If the boy was scared off, the policeman would more often than not suggest sex with him instead. He was fellating a teenager down by the Nile when a policeman crept up and stuck a bayonet against his back. He had to pay him 10 Egyptian pounds, as well as pay the boy, likely his partner.

Another night he got lost in a street maze branching off Tahrir and, looking for his Hotel Suisse, went into the wrong building on the wrong street right up to the sixth floor. This motivated the night watchman to call a black-clad cop, who took him to headquarters, where they had a confused debate in bad English and Arabic, since he couldn't remember the name of his hotel street, and they'd never heard of the hotel. Finally a squadron accompanied him on foot to the Hotel Suisse — as it happened, only a couple of blocks away — to verify that it existed and that he lodged there.

Something disturbingly Cairene happened. A young man with a newspaper-wrapped package in his hand was trying to cross a street, where both red and green lights were interpreted by Cairo's cars as "go," since traffic policemen spent most of their time soliciting bribes, sipping tea, or suggesting sex in odd corners. A car knocked the young man flat, not even slowing down. People lifted him and put him in a taxi to a hospital or morgue. One more little urban life snuffed out, Edward thought. One moment full of life, thought, worry, maybe love: the next gone. The young man had clutched a small parcel in one hand....

In his regular bar, he was attracted to the manager, who was pliable, but kept putting the event off. Finally they made it in the washroom. The manager and his cronies were always offering him cigarettes, and it took him awhile to realize that these were laced with hash. That, and the rotgut spirits, did him in. He didn't wash or shave. Then the heat began: once it was actually 42° C, 108° F. He sat drinking in a cool little imported tavern in the Hilton on the Nile, refuge from his furnace-like hotel room full of buzzing flies. Flies turned him into a landing strip, made him public property.

Perhaps the Hotel Suisse changed hands, because the staff seemed different people. They began staring insolently, making him even more nervous. The maid had given up any pretense of cleaning his stuffy, disordered room: she simply removed the leftover newspapers and magazines that he deposited outside his door. The khámsin filled the room with dust, but she didn't care about that either. The elevator defunct, he had to walk up seven floors.

Frugally eating rice and lentils, he waited for slow-arriving money. He stayed in his room all day, typing letters, killing flies. One night at a tourist bar, a dark, heavily built boy came in, limping yet swaggering. Everyone knew him. The boy's shirt said "Brasil-Rio de Janeiro," so starting a conversation was easy. Edward asked to be rescued from hell. Rifaat proposed that they go to Alexandria; the sea air and cooler temperatures would do Edward good. He accompanied him to his old bar and upbraided the manager and his pals. He helped him to renew his visa in the bureaucratic beehive. He helped him pack. Their taxi careened across the desert Alexandria, the driver and all of the passengers stoned.

Most of the Alexandrian Greeks, Italians, and Jews were gone, but had left reminders. He and Rifaat went out to bar, bazaar, and restaurant, saw Cavafy's house and Durrell's square with its clicking palm trees, ate small clamlike molluscs at a tavern by the trolley-stop. They walked along the seaside corniche; it was warm enough to swim. After Cairo, the sea salved his skin, nerves, and eyes. Even the car horns were more musical.

As Rifaat's told it, he was scion of a rich family dispossessed by Nasser in the 1950s. He'd been a student at the University of Cairo, popular with the girls, a bodybuilder, a judo and karate champion. One day Anwar Sadat made a speech on campus about Egyptian democracy. Rifaat, 19, spoke up, asking why they weren't allowed to elect their own student federations. He was leaving campus with friends when a car sped up behind them. He was able to lap aside, but the car ran down his friends. He fled Cairo. He couldn't register anywhere in his own name or use his own documents, so he lived in apartments under friends' names. When money ran out, he became a male gigolo.

Constantly on the move, he could only communicate with his family through go-betweens.

If Rifaat needed cheering up, so did Edward. He'd noticed less strength and feeling in his lower left foot and ankle. A pinched nerve? Result of a drunken fall? The beginnings of multiple sclerosis? Rifaat's way to treat such maladies, and to keep him off solitary drinking, was to keep him high on hash. But sometimes hash seemed to make him *want* to drink, to come down a little. He was afraid that, while drunk, he'd commit suicide, be robbed and murdered, killed in a fight, or run over. He sometimes wondered if someone in Brazil practiced *macumba* to bring him back, or to punish him for leaving. Rifaat said he'd try to find a sorcerer who specialized in spells. Randy would simply have advised him to stop drinking. Of course. He could stop drinking right away if he had a reason to.

One night he escaped from Rifaat's surveillance, but next day required tranquilizers to banish his jitters. Rifaat nursed him, delicately attentive—a morning kiss, a massage, arms around him. Being with another body when he woke up at night was good, even if it snored. He understood when Edward told him that he felt the same age as he, or younger. "Of course," Rifaat said, "I think of you as someone my own age—why else would I introduce you to all my friends?" Though Rifaat had expensive tastes, Edward didn't begrudge a cent he spent on him: it was like paying a psychiatrist.

Their last night Rifaat came in drunk: Edward had given him *carte blanche* to do it alone. Someone with a British accent had driven him home at 3 a.m. Parting from Rifaat, he headed to adobe oases deep in the desert, where troupes of children followed him shouting "Hello!" When he chased them away, they threw stones at him, which he threw back. Drinking no alcohol—no bars—he went south, stopping at places that he and Randy had missed, like the temple in Abydos, actually seven temples to seven gods. Luxor had almost zero humidity, good for Ruth Beissel, and he thought the ruins would fascinate her. If she came there, she'd be able to visit them easily, despite her arthritis. Luxor was only a small village but in his four days there, he was propositioned 19 times.

At Aswan, the Nile was lake-like. Aswan town was noisy and dirty. Even the 10-year-old boys who sailed felukkas propositioned him. But he wasn't interested in kids that size. In fact, he'd grown uninterested in any Egyptians. One reason was oversupply, which took away the joy of the chase or the charms of courtship. Sex was mere mechanical pleasure, quickly summoned, quickly performed, quickly over. And the *galabiya* was a turn-off; it feminized a boy's body. He was attracted to tight buttocks, box, and legs taut under blue jeans. The *galabiya* did away with all that. Associating them with priests, he couldn't help finding figures in flowing Biblical robes asexual, When he saw naked boys swimming in the Nile, he found their bodies exquisite; when the same boys left the water and put on grubby *galabiyas*, desire ended.

He waited in his air-conditioned hotel room for the weekly boat to Abu Simbel. It turned out to be a big floating two-storey, roofed-over metal raft, pulled by a tug. Nubians and hippies aboard, in mid-lake the tug's motor broke. The foreigners and half the Nubians slept on the upper deck; the others slept amid the cargo. On the upper deck he reposed on the big towel Randy had left him, and heard the Nubians in long white and blue gowns dance to their rhythmic music, so much better, he thought, than the whining, lovesick Arab music, with its tremolos, sustained notes, and endless repetitions. The roof of their ark kept them cool in the day, and the breeze did at night. An old one-eyed man served bread, coffee, beans, and Coca-Cola until it ran out. That was all the food they had, but most had brought cheese and mineral water. While becalmed, he read and passed along a copy of *Whitefaces*, my poetry collection. He and the other passengers had much lively discussion about my poems. It was one way to pass the time if you were stranded in the middle of a lake.

After another tug freed them, they reached Abu Simbel, and got to see more than the tourists who flew in, gaped at ruins for an hour, and flew out. Curators, workers, a few Nubians, plus doctors, dentists, and teachers doing their required rural stint inhabited the village, which UNESCO had built for those who rescued the two temples of Ramses II and his wife Nefertari. Stocked up on bread and fish, the oversized raft uneventfully returned to Aswan. From Luxor, he followed the Nile, stopping at El Mina, which offered greenery, a bend in the river, and a hotel with bath and ceiling fan. Then he was back in the Cairo maelstrom. He'd decided to go overland to Israel, but every time he tried to cross at El Kantar he found the border closed. The Egyptians closed it on Friday, the Israelis on Saturday; elections and religious feasts closed it, too. Between abortive crossings, he travelled along the Red Sea to Port Said, whose reputation for wickedness was remote: they didn't even serve alcohol now. But its Victorian gingerbread houses were pretty; ships towered entering or exiting the canal. Parts of the town were still torn up after four wars with the Israelis. Off drink, he found that his humour had become drier, his sarcasm more biting, and sex seemed a wild absurdity. When he was drying out, he thought he turned into his father: reticent, aloof, timid.

Back in Cairo, he retrieved his typewriter at the Hotel Suisse, and switched to a hotel by the train station. He ventured out to collect mail. Egyptian mail was dependable but unbelievably slow. After three tries, he got through to the official in charge of letters (*chargé de lettres*, they must have called him, in view of his officiousness) and found a letter for Randy. He charged the *chargé* to return it to sender, and he flattened the poor thing with a dozen rubber stamps.

Randy had sent photos taken in Cappadocia. Edward sent extras to his relatives, who wrote back, wondering who the "nice-looking chap" beside him was. The "Turkish guide," Edward wrote them. By letter, Randy advised him that Edward's life seemed to him

> ... absolutely hellish. A good restaurant is no substitute for a home and the warm companionship of caring friends. You're the greatest ad against being "an heir" I've ever encountered.... I wonder who you are slamming in the ribs these days for having a political or social viewpoint different from your own. It must be very depressing — like a prize fighter deprived of his punching bag. How incredible that someone with an ability to think should become as closed minded as any East TEXAN

you would ever find—except closed minded in
an idiotological leftist, anti-American, even anti-
Turkish way.... Don't be mad at me for an entire
year. Limit your rage to 3-6 month periods. Year-
long rage leads to drink, lack of sexual interest,
attraction to dangerous sexual partners, fear of
height, fear of crowded buses, arguments with
cabdriver, bartenders, hotel keepers, etc and an
acute inability to stand temperatures over 85° F.

Randy was debating whether he should bring Ali, of
Cairo memory, to New York. Nominated as Randy's envoy,
Edward was sure that, whatever he did or said, Randy would
find reason to berate him. Over a long session at the Nile
Casino, which wasn't one at all, but an outdoor restaurant that
stretched for blocks along the river, Edward tried to sound
Ali out on behalf of his friend. He asked him if he wanted to
go to the United States, and what he felt about Randy. In one
way, he wanted to discourage Randy's initiative: First-World/
Third-World relationships were impossible. The economic gap
between boy and tourist accounted for most of the robbings,
beatings, and murders of gays in poor countries, though usually
it was not the original tourist, but an innocent later one, who
suffered the consequences. Yet he thought that daring contacts
across cultures were valuable, even part of the First World's
duty: an individual foreign aid program. Randy was offering an
opportunity that Ali might never get again.

Randy perhaps wasn't aware, he wrote, that in Ali he
was dealing with an honest, sensitive, intelligent if dreamy 20-
year-old, fed a diet of romantic Arabic literature. A fair swap
was in prospect: Randy could give Ali experience, Ali could give
Randy the delight of renewing his own youth, as well as sex
and companionship. He was unlikely to stay in New York and
turn into some monster or disco demon on Randy's hands. Ali's
idea of a big night out was to go the Nile Casino and spoon ice
cream.

Edward observed that many gay Third-World boys
preferred foreigners, finding them less aggressive, less brutal
and macho than local males and, after mercenary encounters
with Egyptians, he could see why. In any case, he was sure that

Ali would obey Randy's conditions. Randy described himself as a "silly romantic fool," but he should be. He should not talk about being "realistic" and about "honesty" in his relations with others: that was dated 1960s crap. He should settle for an illusion when the illusion would bring him a little happiness and surcease from pain, and bring a little happiness to someone else.

Shaking off Egypt's dust saddened him. He had ended up finding Egyptians friendly, humane, and civilized, even more so the helpful, courteous, and well-educated Copts. Except for the police, they were tolerant, civilized, and gracious. Yet something was wrong. Moroccans were irascible, aggressive, unpredictable, but when a Moroccan took you as his friend, he was willing to give his life for you. The Turk was serious and honest. The Greek was an engaging hedonist. But the Egyptian? An enigma.

The peasants would never miss him. The only ones who'd know he'd gone would be someone stamping his passport, or closing his file in a ministry. Before he could cross to Israel, the beginning of Ramadan stalled him at El Arish: a power failure, blazing heat, and millions of flies. The town was an extended souk where everyone was an adding machine and kids blended "*shalom*" and "hello" by greeting you as "shallow" — come to think of it, an appropriate greeting for the tourists that passed this way, kibbutzniks and American Jews in air-conditioned buses, raring to do Egypt in one day or one week. An effete breeze rustled the tall fountains of date palms, and dried his sweat-beaded forehead. He walked barefoot in the sand. Two impossibly handsome Egyptians came toward him. They all but collided in the blackness: florid excuses, and they walked on. A scrap of conversation blew past his ears: "...when you're with a beautiful guy, and you want to say `oh, I love you so much', but you can't because..."

When he finally crossed the border, people pushed, kicked, were pushed and kicked by soldiers, fainted in the sun. Palestinians, mostly, trying to get home to their families. Twice knocked off the bus to the Israeli side, he spent six hours trying to get through crowds. A collective taxi took him to Gaza, a rundown town of cooped-up refugees. At Israeli customs, his luggage was torn apart and relentlessly interrogated. In the mêlée someone stole his Portuguese shepherd's coat with its astrakhan collar and three capes. Well, it had been too heavy to carry around in hot weather, anyhow, and he'd intended to give it to some Arab lad who coveted it—but they wanted blue jeans. No doubt some Palestinian in the Gaza Strip thought it would look good on his wife. No doubt it would.

Next day, a new world began with Jerusalem. The nights were cool and the days clear, breezy, and dry. His pension, whose manager was an American Jewish returnee, was filled with people who'd been working on kibbutzim, and with U.N. soldiers, including a raucous Fijian battalion. He prowled Old Jerusalem. Out of kinship with the Arabs, he made a point of datelining his postcards "El-Quds," the Arabic name for Jerusalem. In the Jewish quarter, it was cleaner, relatively uncrowded, and the restaurants were superb. Down to about 60 kilos in Egypt, he began to gain weight back rapidly. During the Sabbath, all the Arab restaurants and bars of East Jerusalem opened out of spite. The old walled city charmed him with its dozen gates and its mosques, Christian shrines, and synagogues, a Babel of races and commerce by day, a dark labyrinth by night.

Yes, the religiosity of Jews, Christians, and Muslims disturbed him with childhood echoes of the Garden of Gethsemane, the Mount of Olives, the Sacred Way. Many religious monuments were aesthetic horrors, especially the Church of the Holy Sepulchre in Jerusalem and the Church of the Nativity at Bethlehem, shared by and quarrelled over by several denominations. In nearby Hebron, the Tomb of the Patriarchs—a mixture of mosque, synagogue, and Crusader church—rivalled them in hideousness. Yet Jerusalem's walls were indeed golden from the local building stone, and when they were lit at night...! Jerusalem was one of those rare cities that were just as you imagined and hoped them to be, turning him back into a religious person as anyone, he thought, but an idiot was.

To the Wailing Wall came bearded, black-clad, white-shawled Jews, mostly Hassidim, who stoned cars that passed through their area of West Jerusalem on the Sabbath, wore beaver hats, didn't cut their children's hair, joined by tourist

Jews in hot shirts and paper beanies. Among the cypresses and cedars of Temple Mount, Arab guides shouted at strolling Gentile sightseers, "No entrance here!", "No shoes!", "No immodest dress" — religion's endless litany of negatives. At the Golden Gate, where Jesus entered the city on his donkey, you could not approach or follow his steps. The silver-domed El Aqsa, westernmost point of Muhammad's wanderings, had been built by Umayyad caliphate; made a church by Crusaders; restored by Saladin, a Kurd; set on fire in 1969 by an evangelical Australian.

Jews stuck messages to God in crannies of their Wall, mumbled and nodded. The Dome of the Rock, with its faVence tile lozenges, unspoiled a ribbon of calligraphy proclaiming God was Great and Beautiful and Only and Supreme. The Rock was the mountaintop where Abraham took his best-loved son Isaac to sacrifice for sacrifice to God in a burning bush. This was the rock where Muhammad on El Burak, his Pegasus, sprang to the heavens and talked to the prophets and God. Scant miles from here, over dry rolling hills, the other one, the man on a donkey, had been born.

A priest told him about the Sacred Donkey. Disgusted by the Crucifixion, the donkey shook off the dust of Palestine, and took a boat (or walked on water) to Cyprus. From there he went to Greece, and thence to Italy, where he died and was buried in his own special church. Ruth had written of the danger of Edward's being reincarnated as a donkey. But you could be a donkey, and still be a saint.

In Nablus, since it was Ramadan, he couldn't even get a drink of water until a store-owner invited him in, closed his café, and served him a Coke in a dark corner. Hebron had an Arab market, crumbling adobe houses, and blind alleys. When he went back to the bus, soldiers in mirrored glasses made passengers stand to be frisked with arms splayed. They snatched a cigarette from an Arab boy's mouth — "because it's Ramadan." They questioned Edward closely about the Lebanese visa in his passport. The Arab boys, seeing that he was a harassed stranger, began to talk to him. Goat-bells tinkled. The ancient valley bloomed behind them. He asked them what they called their city in Arabic. Their answer? "El Khalil." The Beautiful.

In Bethlehem and Nazareth he found Christian Arabs. He climbed flat-topped Masada, where the Zealots, cornered by Rome, had thrown themselves into the abyss. Bathing in the Dead Sea was like swimming in warm olive oil. On the Feast of St. Mary Magdalen, he was awakened by mosquitoes and the muezzin at 3 a.m. Maybe just as well: he'd been having an imploding nightmare. In this one, his mother had a heart attack, and he was carrying her to hospital.

Tel Aviv, repulsively modern, was saved by its seaside and by its remnants of Europe: sidewalk cafés, and good cheap restaurants. But the money he'd had forwarded to Israel in July, designated for the Hapoalim Bank in Jerusalem, was sent to the Israel Discount Bank here. But somehow the bank thought he had left the country, and sent it back to Canada. Temporarily broke, he survived on chickpea dip and pita, and slept several nights on the beach.

In the old Turkish port of Jaffa, hundreds sat on the seawall in the moon-washed nights, or angled for fish from the rocks below. Old Moroccans and Yemenites sold shish kebab and grilled tripe from stalls. Here also were elderly European barbers, shoemakers, tailors, and restaurateurs with exquisite manners, though their culture and customs were dying out. The young Israelis were often disarmingly open—until you began to defend the Arabs, at which point their minds slammed shut.

In Haifa, he visited the world shrine of the Baha'i, a gold dome on a hill, to honour their idea of world harmony, and in memory of his old Edmonton landlady. In Cairo, he'd got a visa to Jordan. Now he got as far as the Allenby Bridge over the Jordan River, reedy and 10 feet wide, making Lindsay's Scugog River look like a mighty torrent. The Jordanian officials seemed satisfied with his documents until they saw the Egyptian land-exit stamp. He hadn't realized that Arab nations considered it to be tantamount to an Israeli entrance stamp, and debarred you. Foregoing Jordan, fixing his mind on an island and a village where he could settle down and work, the donkey embarked for Cyprus.

20

THE U. N. REFUGEE

August-September 1981

His example, at any rate,
some god gave us, to emulate:
no bouleversement *turns him around.*
His world was always upside down.

~ The Sloth

On Edward's second night in Cyprus, a pair of friendly teenagers engaged him in conversation. One of them also engaged the pocket that held his passport and traveller's cheques. He usually made it a rule to carry them separately: this time he hadn't. He pitied the Palestinian or Lebanese terrorist who got or bought the passport: he'd be suspect everywhere. Though he felt naked without documents, the authorities couldn't send him away without somewhere to send him.

American Express largely replaced the money. However, he couldn't replace the passport because Canada's Honourary Consul had gone on holidays for the month of August. He expected that the consul would be censorious. Admittedly, Edward had lost his passport a few times. Seven, to be exact. If it happened once in your life, replacing a passport was instructive, even comical; more than once, it lost its charm. You could avoid loss by avoiding *all* contact with any other human being, by trusting absolutely *no one*, responding to *no one's* overtures.

But what purpose was left in life then, except meditation, masturbation, eating meals, and reading newspapers?

He had hoped to find a mountain town empty now as vacations ended, gain coolness and peace of mind, and work at translation. But he couldn't leave his pension because the police had to reach him quickly if they found the passport. Each scorching day began with the cicadas, which emerged from underground for one season of ceaseless, senseless song. He could tell when the sun had risen, not by the pale, fierce light or furnace heat, but by the first buzz saws breaking into dreams of childhood. He remembered the night-barking wild dogs of Trinidad, chattering street-sparrows of North Africa, the howl of monkeys in the Brazilian jungle. Here his sleepless nights and dull days were relentlessly clocked by the insane, mechanical click of cicadas, which couldn't even be seen even when though they were shrilling a foot away. The lifelike shells of their most recent metamorphosis clung to each carob tree.

Early travellers, who almost unanimously opined ill of Cyprus, complained of the "locust"—which must have been the cicada—and also of snakes and of frogs croaking all night in pestilential swamps. The swamps had long been drained and were bone-white salt flats or high-rise tourist apartments, though the hemophile mosquito remained. On this Greek-Turkish-British island, hordes of tourists flew in from the north, eating fish 'n' chips with the sickly sweet red wine. The all-night buzz of jets, disco beat, the Babel of soldiers and sailors, Arabs, and English expatriates from beach hotels and condominiums. A Cypriot proverb said that to work was hard but not to work was harder.

He read about walled, moated cities; closed, violated mosques; grey minarets; smoke-blackened churches full of old gold icons. Fossil dwarf hippo-bones worshipped as saints' relics, powdered, drunk by the faithful; the stone where mothers lit candles to the milk-giving Virgin: myth, literature, and history merged. Cyprus was the island of Aphrodite, born from the foam at Paphos. A mosque in a palm grove marked where, in the seventh century, Haram, the Prophet's aunt, fell from her mule and broke her neck. The Turks ended Venetian rule after a year-long siege of Famagusta, and flayed alive their general.

Here, after abandoning poetry and before exiling himself to Ethiopia, Rimbaud contracted typhoid fever. Britain "leased" Cyprus from the collapsing Ottoman Empire in 1878, until it cut its losses in 1960 after an armed movement sought *énosis*, union with Greece. After a Greek-inspired coup against President Makarios, Turkey invaded in 1974: partition followed. Now the Turks, 20 per cent of the population, held nearly 40 per cent of the island as a vassal state of Turkey, while the Greek part was an appendage of Greece. The Green Line, the U.N.'s buffer zone, divided the island.

Island of love, they said, though love was also a ruin, its voice shrill, mechanical, like the chant of cicadas or the dead beat of disco. An unfortunate little country, an unlucky crossroad, all that movement, conquest, bloodshed, and suffering the burden of history and of the present, too: the ubiquitous soldiers in their U.N. green, chatting up bar-girls; internal refugees from the Greek and Turkish parts of the island, the external refugees from Lebanon and Palestine with their tales and nightmares of atrocities; the young boys by the harbour and their own dreams of exit.

Tourist trap and sweat bowl, the port of Limassol was something of a sin city. The local boys had a dark mixed Greek-Arab look and wonderful bodies; they were commercial, approachable, and dangerous. The redlight district tired and repelled him yet was irresistible when he couldn't sleep. Snatching sleep often required drinking brandy-sours, but of course drinking produced further sleeping disturbances, especially if he had a hangover. Apart from Valium, the only pill that helped him was Mandrax, which gave him soothing dreams. Doctors, claiming that it was addictive, pulled it off the market, though he could find black-market samples. But, really, the only substitute for sleep was work. If he couldn't sleep, he translated or wrote until he was exhausted, even if by then it was dawn. Dispatching bundles of poems to friends, he hoped they'd retain them. If he died abroad, he hoped that someone later might to read or publish it. Well, nobody cared about poetry anymore, certainly nobody cared about *his* poetry, he considered, so he might as well write, like Constantine Cavafy or Emily Dickinson, for a small circle of friends. But he didn't think even his friends took him seriously as a poet. Yet sharing poems with them was a slender thread that still joined him to life and society — that, and sex.

His cheap pension was noisy with couples coming in for sex, but he was used to such conditions. His most recent injuries had healed. His pain was cerebral. His misadventures and depressions were almost continuous now: he had about two days a month when he felt in control of himself yet without booze, life lost all interest and colour. During the four months he hadn't drunk during the past year he had sexual relations exactly once. Now his main social event was meals. Eating once a day, he dined in an arbour-housed tavern, shaded by the ailanthus, a Japanese import resembling a ferny walnut tree. His staple was mixed stuffed squash, peppers, and eggplant, so simple and filling. With it, he drank white wine they called "Hock," which tasted like Muscatel. Sometimes the heavy meals came at a cost. One hotter than usual day he lay down to doze on the beach. When he woke up, his glasses were gone; luckily, he kept an extra pair.

When he went north on his frequent trips to Nicosia, he encountered a new downtown of parks, government buildings, restaurants, boutiques, and high-rises. Across a filled-in moat, used for parks and tennis courts, was the old, circular, walled city with about a dozen entrances in its crumbling stone and earthwork. Here were sordid bars, patronized by youthful U.N. troops. Apart from tiny businesses like haberdashers and barbers, the city had gone somnolent. There were a few small, dark Greek churches, a few closed grey mosques, the archbishop's palace to which Makarios had escaped after the last attempt to murder him. As he went on, the streets became emptier and emptier, and he came to the barricades, the line where the Turkish advance was stopped. Beyond them, the red flag-and-crescent of Turkey fluttered, but only over eerie blocks of bombed, burned, and shattered buildings, inhabited only by cats, rats, and wild dogs. The walk to the British High Commission, technically inside no man's land, was spooky; everything was ruined houses and gardens overrun by eucalyptus.

You were allowed to cross at one checkpoint only, to the flak of endless argument with Greek soldiers, who wanted to know why you were going. Once across, there was little to see in the shattered Turkish side. More old and ruined buildings, and small businesses, mosques, closed Greek churches, and the appealing monstrosity of a Gothic cathedral, Sta. Sophia. When the Turks took Nicosia in 1570 they put two preposterous minarets on it and turned it into a mosque. He could have stayed in the Turkish zone for up to a day but, since he didn't have proper documents anyway, he only spent a couple of hours. He could have got a two- or three-day permit to go further inland, but he feared he might get stuck there, or have to go to Ankara to get a passport.

The Turks had brought in colonists from the mainland to make them permanent settlers. Before partition, there had been no geographic separation, but a crazy-quilt pattern of intermingled villages. On the Greek side, out of 600,000, a third were refugees from the North, who had been resettled and rebuilt their lives. Now there were at least 50,000 refugees from Lebanon, only 50 miles away, who periodically flooded the island when the civil war there flared up anew; thousands came after Menachem Begin's recent bombing of Beirut. Besides the Arab tourists, robed men and veiled women were everywhere. He met people all the way from Abu Dhabi to Libya, supposedly here on business or holidays but, he suspected, seeing to more sinister matters. Speaking of Israel, a Lebanese told him: "We can wait 200 years, but we shall one day drive the dogs into the sea." The Palestinians posed as natives of other Arab countries. Add to this hodgepodge the planeloads of tourists, and the thousands of soldiers on the two NATO bases that, by a law setting up the republic, Britain possessed forever.

The burnt island was too hybrid, too disturbed, too crowded. The Greek Cypriots themselves were kind, hospitable, gentler and more reserved than their mainland kin. He detected in them a melancholy nostalgia for the vanished times when both races lived together in relative peace. Cyprus had never "belonged" to Greece, or at least not since the Byzantine Empire began to fall apart, and Greek Cypriots didn't seem to hate their Turkish fellow citizens, or vice versa.

He could give no one a reliable address to write to, nor did an interminable Canadian postal strike aid communication.

Nonetheless, he was annoyed with Ian Young, since he thought that he'd not made an effort to sell or distribute *Later*. In answer to instructions and remonstrations, he had got what he deemed to be aggrieved and insulting answers. Writing to Ruth Beissel, he commiserated about the financial problems she was having, and that she had fallen twice in December, once painfully injuring her coccyx. No laughing matter. Why had joker Nature provided us with vestigial tails? She had written of committing suicide. If she went through with it, he would understand why, he wrote, but he would be desolated: she was one of the few people left who inspired him. He hoped that her daughters kept on needing her and letting her know they did. But his opinion on families was unchanged: the family was the primary prison institution, a chain of tyranny perpetuated from parents to children, as the latter revenged themselves on *their* children (and their parents too) for what the parents did to them.

The Canadian dodo had fallen to its lowest rate against the U. S. dollar in 50 years. On the last day of August he went to see the immigration man at the local police station, who'd suddenly summoned him. Maybe they had found his passport. He was sure that it was somewhere on the island, thrown into the rubbish. Since it never rained, maybe it would be found intact. No such luck. The man was nice, but all he said that Edward, since he'd been here a month already, *must* get a passport. So he was off to the capital for the *nth* time, on this occasion to see the Canadian Honourary Consul.

The consul turned out to be suave, immaculately dressed, and spoke perfect English. He did not chide him about the lost passport. They discussed possibilities and hypotheses: his somehow going to Beirut; his going to disliked Tel Aviv or favoured Athens; his remaining here and simply getting the passport by mail from one of those places. The consul suspected that a Palestinian had stolen the passport: Cypriots simply didn't do such things. He phoned Tel Aviv, and Edward spoke inconsequentially to an official.

He treated himself to a little air-conditioned Arab restaurant, and took the taxi trip back to Limassol through the hills. He was exhausted after his day of diplomacy, though heartened by the horoscope he'd read that morning. It had said

that "fears and doubts will be erased and significant changes
occur"; it further advised him to "check Gemini," under which
he read that "attention to details results in recovery of lost article,
could lead to profit, and bring you into contact with interesting,
dynamic individual." So, tonight, without doubt, he'd find his
passport in the hands of a smuggler or terrorist, who'd invite him
to join his group, since, under Cancer, "you receive invitation
to join special group or organization." The day wasn't over. It
could still happen.

But, at the end of the day, he didn't find his passport,
though a guy in the redlight district said he'd help him look for
it. The Tel Aviv official called up collect and they talked for 20
minutes, costing $16: real dollars, not dodos. He had nothing
sensible to suggest. *Edward* must find out if the Greek authorities
would let him proceed to Athens to get a new passport, which
would be quickest, or he must return to Tel Aviv. *If,* Edward
thought, the crazy Israelis let him or he could go to Beirut, *if*
the crazy Lebanese and Palestinians let him. Or he could wait
in Cyprus for Tel Aviv to send him papers to fill out and send
these to Athens, which might take *at least* a month, and require
him to replace the birth certificate that had been stolen earlier,
which would also probably take a month. The most extended
passport they could give him would be for six months, or they
could give him an emergency passport valid only for return to
Canada. Everything had to be checked with Ottawa to be sure he
was who he said he was, and to learn if he'd be granted another
passport. It was probably best to stay put, the official advised.
The easy-going Cypriots would not object to his presence (*they*
knew about refugees), and it was a Commonwealth of Nations
country and all that. But Edward thought he knew more about
the whole thing than the official did, and he could see this affair
stretching out forever while he remained an enisled prisoner.

Laurence Durrell's charming book about Cyprus,
Bitter Lemons, had divided humanity into "nisophiles" and
"nisophobes," island-lovers and island-haters. Edward was now
a confirmed nisophobe. He resolved to stay off islands. Finally
in mid-September, the Greek Cypriot government came to his
rescue, or maybe they just wanted to get rid of him. On his 36-
hour ferry journey to Piraeus he wrote postcards to be mailed

upon arrival in Athens. To Randy—whose plan to bring their Egyptian friend Ali to New York for the summer had come to nothing—he penned a scatological string of them. To me, he wrote of escaping Devil's Island. He could now forget Cyprus, a distant outpost of empire, crossroad of barbarians, leaving it shimmering in the mirages rising from burnt plains, chalk-white and blue mountains. The ship had left behind the boys and bargirls to their larcenies and dreams. A faint breeze blew fresher now. Goodbye, partitioned island of love, the enchantment of ruin and the foam of legends, the welter of hatreds. He remembered tourists and refugees, sleepless nights, carob trees, the bougainvillea's dry flare, the fierce sun and fiercer thirst, the centuries punctuated by the parched buzz of the cicada. In his pocket was what the Greek Cypriots had furnished him with. Good for a year and valid for entry to Greece, the document declared the bearer to be a U.N. Stateless Person.

21

THE GRAVEYARD OF HOPES

September 1981-June 1982

Did these two love? Did they swear sacred vows
of eternal loyalty toward each other? Surely the decencies
of caste and race and rank would preclude that!

~ Funerary Stella

He was holed up at the Hotel Leto, Odós Missaraliótou 15, below Plaka, behind a row of glossy-leaved, bitter-orange trees and a winked-out neon sign. The Plaka district at the foot of the Acropolis was good for male prostitution. He dispatched a postcard of a prancing erectile satyr to me, noting that "you're the same you, and it still looks like you."

At the taciturn Hotel Leto, he was the only long-term resident. There were, however, short-term residents. The midnight tattoo of his typewriter counterpointed their rhythm: comings and goings, exits and entrances, groans and whispers, cric-crac of bedsprings. As autumn passed into winter, he heard on the street oranges plop, squished underfoot by passers-by. From the persimmon tree's dark boughs, bright fruit rotted in the cold sun. Sometimes padding in the torn fur slippers he'd bought in El Salvador four years earlier, he dined on rice-stuffed vine leaves and fish-roe salad, and drank harsh retsina at a tavern where a fig-tree limb with huge leaf-hands stretched through the tavern and out a window.

At the Canadian Embassy, he picked up a pathetic plea for help on Moroccan prison-letter paper from a black prisoner, sent years earlier. The plea was unfulfillable. However, he could help the Honduran sailor, José. They'd drunk in a hundred small tavernas and sailed to islands. They'd fought and fed each other's hopes and fears. They'd only had sex a few times, but José's sly smile and drunken charm tugged at him. Though José rarely asked for money Edward paid for his white wine, rice, and beans. He got temporary shipboard jobs, repaired or painted boats in dry dock, peddled hashish, turned tricks, slept in public squares when it was warm, or in construction sites in winter. Sometimes Edward went down to Piraeus to join him in his sleeping bag, not for sex, but just to have company, or to try to feel what it was like to be destitute.

A pet shop just below Ommonia they liked to pass was filled with parakeets and macaques, kitty-corner from a subterranean porno theatre from which you could hear the metro train rumbling on its way to Piraeus. The shop had two macaws, a blue-and-gold one and a red-and-blue one. Transported from a South American jungle, they balanced outside, chained to horizontal perches, cracking sunflower seeds with their curved black beaks, and endlessly shrieking "*Arara*! Dry crackers!" Edward and José fed them fruit: the two *araras*, Brazilian Portuguese for "macaws." He and José were just as exotic here as the macaws, he thought, just as colourful, alien, and lost.

December had shown warm sun and a deep blue sky. No snow, no frost, no rain: perfect weather for parrots. But one day, as he passed the pet shop, the blue-and-gold macaw was gone, sold to a rich client who'd taken the bird to Rhodes. Its partner stayed on outside the shop, balanced and swung, ate fruit and sunflower seeds. But there was no longer any sun or flowers in that life. He turned vicious and pecked, only rarely crying, "*Arara!* Dry crackers!"

Winter rain came to polluted Athens with its leafless, pollarded trees. As the weeks passed, Edward drank ouzo and ate octopus and potato mayonnaise with José. On a wet February afternoon, the cold wind blowing, he turned up, his shoes sodden sponges. His face's mestizo brown had paled to yellow. Laid off from his job, knowing he'd never get a ship here, he'd saved up just enough money to buy a bus ticket to Barcelona for himself, his cousin, and a friend. He asked for money to buy bread and cheese for the trip. Edward gave him the money, shook his hand, and watched him leave.

Using leftover letterhead from the Hotel Roma in the spa town of Termas de Rio Hondo, Argentina, he noted to Renate Jürgensen that it had been four years since they'd seen each other. Still, he felt obliged to caution her that homosexuals were not for turning. Far too often, women felt that *they* were the ones who could "understand" and "reform" a homosexual, that he was as he was because other women had spurned, been cruel to him, or exploited him, and that if he could only find the "right" woman, he'd be "cured." But homosexuality was not a disease, he pointed out. It was part of the human condition.

The past few months had been tough. In his opinion, the Athens police were overprotective of foreigners, thought them to be incapable of looking after themselves, and sent them to hospital for little cause. Thus, on Christmas Day, he'd awoken to find himself in a bed in the Hospital for Traumatology and Injuries. He made the staff release him the same day. An encounter with a Chilean, who'd earlier hit him over the head with a chair, led to being robbed and a karate chop that gave him a broken ankle that took more than two months to heal. Nor was healing aided by an incident in a porno theatre. Noticing that people were masturbating or fellating each other, he began to participate. But one day he chose the wrong partner, who hurled him into the aisle. He limped out, but the man followed him, knocked him down, and would have beaten him up, had not a policeman intervened.

Many months earlier a letter had caught up with him from his cousin Marg Wansborough, relating that Mrs. Wilford, the mother of his childhood friend Susan, had died. Writing a letter of condolence so tardily, he told Susan Wilford, must seem "rather bizarre" though perhaps it was more sincere than one dutifully written just after the event. He had been writing fewer letters "to the diminishing number of family members and acquaintances I retain there, not because I don't love them, or think of them, but basically because I want to forget Lindsay and be forgotten by it, " and "to end this love/hate relationship I had with the town, not continue it to the grave." Susan had tended her mother constantly during her last years; she had nothing to reproach herself for. Edward did.

> .... I think the dying know, need and deserve the presence and support of the living. If I had known then what I know now, I'd have returned to Canada after my father's death, or at least after my mother took her first stroke, and stayed with her until she died, whatever the unspeakable unpleasantness and personal limitations living in Lindsay wd have had for me. She might not have lived longer, but she'd have lived, and died, easier; I realise now that she died, among other things, of loneliness. There is a law of retribution, or compensation, operative in life, I truly believe, and I am being punished, as I deserve to be, for my neglect of her in her last years of need, because I too am beginning to know what real loneliness and isolation are. And I shall probably die alone, as I let her die, and that too will be just.

Twice he was robbed of traveller's cheques, left almost penniless until he could get money transferred. In January, a young Tunisian slipped something in his drink, insisted on getting him a taxi, went with him to his hotel, and robbed him while he slept. For the benefit of American Express, he collected stories of theft with virtually the same plot as his, most involving Arabs. In February, the traveller's cheques, though hidden among his papers, were stolen while he was out of his room: he suspected the Tunisian. Refusing to pay him until they'd thoroughly investigated, American Express said he'd become a "habitual loser."

He got out, first to the extreme southeast of the Peloponnesus, then to Naxos in the Cyclades, cold and windy, where a boat took him to Rhodes. By the time they reached Rhodes on the 32-hour trip, he could barely stand up. The capital, a walled medieval city, was agawk with Nordic tourists. Small white Lindos on the east coast had a cliff-hanging, over-restored acropolis, and cloying, candy-shop houses. He was relieved to find a tourist-untrodden path, its edges bright with spring flowers, that took him down to tiny, crag-enclosed St. Paul's Bay, where a cake-white church signified that a traveller arrived from Ephesus in 51 A.D.

On Good Friday, that year mid-April in the Orthodox calendar, he reached Kos, just across the water from Bodrum in Turkey. He endured tolling bells, chanting processions, and the bleating of doomed Paschal lambs. Hippocrates had practised his Aesculapian arts in a nearby pine grove. Aesculapius was supposed to appear to a patient in a dream and suggest the remedy for his illness. Maybe it would work for him, he thought. Lately he'd been dreaming of José. No one had heard from him since he'd left, and Edward worried that he was trying to reach him. In one dream, José suggested that he write a book about the horrors of Central America to be called *Neither the Power nor the Glory.*

After a rare good night's sleep, he felt decades younger, and roamed the ruined castle, huge with crenellated, crumbling battlements; dungeons, endless tunnels, hidden chambers. All over were classical and medieval bric-à-brac they didn't have room for in the museum, Greek and Roman ruins, and Turkish mosques, fountains, and cemeteries. It also had the world's oldest, biggest, and sickest plane tree, said to be planted by Hippocrates, falling apart under its own weight.

After depression returned with redoubled force, he passed deck class dozens of islands, always with cubist white, blue, or pastel houses climbing a hillside circling a bay. He intended only to stay a day in Patmos, where the exiled St. John, at the age of 95 or so, heard the voice of an angel and dictated the Apocalypse. In the tenth century, a Byzantine emperor gave the 30-square-kilometre island to St. Christodoulos, who built an immense mountaintop fortress-monastery for protection against pirates and as home to monks. The Apocalypse pervaded the place, the presence and power of the monastery, always looming over you, and of the monks, though at intervals tourists from cruise ships briefly filled the shops with their polyglot presence.

Hydra was the island of artists and writers; Mykonos, of homosexuals; Patmos, of the occultists. He had never met such a band of charming self-convinced nuts. Everyone sought a guru, or had found him. Though most of the people were crazy, they *did* believe in something, and were intelligent, amusing, if often overly intense. On his first night, he met Michael, "the greatest poet in England," who was a Sufi and Taoist (or, as he put it, "a servant of Tao"); a Colombian poet and political exile; and David, a young Australian lawyer who had once been a holy beggar in India, living in Bombay on a concrete slab. All one night they discussed an advertisement that appeared in the world's major newspapers on April 24, announcing that the new Messiah, the Twelfth Imam, the reincarnation of Krishna, the Fifth Buddha, etc., were all one and that he was amongst them, to be revealed to the world in a universally understandable tongue. Alas, the date had come and gone, and nothing had been heard of the new Messiah. At a 5 a.m. dinner, David announced that *he* was the Messiah.

Over the next days, Edward read the greatest poet in England's poetry, which was all about love is all and sex is all and love is sex and sex is love and love is God and God is sex. The poet lived with an English girl who sank into spells during which she stared into another world. Her husband ordered her about as a form of therapy, while she obeyed dog-like. Edward read David's novel and suggested revisions. And Dave, a young half-Japanese Englishman—everybody seemed to be called Michael or David, and since nobody used anything but first names, it got confusing— had spent a third of his 26 years in jail. He smuggled, illegally copied cassettes and records, and sold ersatz tea and coffee with Lipton's and Nescafé labels.

Ruth Beissel was contemplating a trip to India, where she hoped to relieve her crippling arthritis with the aid of the guru Sai Baba. When Edward mentioned he planned to join her there, David, as distinct from Dave, dispensed advice and addresses. He and Michael, the poet, assured him that Sai Baba would help her. They suggested that Edward meet the magus Stephen, the leader of a commune in the village of Lefkis. They went to a party that Stephen and his Greek wife were throwing for a young Frenchman who, after a year and a half, felt he'd been "cured," and was going home.

On a hillside farm with a curving beach he found the magus, a robust man with a great white beard and shock of white hair. They talked by the edge of a well, with poppies blooming all around and the bells of a herd of goats tinkling nearby. Stephen had spirit guides, a Catholic priest named Father Joe and an Arab named Ramadan. Stephen believed that everyone had a "spiral" of past lives, and that when they "died" they merely went to an "ethereal world," where they could observe this world but not often communicate—or only through chosen "vessels"— and where they remained, meditating, Edward supposed, on the experience of their past life, until they either reached the state of perfection in which they didn't need to return to this world and atone anymore, or returned to purge their karma. Reincarnation had always seemed pure horror to Edward. When he remarked that the ethereal world sounded much like the Catholic limbo, Stephen said no, but there was something like limbo in the spirit world: it was the place where the souls of those who had committed suicide lay and watched the lives they might have led pass in dumb show before them, and were consumed with regret. Edward didn't think he'd like that, though sometimes he thought he was there already. Stephen told Edward that he was an "old soul," who was unlikely to return many more times. He knew nothing of Edward's past, yet he pointed out that he'd had "at least three" South American lives.

The next day, Stephen told him, "Beside you stands Ramadan." Then he said, "Now I see someone coming through. I see white hair, glasses, and a moustache. *Something* about the army." After a pause: "and, very strongly, the law." This was, of course, Edward's father, dead these 13 years. Stephen told him that his father was strongly on his side, and was happy in the ethereal world. His father said something like, "Edward, my son, if with my precise legalistic mind I didn't understand you before, forgive me. Now I do, and I appreciate your struggle and your courage." It was wonderful to receive that message and realize that *someone* was looking over him. His mother, on the other hand, was in trouble in the ethereal world over unresolved aspects of her personality, and probably would have to return to earth. Edward supposed he was one of those unresolved aspects.

Stephen also told him that he had healer's hands, and would work with mentally disturbed people. He told Stephen that he'd wish to be a "hidden healer," working good on people without their knowing it, in order to avoid the ever-present danger in people of his temperament to go on an ego-trip, thinking of themselves as responsible for what was really God's doing. If Ruth's arthritis wasn't healed through Sai Baba, maybe it could be through him.

The interviews with Stephen shook him up. He felt he was coming under someone's power, which he fiercely resisted. Whether it was a power for good or for evil he couldn't tell. Maybe Stephen just picked his mind, although that itself was uncanny. During the five years Stephen had been in Patmos, he'd given therapy based on simple country living, weekly prayer meetings, and meditation. Stephen's wife did much casting of the *I Ching* for Edward: how much he should be allowed to participate in the group, and whether it was time for him to join it. Answer: not yet. What Edward *could* do, the *I Ching* declared, was to read and annotate Stephen's 1,000-page manuscript.

Patmos began to disturb him. The locals were mostly hostile or hard to know and, though he thought Stephen sincere enough, his followers sometimes gave him the creeps. They all seemed to think and speak alike, as though they were the products of a mass mind, or zombies, or hypnotized. And his new friends wouldn't leave him alone: everyone was trying to convert him to some cause or point of view. They visited him at all hours, treating him either as an oracle or as a recruit. He couldn't get any work done. An incident occurred that he took as a sign. He'd bought an expensive French magazine, *Le Nouvel Observateur*, to read an article in it on the Falklands. In a restaurant, he put it on a table while, as usual in Greek restaurants, he chose food from cooking pots a few feet away. When he returned, the magazine was gone. He saw a middle-aged woman at another table reading it. He asked for it back and got it, but the pages of the article had been ripped out. He spoke to the woman in French, but she didn't understand, so what was she doing with the magazine? He asked who had torn the pages out. She said the magazine was on her table and Edward had not been in the restaurant at all. She and her husband suggested he call the police. Edward angrily cancelled his meal. Either someone actively disliked him, or the spirits were telling him he should go. He left Patmos the next day.

He returned to Athens via Mykonos. Small, rocky, arid, it offered little besides a charming port-town, and nude gay sunbathing. In Kos, he had written American Express one of the long, furious, publicity-threatening letters in which he specialized, and sent copies to New York, Rome, and its main office in Brighton, England, disgorging the contents of the copious Tunisian file he'd maintained. He wrote of his attempts to recover his money, his observations on the Arab mafia in Piraeus that dealt in traveller's cheques, pointed out that if American Express were holding *his* money and, at today's interest rates, making a tidy profit on it, they had the moral obligation to *do* something. He did not expect action from the Athens police, amiable nitwits who specialized in adultery cases, pornographic movies, and chicken theft. But he noted that he'd been an American Express customer for 20 years and had only thrice lost traveller's cheques. He threatened to go to a competitor, or return to carrying $100-bills in a money belt.

On his return, he found that American Express had money waiting for him. The bad part was an endless round of trips to police stations and a prison to look at suspects. The Athens police were hopelessly bureaucratic. To his embarrassment, they had his letter to American Express, which included his comments about them. From Station "A" they sent him to Station "B," which sent him to Station "C," which sent him back to Station "A." It took the stupidity of a Tunisian to crack the case: he'd gone to an American Express office to cash a cheque. He was asked to wait for the manager, and was nabbed, and a band of other North Africans with him, whom Edward also had to go and identify.

Edward recognized the Tunisian but told the police he'd been drunk and couldn't be sure. He didn't want revenge against the world's poor for taking advantage of, or retaliating against, the world's rich. He held nothing against the boys who stole his cheques; he'd do the same thing were he they. He was simply tired of having been a victim, and of the effects of being victimized had on him, turning him into a lonely, bitter, suspicious, misanthrope who couldn't recognize or enjoy sex or simple friendship when it was offered.

Notwithstanding, he rejoined his sailor friends in Piraeus. If he had to do it all over again, he thought, he'd join the Merchant Marine. In one year of travel, he could have learned more than in four at university. It would have suited him: its womanlessness; its solitariness, each sailor for himself, and yet the fraternal camaraderie; the travel and the drunken carousing in foreign ports. The sailors were overjoyed to see him; the Chilean who'd brained him was now in jail. They called Piraeus *"el cemetario de los esperanzas,"* the graveyard of hopes, and they met every day to discuss possible jobs at a spot, *"el muro de las lamentos,"* the wailing wall.

Edward befriended the luckless and friendless, like a Costa Rican who had come here with his family's hopes and savings, expecting fame and fortune, and found even worse poverty. In the fall, Edward had put him on a train to pick olives in the Peloponnesus. When he returned, he successively was jailed after an innocent involvement with a jewel thief; got into a fight with an Englishman about the Falkland Islands and was sent to a psychiatric hospital; was arrested for overstaying his visa and had his passport confiscated until he got a ticket out of the country; had his clothes and belongings stolen; was jailed for threatening the Costa Rican consul and refusing to leave. Finding him wandering in rags, Edward fed him, housed him, bought him new clothes, got him a ticket to Barcelona via Paris, and wrested his passport from Immigration. The Costa Rican planned to stay in Paris, of course. He was going to be disillusioned, Edward knew, since he was a dark *Indio* type and the French police would take him for an Arab. He saw him off on a Magic Bus.

All this took nearly a week. Why, he wondered, did he attract, or was attracted to, mentally disturbed people, criminals, vagrants? What karma was he purging? Had he been in some previous life a tyrant, a dictator, or conquistador? Nor did he simply like to feel superior. He thought that his relationship with sailors wasn't masochistic, nor was it mainly sexual, though he'd been to bed with many of them: he could give them a little money and they could give him a little pleasure, and even macho

Latin American sailors usually understood this. They liked to drink, and so did he. When they got too drunk, they became violent but he forgave them, and when he got drunk and did the same, they were equally forgiving. Talking about their countries, their politics, or the World Cup, listening to their music, he was with "*mi gente*," his people, reliving his youth and the cantinas in which he'd drank and talked and fought.

He'd done far more in the past two years than get drunk and have his head bashed in. Winston Leyland, always trolling for literary merit and gay content, this year was publishing *Adonis García*. Next year he was to issue another of Edward's translations, *Bom Criolo: The Black Man and the Cabin Boy*, by the nineteenth-century Brazilian novelist, Adolfo Caminho, which told a tragic tale of a sailor's romantic obsession. Add to this the backbreaking task of selecting and translating a massive Latin American gay-fiction anthology called *My Deep Dark Pain is Love:* he had about a month to go on that one.

He was ready for India, if he could only get the translation out of the way, but he worried about Ruth Beissel and her plans to join Sai Baba. The climate might relieve her pain and make her believe she was cured, but he feared she'd relapse after returning to Canada. Then, too, the voyage could be dangerous or exhausting for someone in her physical state. But perhaps she wouldn't go: she kept changing her mind. In a year or two, he'd have to return to teaching, but not in Canada — unless Henry Beissel could get him a job at Concordia University in Montréal, which he doubted. And where, he wondered, was José? By now he must be in a Barcelona alley. Later, he devoutly hoped, he could be found in the *comajones*, the brothels of San Pedro Sula, Honduras, tending bar, downing rotgut, and curing his hangovers with tamarind juice.

Through the raw winter the red-and-blue macaw had lunged from its horizontal bar but never shrieked "Dry crackers!" Spring came, and the plane and mulberry trees sprouted leaves. One day as he passed by the pet shop, he noticed that the macaw no longer swung from its bar. It had died, the shopkeeper said, of some tropical disease no veterinarian had been able to diagnose.

22

IN THE MIDDLE OF THE EAST

June 1982-March 1983

*And if one calls on people only when one needs them
one cannot expect to find them waiting around.*

~ Insomnia

Though Edward sometimes reviled Randy Wicker as a travelling companion, he was eager to regain his company. However, if Randy was going to join him, he needed to know *right away*. He hoped they could meet in Istanbul, where he now was. The bus from Athens had let him out on the sinister hillside where he and Randy had once arrived. His hotel was $4.25 a night. The Turkish word for "hotel" was "otel," making tourists think that the letter "H" had fallen off signs. Tourists were few, another smiling circumstance. The curfew hours were shorter, fewer soldiers were in sight, and blackouts were rare. Turkish food was warmer and less oil-drenched than Greek — the yoghurt dips, luscious fruit, and drinks he liked, and his beloved stuffed vegetables. He even enjoyed sitting in dim cafés puffing and gurgling away at water pipes among grizzled puzzled old men. He got his hair dyed the blackest black it had ever been.

Turkish, he found, was an easy language to learn: bless red-haired, blue-eyed Kemal Atatürk for having abolished the

devilish Arabic alphabet. Two weeks drifted by. One night he
veered far from the lights of Táksim Square, descending Istiqlal,
the main drag, past shops, street vendors, restaurants, louche
cabarets, turning off the avenue into dark cobbled alleys. He
found the Golden Horn, where fish restaurants creaked and
pitched with tides, late-night motor traffic passed above them,
and ferries took workers between Europe and Asia, downward
past a yard filled with jumbled beturbaned fezzed tombstones,
past a fourteenth-century squat Italian tower, and a small white
mosque.

An alley branched to a cobblestone street aglow with red
light bulbs, thronged with swarthy sailors, greybeards, smooth
teenagers, farmers, blue-jeaned workers, uniformed soldiers.
Weary-looking, they prowled, peering in doorways at the
whores: mostly fat, middle-aged, and bored. The women posed
languidly, danced to atonal music, chatted, waited on stairways,
watched TV. Two imploring teenagers bargained with them,
who smiled, refused. It all seemed passive and passionless: no
pimps, no madams, no drag queens. A boy bought ice cream;
cigarette vendors pushed; kids hawked shirts; a cripple begged;
a grave oldster sold pornographic slides. He took the empty
streets leading to the bridge, ate fish and drank wine with the
tired old men in a café, watching ferries cross in the dark.

Turkey had many repressed, lonely young bachelors:
bad news for them, good news for Edward. He learned to
never proposition anyone; simply make eye or verbal contact,
let the other party make the come-on. Someone who started a
conversation in a bar, unless he was just trying to practice his
English or find out about the chances of work abroad, would
eventually propose sex. A case in point was two young men—
hard to guess the age of Turks, because of their serious mien,
the mustaches, and the wrinkles that hot sun, hard work, and
worry imprinted—whom he met. Though Turks were greedy,
rough, and sadistic in bed, and what he liked were men who
were tough but not rough, he spent two nights in the men's
disorderly suburban apartment, having been caught on purpose
by the curfew both times. The experience was satisfactory, but
unsettling. He hadn't slept a wink, but his hosts did—with a
dagger at their side.

He wrote Randy that all relations were based on interest and use; there was always a used and a user, a lover and a beloved. Nothing wrong with this, so long as the used consented to the use. These contracts shouldn't be codified. Americans, he wrote, were compelled to categorize and organize: they'd form unions for johns and hustlers, a club for pedophiles. Why couldn't they let things happen and nature take its course? They couldn't believe in anything unless it was written down as a law or constitution or Supreme Court decision. He pitied them for their desperate need to make public, respectable, and profitable. Randy's talk of gay cemeteries, bowling leagues, and softball teams was typical. Like America's desire to remake the world in its image, its identity politics was innate.

Uncertainty, the outlaw element, that tingle of danger, that element of the chase, of the hunter and the hunted — and one could become the other — made hustling and being hustled, picking-up and being picked-up, exciting. This was one message of John Rechy's *City of Night* or of Jean Genet's *The Thief's Journal*. It wasn't for sexual reasons alone, he wrote, that he was homosexual; it was because he was anti-society, anti-organization, anti-family. Attempts to convert short-term commerce into something more permanent could be heartbreaking failures. With luck, you could develop camaraderie, a "we're-all-together-in-this-fucking-game-so-we-might-as-well-be-friends-and-help-each-other-out-when-we-can." Working through sex to friendship could be managed, yes. If he were smitten, he wanted to go to bed with a boy as soon as possible and get that out of the way. Then perhaps they could have a stable friendship. That was about the best you could expect. Always, always, he wrote Randy, control the relationship.

In a brief sharp war, the British reclaimed the Falkland Islands from Argentina. Neither had the best claim to it, he wrote. *He* did. The Falklands were settled by people from St. Malo, hence the name, *Malvinas* < *Malouines*. His father's family had been Norman, from a small village called Lessay, a few miles from St. Malo. His mother's ancestors were from nearby Brittany, and the French fleets of settlers for Canada sailed from St. Malo. He thus demanded to be addressed as "*Roi et Souverain des Iles Malouines.*"

He had promised to comment on the 1,000-page spiritual epic that Stephen had given him in Patmos. He also needed to deal with a pile of long, long-overdue translations that Winston Leyland had unleashed. Such unpaid work was going to take a while, and Winston would have to understand this, or find another translator. He asked himself why he undertook these tasks? The urge to redeem himself? To feel socially useful?

And Randy.... *Was he or wasn't he* joining him in Turkey? He sketched routes they might take, ruins they might visit, markets Randy could pillage. But when he checked his mail at the Canadian Embassy in Ankara he found out that Randy was going to a Caribbean island. Disgusted, he took a hotel right in the bus terminal, hoping to quickly leave the capital's cold, overcast or drizzling days. The traffic noise was infernal, the crowds claustrophobic. Ankara was a good candidate for the world's ugliest city. Planned, it had outgrown its planner, Atatürk, into freeways, Bauhaus boxes, and shantytowns. A few Greek and Roman ruins, a medieval hilltop castle, and a couple of old mosques confused the picture. The smog was bad: people burned wood or lignite coal. He spent a night seeking a restaurant where he could read his newspaper and letters, but could find only beer halls filled with old men. He started to smoke, which he reasoned would curb his drinking, calm his nerves, give him something to do with his hands, and while away insomnia. He resorted to Mandrax and Valium, rereading two favourite Shakespearian plays: *King John* and *Richard the Second.* He celebrated his forty-fourth birthday with a drinking bout: a panic attack about impending death induced such hypertension that he thought he'd have a stroke had he not gone to a hospital (his blood pressure was 200/160, they said.) He took himself off alcohol.

In the semitropical southeast, he saw the wonders of Pamukkale. The village lay at the foot of calcium cliffs, which dropped in a series of steps, so that the water from hot and cold springs tumbled into hundreds of bathing pools. Ruth had told him she was postponing her trip to India until November. He responded that he'd probably get to Bombay before she did. He was ready for India: more and more he saw everything as *maya,* and he had as little attachment to belongings as a *sadhu.* One thing that didn't appear to be *maya* was mild chronic diarrhea.

After a few hours' exposure to 50,000 fat Turkish poppas, mommas, and screaming brats he fled Marmaris on the Mediterranean, one of the ports in deep windless bays on the deeply indented coast. He prefaced his postcards to Randy with "we could have visited...." The village of Kaş, for example, in the Antalya region. On the road to it the bus stopped in Demre long enough that he could see the church of the fourth-century bishop who became Santa Claus. Not really *his* church, of course, which was destroyed by Arabs, who left it in ruins. Nor was he actually there: his body had been stolen by Italians in the eleventh century, and now lay in Bari. Kaş, arching back from the sea, was like a Greek island: whitewashed, red-tile-roofed homes, a small, curving bay ringed with cafés and restaurants. The people were all Greek, though they didn't seem to realize it. Greece was in fact only two miles away. Izmir, once called Smyrna, certainly had been Greek, until the Turkish victory of 1921, when the town had been torched and women and children skewered in the streets. Instead of Greeks, the town had fig trees, grape arbours, and broken statues.

Knowing Randy's distaste for Christian history, he sent postcards from Ephesus (Efes), depicting the Virgin Mary's house in the nearby mountains, said to be her home and final resting-place. He always enjoyed twitting his proudly atheistic friend, generally keying his postcards to Roman Catholic feast days. He had so far visited five of the seven churches of Asia Minor, as named by John in the Book of Revelation, he wrote. The Virgin Mary's house had been revealed by a German mystic who saw it in her vision, and was visited by Christians and by Muslims, who revered her as Miriam, mother of the prophet Issa. Beside it was a spring whose waters were said to erase 20 years from one's age. He drank of them and reported that it was true: he felt "positively infantile."

Overland, he headed for Konya of the namesake province, with its tomb-mausoleum of Rumi, the poet-founder of the Whirling Dirvishes. In Erzurum, in barren, impoverished eastern Turkey, the women looked like walking potato sacks, and the men wore beards and skullcaps à la Ayatollah Khomeini, who smiled down from the Iranian consulate's walls. Turkey had some of the world's worst hotels; the further east you went, the worse they got. But at the Örnek Otel, for the first time in three months he got an airy, clean, sunny room where he could type in peace. A big table, suitable for writing, and a chair! Enough light to read by at night! A shower that was hot in the morning and did not drip! A private toilet that actually flushed!

The Turkish hotel reverted to type in Kars, a bleak garrison town near the borders of Armenia and Iran. One night, he soiled his bed sheets: embarrassing, but he disliked his hotel so much he was rather glad. In the Kurdish village of Doubayazit, on the Iran border, women dressed in layers of skirts, bands, and sashes in clashing, day-glo colours. By law, Kurdish could not be taught, spoken, or even the word "Kurd" used: they were "Mountain Turks." Long before the Turks swept in, the Kurds had been here. Like the Palestinians or the French Canadians, they were not going to go away. Do—ubayazit lay in the shadow of the snowy extinct volcano Mount Ararat: he reported to Randy that he had seen the animals go into the ark, "2 X 2." He spent two days by Lake Van, a salty inland sea. Van itself was a medieval city: four miles of black stone ramparts at the point at which Turkey dissolved into the Arab world.

He took a tangent to the Black Sea and to Trabzond, filled with Orthodox churches converted into mosques. Clinging to cliffs outside town was the white-walled Sumela monastery where in frescoes St. John the Baptist contemplated his severed head, St. Nicholas destroyed the immoral classical statues, and the Pantokrator reigned in glory. In Sinop, named after the Amazon queen whom Zeus courted and granted her wish— which turned out to be perpetual virginity—he sat under an arbour of Virginia creeper, vine of his childhood. Plane trees aped maples but produced balls, not wings, and had scaly trunks. Mimic maples.

In the provinces, he'd had to reverse the pick-up strategy he'd formulated in Istanbul: here, *you* had to approach. People were pathetically anxious to communicate with the rare tourist, and get news of the outside world, but news was hard to convey. They had only heard of a distant place called "Almanya," Germany, where the best and brightest of their young men had gone. When he said he was from "Kanada" there was a long, reflective silence, then the timid question: "Amerika?" Politically, things had eased: there were no more curfews. On September 6, the day they took a census for the plebiscite on a new constitution, every Turk was ordered to stay put all day and be counted. The constitution was approved.

On the way back from Nemrut Dağ, Nimrod's Mountain, where an insane Roman vassal king had built a place of worship for the religion he founded, whose mostly Greek pantheon boasted himself as principal deity, Edward's taxi halted. A loaded truck had blocked the road. They were in a hill town, Karadut, which meant "blackberry." It was early October. Blackberries grew in every stage from dawn-blue flower to glossy fruit, everywhere by the road. Children offered them to him. He answered the villagers' questions: Where was he from? Is there work? What are the women like? Are you married? How much do you earn each month? How many wives? How many children?

This was a great moment for Karadut — an *almán*, a tourist, in their midst. He and a newfound friend, Mehmet, lay in a field under fig trees. Mehmet asked him whether he was happy here, and Edward said he was. They ate flat, unleavened bread and sweet green figs, red as strawberry jam inside. Beautiful, guileful children came to stare at them, and cautious, brilliantly hued women did, too, from a distance, and bloomered, moustachio'd men. Six months of the year, Mehmet said, the place was snow- and rain-bound. The villagers improvised levers from boards and barrels, and lifted the truck from the ditch. Skullcapped elders murmured *inchallah*. The taxi could go.

Having visited the hazelnut and pistachio capitals of the world, he now toured Diyarbakir, the watermelon one (Dilley, Texas, only *thought* it was), in time for the Feast of El-Kibr. He went to Antakya in the extreme south, where he sent Randy a postcard of the world's first Christian church, said to be founded by St. Peter. Antakya, the classical Antioch, was set in a subtropical valley close to the sea. Once belonging to Syria, it was Arab-speaking. The Arabness began to show in charm, bustle, and aggressiveness. He was starting to leave the slow, grave, taciturn Turks behind.

Near the Syrian border, Harran was an ancient village of mud houses like beehives or termite mounds built on an endless plain like Saskatchewan's. Abraham had paused here in his peregrination to Canaan land: the carp in the local lake were sacred to him, or so they said. A ruined Umayyad minaret, towers, a Roman arch, a well, a castle — all crumbling to earth. He asked his driver in book-Turkish, "Why do they live this way? What's the advantage of living in cones? Why does no other village do the same thing?" The patient, dignified man with a walrus moustache became irked by the persistent questions. He spat out a single word. "*Fakir.*" They were poor.

He had reached the Levant, Syrian version. Aleppo, a city of two million, was wild with smells, colours, noise, and dust. He was pleased to see male hand-holding and kissing in public. People often could speak English or French, though women were veiled and men wore keffiyehs, djellabas, or Turkish bloomers. A world of muezzins, mosques, alleys, and endless souks, a covered market as big as Istanbul's. He saw ruins of the sixth-century Byzantine cathedral erected around the pillar on which St. Simon Stylites had perched for three decades. South into the desert, Palmyra was a scraggly village with six square kilometres of ruins, including a Temple of Baal. We still make human sacrifices to Baal, thought Edward, except we call them "abortions."

Damascus was crawling with Communist "advisers," technicians, and tourists, and P. L. O. members, most of whom friendly youths who drank too much. After the warm days and cold nights of the desert, it had turned rainy. At the Canadian Embassy he found letters from Ruth confirming that she was going to India, but naming no dates, flights, or address where he could find her. A year earlier, she'd given him addresses, but he'd left these back in Athens. He decided to go to India at the start of December at the latest. He wrote Monique de Gaye, with whom Ruth had been staying, that he didn't want to be with Ruth in her first weeks in India so as not to neutralize Sai Baba's healing with his scepticism, or to witness her disappointment when the healing failed.

He slipped into Lebanon, which, after seven years of civil war and the Israeli invasion, the posting of a multinational peace force and a relatively moderate president seemed safe to visit. However, every Lebanese he met was amazed to see him, laughed at his pretence at being a tourist, and wanted to know whom he was spying for. The taxi trip from Damascus, usually two hours, took all day and nervewrackingly crossed seven different army lines. Among the green mountains, the armies of Syria, Palestine, and Israel were fighting for control, and Maronite Christians, Druze, and Muslims battled each other. But Beirut seemed prosperous, if one ignored the empty and boarded-up buildings. The Royal Garden Hotel—apparently the one hotel left open in all West Beirut—charged him an extortionate $US56 a night, enlivened by the sounds of real or imagined gunfire.

The only place he could visit was a Christian town, Baalbek, which entailed crossing Israeli lines four times to questions, gibes, document checks, and rifled baggage. From now on, he resolved to help the Palestinians every chance he got. Not to mention the other oppressed non-nations of the Middle East, like the Armenians, Kurds, Assyrians, Druze, Baha'i, Maronites, Shiites, Alaouites, Sunnites, and Copts. When he got there, Baalbek turned out to be run by an Iranian brigade of "volunteers" who Khomeini had dispatched.

He scuttled back to the relative sanity of Damascus. One night, he got lost in the alleyways of the Grand Souk, when he strayed into what had been the old Jewish quarter. The secret police arrested him as an Israeli spy. He didn't have his passport on him, and couldn't recall the name of his hotel. They tossed him into a jail run by jovial blood-red-and-green camouflaged soldiers. The next day, in a police station disguised as a house, plainclothes police grilled him about Israeli security (Do they eat felafel? Are Jewish girls easy to make?) before giving him on a guided tour of synagogues, Christian churches, and the local offices of P.L.O factions. His hotel was called Abu-l'Houl, "Father of Fear."

He discovered that he could easily get a visa for Jordan, having been refused one in Ankara. From Amman, he wrote Renate Jürgensen that every time he saw an Arab lady with a sack over her head he thought it must be she, and every time he ate a sheep's head—eyes, tongue, brains and all—he longed to share it with her. The second language in Syria had been English; in Lebanon, French; now it was English again. Aqaba,

Jordan's only port, now handled all Iraq's imports, since Iran was blockading its ports. It had one bar; thousands of container trucks arrived from and left for Baghdad every day. A hundred miles north was Petra, the ruined, canyon-hidden Arab-Roman city cut in the cliff-faces of rosy red sandstone. He saw Crusader castles, desert fortresses, and the mud streets, hovels, and tents of a refugee camp. He was going to take a bus through Syria and Turkey to Athens, where he'd fly to India. He picked up a Syrian visa and got his passport stamped at the Turkish Embassy. When he returned to his hotel, he found that his passport had vanished.

A lost passport meant a round of police stations and government ministries in the hope the thing would turn up. This time it didn't. Canada had no embassy in Amman. Everything had to be done through the embassy in Beirut, and everything had to go by courier. The loss, and a bad cold, knocked him out. The chilly weather and unheated hotel room made his cold worse. Amman was nearly dry, but of course he could have ferreted out a bar in the Sahara. Even if one were Lawrence of Arabia, there'd be precious little to do here. Maybe, he thought, he could interview the visiting Yassar Arafat. After a month's enforced stay, a passport again in his pocket, he took a plane for Athens, costing him sevenfold what the overland bus ride would have. He resolved to fly to India in two weeks' time.

When he got back, he could have kissed the Athenian ground. Writing Randy on the Feast of St. Nicholas, the Orthodox patron saint of sailors, travellers, and children, he said that the mindbind of Islam had pressed on him like a corset. It was joy not to hear muzzeins sing, not to know that Allah is *Akbar*, or that "prayer is better than sleep," not to have to walk a marathon to a beerless bar, not to have to repeatedly explain, in Basic English, French, or German, what he was, when he had arrived, what were his religious beliefs, whether there was work or marriageable girls where he came from. It was wonderful to be where he knew the streets, the waiters, the food, to rejoin friends, out-of-work Latin-American seamen like Adrián. The Chilean, a particular friend of, José, *his* particular friend, was a hard-working, hard-drinking ordinary seaman, a big man with a big smile. When he encountered him, Adrián wept that the government had started to deport people like him. Edward bore him off to the palm groves of Crete, where they celebrated the feast day of Our Lady of Guadalupe, the Dark Virgin, patroness of the Americas.

He thought he couldn't take India until he'd rested a bit. He now had a letter from Ruth giving him Bombay and Sai Baba ashram addresses, and telling him that she would set off on November 16, as it happened the same day that he had lost his passport. Any day, any week, he'd get up the energy to join her. He got a letter from Henry telling him that Ruth was annoyed that he hadn't been in Bombay to meet her. Guilt complicated and compounded itself and created deeper guilt and self-disgust.

He developed a hacking cough — cigarettes, plus the fact that the Athens winter was freakish: snowfalls-and-flurries; blizzards on New Year's Eve and the end of January, intercalated with days of dazzling sun, blue skies, and warmth. As the slow snow fell, statues were transformed into people, people into statues, the Acropolis looming on an escarpment, the caryatids dissolving in acid rain. Around Ommonia Square, movie-houses opened in the morning. Rows of black-suited men watched American fuck-movies, their hands stirring in pockets and under newspapers, squirting into handkerchiefs he thought likely were embroidered by adoring maiden aunts. Old men sold sesame rings and spinach pies; other old men talked politics while cats prowled. Under the pale sun, languid playboys, newspaper-readers, and the rare tourist sipped beneath leafless poplars.

A craving for milk made him drink eight half-litre bottles by noon. One reason he drank too much alcohol, he thought, was that he was always thirsty. Milk didn't fill him up, intoxicate him, or sicken him. He disliked drinking water; he liked only things that had a taste to them. One night he got into heated debate with two Palestinians about who was responsible for Beirut massacres. At such times, Edward's towering moral rage either frightened or incited. The men were incited: they broke his nose. For a supporter of the Palestinians, he ruefully reflected, he certainly seemed to have bad luck with them.

When he could read again, he had to deal with Himalayas of mail, foothills of new Latin American material to read, appraise, translate, annotate, type up. He proofread the lengthy *My Deep Dark Pain is Love*. Through the summer and fall, he'd also been correcting Stephen's vast single-spaced manuscript. He had sent the bulky object to Patmos, only to have it bounce back. He posted it again, and to hell with it. Stephen would never find a publisher anyhow. His correspondence with his admirer, the wealthy English collector Anthony Reid, also met with misadventure. Reid, whose library holdings included hundreds of gay erotic drawings encased in morocco albums, had invited him to fill up a blank blue-bound book with handwritten poems: *"Using only the right hand pages...* please write in any original boy-poems of your choice (your *own* poems, of course) but write them *IN INK*....Hopefully ALL will be about BOYS....A TITLE for the book... should have the word `BLUE'."* He promised a fee of £100 on delivery; if Edward came to visit, he would be given a bedroom suite overlooking a lake, introductions to friends in London, choice film-shows, unlimited motor tours, not to mention some delectable boy-love collectibles. Edward lost both letter and book in Beirut, so the collector was out £5 plus postage. Reid sent him a photocopy of his letter but refrained from sending another blank book.

He thought of *Later*, the book he'd brought out with Ian Young's Catalyst Press. In four years, he'd not asked for a financial statement or the fate of the 500 copies whose print run he had paid for. He now asked if there were any proceeds he could apply to subsidizing a fourth book. To me, he wrote that he had not discarded my poetry collection *Madwomen*: it rested in the asylum of a valise stuck in a dusty basement cupboard in Athens while he toured the Middle East. Byron Black, last heard from six months earlier, sent a huge batch of zany visuals from Japan. It was too much. Dealing with correspondence took time.

Letters and work helped to counter anomie, and combat satyriasis. He could go for long periods without thinking much about sex, but when he was in heat, he was ravenous. Erotically roused, he could masturbate several times a day and still want sex. But he didn't know what produced the cycle. Alcohol? Pornography? Something. Sexual contact was like a spasm of life fighting off death. When he yielded to it, it saddened him: he'd hoped that age would free him from desire. But even greater than sexual desire was sexual curiosity.

It was now late February. He was ready to go. He bought a plane ticket. But he first had to renew the three-month passport he'd got in Amman in order to get a visa for India, and the Embassy delayed and delayed. He had to send for money, which took a week. He had to get rid of countless small belongings. He bought guidebooks and snatched everything the Indian tourist office handed out.

Meanwhile, his friend Adrián had returned from picking oranges in Argos in the Peloponnesus. After a taverna meeting, they parted at midnight. The next day, Adrián phoned that the police had picked him up. When Edward brought him some cigarettes, the police told him that Adrián would be released; he should come back that afternoon. When he did, Adrián was gone. Edward assumed that, released, he'd returned to Argos.

Randy wanted to know why he hadn't joined Ruth in Bombay. Replying, he cautioned his friend to cease nagging. Didn't he think that, what with his parents, the Roman Catholic Church and schools and universities, that he'd got enough advice? Three weeks later, he learned that Adrián was still in jail, and about to be deported to Chile. At Adrián's request, they had sent him to Israel where, arriving grimy and penniless, he'd been packed back to Greece. With difficulty, Edward got permission to see him. Adrián, a bitter opponent of the Pinochet regime, was terrified of being returned to Chile. Only Edward could rescue him. He thought, "You've abandoned so many people who've loved you or whom you've loved. Now you have another chance to save someone. Do it."

They wouldn't let him buy Adrián a bus or boat ticket to another European country since they thought he'd get off at the first Greek stop. They wouldn't let him buy a return plane ticket to, say, Rome, since they didn't want him to return, nor would they give Edward his passport so that he could get a visa. No European country would let him in by air without a visa or a return ticket. Finally, Yugoslavia agreed to take him. The idea was to get him there, then proceed to Italy. But only after he threatened to sue did the Yugoslav airline let them board.

On February 24, Belgrade admitted them, but the Italian Embassy said Adrián needed a visa, only obtainable in Chile. Edward got him into Italy by taking a night train to Trieste, where the sleepy immigration official didn't even look at his passport. In Venice, Adrián wanted to return to Greece on a ferry with him, but Edward, giving him money, made him stay behind. He hoped he'd reach Greece undetected, or find work in an Italian port.

Exhausted, he instructed his Lindsay, Ontario trust company to telex $2,000 to Bombay. He reset his departure date for March 12, but sensed that Ruth was no longer there. In any event, he was going now.

23

FORMS OF APOLOGY

March-June 1983

*And this is the millstone I carry around my neck. It is also one proof
I have of the existence of the Devil,
and I think that you have already guessed his name.*

~ The Millstone

The plane brought him to Bombay on a Sunday morning.
After a frigidly air-conditioned, sheetless night in a Muslim
boarding house, he learned from the director of the Goethe
Institute that, following her stay at Sai Baba's ashram, Ruth had
left India barely a week earlier. To the very end, she'd expected
Edward to appear. He spent the next three days depressed that
he was alone in this enormous country. In a surly postcard to
Randy depicting a sculptured panel of a man copulating with
a horse, he said he was shocked at the multitudes living on the
street amid skyscrapers, possessing only a sack, a straw or rope
mat on a pallet, or a hut of cardboard or sacking.

He booked deck-class on a boat that took nearly a day
to reach Panjim, the capital of Goa, a small, still markedly
Portuguese city on the river near the sea. Baroque gold-altar
churches and the remains of St. Francis Xavier in the Basilica
of Bom Jesus were a few miles upstream. On the globetrotting
typewriter Ruth had given him, he painfully explained why

he had funked their rendezvous. He had let her down, and failed her when she'd most needed him. Yes, his behaviour was inexcusable and seemed inexplicable but.... He wished to avoid rhetoric, excuses, rationalizations, and self-justifications. He promised to keep his letter short and to the point. Then he wrote write several thousand words of excuses, rationalizations, and self-justifications.

He recapped his travails and traumas of the previous year and, backing and filling, asked whether he'd maliciously wished to let her experience alone the horrors of an underdeveloped country, since he had warned her of them and she had made so light of them. A desire to rub her idealist's nose in the fact that India was not engaged in a lofty spiritual quest, but in a quest for survival, and that corruption, violent crime, injustice, and indifference to suffering were rife? From Kipling and Forster to V.S. Naipaul and Salmon Rushdie, books had made him think that India was inscrutable and perilous. Even in the Indians he'd liked, he sensed something treacherous and obsequious. He distrusted all religious leaders and cult figures, especially based in an ashram. He wasn't cut out for meditation, or to join a troupe singing through villages.

The rule in this climate was to get up very early, drink vast quantities of liquids, stay out of the heat, and keep oneself busy. Also avoid alcohol, difficult to do in Goa because every second building was a bar or wine-shop. Menu items were an inexhaustible puzzle, though everything he ordered seemed to come out a curry in the end. He was losing weight, because it so hot he didn't feel like eating more than once a day, and suffered from trickling diarrhea.

Half those in the mostly rural union territory of Goa were Roman Catholic, but Portuguese influence was dying out 22 years after its "liberation." The land was lush, reminding him of Brazil. The young spoke English and Marathi. The courteous, gentle, reserved, and helpful old men were pleased to speak Portuguese with him. Tourists included the usual unwashed rock-oriented, druggy, or religious-freak European hippies and bankrupt beachcombers, with their cutoff jeans, and backpacks. They lived, it seemed, by smuggling, drug peddling, panhandling, or robbing one another.

Goa was cheap. Economizing was becoming important to him. One could run through any amount of money if you were out of the country, he thought, and the people looking after money were neglectful. His private income wasn't such a fortune as people thought. To manage money properly, you had to devote your life to it, and then you didn't have time for anything else. He had no regrets: inflation would have eaten it up anyhow, and he preferred to see the world rather than crouch in Canada counting pennies.

Letters caught up with him. From Japan, Byron Black sent one adorned with ironic rubber-stamps—mail art and rubber-stamp art were among his many enthusiasms —and included colour photos of a Filipino boy named Marlin Oliveros, his new partner and video assistant. Byron had taught in a photographic college in Osaka for four years, and was planning a trip to Thailand to videotape the Karen rebels on the Burmese border. A stranger, a Toronto theatre director named Sky Gilbert, introduced himself as a producer of plays based on the poetry of gay writers. He wanted to stage Edward's work too, this one for spring 1984. "I think you are Canada's Cavafy," he wrote, "which is quite the highest praise I can think of for a poet."

A letter from Henry Beissel made him recall that during his French visit nearly three years earlier, Henry had accused of him of treating children maliciously. This had rankled. True, he tended to be sarcastic and ironic, and children did not understand irony, his anyway. Admittedly, he was not particularly fond of children. Like dogs, they were noisy; they demanded too much attention; and they were always underfoot. If he'd been malicious to Henry's little Klara, maybe it was due to envy. He would always live alone, but Henry had managed not only to set up a new hearth but to sire a child.

For the past few years, he'd been translating for Winston Leyland's Gay Sunshine Press, but translation wasn't the niche that he hoped life would craft for him. He didn't necessarily find life tragic, as Ruth claimed he did. He found it meaningless. The secret was that there was no secret, the meaning, that there was no meaning; the mystery, that it would always remain a mystery. Strolling along a beach, he read a message misspelled in the sand, waiting to be erased:

It is called water.
It is in Colva.
We are called heapy.
We all come different place.
Hear the boats, coming ang going.
Thank you.
He transcribed this on a shard of cardboard, a material only slightly less impermanent.

Madurai, epitome of the temple town, was in Tamil Nadu, an algal, fetid tank with a ruined sultan's palace. Ten thousand jingling rickshaw-drivers rang bells and tapped their handlebars outside his hotel window. A thousand sacred cows ate and excreted, upset fruit carts, blocked cyclists and pedestrians. This was a cowtown for sure.

The temple of Minakshi was festooned with coloured figures of gods, beasts, and mortals. Thousands of soaring brutish pyramids were alive with painted, intertwined deities, all similar, all different, a triumph of rococo, no inch undecorated. Wrinkled temple elephants with the smug contemptuous faces of priests would, for five rupees, scoop up your offering of fruit and present it to the elephant-headed god. Courtyard within courtyard held carved dim columns, dank silence, the smell of hashish and incense, padding barefoot fat white-robed priests and devotees with flame-marked foreheads. In the sanctum sanctorum's barely visible darkness resided the lingam and the yoni.

He spent his first night in a downtown guesthouse that possessed a finely detailed view of the hellish pyramid, and was constructed above a stable for sacred cattle that munched, shat, and behaved like normal cows. They mooed all night. Cows slept little. So did Edward.

The opium he'd bought visions, though less vivid than the pyramids. The next day he moved to another bell-janglers' corner hotel. At a newspaper stand, he found Ravi, a fresh-faced 15-year-old. An English-speaker ("One of the only ones you'll find here, sah") born in Sri Lanka, he dressed in the navy shorts and thin white shirt of his breed. "Anything you want I'll get, I'll show you, I'll bring you to see. I'll do anything!" Edward noted the hidden promise in the double-edged words, also noted a protruding tooth, mused on whether it might interfere with the act he fleetingly contemplated. He made a date to meet him the next day, and promptly forgot him.

But Ravi did not forget. Next afternoon he was there by the news kiosk. "Why didn't you meet me today? I'd planned..." He let himself be taken in a hired trishaw-jangler to a ruined palace. Surprise: it was beautiful in its tiled and stalactite dereliction. Next morning, early and hot to trot, Ravi was there with the rickshaw boy. But Edward had a traveller's cheque to change, which meant paying the driver for an interminable stay parked by a bank. Tax-clearance to get for Sri Lanka required trips to the "English" side of town across the river (broad streets, lush gardens, avenues of flame trees). While there, Ravi simply had to stop at the "best" hotel since he'd always dreamed of breakfasting there. Inside a cavernous Edwardian club with cummerbunded waiters and decapitating ceiling fans, Ravi ordered bacon that he no more than nibbled. He highspiritedly played his nagging theme: "Take me with you to Sri Lanka. If you can't, at least take me to Rameshwaram. I've never been anywhere but Madurai except Kodaicanal. Take me to Kodaicanal!"

Kodaicanal? Said to be a small cool hilltown, four hours away by bus. It was "Kodaicanal" until at last Edward said, "OK, we'll go to Kodaicanal tomorrow morning. Meet me at nine." Then, weary of grateful chatter, he told the rickshaw-boy to find him an arrack shop. Ravi drank his first arrack, made from sugar cane, rice, or coconut, his first *toddy*, fermented palm sap. Late that afternoon, in Edward's hotel room, he said solemnly, sweetly, "Thank you. I'd do anything for you." Before he left, he bent over him in bed and kissed his cheek.

Next morning, Edward rose, determined to avoid Ravi. He lingered in the arrack shop at a long table lined with dhoti-clad untouchables who spat on the sawdust floor. He drank until the heat, flies, cows, and jangling cycle bells were bearable, even pleasant. Noon came. By now, he thought, the boy must have understood that life was one broken promise after another. Nothing could be. He went back to the hotel.

Ravi was waiting for him there, resentment blazing in his eyes. "I've waited three hours here for you. What happened?" But at once his mood changed. After all, Edward had come, he was *there*. There was still time, there were many buses. Ravi laughed: "Me mommy said that I can go, and I borrowed these trousers from me very best friend, because I don't have, and it is *cold* in Kodaicanal." But Edward had soured.

"It's off. I'm not going."

"But why? You promised."

"I don't have the time."

His head throbbed, throbbed in the heat. He shambled slowly up to his room. Ravi followed him, and began to cry.

"But I told my mommy! But you promised me! But me friend's trousers...But you promised! I thought you liked me. You said you was me friend."

Brutally, Edward answered, "You're a little boy. I've no time for little boys. I don't want to spend three days with a little boy!"

"OK, a little boy, but you said... Me mommy...."

Even then Edward wanted to take him in his arms, say, "My boy, forgive me. Can't you see I'm drunk?" and cry with him, saying, "All right. We'll go. I'll sleep, and we'll go up this evening."

Instead, he said, "You can't even do the things I like!" He unzipped his pants, seized the thin arms, yanked him forward, thrust down his head. Ravi did not have to kneel, he was so small. He wept and said he'd never done *that*.

"Oh, I know you have!" He watched Ravi's mouth close on his penis. He twisted, bumped, ground, and pumped, then pulled away and yelled, "You little queen, get out of here. You can't even suck cock! Get away!" He pushed him off, peeled 100 rupees from his pocket roll.

"But me mommy...But you said..."

"Get out!"

He shoved him out, Ravi retreating.

The next morning, he resolved to explain everything. But first, he had to hit the arrack shop. The hot hours passed. He managed to regain his hotel, pack his belongings, pay the bill, take a rickshaw to the bus station. Yes, there was still a bus going up to Kodaicanal.

He arrived at nightfall in one of the retreats the Raj knew how to contrive: a dredged lake for boating, horse trails, a race-course, a cricket pitch, stone churches, evergreens, and English flowers. He spent the weekend thinking of how he'd make it up to Ravi. He strolled round the lake he might have boated on with Ravi, he rode the horse that Ravi might have ridden.

Back in Madurai, he avoided the temples and the arrack shop. He switched hotels and spent his time in the "English" part of town. He thought he might run into Ravi but he didn't, and he couldn't remember the name of the slum he lived in. He left for Rameshwaram and the ferry to Sri Lanka, feeling as if a millstone were around his neck, the one in the Douay version of Mark 9:42: "And whosoever shall offend one of these little ones that believe in me, it were better for that man that a millstone were placed around his neck, and he were cast into the sea."

24

PERJURED EDEN

June-July 1983

The traveller leaves the island. Classic theme:
ships, garlands, handkerchiefs' supreme adieu.
This time, though, the scene's different: airport venue
crowded with hungry refugees — the dream
become nightmare. Time to wake up. The boy?
Back in his small village picking up his small life.

~ Farewell, Dear Reader

Sri Lanka, one of whose epithets was "Land without Sorrow," looked good after he had taken the slow ferry, but trouble was in the air. In the north, Tamil Tigers had raided army depots, and destroyed buses, even a train. The Sinhalese, who controlled the army and police, exacted revenge. Anti-Tamil riots, arson, and carnage spread. This, he thought, was the latest yank in a tug of war between the majority Sinhalese and the minority Tamils, including a million who held no citizenship or passport, only a card allowing them to live in or travel to India or Sri Lanka. The Tamil Tigers was a loose name for assorted insurgents taking part in a civil war that was two-and-a-half-millennia old.

After Colombo, the ugly capital, even the poorest farmhouses looked neat and clean, and Sri Lankans seemed to him less sly and devious than Indians. The weather was lovely because the monsoon had been weak, a disaster for farmers but a boon to tourism. Prices were ridiculously low. Boy guides offered him a tiny entry into their world. They got free hotel accommodation in the towns to which they led tourists, ate meals with them, earned a small stipend or "gift." Hotels didn't even blink at a boy's presence, though the president had declared that "socially unacceptable" behaviour carried with it a 20-years prison term.

From the hill town of Nuwara Eliya, he climbed to Adam's Peak, where legend had it that the Buddha's footprint was stamped, and to Bodhygaya, where Buddha had sat under a bo-tree until enlightenment arrived. On a long snaky street, bazaaring its way under the mountain peak, he tasted boiled cashews in a banana leaf, and buffalo yoghurt in clay bowls. Pedro's Hotel had rattan armchairs, and fading portraits of the young Victoria. Guides took him in a hired car to the "World's End," where the mountains fell sheer. In pine woods he rested amid mist like reefer smoke, ate birdnests of noodles, and visited tea plantations where bright-skirted Tamil women bowed. Descendants of the untouchables, despised of the despised, dark quiet men with elongated names and equally long addresses.

He found beaches of reefs, coral, bright fish, and blue water on the south and southwest coasts. In the Muslim town of Hambantota he saw a green-and-white-breasted mosque, a pomegranate tree beside a cool pool in its courtyard. He ate buffalo curd covered with a yellow crust, and sea turtle eggs — the leatherbacks swam thousands of miles to lay them. He drank Lion stout, and noticed how bo-trees throttled palmyras. The bo-tree sent its clinging tentacles down the trunk of the spiky tree that yielded palm wine toddy, sugar, and roof thatch, sucking out its soft sweet substance.

On the way back to Colombo, as he toured ruined royal Buddhist cities in the island's centre, the bus careened toward the main and only street of Dambulla, a straggling town noted for fifth-century cave murals. The bus stopped. He descended, and the bus reeled on. Burdened with luggage, he looked dazedly about him for a hotel signboard. A brown lizard boy lounged against a stone wall, half-hidden by hibiscus, and briskly detached himself. Edward followed him.

Herath, a buck-toothed Sinhalese lad, insisted on going with him to the caves, where monks raged at him because he tipped, not them, but an elderly man who showed him the cave's features with a flashlight. At nearby Sigiriya, they viewed a ruined castle built atop an enormous rock 1,500 years ago by a mad king. He gave Herath 50 rupees, about $2 U.S., for his services: an enormous amount for Sri Lanka. Herath wanted a pair of blue jeans, and was disappointed when Edward told him he had only two pairs, which he needed, and were anyway far too big for the boy.

He wanted to sneak away the next morning, but Herath was waiting for him. Actually, Edward was starting to enjoy the company of this country boy who, with a shy little smile, asked his many questions in fluent broken English. They saw Gil Vihara, where in the chartreuse jungle a rock-cut, stonily smiling Buddha was gigantically threefold: teaching, meditating, reaching Nirvana. Herath, who ineptly found them a remote hotel lacking ceiling fans, had never had close contact with a foreigner, had never slept in a hotel or eaten in a good restaurant, had never taken drugs, and had no sexual experience whatever.

The first time Edward took him into a bar, Herath was sure that the customers would assault him. His conviction strengthened when a blind-drunk old man collapsed at the next table, fell to the floor, and was lugged out. But Edward convinced him that he should learn about such things. "You're a man now. You can drink..." Soon it was Herath who always wanted a bottle of beer, and who proposed that they smoke marijuana. With the pocket money he gave him, Herath bought a few grams of the cheap, potent kerala grass. One night he came back to find Herath sitting on his bed, blissfully smiling, his eyes like stars. "Oh, Eswar" (he always said "Oh," when surprised or delighted, and could not pronounce "dw"), "it's wonderful." Later, a bit paranoid, he had to be dissuaded from flushing his *tola* down the toilet. When he'd smoked it all, he decided that grass was a bad habit. Herath called his mind his "computer": "I want to keep me computer clear." He was full of desires. He ordered tiger shrimps because he'd wanted to try them. Another day, he suddenly coveted a pair of corduroy trousers, and stirred up the whole bazaar to find them. If Herath's wish list had consisted of selfish whims or attempts to exploit him, he would have objected, but they were only childlike impulses.

And Herath sharply bargained down the prices of hotels and cafés.

Herath told how he left home. The year he turned 15, the monsoon had failed, and the rice he and his father planted shrivelled in the paddies. His father couldn't see the point of Herath's going to school. His mother secretly had to give him the one-and-a-half rupees, about a dime, to buy a copybook. When she couldn't buy a replacement, he had to quit. He helped his father in the fields from dawn to dark. But the monsoon failed again. He left home.

The sight of bare-breasted, bikinied tourist girls on the beach excited him. After many explanations about sex, they conjoined. Herath tried to avoid climax, but Edward said, "Give me your milk." He had never seen anyone come so copiously. "Now you know there are other ways of having sex," he told him. Herath smiled, closed his eyes, and instantly went to sleep, warm, soft as silk. The next day Herath was humbly grateful. He asked, "Is this what they call homosex, Eswar?" But he still wanted to try women.

Lalkudah-Passekudah was an east coast town on a bay of coral reefs and technicolour fish, where they went out in a glass-bottomed boat. Herath delightedly snorkeled for the first time. The resort restaurants at the height of the season had forgotten delights like tzatziki and guacamole, stuffed crab, and tropical fruits like the savoury but infamously stinking durian. But the town was Tamil, the local people were tense, and Herath couldn't speak the language. They took buses far south to Arugam Bay, a mostly Muslim beach resort by a long curving bay of white cliffs and yellow sands where they could swim in the calm water of a tidal lagoon.

The eve of Full Moon Day, a monthly Buddhist holiday, was as bright as day. Sleepless, they walked for dusty miles on a road that led to a triple shrine of temple, mosque, and *stupa*, reconciling Hindu, Muslim, and Buddhist. Tamil celebrations were underway, the Hindu feast of Shiva, and his son, Murugam, god of war, which involved piercing bodies with needles, daggers, and pointed objects in cheeks, tongues, and hands; suspending people by the mouth from huge hooks; flagellation, fire-walking, lingam-worship. Truckloads of drunken Tamil boys

zoomed past them. He and Herath veered off the road to sit in a
tangle of sea grape on a dune by the dark, sparkling sea. Herath
had breathed, "Not Arugam Bay. This place is paradise."

The next morning they went to the village of Pottuvil.
In a bazaar, Edward changed a traveller's cheque and Herath
searched for a gold chain and corduroy trousers. He also wanted
a swimsuit. The things a boy needed! But there was something
wrong in the shifty village, and in each merchant's face. Edward
read that Tamil separatists had ambushed Sinhalese soldiers
in the north. He tried to forget it with a blue and gold day of
swimming. The surf was up and the surfers were curling along
the crests, the palm-thatched bar open to surf spray and salt
wind at the point of land where the sea was wildest. The place
was thronged with single-minded Australian surfers. Surfing
was something that Edward had been too unathletic, stodgy,
cautious, and myopic to take up. Beyond the wattle and bamboo
walls the perfect wind was blowing, the perfect wave. Beside
him was the perfect boy, talking eagerly to strangers, quaffing
beers. But curfew had been declared across the island from 6
p.m. sharp. Edward's transistor told him that Colombo was
burning down, and that riots had started in other towns.

In reprisals against Tamils, many had been killed, their
bodies burned by the army. Now curfew was declared for 4 p.m.
The hotel owner told Edward he should get "that Sinhalese boy"
out of town. Edward wanted to send him back the way he'd
come and proceed alone, but the violence had engorged the tea-
growing hill towns with mixed Sinhalese and Tamil populations.
The route to Colombo through them was the shortest.

By three separate busses, passing through shutdown
villages, they headed for Badulla, a south-central market town.
A middle-aged Tamil businessman, moon-faced, full-bellied,
and full of himself, joined them at a silent small town of boarded-
up streets. As they neared Badulla, a mob of laughing, shouting
young men in red-and-green flowered sarongs blocked the bus.
They demanded the passengers' names and races. Many who
looked Tamil shouted "Muslim! Muslim!" The businessman
swore he was Sinhalese, but they had no trouble recognizing
a Tamil. They dragged him out, and began to stone him. The
man's eyeballs rolled like agates tossed by boys in a game of

pitch. Edward began bellowing at the bus door to let him go. The mob rushed up, shouting, "Kill the Englishman! Kill the white man!" Herath told the driver that if he did not drive on, he'd hijack the bus. They bulled through the mob, knocking people sideways, leaving the Tamil to his fate.

They passed the smoking ruins of a car, a charred body at the wheel. Around a curve, they saw Badulla in the valley below, smoke rising. The crowds thickened. They reached a bridge, the smoke now dense, the sound of gunfire near. On foot, they crossed the bridge. Pleading people loomed at the windows of a burning building, the mob screaming that they were Tamil Tigers trapped in their hideout. A hotel turned them away, suspecting that Herath was a Tamil. In another, the lobby was filled with gabbling foreigners. They climbed a hill, from which people watched the scene below. They found a kind old bachelor who agreed to take them in. They asked him if he was not afraid. He replied that he'd already lived long enough. That sleepless night Herath wept, "Where is me mummie? Where is me daddie? What they think happen to me? Maybe they burned down. Maybe they dead." In the morning, they asked the old man if he was going to join the looters. He said, "There's nothing I want any more."

Except for the big stone courthouses, churches, and government offices, the town had been incinerated. Everything—Tamil, Sinhalese, or Muslim—was gutted and charred, still smoking. Everyone running in panic at the least rumour, some looted what yesterday's looters had left: sheets of zinc, tables, doors. Edward counted six burnt cadavers in what was left of cars. At the terminal, buses were running to the next town, Bandarawela. There, a Sinhalese told them of the Hotel Souveni.

The hotel, perched on a hill, had no electricity or water, but the owner, a Catholic, his wife a Buddhist, welcomed them. Herath watched TV and played billiards and they could walk in the fragrant hills. For two days, they watched mobs burn down Bandarawela. No one tried to put out the fires. Just after they arrived, they'd seen mobs coming to burn a *kovil*, a Hindu temple, at the foot of the hill, smashing everything they could. The *kovi* burned all day and night. A stench rose from where arsonists had locked two priests among the multi-armed statues of Shiva and Kali.

Safe for now, they savoured the hotel's salted rice with jaggery and cinnamon for breakfast, and dinnertime mounds of rice with multiple curries. The TV repeated messages from some Minister of Disinformation, the BBC shortwave intoned that riots were spreading, hundreds were dead. Edward went on reading *La Viellesse*, Simone de Beauvoir's masterpiece, perhaps the most depressing book ever written, making him almost long for a quick fiery end. The next morning, curfew was relaxed, and they caught a bus to a charred little junction-town, and then another to Nuwara Eliya, where Edward had been happy a month earlier.

His former hotel was unharmed, though the Seventh Day Adventist Church across from it had been razed because the pastor was a Tamil. From the hillside Alpine Guest House they again saw the town in flames. Most of the food had run out, and so had cigarettes. Beer ran out. Then the curfew lifted. In one downtown shop, he saw a huddle of carbonized bodies. The old Grand Hotel was untouched, but all the funny old English pubs were gone. He encountered the guides he had been friendly with, but they knew that tourism would not return any time soon. He left them all tips. None of those he talked with said they couldn't recognize anyone in the mobs, who appeared to have leaders, consulted lists, and pointed out buildings. Wild rumours always involved the Tamil Tigers. "The Tigers attacked the train from Nuwara Eliya to Kandy and killed all the passengers, " "The Tigers sent a suicide command to burn down all downtown Colombo..."

They managed to get a bus to Kandy, capital of the hill region. The riots were winding down: a mere few dozen Tamil buildings had burned. In this Buddhist centre, monks strolled in banana and tangerine robes through the bazaar, tittering and twittering like parakeets. Under the rain trees they marched single-file, staring straight ahead around the artificial lake where bodies floated. To Edward, they seemed like gorgeous blossoms growing from the dark humus of human suffering. Unlike poets, who were epiphytes — self-sufficient plants taking nutriment from the air — they were saprophytes, demanding a sacrifice of human flesh to attain their detachment and serenity. He wanted to hit them over the head with the umbrellas they always carried.

They stayed at a boarding house, where they could stroll on side roads. On their final night, Herath prefaced the adjective "last" to all their activities: "Last beer!", "Last meal!", "Last sex!" The next day Edward put him on a direct bus for not-very distant Dambulla. Herath told him that he'd always remember him, that he was sorry for all the money he'd cost him, thanked him for the gifts, hoped he'd see him again—though in another country, knowing that Edward would never return to Sri Lanka. When the time came to go, Edward felt he had seldom become attached to anyone so quickly, and could scarcely bear to part with him. It was like losing a son.

Colombo was curfewed, thousands of tourists clogging the hotels. He walked block after block of twisted, fuming ruins. Every undestroyed business was shut, but next day he could book a plane ticket. Stunned citizens were starting to emerge. He took a train to Negombo, a port city near the airport. Arriving after curfew, he battled verbally with army guards. The next day he strolled around the mostly burned-out downtown. As he passed a restaurant, a pet monkey tore his shirt and grabbed his newspaper. Enraged, he had a Peter-Sellerish row with the restaurateur, who screamed that he'd murder him and throw his body out to sea, "like we did so many last week!" Edward screamed, "Sinhalese vultures! Sinhalese murderers!" When he subsided, he was ruefully aware that he'd generally found the Sinhalese much more approachable, personable, and charming than the caste-ridden Tamils. But he also remembered what he'd seen.

The airport was like a refugee camp: thousands of waiting Tamil families slept on the floor. Their flights were delayed. By now, Herath would be back in his small village, where Edward's $60 would burn a hole in his pocket: paltry return for a two-week tour of arson, pillage, and murder. At last, the bundle-laden travellers were processed, passports stamped. They filed across the shimmering tarmac, down a broadloomed aisle, seated themselves, strapped seat belts. The tiny plane of Garuda, the man-bird who was Vishnu's mount, trundled down a runway, rose through the air, touched down an hour later at Tiruchchinapalli.

25

ALONE IN THE CROWD

July 1983-October 1984

But there are things one chooses not to see
(though they remain there); vision is selective,
and charity must be...

~ The Living Sheet

Tiruchirapalli was rife with gates, temples, and bazaars, all temporarily to Edward's taste: nothing in Trichy was burnt, cancelled, or in chaos. While wandering the plains of Tamil Nadu, he spent a few hours in Madurai, waiting for a night train. He could have looked for the boy Ravi, but he didn't. He killed time near the railway station, eating pakoras and drinking rum.

When he boarded for the 40-hour trip north, the tariff included a sleeper — not that he could sleep. Once in New Delhi, he dodged bell-dinning horse-drawn rickshaws, autorickshaws, and bicycle rickshaws. Despite the bearded, beturbaned Sikhs and ahimsaic Jains of its mix, Delhi retained architectural reminders of its Muslim origins. These appealed to him, as did the leafy avenues and the imperial relics of the Raj, but they didn't make him linger. He sped northward via Chandigarth, the Punjab capital, to Simla, the mock-English, cool, mist-shrouded hill station that had been the Raj's summer seat. Simla's huge apes gestured obscenely, stole food from hotel rooms, and clattered around on rooftops all night. One morning an ape peered into his rooftop room. He'd have invited him in, he wrote Randy Wicker, except for fear of AIDS.

Shrines, castles, temples, and hot springs along the way, he reached Kulu, which stretched along the upper reaches of a gorge. Monique de Gaye lived here at Swami Shyam's meditation centre. Edward had often dispatched postcards to her—even if he found that writing in French, that cerebral language, always made him feel as if he were turning into *Le Monde*—but feared that he would find the dissatisfied woman he'd known in Montréal, that they might have nothing to say to each other, speak at cross-purposes, or come to verbal blows. But youthful, radiant with health, she'd lost her old restlessness yet retained her vivacity. She had a pleasant little pad, and the ashram's atmosphere seemed devoid of religious mumbo-jumbo and military discipline. They took a cab out at a road's end for a scan of green mountains and abrupt declivities. Someone offered to sell them marijuana to enhance the view.

Swami Shyam, as moderate and reasonable as a swami could be, was not disposed to cloudy claims and Hindu ritual. All the same, Edward thought that converts, like drug addicts, wanted to spread their addiction. Addiction was on his mind because he'd been travelling with—and in Kulu, trying to evade—Marc-André, a young Québécois junkie. Marc-André alternately tried to kick the habit and to seek for smack. No sex was involved; Edward was *his* guru.

North of Kulu, Manali was a trek base and freak centre where pot grew wild by every roadside and Afghan "freedom fighters" supplied poppy juice. But Edward preferred Dharamsala, where the Dalai Lama, no junkie, lived in exile. He saw spinning prayer wheels and hundreds of red-robed monks, took steep climbs, heard tinkling temple bells. He moved north through stone deserts, sharp or shattered peaks, and fortress-like farmhouses. At Leh, the valley capital of Ladakh, monasteries sprouted from hillsides.

Srinagar, the main town of Kashmir, had medieval mosques, Moghul lotus gardens, buzzing bazaars, wooden houses with overhanging balconies. On the seven-bridged river and maze of waterways and floating vegetable patches on rafts, hand-paddled water taxis and houseboats were noisy with boys, who tried to sell him their wares, including themselves. In the sacred cave of Amarnath stood Shiva's tall, naturally formed ice lingam. Garlanded with flowers, lingams could be found in many temples to Shiva, symbolizing his reproductive aspect. The lingam was usually black stone, always dripping oil. Think, he wrote Randy, how well-lubricated it would be. The lingam also reminded him of the massively endowed Roosevelt, a black man whom he and Randy had known in Austin, Texas. At the time, Edward had never thought of *him* as an avatar.

Pahalgam, down poplar-lined roads, was a mountain village selling carved walnut lamp-bases and papier-mâché. The nights grew frosty, the days under a pale distant sun like a Canadian autumn, the enormous plane trees, like maples, turning flame-red, slowly shedding their leaves. He stayed in a ski-lodge-type hotel with a roaring log fire in the common room, hot water bottles, and thick eiderdowns. A month later he was in another Tibetan town, Mussoorie in Uttar Pradesh, a hill station on a horseshoe-shaped ridge. He had found himself in a vast emptiness and austerity. He entered Pakistan, which had moved deep into a dream of Islamic purity. But people were helpful and hospitable, the country seemed more comprehensible, orderly, and better run than India.

Early in 1983, he wrote me: "Dear Brother-, Mother- and Otherland (or has Other arrived yet? If so, my commiserations. But you *wd not* follow my advice, or the path I blazed for you)." The Other, my son Malcolm, had in fact been born. Edward was writing at 3 a.m. while munching tangerines and dried mulberries, warmed by a small kerosene heater with a spectral blue flame in the land of the Ismailis, followers of the Aga Khan. He was now ranging across the Northwest Frontier on the borders of Afghanistan, Russia, and China.

A highway took him across desert plateaus and narrow gorges to the market town of Gilgit, an oasis in a wide mountain-rimmed valley. Past Gilgit, Hunza was the model for Shangri-La in *Lost Horizon:* jagged-peaked mountains, a rushing river far below. Rippling terraces cascaded from the snow line, poplars cutting verticals. The Hunza people, Ismailis, spun wool, tended herds of yak, cattle, goats, and sheep, and grew corn, apricots, wheat, and walnuts. In Chitral, he found the Kalash, the white-skinned supposed descendants of Alexander the Great's Greek warriors who, practising an ancient religion, were the last holdouts against Islamic missionary zeal. The Kalash made a dreadful wine, the nearest thing to alcohol he could find.

Peshawar was the last city before the Khyber Pass, the centre of the Afghan insurgency and the refugee influx, bazaar after bazaar in narrow lanes; smuggling, drug trading, and arms dealing a way of life. More than half its million people were by now Afghans. The tribal society reminded him of Morocco: febrile and dangerous. Three hours away in the mountain valley of Swat, carved Buddhas gazed from rocks among giant pines and wooden-beamed mosques. He recalled a satirical ditty that a nineteenth-century Montréal journalist had penned in the *New York World* on noticing a press dispatch headed "The Ahkoond of Swat is dead": "Mourn, city of Swat! / Your great Ahkoond is not." Typical, just typical, Edward snorted, a hack writing a "humorous" poem about Swat, unaware that any Canadian city was more provincial and chauvinistic than Swat could ever be. In expiation, he visited the Ahkoond's palace.

You knew where you stood with Islam, a religion with a rule for every occasion and the right way of doing everything. He'd bought a book, *How to Say Your Prayers*, containing 144 pages of rules on the correct position for defecation and urination before prayers, bans on eating radishes, onions, or anise before praying, an injunction against farting in a mosque, which invalidated the prayer, and a prescription for the length of vowels used in saying "*Allahu akbar*."

The Islamic Republic of Pakistan had made him feel like a bubble boy. Via Karachi, he returned to India after two drinkless, sexless, though not drugless, months. Now he could see women with faces and bodies, and get a drink again. He didn't like what he saw in Amritsar, site of the Golden Temple, sacred city of Sikhdom. Driven out of Pakistan, the Sikhs now battled their Hindu neighbours. Amid nightly curfews, half-a-dozen murders occurred each day.

After an obligatory visit to Agra and the Taj Mahal, loveliest of mausoleums, he went on to Madhya Pradesh. Bhopal, its capital, was an old Muslim town of narrow alleys, turrets and arches. The mosque's minarets were dotted with pigeonholes, its cool marble floor a chessboard of black and white praying-squares where hundreds of young boys in white skullcaps chanted and squatted like cross-legged pawns. By a lake bordered by rain trees, or in a deep landscaped ravine, families sat at night, and lovers strolled among flame-of-the-forest trees. He strolled, the scent of frangipani and flowering mango in the close night air. Amid laughing friends, a boy in the bazaar shouted "I fuck you?" In the village of Khajuraho he contemplated mystical conga lines of sex: a man exuberantly copulated from behind with his horse; his engorged friend awaited his turn while a startled female witness clapped exquisitely moulded hands over eyes.

He plunged south to Mysore. Pondicherry on one coast, and coconut-fringed Kerala on the other, were respites from anthill cities. He only felt calm when he sat alone in a cool, quiet hotel room, or in some dark, empty bar. Other times, he suffered from near-panic claustrophobia: markets, bus terminals, and train stations were to be avoided even in the best of moods. From Mysore, he reported to Randy that he'd found *their* church, St. Philomena's, and was sending five postcards of it to sanctify Randy's "junk shop." How wrong of the Pope to de-canonize her, or declare that she'd never existed. He'd seen her hand, miraculously mummified, with his own eyes.

He was on his way to alpine Ootacamund, a.k.a. Udagamandlam, more commonly called Ooty. From there, he sent Randy an annotated "Welcome to Ooty" brochure. "The annual flower show organised by the government and the Dog Show of the South Indian Kennel Club held here in May every year are major attractions." He urged Randy to attend. "A mini train for children will be ready soon at an artificial lake." Randy should bring all his children along.

Ooty was crowded with the start of the Indian summer-vacation, the Tamil New Year, the horseracing season, and a visit by Sai Baba, Ruth Beissel's guru, with all his camp followers. He fled to nearby Kotagiri, a hill resort among coffee and tea plantations. Restful Kotagiri had 19 Christian churches; for Randy's benefit, he dispatched a flyer for the Queenshill Guest Home, a member of the Nilgiri Christian Guest Homes

Association, whose proprietors offered reduced rates "For full-time Christian workers." Avoiding Easter celebrations, he set off for a wildlife sanctuary in the region abutting Kerala and Karnataka, where he encountered elephants, monkeys, wild boar, a few deer, giant squirrels, sambars, bison, crocodiles and, one day, an armoured medieval animal — a pangolin. He thought it was much like himself.

Feeling more cheerful, he ventured to Vijayanagara, in arid, torrid territory. He sent me a postcard: "Dear Razor (hopefully) Blade" (he'd always preferred beardless men) from Bijapua on the feast day of the Immaculate Virgin. The stone statue was 1,003 years old, and, like those of Jain saints, symbolized total detachment from worldly possessions. He thought that Jainism, like Buddhism, was "less nutty and repulsive than Hinduism, but not much."

For many months, letters had flown after him. Winston Leyland sent parcels of Latin American books, and forwarded reviews of *My Deep Dark Pain is Love*. The Victoria and Grey Trust Company in Lindsay reported that his account had earned $1,504.67 in interest, down from the $3,467.47 at the end of 1982. From late March until April 1984, a Buddies in Bad Times production of *Lacey or Tropic Snows: Theatrical Tales of a Canadian Exile in Brazil* had played in Toronto, and Edward heard about it from several sources, including Sky Gilbert, its producer and director. The show's set featured a Brazilian honky-tonk and a circular satin bed. Among the musical numbers was a song-and-dance version of "Let It Snow," with four Santa Clauses. The cast included a Colombian from Barranquilla. Audiences were sparse, and the *Globe and Mail*'s critic sourly noted that Lacey had the gall to criticize Lindsay from the safe harbour of Rio de Janeiro. *The Body Politic* condemned Lacey and Gilbert for being depressing. The theatre reviewer for the weekly *Now* said, "neither biography nor art is worth the energy that Gilbert and cast put in" and that "Lacey is bland, so is his verse, and so are most of those around him...."

By Canada Day he was in Nepal, the world's only Hindu kingdom. The main square of the little valley capital, Kathmandu, had street markets, shops with pagoda-like roofs and sculpted doors and windows, and temples with roof struts even more explicit and varied than in Khajuraho, though exclusively heterosexual. He lingered: the exchange rate was favourable, helped by the global rise of the U.S. dollar. Kathmandu had cocktail bars, specializing in the Rum Doodle and the Annapurna Sling, but closed down at 9 p.m. He longingly recalled filet mignon dinners with champagne, at 4 a.m in Buenos Aires, and Mexican red-light districts alive with music, drink, and laughter every hour of the day.

In Kathmandu, rats racing under his floorboards kept him awake, as did his fellow guests running around their rooms. Or maybe Valium and alcohol were working against him. He burned mosquito coils to avoid being eaten alive, and gashed his skull twice by hitting a projecting shower pipe set at head level. Dogs barked from all points of the compass. Though as a boy he'd had a dog, a rotund spaniel named Thumper, he had come to class this tamed wolf with the fly and the mosquito. Even one distantly baying dog could wake him from the soundest sleep. He had agreeable fantasies of leaving poisoned tidbits for them, and if the tidbits fell into the hands and mouths of a few children, that, too, would be desirable, especially the little monsters in India who'd trailed him, chanting "One rupee! School pen! Bye Bye!" When he went to get his visa renewed, the official asked him, "Why do you keep staying on and renewing for one or two weeks at a time?" "Oh, the roads and rails are blocked right now in India because of the monsoon," he answered. "But the monsoon lasts till September," the man pointed out. "I just don't want to go back to India," Edward confessed. "I understand," the official sighed.

Any visitor to India, he wrote Randy, "should put sex away in a locked compartment of his mind, among the forgotten things." Of six Indian sexual partners, three had been clinging vines; one tried to blackmail him, one tried to rob him, and one did rob him. How could you have sex "with people you saw crouched by every roadside, street, or beach, with a slowly lengthening turd uncoiling from between brown buttocks, or a turbid puddle of water slowly forming between their legs?" One day he'd seen "a dog lustily devouring a young boy's ordure as it was coming out, snapping it up, hot and delicious, almost before it hit the ground." He also hated ceaseless wheedling, Indian

English, stares, even people saying "hello" — always a prelude to a sales pitch. He suffered from thermophobia, phonobia, and demophobia.

Three-quarters of Kathmandu's beggars, and the mad *sadhus* around the temples, came from India. The Indian tourists who arrived were Anglophile, yet xenophobic. He couldn't stand retroflex-consonant-studded Indian English with its "What is your good name, shar?", "What your wark, shar?", "What is thee time, shar?", "What is your native place, shar?" His main respite from Indian incursions was a room-boy who massaged his aching muscles. From a poor village, he became, for a small financial consideration, Edward's sex object. He provided him with company, the warmth of a human body, and a bit of affection. Even when naked the boy, a Brahman, never removed his sacred thread.

His hotel specialized in Indian tourist groups: he was repelled by saris, *tika* spots; the smell of curry cooked by upper-caste servants so that their masters could eat undefiled food on undefiled plates, prepared by undefiled hands; the sounds of flushing toilets, washing of clothes in showers; and the hawking and spitting as people rose to perform ritual ablutions before their sunrise *puja*. One night, two roomfuls conversed in shouts, with open doors. He slammed both doors shut, reminding the guests that they were not in some Bombay tenement, and their rights ended at the point at which his elbow began. The men closed in to beat him up, the bejewelled women shrieked, and he retreated. He left the next day.

Resuming his travels, it seemed to him that everything in India was too much: the sun too bright, the dust too dusty. It was a country that made all human effort except the Oblomov reaction — retreat to bed — seem meaningless. He sometimes stayed in his hotel room for days at a time. Hinduism preached scornful imperviousness to anything that belonged to the other, outer, sensory world of *maya*. Nothing could be improved, nothing could be changed. It would go on forever, time out of mind. But a poet had to be hostile to Hinduism: he could not function without *maya*.

From Delhi, he boarded a fast air-conditioned train with dining car, stewards, and reclining seats. Each station had its vendors of *chai* and cakes, its kiosk, its homeless beggars, a stationmaster watch- and whistle-proud, a white-and-black board announcing name and altitude, an old clock still keeping time. As they crossed hyacinth mountains, or the yellow scrub of desert, infallibly from every shack and village children waved. Travellers were travelling into distance; children were travelling into time. Hello, hello, they called. Goodbye, goodbye, travellers said as they vanished.

Seventeen hours later, he woke to Bengal's insistent, excessive green-blue morning. Villages, stations, jungle swamps, ponds, and rivers flashed by. Descending at Howrah Station in Calcutta, he saw mountains of garbage left over from a sweepers' strike. "*Chai, babu,*" water, sir, came from a small, fly-clustered boy lying in the sunlight beside a drain, curled under a torn, fouled blanket, a tiny red loincloth covering the swollen belly and staring ribs. Edward shifted him into the shade, pressed 10 rupees into his palm. He ought to have taken him to Mother Teresa, but he was too depressed to manage it. He fled when a crowd gathered round and began to jabber at him. When he returned that night, the boy was gone.

Geckos chuckled that night; serenity came in small doses in the morning with the caw of the first crow, the first bather at the muddy *ghat*, the first pause on the bridge over the Hooghly. It came in the small dark bar where the beer was tepid but the fish tasted fine. He tried to remember the little decencies people preserved: the small service rendered, the small change returned complete, the small smile.

Calcutta was the place where you began to feel that the Far East was near, but an airline strike began, and a religious holiday closed the city down for nearly two weeks for. He went to Orissa's beaches, paddy fields, coconut and cashew plantations, and repulsive temples. Finally he could leave. At the Dum-Dum Airport, minutes before his flight, he wrote Randy that every one of India's 750-million harassers, hasslers, hustlers, and wheedlers spoke with exactly Randy's whine, the same precise pitch, the same nasality. Now he needed to go to the washroom. Calcutta had, in the Biblical phrase, turned his bowels into water.

Living in boathouses, houseboats, house-and-boat houses, the Bangladeshi were dignified and generous. He entrained from Dhaka to Khulna, traversing the Pedma, which the steamer took an hour to cross. Down the river floated green eyelets of water hyacinth, water lilies, and the remains of bodies from Benares. Bangladesh had the largest delta in the world, the tributaries of the Ganges wending into the Bay of Bengal through mazed marshlands and mangrove swamps. From a boat rail, the country slipped by, dark land melding with velvet sky. Other passengers asked him if he were married, if he had a son. He told them no. A male procession, young and old, came to ask wonderingly, sadly, all night long, "But if you don't have a son, who will say the prayers for you when you are dead?" The boat stopped at river ports: a dusky feral swell; earnest young soldiers; veiled, sari'd ladies; children playing, asleep, being fed, being weaned. All the world in groups: families, friends, gossiping women, card-playing men. Edward, alone among them: rich, of course, suspect, perhaps crazy. The ship bore through delta channels toward the indented coastline. The horizonless river flowed into its sea.

In Dhaka, he met Shawpan ("Dream"in Bengali), a 17-year-old tout who took him to the Blue Nile Hotel on New Elephant Road. He gave him a few days of knowing where his next meal was coming from. In time, often breaking into tears, Shawpan told his story, backed up by letters Edward read. If anyone had ever been betrayed, bluffed, cheated by a wild card from the top of the deck, it was Shawpan. A cyclone killed his parents, and an old woman had found the four-year-old wandering on the river mud flats. When he was 10, he found another little boy wandering hungry by that river. He took Ali to the woman. He and Shawpan slept in each other's arms.

Years later, they moved to Dhaka. An Austrian tourist took up with Shawpan, then fell for Ali, now 12 years old. Under the pretext of adopting both boys, he painted a future for them all as a family. He got Shawpan to arrange documents for his "brother," and whisked Ali off to Austria. When Shawpan telephoned Vienna, the Austrian said, "We no longer need you." His brother broke in to say in Bengali, "Buzz off, Shawpan."

Such everyday Third World tragedies made Edward despise his fellow gays. He told Shawpan that tourists might listen to him, but had problems of their own, didn't want to understand Bangladesh, and would forget him sooner or later, probably sooner. He, Edward, could only do things like take him for a weekend to the port of Chittagong. Shawpan showed him the scars on chest and belly where he'd been burned with acid during the 1971 war that had severed Bangladesh from Pakistan. He showed him something else, and when Edward demonstrated the ways one could play with it, he was indignant: "You've only got eight days here. Why on earth didn't you teach me this a week ago? Don't you know that I almost come in my jeans half a dozen times a day? I'd have kept you busy." Shawpan had met an American girl named Lorraine. He bragged that he'd come seven times the first night with her. She was now in Nepal: he would go there — if only she'd invite him.

Edward was bound for Burma, a.k.a. Myanmar, land of seven-day visas, where travel had to be booked through a monstrous bureaucracy. Currency controls didn't work: the black market for cash was three times the official rate. Rangoon was a dilapidated nineteenth-century city where faint traces of the Raj remained. The Burmese, with their amiable, open character and handsome faces, reminded him of Tibetans, but the country was rubbed raw by a military clique: nothing worked. He informed Randy that on the next day, October 26, he was leaving for Bangkok.

Part Three

PASSPORT CANCELLED
1984-1995

House and inhabitants, rejected, longed-for,
expelled from memory, are you: you roam
without a resting-place on earth, yet bearing,
tortoise **extraordinaire,** *your prison-home.*

~ **The House**

26

LOVE IS SO HURT

October 1984-December 1987

the past is filled with chances missed,
old loves, lapsed friendships, loved ones lost,
the future is a formless mist:

and I am slowly getting pissed.

~ Aduh

He'd thought that Thailand would be a place where he could rest. Thus he arrived in Bangkok, whose impossibly long Thai name meant the City of Angels, Great City and Residence of the Emerald Buddha, Impregnable City of the God Indra, Grand Capital of the World, Endowed with Nine Precious Gems, Abounding in Enormous Royal Palaces which Resemble the Heavenly Abode Where Reigns the Reincarnated God, a City Given by Indra and Built by Vishnukarm.

Inside an hour, he decided that Bangkok was the worst city in the world. Set in a windless swamp, it certainly was the hottest. He climbed hundreds of steps to the bell-shaped gilt stupa of the Golden Mount, where urban vastness lost itself in heat haze. The Chao Prya, a silver river under a sooty sun, bisected the city. On it, rice barges and long-tail boats crisscrossed; it wound through slums, slipped past mansions, skyscrapers, hovels beneath the flyovers, stilt houses of shellacked teak, polychrome temples, broad treeless avenues and squiggling alleys. The excesses of Bauhaus bumped against endless rows of Chinatown's squat cement-block shophouses. In Patpong, everything but passion was on display in the dirty-pastel, multistoreyed brothels, hundreds of numbered bonded girls behind glass. The Thai were, the saying had it, "the most charming people money can buy."

Exhaust fumes mounted to the pale sky; traffic roared, blared, and blatted, motorbikes fought trishaws, minicabs, and jammed buses. Extant sidewalks were tilted and potholed, festooned with eating stalls: relief overcame him when he saw something on his plate he could recognize. The scents of the city: exhaust and filth, fresh-ground coffee, marsh, shit, acrid trickling sweat, rotting fruit. Swarming markets sold Dior t-shirts, aphrodisiacs, fake Rolexes, fried rats, water beetles, chicken embryos, mooncake and starfruit, snake blood, lotus seeds.

Taking the Phrya Empress downriver, he passed bobbing islands of water hyacinth with spiked blue towers, flushed twice a day by tides. Black chains of barges floated too, laden with sand or cement, each with four eyes of tire rings that stared him down. He watched wat and wat-nots go by, and the monumental simpering image of Prince Siddhartha. At the Krong Thon stop, he drank and wrote poems. The disagreeably sweet, agreeably potent rice whiskey was much cheaper than beer.

He sought out Byron Black, who had arrived earlier that year to make instructional videos for a university. Snappish from the start, he resented Byron's attempts to make him adopt Thai ways. Byron had been taping videos of the Karen rebels who battled against the Myanmar regime, which had pushed them into a corner in the Burmese border state of Kathulé. In Bangkok, Byron introduced him to some Karens; he saw others tapping towering palms. They clambered up, drove a nail in near the crown, hung a gourd, and slithered down. He reflected that some boys liked to shinny up trees. Some boys were afraid to.

Through Byron, Edward met Dean Bishop, an expatriate American from Washington State. Dean had served with the U.S. Army in Germany, studied Asian languages in Paris, and ended in Cambodia, quitting Phnom Penh shortly before it fell. Settling in Bangkok, he helped Cambodians fleeing the Khmer Rouge butchers. He sold Thai jewelry and Burmese handicrafts in Penang, Singapore, and Bali, and Cambodian silver boxes copied in Indonesia. Meanwhile, Winston Leyland had come from San Francisco to meet him. After they met, he concluded that Winston — an Augustinian monk turned Buddhist — had remained a priest. Winston found that anyone talking to his translator, couldn't get a word in edgewise, but was half-glad not to.

His National Trust account in Lindsay had shrunk. He set off to spend the last of it in Indonesia. In northern Sumatra, he lodged at Lake Toba, the world's largest crater lake. The Bataks of the mountainous interior, once headhunters and cannibals, were fervent Catholics now. In one of their villages, to the flicker of fireflies and the tree frog's chirp, young men gathered in a *tuak* shop to drink the white viscous fluid from palms, and he heard the same songs of the yearning heart he'd heard in the *fado* bars of Lisbon and in the Andes. The music was unearthly.

Oh, my father. You were a singer.
You wanted me to be a troubadour.
Now you would be happy, father. I am a singer.
But father, you are dead.

In mid-lake lay big, wedge-shaped Palau Samosir, isthmus-connected to the mainland. Mounds of tiny fish lay on the dock beside hairy red rambutans: vegetable tarantulas. On Nias Island, with megalithic dolmens and menhirs everywhere, there was no electricity, no road, no noise, only a huge surf breaking on the beaches, and a small boy's devotion. Akan, a frail, motherless 12-year-old, the cook at the hotel where Edward stayed, called him "papa" and held his hand. Another guest, a young Italian woman, also cleaved to Akan. She needed something from Edward, he thought, and he needed something from her. He thought he could ask nothing better of life than to stay and raise Akan with her. But of course it couldn't last. He'd already had his chance for a son, and thrown it away in Brazil.

The central highlands Sumatran city of Bukkitinggi, just below the equator, was home to the Minangkabau, orthodox Muslims, though women owned and managed the family property. Young men walked intertwined like two halves of a whole, hand upon shoulder, arm in arm, arm around waist, romping home from school, loafing on street-corners, ogling unapproachable girls in veils and wimples. Above rusty iron roofs, volcanoes were conical, green, and jagged, notched at the top. Sometimes they rumbled or flashed fire at night, and the air filled with sulphur, borne on the same wind as the fragrance of frangipani and night-blooming jasmine.

From West Sumatra, a cruise boat sailed him past the dead volcano Krakatoa to Jakarta, chaotic, squalid, and sprawling. He bussed through the mountains to Bandung, a big city full of young handsome Sundanese. He thought of these students' love of "bluyins," the acme of fashion when complemented by T-shirt and running shoes. He'd pause at a shop where the stovepipe legs of deep-discount bluyins funnelled out in the wind. In Pangandáran, a south-coast, black-sand beach resort with booming surf, he rode pillion on a motorycle-taxi, his arms around a firm waist, drinking in the odour of the boy's body. He let the world fly past him. They were going to pick magic mushrooms in the meadows among the buffalo dung. The boy was going to be trouble. Yes, but so what?

In Jakarta, he'd got the telefaxed last of his legacy from Lindsay: $1,448.09. He was relieved: it seemed to him that a private income had paralysed his will, made him alternately neurotic and complacent, penny-pinching and spendthrift. On the way to Bangkok, money almost gone, he paused in clean prosperous Singapore. At night, Bugis Street filled up with café tables, and the drag queens thronged.

Back in Bangkok by May, he needed a job and somewhere to live. The second requirement was quickly met. Byron invited him to stay at the "clubhouse" he rented on a quiet lane off a major road intersection in the Thonburi district in north Bangkok, near the Krong Thon Bridge where Edward liked to ruminate and find boys. Once, lying there drunk, he heard a couple of the boys he'd been with gloat that they'd cleaned him out. He came out of his stupor to tell them where more was hidden.

His tiny clear handwriting was useful in proofing texts, tests, and *Today's English*, a Thai-English magazine put out by the Serm Lucksutr (SLS) Language and Computer School. His boss, Sanguan Wongsuchat, "Mr. Wong," paid him US$2 an hour.

Even at this wage, he could save a little, provided he did not drink.

The singsong of Thai disturbed him as much as the twittering of birds: he'd had to move out of a lodging place because a mynah bird and a cockatoo chattered all day. It wasn't easy to remember monosyllabic names like Miss Keen, Mr. Chao, Miss Ae.... Once, after a night's drinking with Byron, he yearned for soup at half past three. He marched up to a startled Thai and shouted, "*Sopa! Sopa!*" He was sure that "*Sopa*," like "Stop" or "Hello" was universally understood. If he'd been picking sides in a sports contest, he would have packed his Good Team with Brazilians, Portuguese, Mexicans, Greeks, and Indonesians. The Bad Team would be Spaniards, Italians, Indians, Texans, and, of course, Canadians. On which team would the Thai play?

Of Bangkok, Byron's friend, Edith Mirante, an American journalist and painter, had said, "At last, a city as chaotic as I am." But he needed places more orderly than he was. The Thai were the people of the smile, so unlike the Canadian scowl. But their good manners hid hypocrisy, he thought. They said "yes" when they meant "no." They agreed with all his criticisms, lied charmingly, and valued ceremony, cleanliness, and dressiness: things he'd always avoided. Amid the innumerable irritants that besieged them, manners, and laughter were their safety valves.

That summer, Jourdan Arenson, a young man from the San Francisco Bay area, arrived at Byron's to find Edward on day four of a week-long drunk, infected scabs on his face, blabbering and slobbering. His clothes were filthy, his hair greasy, swollen bruises on his forehead and knees. He didn't know day from night. He ranted at neighbours in Hindi and Portuguese ("They can understand it if they want to!") Then he sat in brooding silence and chain smoked with quivering hands. When his friends tried to clean his wounds, he barked, "No! Leave them alone. They will heal." Sober, he was for Jourdan an ideal guide to the Wild East. Seemingly omniscient, he astonished him with memory feats: he could recite 40 lines of Robinson Jeffers flawlessly.

"You think you'll find yourself in other people but as time goes on you don't find it," he told Byron. "All my life I wanted to have a friend who would drink with me and control my drinking. If I got drunk he would help me home. You find it when you're young but you can't find it when you're older." One night, he came back with a cut on his forehead that required seven stitches. "Can't you see it? I just don't care about myself anymore," he said. Alerted that he had passed out, his friends scraped him off the pavement, his striped jersey riding around his neck, his trousers almost off. They bundled him into the back of a pickup truck, struggled with his dead weight up steep stairs. Once, when he was about to set off, they tied him to a pillar in his bedroom. When they hid his passport and money, he'd get drunk on credit. Disgusted, Byron gave notice that he had to leave.

He simply moved across the road to the house that Dean Bishop rented, where his letter-writing was accompanied by shrieking mynah birds, kekking frogs, and screaming katoeys — or were those the mynah birds again? Among residents were Dean's former boyfriend Sak, and his taxi-driving brother, Pap. Uncountable pals slept or stopped over, and often sat down happily to dinner at 3 a.m. In this unstructured family, Edward ("Ed Wad" to them) at times thought he'd never been happier. He'd awake to find a dozen slumberers sprawled on the living-room floor. Among the residents was Edith Mirante, a passionate opponent of the Myanmar regime. Originally from New Jersey, she'd gone to Chiang Mai, Thailand's second, much smaller city, to befriend Karen refugees. Edward reminded her of Steven Maturin, the polymath wanderer in Patrick O'Brian's seafaring novels. After she left, he slept in the room she'd occupied, calling it the "Joseph Conrad Suite," which he renamed the "Constantine Cavafy." Writing a note to her, serenaded by gibbons, he called it "an island of peace amid the chaos, & permits me to recentre myself in the immortal sabbath of meek self-content — but I am a mere passing guest spending the night there, a travelling salesman based in the room of the absent daughter departed to study at college...."

He adored Sak and Pap for their exquisite bodies, especially Sak. In doomed adventures, Sak was the picaresque hero Edward had always yearned to be. In the aftermath of a brief physical involvement, Sak treated him, he thought, with a mixture of brutality and flower-petal delicacy. For Dean and

Sak, he often left contrite notes after drunken outrages, though sometimes with an edge of defiance: "When I drink, I mind *my own* business. I take special care *not* to bring my bar problems back home." Not so. Once he audiotaped him, their dialogue punctuated by pops, clinks, gurglings, pourings, and long silences.

> *Sak*: Why do you drink? We all want to know the answer to one question. Can you answer that question?
> *Edward*: Please understand. No, you don't understand.
> *Sak:* I don't understand what are you talking about.
> *Edward*: You did not understand.
> *Sak*: The problem is you like to drink. You must talk about that.
> *Edward*: I do talk about that.

On his thrice-yearly treks to Penang to renew his visa, he was never sure that the Thai consulate would do it. Penang was dull, but only dull in comparison to Bangkok. One day, he encountered Jourdan, also renewing his visa. As they walked together, Jourdan noticed that each sight irritated or enthralled him, and each triggered a reminiscence. He recounted his experience at the Stockholm Hotel in Bangkok, where two boys he'd picked heatedly argued about which one of them would on top. Neither wanted to be on the bottom. He considerately let them *both* get on top. As they ate, red ants bit Jourdan's ankles under the table, prompting Edward to expound his theory that the concept of reincarnation could only have originated in the tropics.

His travels on the Indian subcontinent nightmarishly returned to him. Indira Gandhi's Sikh bodyguards had assassinated her and, a week after her death, a toxic cloud from the Union Carbide plant in Bhopal killed 2,000 people and maimed 150,000. Begging letters arrived from boys. They yearned ("I sleep by myself so lonely"), implored him to remember them ("Long ago that we didn't see each other. And I thanking about you very much"), reminded him of their devotion ("I just kiss your picture every night. I do not know what to say again. LOVE IS SO HURT.")

Tearfully, he told Dean that the Third World would grind out their talent, beauty, and pride, and quoted from Vachel

Lindsay: "Let not young souls be smothered out...." Herath had written from Sri Lanka that he was "going thru last stages of a man can survive. I'm begging you for the last time if you can kindly send me some money to maintain." Edward sent him a money order, which disappeared in the post. It seemed ironic to Edward that, now that he had no private income, hopeful "sons" were turning up everywhere. Not all were former sexual partners. Thinlay, a young Tibetan refugee he'd met in India, fondly recalled their time together. In Tibet, Thinlay would have become a monk. His father rose at 4 a.m. to pray before the family altar, but his sister had become a cabaret dancer to help support the family. Thinlay wrote, "Please give me suggestion otherwise my life will uselessly exhausted at this place." On his behalf, Edward wrote to an academic acquaintance in British Columbia, where Tibetan refugees had settled. He got no reply. Thinlay would continue to live, as the boy put it, like a "Frog in a Well."

Shawpan wrote from Dhaka, telling him that "I did not find none as my best friend in this world except you." He was "quite hopeless and helpless and seeing deep-dark around me." He begged to come to Bangkok. Could Edward "spread your gracious hand to do some thing for me"? In March, Shawpan sent three separate copies of a letter to better the odds of receipt. "Perhaps if I say that I love you with great force and desire you can understand how I feel." Edward let months pass before sending a long, dithering reply. Shawpan might think he was rich, but he wasn't. "What you and I did together, what I taught you to do, once, is one of the oldest games in the world; millions upon millions of people have done it millions and millions of times, and it does not mean love"; it had been "just a night's pleasure and release between two friends. It's only because you had never done it before that it seemed so important to you." In mid-letter he reversed directions. Yes, if Shawpan still wanted to come, he'd be happy to see him. He hoped that Shawpan could borrow the cost of his airfare.

In late October, writing to Randy Wicker, he took stock of the past decade. He thought that he'd undergone "merely the birth struggles of the new `me,' the metamorphosis of the insect into its new phase" that would "evolve to old age and death, more serenely & philosophically." People like Randy and Byron, "for all your goodwill and tolerance and patience and true lasting friendship you bore and bear me (and I bore and bear you in equal measure) have never understood me or my purpose or feelings or anything that goes on in my head at all." All human contacts "have their dangers and, more important, their limits: you can never really know anybody but yourself."

Dean had no phone, but there was a corner booth. Because of groundwater and floods, people were always getting electrocuted in phone booths. In early May, a freak storm dumped nearly 20 inches of rain, and the household was marooned for days. Even on rainless days, it took Edward a motorcycle-taxi ride and two buses to get to work. On days off, he rose, slipped into shorts, sandals, and shirt, and tiptoed past where Dean drank last night's coffee and read last year's newspapers. He crossed railroad tracks, followed a lane through dew-drenched greenery and slanting sunlight to a forest wat and a pink- and-blue lotus pond, the heads of palms stirring in the breeze. He stopped at a coffee shop where the condensed-milk coffee tasted like chocolate. Opening a pack of Falling Rain cigarettes, he looked at palms and the bronze-blue sky, thinking, "This is my world, this is the place I chose." The first customer of a bar, he bowed when he left, joining hands to breast. He strolled into swampier jungle to the house at the bend where Miss Lek, forewarned of his coming ("The farang he is drinking coffee at the wat!") was waiting with two weeks' worth of laundered clothes. Or he went past wood-zinc shacks with latticed windows to a roast-chicken place where the three cheery girls made endearing, baffling allusions to the night before. He could visit Marlin Oliveros, who had moved out of Byron's house and lived in a stilt hut but, no, he'd still be asleep with a girl. Instead, he passed market gardens and women selling "swamp oranges," pomelos, the sweet grapefruit big as melons. Big snakes devoured small snakes in irrigation ditches; trucks passed, crammed with soldiers and uniformed schoolgirls. He paid his respects to the village goat, and to a temple in the shape of a dragon, boat, and bird. Then to the Wat Chelo landing where he drank and watched the longtail boats come and go. He discovered a network of pathways or plank walks winding miles through swamplands. So all of Bangkok must have been once.

At Serm Luksutr, he covered up his AWOL binges by getting his friends to phone that he'd gone to renew his visa. He'd just re-read *Bartleby the Scrivener*: like Bartleby, he felt like saying, "I prefer not to." No team player, he vexed Bruce Anderson, an American whom Mr. Wong brought in to edit his magazines, and was fired in March 1986. In late April, he had a nasty fall. Frightened that he'd never walk again, he allowed Dean and Pap to carry him to hospital. There, he requested "medication," which the staff interpreted as "mediation." While Dean was away, he sometimes binged for weeks. He told Dean where to send his papers upon his death. It was in this context that Winston Leyland paid a second visit to Bangkok.

One night after he and Winston went off together, Byron got a phone call from Winston, asking to be rescued from his roaring-drunk translator. Fighting traffic on his motorbike all the way to Patpong, Byron found the pair in a club featuring two sleek go-go boys jacking off on a platform. After, the sleek go-go boys hovered, ignored and bored. The trio headed for a dank hotel where, in a dingy coffee shop at two in the morning, Edward and Winston recalled little bars in São Paulo, or the way they made late-night soup in Rio.

Winston urgently needed galleys of books proofread but Edward abruptly decamped for Penang. Winston returned to San Francisco empty-handed, but got the airmailed galleys — only just in time. They corresponded about Edward's translating *A Sombra dos Dias*, a novel by Guilherme de Melo, based on the gay newspaperman's life in Mozambique. Winston offered him $2,500, of which he would pay $1,000 on signing the contract, the balance on completion the following March. Edward was also dealing with Ian Young, the distributor of *Path of Snow* and publisher of *Later*. In seven years, Edward complained, he'd not received a royalty statement. He took to calling his friend "the late Ian Young." After an exchange of letters, Ian sent him copies of both books and $300.

To Dean, he wrote that he had thought of killing himself, "*terminer, de toute une fois, ce travail, cette angoisse, ces troubles. Mais je résiste, et je suis fort. Sois fort aussi.*" Only living with Dean had saved him the previous year. Dean's kindly patience, however, snapped in August. He evicted him. This coincided with the loss of his passport, which he'd shed in Songkhla, a mostly Muslim east-coast port in the extreme south of the isthmus, home to pirates and plunderers, otherwise known as its fishing fleet. He lost his glasses there, too: Khun Manit, his new, part-time employer, gave funds to replace them. He was forced to accept Manit's offer of free accommodations and full-time employment at his school amidst the Silom Rd.-Patpong ugliness. *Sans* passport, he avoided the police from August until the end of October. Meanwhile, he pledged to translate the monstrously long Melo novel by early the next year.

He repaid Manit's help in extra work. His lazy unpunctual students were at least respectful, though they had a 10-second attention span, and were afraid to give any response that was not the exact response everyone else gave (100 people all replying, "I look TV last night.") The girls were the worst: shy, perpetually giggling. All the Thai wanted to do, he thought, was to lovingly memorize a guru's every utterance, and spew it back on an exam. Since students' first names were hard to recall, and people usually didn't use last ones, he experimented by addressing them by numbers.

To escape workplace claustrophobia, he strolled through big emerald Lumphini Park, among rain trees and flowers, freshly-turned earth, and a blue-fountained lake. Thousands of Chinese, *farangs*, and Thais jogged, T'ai Chi shadowboxed, or swayed rhythmically to canned music. Each hour on the hour, loudspeakers blared out the national anthem, a jazzed-up Marseillaise, and the dancers and joggers froze like the statue of King Chulalongkorn that stood just beyond the park's portals.

His spirits had lifted briefly when he saw a newspaper photo of his old mentor, Professor Barker Fairley. He wanted to write and tell him how much he admired him as a person and a poet. But something held him back. He thought of another mentor, Robert Finch, who was said to be issuing a Collected Poems. If so, he was going strong at 86. He heard that Henry Beissel had suffered a heart attack. Edward considered that he was almost sure to suffer a heart attack himself some day. He gave himself 10 more years — at most.

The Canadian Embassy's library holdings included decade-old copies of "current" magazines, and no Canadian literature, unless you counted telephone directories, *Who's Who in Canada, The Canadian Social Register* and umpteen volumes of *The Criminal Code of Canada.* He'd become a trial to the Embassy. In Ayudhya, known for its temples, ruins, and crime, he'd been robbed of traveller's cheques and passport. The Embassy gave him a scolding. By October 1986, he'd lost five passports in Thailand. After Songkhla, the Embassy nastily told him that he might get, not another passport, but a travel document allowing him to return to Canada, one way. When, about the end of October, he did get a passport, it was only valid for six months. By the time he received it, he'd overstayed 72 days without Thai documents. After he paid a hefty fine, the immigration police gave him an extension.

On the way to Penang in early November, he stopped at Surgai Kolok, just short of the Malaysian border which, he wrote Dean, was "like the Mex. border towns of my long lost youth. I had a marvellous time in & did all the things I shdn't, without losing money, glasses or passport; it was small enough to be *un*dangerous & primitive enuf to be picturesque." He spent a few days in the cool, damp Cameron Highlands, where he did not mysteriously vanish, as had Jim Thompson, the legendary American businessman whose house was one of the sights of Bangkok, had done one weekend in 1967. He wrote Dean, "All things considered, I'm lucky, but how much longer can one remain lucky?"

He got his question answered in Songkhla, where a three-week binge ended when he was struck down in traffic. His forehead deeply gashed, he returned to his room, put a plaster on, and fainted. He woke up hours later to find pillow, bed sheets, and mattress drenched in blood. At a hospital, they stitched and X-rayed him, told him that he'd lost at least two litres of blood, and attached him to an IV. They kept him off food and water. "Doctor order," the nurses said. On the morning of the third day, maddened by thirst, he tore out the IV and donned his bloodstained clothes. Barefoot, vainly chased by a policeman, he fled the hospital, chug-a-lugged six orange sodas, and returned to the still gory hotel room, where he lay for two days until he felt well enough to get his hair dyed raven-black again.

On his last night there, he sat at a market table at sunset. A man approached unsteadily, swollen somehow; his face red, yet pale. Sixty years old perhaps; clothes clean but shabby. In slow good English he said, "...I suppose your problem may be the same as mine. I drink all day and every day. I am careful. I drink slowly so as not to get drunk. All day long. All the long day. Why do I drink? Oh, I cannot stop. Useless. When I drink, I am—happy. I float above it all, this pitiful human life. I was rich once. My children have grown and left me. I had a house, a business once. My wife divorced me. I have—a broken heart. Now I live at the wat. They give me shelter, they give me food. They don't care that I drink, since I'm not a monk. And when I have the money, I drink." With that, he bowed and was gone.

Manit's guide on a visit to Chiang Mai, he continued alone north by riverboat up to the Golden Triangle, the meeting point of three countries, and to Mae Sariang, set among green mountains. A Burmese town, open to Thai but forbidden to *farangs,* lay just across a few yards of foaming, tumbling river. Then back to Chiang Mai, and to a mountain doubling as a national park, on the peak blackberry bushes and rhododendrons. He bussed through tribal villages to Mae Heng Son, a two-street border smuggling town, thence back to Big Ugly. During his journey he had visited hill-tribe villages whose people reminded him of Guatemalans, Peruvians, or Bolivians. But, though he ate and talked with them, it was as if he had been wearing a space suit—or they had.

Byron had contracted a paper marriage to a co-worker variously spelled Miss Nu, Noo, or (Byron's version) "Gnu," a capable girl who was Marlin's recently acquired girlfriend and helped to manage Byron's household. In November, Byron struck a woman who'd dashed in front of his speeding bike. After she'd died of injuries, he had paid a large sum to her family and set off with Marlin to show his videos in Canada. Meanwhile Edith Mirante—Edward had narrowly missed her during his northern journey when she'd been en route to a press conference given by an opium warlord who operated in rebel-held territory—had been jailed, fined, and faced expulsion for illegally crossing into Burma.

By juggling tourist visas, eked out by short extensions, he got through his six-month residency. At the end of April, his recent Canadian passport was renewed. Before Christmas, he'd approached his former boss Mr. Wong, who received the prodigal almost tearfully: he'd had no efficient proofreader since Edward's firing. A mountain of tests and texts awaited. He began to level it, from January working full time while still dwelling in Manit's school. To Dean, then in Indonesia, he sent a copy of the Melo novel for his opinion, enclosing the bulky manuscript in bloodstained cardboard: "seals of my own sacred blood (precious relic), souvenirs of my latest accident." He quoted a Mexican song:

> The house was red
> And freshly painted;
> With Rosa's blood
> They gave it a new coat of paint.

He half-drifted into, half-engineered, a drunken episode to precipitate a full break with Manit, and rejoined Dean's household. To Edward, the implicit contract with Dean was framed thus: "I have no family any more, so *you* are my family, and we're all in this together, so let's all cooperate and help one another out. I know I'm falling apart mentally and physically: *don't* try to stop me or hinder me or limit my liberty, because I'll simply react with worse misbehaviour; just try to protect me as much as you can, and I'll try to see that my actions don't bother you too much." This bland exposition understated the sheer amount of effort it required to save his carcass.

His interest in sex had decreased proportionally to his interest in people, he thought. Once sex had cast a "diffuse glamour"on everything and everyone. Now he saw only its charmless banal repetitiveness. Much of the nebulous complex of emotions people called "hope" was bound up with sexuality: the hope that another would rescue one from the desert of self.

At the end of January, he wrote Byron and Marlin, then in Banff, Alberta, that in the eight months since they'd gone, it often seemed to him that they'd never left. He called his white mongrel bitch "Byron." Reversing a lifelong policy of dog loathing, he had reciprocated her affection ("love, freely given, is never to be sneered at or rejected, from whatever source.") She had produced a dozen puppies, which she and he were endeavouring to feed: he supplied bony chicken parts from the market, and she transmuted them into mother's milk. Her sidekick, "Marlin," a black male who never mated, walked with a limp, wagged his tail sideways, and refused to be touched. The only pup that remained unadopted, because she was hideous and hairless, became charming and frisky. Edward called her "Miss Noo." He could not give news of their adored kitten, "Lacey."

Downtown, he'd been arrested for jaywalking. The policemen looked ferocious as they shoved him and others along the street to jail. But, no, they steered them only to the lobby of a cinema, where a policeman accepted payments for fine. One Thai begged so piteously that Edward gave him the 10 baht he needed. The others had IDs, but all Edward had was a bookshop V.I.P. card (entitling him to a 20 per cent discount.) But the cops accepted it, writing out a receipt to "Edward Ratsey."

At the Canadian Embassy, he heard two U.S. Embassy officials discuss the case of a woman nabbed while returning from Burma. He introduced himself as a friend of Edith. They suggested that he should go to Mae Hong San to intercede, since "Canada has great prestige with both the Thais and the Burmese, as a helpful but uninterfering nation, and you seem to know more about the matter than anyone." In any case, nothing amiss would happen to Edith, they said: the Thai would not do anything crazy like handing her over to Myanmar. As it turned out, she was deported from Thailand. Allowed back a week later, she was ready to cross and recross the Burmese border.

Another binge led to a long, drying-out meditation on dharma, karma, and death, so frightful that he took Dean's advice and joined AA, which met in the rectory of Holy Redeemer Church. He'd feared Alcoholics Anonymous consisted of businessmen and boosters, but these were varied people, simply telling their stories: the decline, the fall, the hitting bottom, the slow ascent. Suffering-death-and-resurrection tales. And truly, every time he binged and slowly recovered, he felt he'd died and returned from the grave.

His elderly relatives were dropping off fast. His cousin Jan had found Marion dead in the bathtub the day before he'd been run down in Songkhla: he wondered if it had been a last warning from her for him to mend his ways. His cousin, Marg Wansbrough, informed him that an uncle, Clair Murtha, his

Aunt Phyllis's husband, had dropped dead. Edward had often told his Thai friends that his family was dead to him. Now some of them really were.

Lots was wrong with Bangkok, but above all it was wrong for *him*. He needed to break the monthly cycle of binge-hangover-absence from work-overwork to make up for lost time.He began to canvass for a place to stay in Canada. One possibility was Marg's home. From time to time, the Royal Bank of Canada had contacted her, concerned that he'd withdrawn massive amounts of money. Since he'd stayed with her and her husband Sandy before, they knew he was "a rambler," up all night, asleep all day. Worried about AIDS, unsure about how it spread, worried, too, about his influence on her kids, fearing that he might stay on indefinitely, Marg tried to put matters kindly but plainly. She offered to house him for a couple of months, but had stipulations. Smoking was a no-no: she and Sandy had allergies. She hoped that he would take a blood test and offer proof that he was free of HIV. Possibly he could rent a trailer at their place: he could use power from their house and park in the laneway....

Winston had sent a contract for him to translate a French translation of a medieval Arab miscellany called *The Delight of Hearts*. He reminded him that the Melo translation was due by the end of April. When it didn't arrive, Winston phoned the Canadian Embassy in early June. Though Edward was around — he had picked up mail — he remained unresponsive. Winston cancelled the Melo book at considerable cost. Now he needed to know about the *Delight of Hearts* translation, since he'd paid up front for publishing rights: if didn't get the book out by the end of 1988, he'd lose the money. He got no reply.

Mr. Wong fired Edward again after another binge. In November, he lost his glasses and money, and woke up in the drunk tank. From Bruce Anderson, with whom he'd been reconciled, he obtained a letter of recommendation on behalf of the Serm Lucksutr Company, which diplomatically noted, "His presence was always looked forward to and appreciated by myself as by the owner-director of SLS, Mr. Sanguan Wongsuchat." While at SLS, Edward had "advanced to the position of senior proofreader of all testing and test preparation materials. A contributor to *Today's English*, a bilingual magazine for advanced readers, Mr. Lacey also helped at transcription and teaching preparation; he "was also Mr. Wongsuchat's personal consultant as regards the English language." SLS regretted "the termination of his employment" and extended "the very best of luck."

He took make-do jobs at English-conversation schools. Friends being God's apology for relatives, he turned to Ruth Beissel to blaze a path to Canada. Seeking a better climate for her crippling arthritis, she had gone to Mexico, joined in Cuernevaca by Renate Jürgensen. She'd invited him to join them there but he had trouble even scraping up the price of a cheap ticket to Montréal. On November 19, he got the Canadian Embassy to contact her so she could send the fare. When the money arrived, he was still 700 baht ($36.17) short: the Embassy made up the difference. He approached the Thai income tax office, fearing that he'd have to pay thousands of baht. Heeding Dean's advice on how to deal with tax officials, he successfully acted deferential, confused, stupid, and poor.

He left Thailand owing Sak a month's rent, and so precipitously that he didn't dry a load of laundry. He didn't have time to pick up his 1959 Olympia manual portable typewriter from a repair shop. Previously used by, successively, Ruth's mother, Ruth, Henry, and Angelica, it had accompanied him around the world for nearly 15 years, used to turn out two books of poems, three books of translations, and innumerable reviews, articles, letters, and poems. Well, Sak could keep it or sell it.

When he departed, banners were being strung up to commemorate the sixtieth birthday of the king. After Marlin took him to the airport, the Thai exit card was headed "Leaving the Kingdom." The plane lifted from the rain-slick tarmac, sliced through the always 90-degree, always 90 per cent humid atmosphere — if sweat could be called atmosphere. It rose above red-and-gilt temples, river, canals, tile roofs receding, then green swamp for endless miles. As it rose, he realized that whatever happened, whatever he did, had done, did not do in life, whatever his sins of commission, or omission, he would never, never have to go back to that terrible city.

27

DO YOU HAVE ANYTHING TO DECLARE?

December 1987-February 1990

I am in Montréal

— cold, Nordic, reasonable —
under the mountain's shadow:

the saman tree is darkening and
the lotus pool is gone; it's
sunrise there, nightfall here.

~ International Date-Line

Flying against the sun, his LOT plane took Edward to Montréal across 12 time zones. He stopped first in Tashkent, then in dawn-hour Warsaw, where he drank cherry brandy and tried to calculate the market value — black, white, and grey — of the zloty. When the pilot announced that they had crossed Canada's coastline the Polish passengers applauded, much to his disgust. As they reached Mirabel airport, the fields turned bone-white, and the Poles anxiously murmured, "Where's the city?"

Because he was appeared fresh from the Thai poppy fields, officials spent two hours sifting his luggage for drugs. A black spot appeared on the X-ray screen.

"What's that?"

"A bundle of wet clothes."

They dragged it out. Sure enough: wet clothes. The officials were also piqued by a heap of rancid spiral shells that he'd plucked from a Malaysian beach.

"Are these shells... er... alive? Canadian law forbids the importation of living molluscs."

"They're not molluscs."

"Oh, I see."

Having given migraines to the officials, he took bus and taxi to a redbrick apartment building at 6430 Sherbrooke Ouest, in the west-Montréal purlieu of Notre-Dame-de-Grâce, N.D.G.: "No Damn Good" in local parlance, and in Edward's. Myrna Beissel at first didn't recognize the grey, wobbly, tropically clad figure with damp overweight luggage. He looked as if he needed feeding. She set about frying up a leaning tower of potato pancakes. Smoking all the while, he engulfed the first stack. Myrna kept frying. Edward kept eating.

Myrna's charities were augmented when her mother returned from her Mexican stay to the small overstuffed apartment just before Christmas. Angelica lived a few doors away, and to Edward seemed as energetic, lazy, and talented as ever. The slightly younger Myrna, now 27, had emerged from the rough chrysalis of her teens to become an efficient, poised young woman who'd turned out far better, and happier with herself, than he'd ever hoped. Ruth's arthritis had worsened (he'd bought her a Tibetan wall hanging entitled "The Demon of Suffering.") Her sojourn in India had left her sappily mystical, he thought.

The standard of feeding had always been high at the Beissels', but their hothouse life irritated him. Their female passion for order yet complication warred with his penchant for disorder yet simplification. They were forever making work for themselves, he thought, moving things around, putting them away, taking them out again. If he always drank coffee in the same mug, and only drank coffee in it, and no one else drank from it, why did they have to wash the damn thing half-a-dozen times a day? The air of Ruth's bedroom was sometimes blue, not just from the pack of menthols he daily smoked, but from their rows. At night her laboured breathing kept him awake; all the Beissels drove him bonkers with their chaffing, chatter, twittering endearments, their maddening femininity. The Beissels were dear, and certainly near, and he blessed them for their help, but living with them made him feel like joining the Trappists. He'd get up at 4 a.m. to read, write, translate, and enjoy the silence.

Ruth, who'd rejected her native Germany for Canada, was irked by his rants against the "non-country," noting that the non-country had instantly granted him monthly welfare payments. He'd always been a "crazy charmer," funny, generous, encyclopedically knowledgeable, but now he was rude, sour, bitter. For him, Canadians were pathetic, pallid, juiceless, useless mugwumps, and Montréal was a parochial Frigidaire. When he young, it had been the city of spires, but since he'd last been here, its mayor, the *grandeur*-prone Jean Drapeau, had taken a wrecking ball to it. He asked himself, "Could I ever have imagined that Romance & Possibility — infinite Possibility, that goddess that haunts all bars — awaited me here?"

It irritated him to know what people were saying. To have to interpret everything imaginatively, investing it with new, alien connotations, gave everything peculiar weight and import. Which was why he liked to live in foreign countries. When he wasn't reeling back, reeking, after three-day binges, he made desultory attempts to get a job teaching English as a foreign language. He wrote Bangkok friends that he'd "settle down for a long winter's hibernation, & think at times of you people & the sweltering heat, the insouciant grace, the nonchalant tolerance, the easy, enigmatic smiles..." The railroad flat sublet he took in the spring on rue Chomedy, a slapshot away from the Montreal Forum, suited him better than the Beissel home — or perhaps the lithium that Ruth's psychiatrist prescribed had reported for duty. Two of his *colocataires* were young men from Ottawa who wanted to become rock musicians. The third was Bou-Alem, a Berber refugee claimant from Algeria.

For Winston Leyland, he Englished *The Delight of Hearts*, rapping out hundreds of anecdotes, footnotes, and rhymed, metrical versions of poems in praise of boys and wine. *Delight of Hearts* merely worked off the advance he'd accepted for the abortive Guilherme de Melo book, but welfare payments covered meals and rent, and Québec paid for the lithium and for new glasses. He considered social assistance to be his due. By his calculations, Canada owed him at least $75,000, counting the estate taxes he'd paid after his mother's death. What he'd forked over since then in withholding, capital gains, and property taxes. This didn't count the 30 per cent depreciation of the "Canadian dodo" over the same period. The External Affairs Department had the temerity to demand what it had paid for part of his air ticket from Bangkok.

April had been sunny, but ended with pissing rain. Mother's Day came, and by May's end, trees were greening, and tulips, narcissi, daffodils, and dandelions were out on Mount Royal, Meanwhile, Angelica secretly planned to wed Francesco, a chubby pastry cook from the Dominican Republic. Only he and Myrna knew about it, though Myrna let it slip to Ruth the night before the event. Henry learned the next morning, too late to attend. That day, a flustered Angelica gathered her skirts in a mad dash for a taxi, only to wait endlessly at the judge's chambers for tardy Francisco. From the bridal bouquet, Edward chose a rose for his lapel. Afterwards, everyone ate a big Greek garlicky meal. Soon he was advising Angelica on how to deal with men of Latin temperament.

As for Henry and Arlette out on his country estate Ayorama Cottage, across the Ontario border ("How many serfs do they own?" Edward asked), he sensed that his old friend considered him a case history la Freud or Krafft-Ebing, and a sponger as well. He'd heard that Klara, whom he'd last seen when she was three, threw a tantrum when she heard he might be heading her way. But after a chance encounter, Henry took him out to Ayorama, a forest-enclosed, cathedral-roofed house, sweeping lawns, and lily-edged, reed-islanded pond. When a neighbour dropped by, Edward said, apropos of nothing, "I am a homosexual." On the drive back to Montréal, he shocked his host by saying, "Henry, I envy you. You have people who depend on you." Meanwhile, he and Ruth remained the best and most acrimonious of friends.

Winston Leyland was urging him to give up booze; he replied that he now drank in moderation. He'd never had serious problems, he said, except when his surroundings were "extremely alcoholised," or he was unhappy. The key to his drinking, he wrote Randy Wicker, was his manic-depression. You drank if you felt too high, you drank because you felt too low, you drank when mania, paranoia, and depression rapidly alternated. He compared himself to Malcolm Lowry, who drank to induce a creative frenzy.

He remained a presence to his family. His cousin Don Blanchard was reminded of him every time he had to undergo security clearance in the military or public service, when his name always seemed to pop up. For some months, Edward had received no answers to letters he'd sent his family. He finally telephoned Marg Wansbrough. He could visit them if he wished, she said, but he sensed a No Welcome mat had been put out. After his parents' deaths he'd dispensed gifts and loans. He'd sent them his books; they knew he was gay. Often, they'd barraged Canadian Embassies for information about him. Now they didn't seem to want him. This was what homosexuals faced, he thought. However tolerant straights seemed to be, they never accepted your gayness. They thought of it as a foible, a flaw, or a phase to be outgrown. When you didn't outgrow it, watch out! They turned on you, or turned their backs on you, and he didn't know which hurt more. Maybe, being local yokels, his family envied his vagabond freedom. Maybe, Catholic puritans, they were only waiting for the moment of his downfall to wither him with scorn. Families, Brazilians said, belong in photograph albums.

After four years of near-silence, he and Randy had resumed their half-fond, half-pusillanimous exchanges. In a Christmas newsletter, Randy, who lived in Hoboken, just across the Hudson by subway from his shop in Greenwich Village, had noted that Marsha, a black transvestite hooker he'd befriended, had paint-sprayed his kitchen and shattered half the glasses. Next to this news, Edward glossed: "I unfortunately never was lucky enough to meet Marsha, but she sounds just my type! I've always wanted to do all that, and more, to R." Randy was nursing his companion, David Combs, who was slowly dying of AIDS. Edward thought that David had nagged, bullied, and exploited Randy. But, he wrote him, "we don't choose the gods we serve, nor do other people generally recognize them." But the waifs and strays Randy had picked up...they were trash! People like him and Randy, he wrote, required stronger, or at least supportive, people. Randy's succubi were robbing him blind, their ingratitude and greed binding him to his Ixion's wheel of work. "NYC's hustlers & conmen are the world's most cunning, experienced & exploitative, & it's ironic (karma, again) that they shd be able to spin their cobwebs of emotional blackmail & economic scams/

schemes around one of the most brazen, weathered, cynical old NYC hucksters." Both he and Randy dreamed of permanent relationships, but impermanence and instability was the human condition: no pleasure without pain, no permanence without change. The only stability was instability, the only security was insecurity: no beauty without ugliness, no happiness without sorrow, no good without evil, no life without death.

The thought that he might have contracted AIDS nagged him; a blood test turned out HIV-negative. Twelve thousand delegates had come to Montréal to attend an AIDS congress earlier that year, and he'd picked up bushels of paper handouts and, condoms. Six months after the congress, he acquired a skin rash on his legs that began with itchiness or redness, then became a leathery thickening or brown discolouration. It wouldn't go away. He had a biopsy, a CAT scan, a battery of tests. He wasn't diabetic; he didn't have leukemia. He might have dismissed it as just another epidermal mystery, had not AIDS been on his mind. Though the rash might have been psychosomatic, he couldn't believe that even his mind could inflict such an ailment. Ruth thought he was a terrible hypochondriac, but even hypochondriacs had things go wrong with them. The dermatologist thought it was a fungal infection. It couldn't *possibly* be Kaposi's sarcoma....

To furnish their apartment, his fellow tenants scrounged in Dumpsters, got gifts of abandoned furniture, and soon accumulated box-springs, sofas, and legless tables. The rock musicians celebrated getting a gig with two non-stop days of noise and drinking, cheered on by three or four — by then he was seeing double — Inuit prostitutes. Bou-Alem harboured a fellow Algerian refugee, and added two young French-born Algerians who were awaiting a plane back to France. No sooner had they departed than the rent cheque bounced. Since they paid the rent separately, everyone blamed everyone else. The building's managers targeted Edward, from whose account the rent was paid. But the bank had forgot to credit a deposit he'd made. He bullied it into making good the bounced cheque.

Some tenants moved out; others had to be found. They settled on a fine-arts student who wanted to redecorate the apartment, and a teenager who only owned a noose hanging in his window. Edward's own large room was almost as Spartan, with a bed, table, royal-blue sofa, and chair. The flat, he wrote, "had the delicate equilibrium of a railroad terminus. "

The little-magazine editor Frank Manley, a fan of Edward's published autopsies on Canadian poetry, hoped to get him to review books. Turning up, he found him youthful-looking, though much older than the youths around him: he wondered whether a portrait of Dorian Gray was stashed away. The world cared not for Canada, Edward intimated, let alone Canadian poets. As a calling card, Frank had brought his own chapbook. As Edward flipped through it, he happily spotted a translation from Anglo-Saxon, and discoursed on Old English poetry and its gnomic naming devices.

Bou-Alem moved out. Ryoko, a Japanese-Korean new-comer, Edward quickly diagnosed as psychotic. The would-be interior decorator, who dressed in black leather and storm trooper's boots, occupied the bathroom for hours, brought home tricks, and subjected the rock musicians to volcanic eruptions of classical music. A Jewish poor-little-rich-girl moved in. Ryoko roamed the apartment, moved furniture about, disappeared with boyfriends for days, and babbled in a mix of three languages. One pre-dawn, he returned to find her grappling with a dozen of Montréal's finest, who'd been summoned by neighbours after she'd tried to break up the flat. The Montréal police, despite a well-earned reputation for brutality, carted her off to a hospital, from whence she returned to Japan. Someone broke in and stole an electric guitar. People "forgot" or defaulted on their share of the rent, phone, and gas bills, and the noose-boy defected to Ontario. The Jewish girl and one of the rockers wanted to move out together, and no one could stand the storm-trooping Romantic. Edward put a sign on his door: *"Je ne suis pas là — ni ici non plus!"* I am *never* in!

Soon after he had returned to Montréal, I'd got a mangled packet of poems from him, and was amazed to see the return address. At best, he'd been a maddening correspondent: if it wasn't a crammed, cryptic postcard with no return address, it was a prolonged patch of dead space. Now came a gargantuan epistle in cockroach calligraphy — he could have had a career as an inscriber of the Koran on matchbox covers—*and* 107 poems. Letters from Montréal to Scotsburn, Nova Scotia, began to arrive with dates like "35th Martober, 2531 (Buddhist Era)." I placed some of his translations of the Portuguese poet Fernando Pessoa, or his heteronyms, in literary journals.

A question exercised Edward. Who could be his literary executor? He wanted *something* to last. Fifteen years earlier, he'd made a will naming John Robert Colombo. But he thought that John had dismissed him as a *poéte manqué* who hadn't pursued a career. Would being an executor burden him? Would he take it seriously? He'd considered naming Henry Beissel. But Henry might be homophobic. As for Winston Leyland, *he* was too gay-centred. Henry might suppress the gay-themed poetry he'd written; Winston might suppress anything heterosexual. Knowing that I was incapable of censorship, he asked me to serve. We met face to face when I turned up at his Chomedy flat one evening in November. We hadn't seen each other in at least a decade.

Papers were scattered across the floor of his room in the vast flat. In a dive on St. Catherine Street, with fierce imprecations he drove off a First Nations woman from a table he wanted. Unable to talk amid the uproar and shattering glass, we removed to a Persian restaurant for dinner, and to the Blue Angel Café, which we had last visited, it seemed, a century earlier. For his Old Time Country Music Club of Canada, "Country Bob" Fuller still garnished his gargantuan overalls with a safety pin, an elderly man still sold chewing gum, combs, and toothpaste at the washroom door, and at midnight we still got free hot dogs.

Later, Edward wrote that I could not imagine the pit into which penury, manic-depression, and the consequences of a New Year's drinking bout had cast him. Enclosing a copy of his will, he said that he felt suicidal. Alarmed, I telephoned him. He was still alive.

Bou-Alem rescued him. He broke the Chomedy lease and found him new digs. By the start of February, he was installed at 3433 ave Laval, app. 6, near Sherbrooke St. Parallel with Laval was St-Laurent Blvd., the Main. His ground-floor room held a small electric stove, a sink, refrigerator, chairs, table, a soft bed, and no neighbours under him upset by his nocturnal pacing.

Next door lived a melancholy Lebanese, from whose room he
heard Arabic melopeias, or the discreet but unmistakable sounds
of sexual intercourse, the "normal" kind. He did his laundry by
hand, partly because he couldn't understand, either in English or
French, washing-machine instructions. He used the corner booth
if he needed to make a phone call.

     Needing a typewriter, he acquired a Japanese-made mess
of wires and plastic, replete with features like an automatic spelling
corrector that beeped at every mistake. Since it contained little
of his vocabulary and personal abbreviations, British spelling, or
foreign words, it constantly beeped to remind him that "bot" was
not a proper Engl. word—nor was "Engl." It had never heard
of a botfly, though it behaved like one. Its automatic memory
instantly spewed out stored gibberish whenever he accidentally
activated it by pushing CODE plus the letter "t," which was easy
to do. Unerasable caps were triggered by merely brushing a key.
Nor could he eradicate "Mr. Sea Dere sur," which he had typed
to test the spelling-correction function. "Never buy a mACHINE
BEYOND YR OWN TECHNOLOGICAL CAPACITIES." It
gobbled up ribbon cassettes, and came with a manual in Japlish.
It was supposedly portable, but he could imagine just what one
ride on an Andean or Himalayan bus, or an Indonesian ferry boat,
or even a Bangkok *tuktuk*, would do to it.

     Winston had in mind a translation of a manuscript called
La Prairie des Gazelles, an anthology of short medieval Arabic
amatory poems. Although he translated a sample, he saw that the
thing was untranslatable, and Winston agreed. So he was off that
hook. He was still supplying his admirer, Anthony Reid, with
hand-copied poems. The connoisseur called their arrival "the
great event of the year and I have been hugging myself with joy
and satisfaction ever since." Though married and a father, Reid
required poems of boy-love and nothing else. When Edward
included a few poems with no gay content, Reid miffed him by
consigning them to a folder labelled "Ephemera."

     Randy wanted to see him. Edward wondered whether
he wanted to gloat over his "dethroned, exiled, and diminished
condition." He now arrived. Edward meaningly took him to the
Botanical Gardens' poisonous-plants section, though he thought
that their ecological niche was a masochistic greenhouse. As a

case in point, he flagellated himself by writing a long anguished poem, "The Millstone," about the episode with Ravi in Madurai. A moment of reconciliation occurred just before Randy left. Many years before, Edward had acid-scarred his friend by writing, "Randy, you want to be loved, but you are not lovable." This evening Randy lay, eyes closed, on a hotel bed. Edward stood at the foot of it and, recalling those hateful, hurtful words, said, "I'm sorry I wrote that to you. You are lovable, and I love you." Randy didn't open his eyes. Instead, he said softly, "Good night, Edward."

At the summer's end, Ruth invited him and a kindly, earnest Prussian named Inge Fiedler, a lifelong friend visiting from East Germany, to help on a bus trip to the Saguenay and Gaspé. They took turns at getting Ruth aboard buses; one went ahead of her and pulled, the other pushed. They enjoyed the journey to Chicoutimi and Tedoussac and then to Matane and Percé, a land of river, lake, sea, woods, and mountains. He ate ravenously, acquired a tan, and stayed sober.

He bussed to Toronto, where he saw that the Chinese had managed to turn Dundas St. West into a would-be Bangkok street market. His chief destination was southwest, to the city of St. Catharines, where nuns were taking care of Aunt Helen, his father's 87-year-old sister, the last in his paternal line. Silver-haired, with a lined, pouched face, she couldn't see or hear well, but was delighted at the reunion. She seemed to him more tolerant: age *did* improve some people. In straggling, spindly handwriting she afterwards wrote him, "It was possible for me to see that you had been ill, or in an accident as you referred to being rescued."

He was back to his normal weight, his blood pressure was lower than 15 years earlier, his tachycardia had vanished, his fungal skin ailment had eased. His translation of *The Delight of Hearts* had been published by Gay Sunshine Press in the fall of 1988. He had revised a manuscript of poems, and written a few new ones. A few translations had appeared in magazines. He'd stopped taking lithium. He had written a will, and named an executor. All to the good.

In November, Frank Manley and I dropped in at his rue Laval digs, a pot of boiled couscous—his staple—atop his little stove. On the same stay in Montréal, I lured him out to a vegetarian dinner with Monique de Gaye and her good friend, an agreeable Jewish girl named Kathy Finkel. He'd last seen Monique in Swami Shyam's Meditation Centre at Kulu in the Valley of the Gods. Once she'd seemed soft-focussed, self-willed, and absent-minded, but now looked radiantly at peace with herself. After our wholesome dinner, Edward's head sheltered against frigid blasts by giant earlugged Nepalese headgear, we went to Kathy's apartment for talk and *tisanes*.

He was restless. For potential employers like the Canadian University Service Overseas (CUSO), he got a letter of reference from Mary Jane Cook, the Texas university friend who'd now retired from running a graduate ESL program in Arizona. She wrote, "I have never encountered anyone whose competence as a linguist comes even close to Edward's." With a new passport in hand, he mulled over places he had been, places he might go. Finding a job anywhere would not be easy. His C.V. looked suspiciously erratic, and his age and marital status counted against him (unmarried at 50 = homosexual = *already must have or will develop AIDS*.) Among nibbles was a university in Saudi Arabia with fabulous pay, which wanted to see him at their office in Houston, Texas, for him roughly equivalent to a Jew turning up for a job interview in Nazi Germany.

He recalled how in Southeast Asia the wise old teacher was revered—"when the guru went dotty," he wrote, he was taken for a demigod, and his mutterings and ravings were treasured as oracular utterances." As he was thinking about this, Byron Black began to boom Indonesia's prospects. Shortly after Edward's return to Canada, Byron had been a guest of Randy Wicker, put on a video show in Manhattan called "Homesick for Everywhere," and then taken a job with American Language Training (ALT) in Jakarta. Indonesia... gorgeous, variegated, the country he'd liked best in Asia. Byron promised to take care of him "as long as you don't act like a Spoiled Baby." By the fall of 1989, the chance of a job with ALT had become so imminent that Byron, about to shoot a video in Japan, gave him an address should he arrive while he was away. He moved out of his Laval apartment and back in with Ruth. In February, he left the country. He didn't phone to say goodbye to me or anyone else because, he later said, he disliked announcing his comings and goings, and equally disliked farewells. If they were to be final, they were too fraught with meaning and emotion. If they were not final, they were bathetic and pointless. And who knew which they would prove to be?

28

THE TERRIBLE CITY

February 1990-January 1992

Now as my cell-lined plane floats high
across the wide placental sky,
why am I still afraid of living,
still afraid to die?

~ Now

From Montréal, he flew to Vancouver, where he bought 200 duty-free cigars for Byron. After a sleepless transoceanic flight, Cathay Pacific, grazing apartment windows, touched down in Hong Kong. He had no time to join beer-swilling students in the bars and noodle houses. Repressing the fact that silkworms were boiled alive—he'd always empathized with creatures usually immune to human sympathy—he bought metres of raw silk for Ruth and Myrna, and hastened to the airport. In Singapore, still in the midst of Chinese New Year, nearly every hotel was booked. At the Indonesian Embassy, he got a six-month visa, and chased down the local contact for American Language Training. These delays made him cancel his flight to Jakarta—Byron was disappointed when he turned up to meet him—and booked another. Before it left, he strolled to the red-light district, relieved to find it extant, with bright dollhouses of Chinese, Indian, and Malay dolls, and vendors of aphrodisiacs and antibiotics. Bugis Street, the shabby home to all-night dives where transvestites paraded after midnight, had been demolished, but was being rebuilt after an indignant outcry.

Then, finally, he was in Jakarta. He hoped that the taxi-driver knew where he was going. Jakarta, at least thrice the size of Montréal, had hundreds of *kampungs*. In one of these urban communities, faraway Condet, Byron Black lived. Wheeling through blank streets for an hour, the driver at last located the southeastern suburb, and even the nameless, narrow street Byron lived on, and the door of his small ramshackle house.

After they'd tried to catch up on the many years since they'd last met, Edward repaired to his mosquito-netted bed. He couldn't sleep. From the bamboo jungle he heard a rushing creek, hoarse cries of "*Mee!* from wandering noodle hawkers, early-rising muezzins competitively called the many faithful to prayer in different keys and durations, sounding, as William Burroughs said, like "a mad tobacco auction." The spectral humming of the 99 names of Allah, like a swarm of angry bees, formed a duet with the ear-shattering drone of low-flying planes from the nearby military airport.

The 18-month contract that he'd signed was no sinecure. A "Model Native Speaker and Teacher of English as a Foreign Language," he had to buff up his rusty skills, instruct up to 30 hours a week, master new teaching methods and textbooks, mark tests and homework, keep records, draw up reports, attend meetings. He got a starting rate of $1,250 a month: in Indonesia, the couple who kept house for Byron got $40 a month and thought themselves well paid. His rent at Byron's was $60 a month, less a deduction for the cost of the cigars. He could gradually pay Ruth the $31 it had cost her when he phoned Jakarta, the $400 she'd lent him for the trip and, going back to 1987, a debt of $850.

Byron had inherited military habits from his father. He got up at 5 a.m. to go jogging, waking Edward, and barrelled off on his motorbike at 6:30 a.m. to teach ALT classes, to create art postcards, or to make audiotapes or videos. Edward had to commute up to three hours across a gridlock sprawl. In this *ville tentaculaire*, the Cyclopean eye was Cililitán, a bus terminal with a produce and fish market spilling into the streets. When he got back about 11 p.m., Byron would be avid for conversational combat. He videotaped their talks. Though they understood little, the houseboys liked to listen to Edward's soliloquies.. He did not bond with Byron's on-site primates, the fierce Mahmud, "King of Beats"; Miss Mina, a.k.a. "Shit Fur Brains," tiny and buck-toothed, with a fierce shrill shriek; and Charles Darwin, looking lost in thought as he spent the day masturbating.

Byron was the only foreigner in Condet, a "village" of half a million. Condet's whitewashed, red tile-roofed homes lined roads of sucking clay. In its cooling orchards grew the jackfruit, its huge bulk and weight held by each small fragile stem from the trunk of the tree; the white-fleshed snakefruit, which had a scaled skin and tasted like a crisp apple; the delicious, malodorous spiked durian, which, if it fell on you, would kill you more surely than any coconut. If Jakarta sometimes seemed like a fever-dream, for Edward it had the negative virtue of not being Canada.

On weekends or holidays, he escaped filth, rats, diarrhea-inducing drinking water, slums, freeway tangles, and Mussolini monumentalism for the green calm land of the Javanese. He asked himself why was he not allowed to live in such places. Why must he always live in places he least liked? Once he ranged onward to the west-coast Sunda Strait between Java and Sumatra, his destination Anak Krakatoa, "Son of Krakatoa." Anak's dad had erupted in 1883 with the strength of 100,000 atom bombs, sent a tidal wave around the world, and lowered global temperatures for three years. The volcano had ejected so much matter it had collapsed, seawater flooding its crater.

His beachhead was a palm-hut resort on a sandy unpeopled coast. An all-day trip through rough seas gave him two hours on the new island that had risen. Standing on the hot dark sand amid pampas grass and casuarina pine told him that this land hadn't been there 60 years before, that in turn it had risen to replace two volcanic craters that were now 900 feet below the sea, that it reconstituted the original cone that had preceded all of these, which had blown itself up some 1,600 years ago... *ad infinitum*. The fumeroles on Anak Krakatoa smoked with sulphur, and the small deep crater yawned yellow and green, like a bursting boil. In the 1970s, Anak had tossed out red-hot rocks the size of Cadillacs. Now the son of Krakatoa was taking a nap.

In late April, toward the end of Ramadan, ALT dispatched him to Banjarmasin, a Muslim city on the south coast of Kalimantan, more familiarly, Borneo. The Banjars and Dayaks had been coastal pirates or headhunters until well into this century; here Chinese and Arabs were the foreigners. For 10 weeks, at one of the schools ALT ran with local partners, he replaced a staffer on holiday, supervised the Indonesian teachers of 200 students, wrote a newspaper column, and did a weekly radio program. The Muslims were hardline, but friendly and courteous. The mostly Christian Chinese ran the school: most of the students were Chinese, anxious to learn, touchingly grateful for the help he could give them. The newspaper column and radio program proved to be fun. The townspeople thronged any event he organized.

Banjarmasin, full of blue and green mosques, shops, and markets, was crisscrossed by rivers and canals chockablock with speedboats, steamers, cargo boats, and houseboats. Though close to the sea, it depended on river trade. It was easy to take speedboat trips far inland and, nearer, the little towns of the artistic and hospitable Dayaks. The houses of the Malay, once-piratical Banjars were filled with what trade brought them: Chinese porcelains, Arabic metalwork, Hindu statuary. Everything was built on stilts on marsh and reclaimed land; tides flooded streets near the narrow river, a tributary of a tributary. At three degrees below the equator, the climate was better, or at least no worse, than Jakarta's. He dined on crocodile kebabs, river-turtle steak, and sea-turtle eggs when, self-catering, he wasn't at war with sugar ants. They devoured even his clove cigarettes.

The dry laws decreed that you couldn't buy beer or liquor to take home. About a dozen places were licensed to sell beer for instant consumption at exorbitant prices, closing early. But one spot, strategically next to the police station, stayed open till 1:30 a.m., commanding a view of river, market, and blue hills. When Edward left work about 10 p.m., it became his refuge. The place had "hostesses"; one of them, a Balinese girl who spoke good English, became a confidante. She was as lonely as he.

Though Banjarmasin was hardly idyllic, he rankled at ALT's next posting: director of courses for at least six months in the West Kalimantan city of Pontianak. ALT's Banjarmasin partners hinted at impending trouble. The first problem, though—a delay in opening the branch—was a boon, giving him three weeks to go to Bangkok. He found that what he'd termed "the terrible city" had lost its dark magic: it was just a place, the Thai just a people. He took satisfaction that Bangkok hadn't destroyed him. Friends like Dean Bishop were absent, but he looked up Mr. Sak, who had begun to look paunchy.

Pontianak meant "the vampire," the spirit of a woman who died in childbirth and returned as a lovely phantom, though trailing putrefying entrails, who seduced young men to their doom. The air seemed to drip from bearded trees, while bats squeaked and twittered in twilight and a thousand swallows flew. Pontianak was like a city of wronged female ghosts. Outside town, the numbed, doe-eyed Javanese whores in their *complex* stared through rain from painted doorways in a fetid emerald swamp. Pointed at Sumatra, on a delta of the longest river in Indonesia, Pontianak was smack on the equator. Sudden rainstorms flooded the city in minutes. It was Conrad, Greene, or Maugham territory, the white man going to drink, rot, or madness. In inflated moments he thought of himself as Ovid in his Black Sea exile, César Vallejo in Paris, Keats dying in Rome, one of a roaming tribe who, self-condemned, scudded like foam in the river. In this mood, he let his mind drift to skating rinks, potatoes, milk, cheese, chocolate. He thought, like a throbbing toothache, of a boy in Rio de Janeiro.

Low, red-tile roofed buildings on unstable subsoil straggled along banks of the mile-wide river. A vertiginous boardwalk, eaves and colonnades overhead, took him past squat shophouses to a riverfront slum. Slow roads led in unpromising directions. Though the river carried timber and rubber from the interior, there was no fast or easy way of getting inland. The government's conflict with Communist guerillas compelled him to obtain travel passes, and repeat the process at every river stop. He did get north to Sinkawang along the coast, a small Chinese city in low, rolling hills near rustic beaches and warm, waveless water, and then into the cool jungle slopes of low mountains that spanned the border with Malaysia, and an almost abandoned hotel set in acres of landscaped gardens, the huge dry swimming pool mossy in the sun.

Pontianak, laid out on a hopeful grid, tried to be attractive with flowery parks and wide streets lined with red areca palms and traveller's tree, but cars, motorbikes, rickshaws, and bicycles made for clotted traffic. At sundown, a thousand cafés sprouted sidewalk chairs and tables. Only anemic beer was served or sold in corner stores but, luckily for him, liquor could be bought in supermarkets and hotels. He ate *padang*, indigenous ancestor of the *rijstaffel*, foothills of small curried dishes around a mountain of rice.

The water was unpotable, and the narrow canals were glorified drainage ditches. Since canals were everywhere, he had to be wary at night lest he put his foot into one, or fall through a rotting spot on a boardwalk. When the tide went out the city stank of shit, fish, and wet earth. He could not get his mind off decay. In the cemetery were the frangipani's starry blooms, gnarled branches, and leaden leaves, and in the shade the blue, green, or purple crocuses springing from the red-earth dankness like knives.

Lacking much in common with expatriates—missionaries to the Dayaks, engineers embarked on building roads, businessmen meeting at a hotel bar's Happy Hour—he could only commune with one colleague, a Malaysian whose English was a little rocky. The local Malays shelled him with predictable questions. Perforce, he had to learn Bahasa Indonesia, a grammatically simplified, lexically enriched version of Malay. Like German, it was literal-minded (a stocking was a "footshirt," a toe was a "footfinger"; a signature was a "handsign"), yet full of petrified metaphors (prostitutes were "butterflies of the night"; a sponge was "the flower of the coral"; the money in his bank account didn't bear interest, it "flowered"). It disturbed him to discover that the "until" was also the verb "arrive," and that "when" was also "time."

The Chinese of Pontianak, more than half the population, were forbidden to publish in Chinese, use its characters, or mount decorations like lanterns and dragons; they were banned from celebrating New Year's, the Month of the Hungry Ghosts, the Mooncake Festival, or dragon dances; they had to take

Indonesian names in addition to their own. He remembered the
wholesale expulsions and run-amok massacres of them in 1965.
Yet he didn't like the Chinese. Though some of his best students
were Chinese, he fumed that they considered him a potential ally.
No! He was no ally. Certainly not of his boss, a caricature of the
grinning Chinee whom, as Byron noted, "stuffed a California
Fried Chicken fast-food joint, a business college, a Yamaha Organ
school and oh yes an English-language school into one riotously
busy building." Byron sent him a newspaper clipping about a
series of dismembered bodies found around Pontianak, scribbling
in the margin, "Anything to do with you?" In early October, ALT's
Jakarta director, A. K. (Sonny) Carlsen summarized the disturbing
reports he'd received about his course director. Edward annotated
them:

> (a) on five occasions you have failed to show up
> for class claiming sickness or just unable to teach
> and on two of these occasions you failed to notify
> the office beforehand that you would be unable
> to teach causing last minute cancellation of those
> classes.
> *3/1*
> (b) of late you have been generally uncooperative
> in participating in the extra-curricular activities
> of the school.
> *there are none*
> (c) you are drinking excessively which has
> become noticeable to your colleagues,
> employers and to the neighbourhood you live in.
> *my own business*
> (d) you left the Pontianak area for an extended
> period of time (3 days) without notifying your
> employers where they might get in touch with
> you thereby creating anxiety for them as they are
> officially responsible for you if anything happened
> that would need to be reported to the authorities.
> On your return, when asked, you thought it best
> not to disclose where you had been.
> *... absolute nonsense*

To Ruth Beissel, he expressed the hope that Myrna would make a go of a hairdressing business ("Ah, but in lovely Canada, so many licences, so much red tape, so many health regulations. Here you wd just set up a stall with a few tables & chairs on any free stretch of pavement, get our yr wok, & start frying.") I sent him a snapshot of my six-year-old son Malcolm smelling a flower, which he told his colleagues was a childhood portrait of himself. He derided me for reducing "all human beings to the lowest common denominator of their foibles and weaknesses (food, at best, for gutter gossip.)" He dismissed the idea that his work might interest posterity, in the process satirizing Henry: "It's all really not of the slightest importance, *sub specie aeternitatis* (as the Bard of Buchenwald wd piously sigh, lifting his hoary noble head with an enigmatic, melancholy smile & shake of the mane, for a soulful gaze at the cold Canadian stars)." From Bali, Dean Bishop brought up old business involving their mutual friend Sak, "who said he saw you in Bangkok and you asked him if he needed the $200 you were going to give him. He's sorry he didn't say yes and now asks if you can send it to me." Dean invited Edward to read some of his books in Bangkok, should he care to drop by.

Conflicts with his Chinese boss reached such a head that he went on strike, barricading himself in his room. ALT recalled him to Jakarta.

While, half a world away, Desert Storm kicked up sand in Kuwait and dropped bombs on Baghdad, Edward set about losing his job. This took a certain amount of doing, since ESL schools were tolerant harvest homes for misfits, misanthropes, remittance men, and burnt-out cases. He skipped classes and perturbed students with his wilfully peculiar behaviour. When Byron pointed this out to him, he answered, "You have taken away the last of my self-confidence." Byron videotaped him strolling around an open-air market, buying a fruit drink from a stand, discoursing about Islam. The amiable outing was a rarity.

Byron's account. One Saturday afternoon Edward was staggering along a residential street. He lay down for nap. A housewife observed a white man curled up in her driveway. Alarmed, she asked whether he needed help. "Oh, no," he replied, "I'm just resting here. I'm a teacher at American Language Training, just down the road." The woman phoned the school. They came round to scoop him up. Back at the office, he shed his clothing and cavorted Tarzan-like. Even ALT had reached its elastic limits. Byron was angry: he'd taken pains to secure the job for Edward and, briefing Sonny Carlsen about his past, had assured him that he'd reformed.

Fired, Edward set off for Bangkok, forced to send Ruth an S. O .S. for the airfare from Kuala Lampur. In a postcard to Edith Mirante, he attributed his Jakarta debacle to ALT's "high-pressure, over-structured & -organized style & methods, which make one seem & feel perpetually busy even when one wasn't; perhaps it was just living w/ Byron & all his powerful yet irremediably scattered energies." Or maybe it had been the six months in loathsome Kalimantan. The "powers-that-be did not like my self-assertiveness, & put me under a kind of probation. This, predictably, led eventually to a spectacular blow-up last month..." While waiting for money to arrive from Ruth, he stayed in a hostel run by Holy Rosary Church.

In May he turned up in Bangkok with one solitary baht in his pocket. He resumed his old job with Mr. Wong in the city core, tiring his mind and eye nine hours a day, six days a week, writing, editing, and proofreading *Today's English*. It took hours to get to his job from the nearly empty house lent to him. Mr. Sak tided him over financially till the end of the month. He wrote me that "Things went wrong in Jkta (office politics, etc.)" and, at much greater length, to Byron, who replied that he was

> ... intrigued by the elaborate spiderweb of rationalization and justification you are a-building to render your antics perfectly understandable, even something so predictable and in character that it's simply outrageous that the Big Bad Boss should not, well, learn to put up with it. I've actually noted this kind of accomplished building of a defense in others, mainly alcoholics. One example I recall discussing with you was how, after Götterdammerung and Swish-out, Wasmin mentioned to me (in confidence) that you had tried to fondle his wee-wee. To which you responded "Well, why did he have it out?" which was a very revealing, if clumsy, attempt

to turn the event around. For all I know you look back now and distinctly recall being seduced by that naughty office-boy....

He'd attracted many boys met on buses or trains. They sent him wandering, wondering aerograms. Addressing him as "Edward Lancey," a boy named Muhammad wrote:

Remember that I met you In "Restaurant Begadang" In Jalan Pakimura Pontianak. I always member with you although you didn't at Pontianak any more. When I was job In Resaurant Begadang you always helped dan taught me in Ingglish. You were kind to me.

Some month ago I went to your course place, ALT. I was looking for you, but didn't to met you and than I ask any body that taught Ingglish there. I asked them does Mr. Edward still tought Ingglish here. They answered Mr. Edward doesn't tought here any more.

Mohammad ended hopefully, "I think you don't forget with me and you don't forget with my name (MUHAMMAD MULYADI). If you still live in Pontianak I will live together with you."

As Edward's birthday approached, he dreamed of Ruth. They were in the Greco-Roman city of Pergamum, a small town full of classical ruins in western Turkey. They were staying in a huge, posh, medieval castle or hotel, and he was worried about what local attractions he should take Ruth to see in the time available, including several that the real Pergamum didn't possess. This was, he wrote her, one of his frequent "guide" dreams involving those who were alive or, like his parents, dead. He thought they reflected his guilt that he didn't do more for people.

Writing to Dean Bishop at the end of the June, he said that he was "still bathed in a mild euphoria" over the return to Bangkok. "I liked Indo., & it is a much more beautiful country, & a quieter, more soothing culture, than Thailand, but I found Indonesians too predictable, too easy to understand, too rigid & conservative & religious & moralistic, and, above all, less vivacious & `interesting' than I tho't they'd be." Thai, however, "zany individualists, understand me (psychologically if not linguistically) & my follies."To Dean and others, he claimed that, unlike dull, puritan Jakarta and boorish Borneo, he relished Bangkok's raw vitality and weird syntheses.

He was also "happy so many people remember me & seem glad to see me back." He settled accounts with Mr. Sak and, paycheque in hand, hastened to Penang, Malaysia, to pay a fine at a consulate for a Thailand overstay, and to acquire a three-month visa. He resumed his benders and all that went with them: missing workdays, getting robbed, drunken-sailor spending. To Dean, he wrote that it was "some penance or self-punishing ritual I have to go thro'." Once, when Dean had returned to Bangkok, a boy delivered Edward home in a wheelbarrow, announcing, "Here's your father!" Once he fell on railroad tracks, bloodying himself. Helped home, he declined to see a doctor but, minutes later, asked Dean to take him to a clinic. He showed Dean where his will was kept.

In the early hours of August 1, 1991 no friends in a pick-up truck were around to scrape him off the street. As he lay in a stupor, a speeding vehicle rolled over him. But this was no routine hit-and-run. Gathering him up, the driver dumped him at the door of a hospital emergency ward. Edward's leg, most of his ribs, and collarbone were broken, his skull fractured, a lung punctured.

He had attained the status that an Indian astrologer once predicted would be his at age 54: a monk possessing nothing but his robe and his begging-eating-drinking bowl. With Edward in a coma, Dean wondered whether he should ask that the plug be pulled. But he rallied, and by September was off the respirator. Dean visited daily whenever he was in town. Marlin Oliveros came, as did Mick van Ness, an English-language teacher who'd been in Indonesia. After vigorous prodding by a teenage nurse, Mick reported, Edward opened one eye. "We can do better than that," the nurse said, jamming one eyelid close. He opened the other eye.

He seemed to have lost half his body weight. His left leg was in plaster, and his hands were strapped to the bed. When he managed to feed himself, food bubbled up through a tracheotomy hole in his throat. Struggling to get his arms free of restraints, his body writhed. From time to time a nurse suctioned out green slime. The nurses urged his visitor to bring condensed milk, talc powder, and "tissues, lots of tissues." A square hole in his leg's plaster cast oozed pus. Yet, recovering rapidly, one day he swung his legs over the bed's guardrail, hissing that the Viet Cong would ship him off to North Vietnam. Dean wondered whether the dottiness was an act designed to fool his friends into thinking that his crushed skull had scrambled his brain.

He was shuffled from ward to ward. One day Mick found him in an overcrowded bay. He had lost his glasses and provided strict but senseless specifications so his friend could find a replacement pair. Mick lent him his own glasses to see how they'd match. Edward liked them so much he resisted giving them up. Given a newspaper to read, he nearly rubbed his eyeballs on it, half the time holding it upside down. While a nurse positioned his body so she could change the sheets he tried to grab her breasts. Mick suggested he hire girls from the Patpong red-light district. "You féén he wan fuck me," confided the sister.

By mid-December, his leg wound stopped oozing. Near the end of the month, Byron, on the way back from a family visit to Texas, videotaped him. "Eddie, how you doing?" Though grizzled, unshaven, haggard, Edward looked better than he had a few months before when, Byron remembered, his scarred head had seemed like one of Frankenstein's early drafts. "I've got to get out of here," Edward said hoarsely, as he bent open Byron's gift, a paperback copy of E. L. Doctorow's *World Fair*. He observed he found that the days went by "on wings of lead."

Byron noted that, in the restless aftermath of surgery, Edward had been a "rambunctious bronco." Edward smiled. Unaware that his friends had sent the Canadian Embassy money for his expenses, and were conferring about him, he said, "People shouldn't worry about me." Speaking from long experience, he added that the diplomats "try to get you out of a situation and then tell you how much you owe them."

"I'm feeling much more normal," he added.

"You were never normal," said Byron.

When the hospital gratefully discharged him in January, he stayed at Dean's house in a sleeping bag that his host had to wash every day. Dean asked him if he felt he was getting back to normal. Edward replied with a question: "What is normal?"

29

"DO YOU THINK I AM MALINGERING?"

January 1992-June 1995

I wonder what I'll look like as a skeleton.
Well, I guess, like every other frame;
a skeleton's a skeleton by any other name;
and we're pretty much the same
beneath our skins
for every skeleton grins.

~ Halloween Poem *For Fraser*

At half-past two in the morning Halifax International Airport was going through the motions. I was there, trying to spot Edward.

Since his near-fatal mishap, the Canadian Department of External Affairs had dunned his friends for money to cover his hospital bills. Randy Wicker had wired money in New York; so had Winston Leyland in San Francisco. Byron Black in Jakarta declined, still furious that Edward had squandered the chances he'd given him. In early January, I proposed to send a one-time sum. Or the diplomats could ship him to Canada, and I'd accept delivery. Cutting its losses, External Affairs chose the latter. In late January we spoke across 24 time zones.

"Well, Edward," I said, "I hear you're going to be joining us."

"Presumably."

Now a Canadian Pacific Airlines employee tumbrelled a wheelchair toward me. In it he sat, grizzled and ashen, hands atop a giant vinyl suitcase straddling the armrests, one leg in a cast, a granny shawl over his shoulders.

"Fraser!" he said huskily. "Thank God you're here." The employee smiled. But we were not quite finished. Edward thought a flight attendant was holding an emergency passport for him. She wasn't.

During the uphill and down dale trip an hour and a half due north, lights of hamlets glittered like ice shards in the ebony night. The car's labour was matched by the motor of Edward's mouth. He thought he was in the adjacent province of New Brunswick, and knowledgeably described its natural history. Arriving, I gunned up a gully-prone lane, skittering over the icy front yard past a big disused barn. Looming above the snowbound lawn, leafless elms leaned across our sprawling white-porched house. A volley of barks: our poodle doing his duty. The barking roused my wife Alison, who groggily appeared in a nightdress. She saw Edward to a bed-sitting room, my mother's sanctum until her death from a heart attack the previous summer.

Over time, Edward grasped where he was. He was not in New Brunswick, nor in Bermuda. Bangkok was not in Brazil, Ecuador, or British Guiana. South Asia was not Brazil or the West Indies. He found it hard to accept that Thailand was in Southeast Asia, that French was not its main language, or that Vietnam was not ruled by an emperor. Alison was not his aunt, nor was I his Uncle Joe. About the past two years he claimed to recall nothing. Digging deep in his suitcase — packed to bursting, gaping at the zipper — I discovered few clues. A cancelled Kuala Lampur-Bangkok airline ticket made sense. But what was the point of a ticket stub for a bus trip to Brasília? A plastic bag of seashells? A sweat-stained paperback of C. J. Koch's *The Year of Living Dangerously*?

His assets, held in a Montreal bank account, amounted to $6.44. Our family doctor attended to the hole in his chest. Soon Alison was changing dressings over green-grey ooze, frustrated to tears by what seemed wilful lapses in memory. He claimed that "malign spirits" had mislaid his papers. He declined to put on antibiotic ointment: "I don't feel I need it." For a time, he was incontinent, blaming it on dreams in which, unencumbered by a plaster cast, he gambolled in a forest glade, peeing freely. A session to fit Pampers on him proved so embarrassing we abandoned it by mutual consent. The bedwetting abruptly ceased. Since his clothes were suitable only for Bangkok, Alison bought him a track suit, which also served as a set of pajamas. Only with difficulty could we dissuade him from wearing suit and slippers in the subzero outdoors. In fact, he saw no good reason why he need ever take off his suit. He pointed out to Alison that he had always looked like either an aristocrat or a rummy.

He was a question mark to our rural neighbours. The farmer who ploughed out our lane spoke of the impending task of clearing stones off fields. Edward smiled in quiet bemusement. "Why," he asked, "would you want to clear stones off fields?" Sequestered in his room, he rejected radio, television, and our pets. "Anyone who would give house room to a dog," he stated, "would give house room to a mongoloid idiot." He thus managed to insult both our poodle and Alison's mentally handicapped brother.

Quaking, he scolded our son Malcolm on his unsuitable choice of friends, a wrathful stabbing finger invoking divine wrath. Though indignant, Malcolm considered our guest as blustery weather that had blown in and would soon blow out. He was right. Edward subsided to one rage a week. He monotonously apologized for causing inconvenience, and offered to walk the 20 miles to a hospital appointment. Eating hugely, he copiously salted, sugared, and peppered in no particular order, crossing knife and fork to cut spaghetti into vermiform segments. He began to shave, take baths, and make his own snacks. He mastered the art of putting on a seatbelt.

His leg fractures healed around the steel plate the Bangkok surgeon had implanted. Broken ribs, shoulder, and collarbone were now sound. As for his eyesight, he saw two images slightly diagonal to the other, telling an ophthalmologist that this was due to having been forced to stay in a hospital bed. While an abscessed tooth was removed, he told the dental surgeon that dentists extracted far too many teeth: as I drove him back through a grimy industrial town after Valium and narcotics, he noted, "What an attractive town Trenton is! Just look at those smoke plumes!" He was entranced by the license plates of passing cars. "`Nova

Scotia: The Ocean Playground'! What a wonderful thing to put on a license plate!"

During a stay in a nearby hospital, he donated the walker the airline had given him, suggesting it be called the "E. A. Lacey Memorial Ambulator," and chatted matily in Spanish with his doctor's Mexican wife. He submitted to a therapist's questionnaire:

> *Q:* Would you like to perform skin grafts or catalogue a collection of law books?
> *A:* Both.

When a nurse asked him about his bowel movements, he replied, "I am an infrequent defecator." The staff called him "The Professor." Some objected to the reading matter that Winston Leyland had sent him, *Gay Roots*, Vol. I, a massive paperback anthology whose cover showed an exceptionally well-hung young man. As for Edward, he threw a glass of water on his ward-mate, a loud stroke victim. Meanwhile, I was trying to figure out where he could go next. He had to go somewhere. Soon we were to sell our home, pack and ship several tons of belongings, find a place to live in Toronto, and get ourselves and our pets there. An Easter card arrived from Rosalyn Paleff in Toronto. Renate Jürgenson sent from Germany a tin of chocolate biscuits, a brochure about Oldenburg, and a pair of her panties. Randy Wicker in New York and Ruth Beissel in Montréal were in touch. But none of these friends could possibly take him in.

Peterborough, the "Queen City of the Kwarthas," wasn't far from hometown Lindsay and only two hours' drive from Toronto. An institution there, which we thought might accept him, demanded he take an HIV test: he found it inconceivable that he could have contracted HIV. Alison got paperwork in motion with Peterborough's social agencies while I lobbied Edward's cousins, whose names I'd extracted from shreds of correspondence. Speaking to us from her home near Lindsay, Marg Wansbrough, the daughter of his Uncle Joe—the right Uncle Joe—declined to help: her husband Sandy was convalescing after surgery. A public servant in Peterborough named Don Blanchard agreed to pick up him on his arrival, and take him to stopgap lodgings.

It was early May. Alison supplied him with a thick binder of key documents, including a typed chronology of his comeback. He'd mellowed about the poodle, describing him as "a European heiress down on her luck." His wounds had healed, he was mobile, he was *compos mentis* enough to ably edit a sermon Alison was to deliver at a local church. I flew with him to Toronto. At Pearson Airport, I took him to a minivan booked for the journey to Peterborough. He got meekly in.

If some malign spirit had contrived to place him in a milieu customized to madden him, Brock Mission would have been a good choice. The mission's rules of engagement bristled with commandments and prohibitions; its ministers seemed to him fanatical and intrusive, its helpers preachy heretics; he demanded that an unpreachy Catholic priest, Muslim imam, or Buddhist monk be summoned. The Mission confiscated his copy of *Gay Roots*, Vol. I. His stay ended abruptly when he made a disparaging remark about Canada and a patriotic youth took exception. Edward threw a cup of coffee on him.

The Family Counselling Service, Edward's overseers, relocated him to a shared-accommodation "home" where he took up menthol cigarettes, pinching them between two fingers, taking lung-dredging drags. He was expelled. Peterborough Manor, a comfy residence for retirees, gave him a week's respite. This was more like it, a good place. Alas, he was shunted to less sumptuous accommodations. Recalling the Manor's blessings, he sadly glossed a brochure with compliments. "A charming country residence specially designed for people who treasure their independence and privacy." *Yes, I was respected in my room and left alone by other patients, who went to bed early and slept and got up noiselessly.* "Laundry and cleaning chores are a permanent part of your past thanks to our efficient housekeeper." *Laundry was done, dried and returned promptly.* "Enjoy menu selection in the warmth of our formal dining room." *Ate in my room; meals prompt and complete and usually delicious.* In his new, unsatisfactory digs, Meals-on-wheels kept him in grub, though he fired his bed-maker on her first day, for "intrusiveness and incompetence." July passed in a haze of distant and recent memories, of personal belongings lost, found, and lost again, of puzzling impending, then postponed or cancelled, assignations and appointments with bank tellers, speech therapists, and doctors.

He marked up Alison's chronology of his months in Nova Scotia. "By February 4 you no longer were intensely irritated by the cats and dog." *They were so noisy.* "By February 11 you stopped giving Malcolm constant orders and scoldings and treated him as most adults do." *He and I became quite friendly, on a casual basis.* "You no longer tried to go out to appointments in trousers that would not do up and exposed you below the waist." *Uncharacteristic behaviour from me: regrettable.* "February 26 to April 8 you were in the Extended Care Unit at Sutherland-Harris Memorial Hospital." *I have good memories of the Extended Care Unit, and wish I'd never left it. Don't remember how I left.* "By May 6 Edward, it was very exciting to watch all this happening. It was like watching a skeleton becoming clothed with flesh and muscle, and starting to operate like a real human being again. Some of it we helped with, but by and large it was your own work on yourself, and you deserve an enormous amount of credit." *No "work," and if you could only see how I've gone downhill since then!* He wanted to meet Third-World young people, who were respectful, quiet, and meditative. This hellhole, gabby day and night, was *as bad as the Brock Mission.*

Running out of housing options, the FCS resorted to the Fairhaven Home for Senior Citizens, which could spare a bed for six months. Soon he was yelling and shaking his fist at a roommate. Given his own room, He blocked his door and hurled imprecations at staff. He assailed neighbours whose TVs were turned up too loud, or who occupied the common-room chair he favoured. He threatened to jump out a window, or into the river. When he wobbled off the grounds, he had to be retrieved. The staff gave up on getting him to clean his room or change his pajamas.

We visited him in early September. I relayed the news that Byron Black planned to publish *Third World: Travel Poems by E.A. Lacey.* He took little notice, but grinned when I played Byron's audio-letter in which the sounds of a Sumatra boar-hunt segued into a narrative of how one of Byron's pet monkeys had bit a neighbour's kid. After we returned from downtown, I noticed a computer printout taped to a corridor wall, passages beginning, "I love Canada because..." How nice it must be, I said, for Edward to regularly see such sentiments. When I pointed out two tiny Canadian flags mounted on a cleaning lady's cart, he advanced on them with surprising speed, yanked one out, and tried to tear it apart with his teeth.

When he had returned to Canada back in January, Canadian Pacific Airlines had alarmingly phoned his cousin Don to say that they had a passenger named Edward Lacey in bad shape, and didn't know what to do with him. They said they'd phone back, but didn't. After Don had delivered him to the Brock Mission, he began to get daily phone calls from the panicky FCS, who wanted him to pay his cousin's expenses. On a visit to him, Don and his wife Sharon bore the brunt of a quivering rage at their neglect of him. To social workers, though, Edward declared that he had no wish to associate with his relatives.

John and Ruth Colombo journeyed from Toronto to offer books and their own company. When they took him out for a meal, he said little but ate much. There always had been something reptilian about him, they thought; now, it appeared, only the lizard part lived on. When Robert McCaldon, a long-lost college pal who'd become a forensic psychiatrist at a penitentiary, phoned he discovered that Edward had not lost his French and Spanish, but his speech seemed near-robotic. Alerted by Robert, another college friend, Paul Weingarden, also phoned. Edward told him he wanted to die.

In mid-December I visited him. Steady cab customers that day, we went to a downtown café, where Edward scoffed two burritos. In a used-book shop, I parked him next to André Gide paperbacks but he showed no interest in taking one home. "They should have let me die in Bangkok," he moaned. His Bangkok acquaintance Edith Mirante sent him a copy of her just-published book, *Burmese Looking Glass,* inscribing it, "For Edward Lacey, my dear friend and fellow wanderer of the unsafe path."

He'd been agitating to go to Québec, which he said would halt his decline. In Ontario, *"C'est pas mon peuple pas ma langue icitte."* The English language was alien. Québec had no wish to take on one of Ontario's own, but the village of St-Isidore-de-Prescott in eastern Ontario at least was French-speaking. By early March he was booked into Villa LaPalme, a seniors' residence there. His social workers, who perhaps quit early that day to celebrate, packed him aboard a bus. From Ottawa, Guy

Courteau, Villa La Palme's administrator, took him the 40 miles to St-Isidore. A roadside hamlet in flat countryside unflooded by the St. Lawrence Seaway, it was dominated by a tall-towered feed mill. In the lowslung brick residence, having insisted that he could only recover among Francophones, he now refused to speak French: St-Isidore's was not real French but a "dialect." He claimed that he wanted to return to Peterborough.

He was heard hammering on a portable typewriter that Guy Courteau had bought for him but whatever he'd typed vanished, possibly spirited away by malign spirits deputed to follow him. The nursing staff was awed his letters from such exotic places as Bangkok and Toronto. From Jakarta, Byron updated him on the monkeys: Charles Darwin had "lost an eye in combat and still carries a grimace rather reminiscent of your worried expression when something is weighing upon you," and Maman, a male pigtailed macaque, had "tried to murder the baby of Rosé, immediately becoming persimian non grata."

Henry Beissel was startled to learn from Ruth that Edward was living just down the road from his home. He was appalled that a man of high culture would find himself in a place that had none. Henry, who had long regarded his old friend as a medieval flagellant who went about the world equipped with a knotted rope, told him to get out of bed, dress, and most important, clean himself. He took him home to rural Ayorama Cottage. Henry's wife Arlette had last seen Edward five years ago. Their daughter Klara wasn't home — just as well, because ever since they had met in Provence she had loathed Edward, or so Edward believed. Angelica and Myrna were in western Canada.

In mid-September, Alison, Malcolm, and I came to visit. I asked how Henry had seemed to him. "He's improved," he said. We took him for a drive. When we parked in a field, his legs were sturdy enough to support him on a brief ramble. He remarked, "I suppose I should be thankful for small mercies. But they seem so very small." We agreed that the sooner he got therapy the better, and that the intellectual stimulation of a big city would benefit him. Edward's local doctor was of the same mind — but only if the patient cooperated.

For the past year, Alison had played catch-as-catch-can with his medical files. Would he get therapy in St. Isidore, or through some outreach program, or get relocated to a brain injury program? We settled on the Queen Elizabeth Hospital, a big squat box on wide, hospital-lined University Avenue in downtown Toronto. By late April 1994, Edward was in it.

The hospital specialized in rehabilitation. At a therapist's bidding, he made meals of vegetable soup and cold-cut sandwiches, and wrote lists of Portuguese numerals (*três, quatro, cinco...*). By the end of May, staff reported "considerable progress." Rosalyn Paleff, visiting, at first didn't recognize him, but then his eyes and smile became those she had loved when they both attended the University of Toronto. As they reminisced, he said she "had become the person he always thought she would be." When she tried to make contact with him later, she was told he wasn't taking calls.

He had turned mulish, in staff parlance, "non-compliant." He didn't believe he could get well in "wrong" Canada, and would only be "right" upon return to the Third World. Wearied by this mantra, I wrote him a memo, queasily aware how often Edward had turned friends into scolds. "Nothing will change for you because you've decided that it cannot change. The corner you're in must be hell, and require an enormous amount of psychic energy to maintain, but it's also a secure hell in which you absolve yourself of blame, guilt, responsibility, or work." After he'd read this, he asked mildly, "Do you think I'm malingering?"

When I took him to a used bookshop, he dumbly stood among the shelves, declining to browse. In a Lebanese restaurant, he sampled the buffet sparingly, saying, "Why do people have to eat when they order food? Sometimes it's enough to just look." In his room, I noticed a tall heap of photocopied typescript, which turned out to be the manuscript for *A Magic Prison*, a collection of letters to Henry Beissel and his family over three decades, the idea for which had evolved out of talks between Henry and David Helwig, who'd been a fellow student at the University of Toronto. Henry had supplied the letters and written an introduction, David had edited them, and Edward had agreed to their publication. Meanwhile, thanks to Alison, his "comfort allowance" from the Ontario government was upgraded to slightly larger "Family Benefits"; she got us Power of Attorney to legally act for him; and set up a bank account we could co-sign. We took on the quasi-legal status of "Advocates." To spend enough money so his bank balance wasn't large enough to make the government reduce payments was near-impossible. He had few needs and no wants — except those that money couldn't buy.

An infection developed where a metal plate had been implanted in Bangkok. On Canada Day, surgeons successfully cut out the infected bone and did a graft. When we visited, he instructed our son — when Malcolm wasn't performing calisthenics with pieces of medical furniture — on points of grammar. When he returned to the Queen Elizabeth, we took him out for some fresh air. Malcolm occupied himself by chasing pigeons. Edward remarked, "He is aggrandizing his territory."

A long-lost distant cousin on his father's side surfaced, a retired accountant with a clipped moustache named Basil Mulligan, a lover of bridge and churchgoer, he made himself agreeable with small gifts. By early August, Edward was living on borrowed time at the Queen Elizabeth. As his social worker put it, he had withdrawn "to the point where we have to work hard to keep on our minds that he still existed on the floor." Alison was the only one who could get him into a shower.

I turned up to take him to his new home, his eighth address since his return to Canada. Wasn't that what he'd always done — gypsy around? His suitcase and a supply of Prozac were in readiness. So, more or less, was Edward. A muscular Jamaican nurse bid him a cheery farewell. "So long, my sweetheart. You are my sweetie, aren't you?" Grimacing, he almost, almost smiled.

Near Allen Gardens' patch of green, Pembroke Street ran off Dundas St. East near Sherbourne St., stomping ground of indigents, winos, streetwalkers, and crackheads. Just up Pembroke was a strip bar, but Edward had no interest in bared female flesh. Or in much else in 41 Pembroke Lodge where his fellow lodgers, most of them in chemical straitjackets, lingered in the basement common room, chain-smoking, bleeding the coffee-maker, and restively waiting for the next meal. One was a tall moody queen in hair curlers and razor burn. "Seems like a nice gal," I said. "She's a pain in the ass," Edward replied. Someone stole his clock-radio, not that the loss mattered much: he never listened to it, and had lost all interest in time. For $528 a month, which took much of his Family Benefits, he got (a small) room and (fatty, plentiful) board. A seldom-seen Filipino couple operated the place. Another Filipino, "Junior," a slim wiry fellow of indeterminate years, did the cooking, cleaning, and much else. Edward once remarked, "If I got a million dollars I would give it all to Junior."

Byron airmailed a newly-minted copy of *Third World: Travel Poems by E.A. Lacey.* Above the imprint of Blacky's Image Lounge, Jakarta, the laminated white front cover showed a cloud-swathed photo image of the earth as seen from outer space. Byron contributed a candid preamble: "He was a handful. He is a fine poet. He was my friend." Appendices included letters from other friends, one of whom, Jourdan Arenson, noted that he'd seen in Edward and Byron "two very different manifestations of homosexuality — the goofy and the melancholy." The volume closed with a rubber stamp of a monkey's face. Pasted in were colour snapshots of Edward in Bangkok poses: being scraped off a sidewalk, dumped into the back of a pickup truck, trundled up a staircase. The back cover showed him atop a Jakarta high-rise, hunched on a cement barrier, eyeglasses in hand, frowning into the lens. Edward had little to say about the book. When Alison suggested that he reply to Ruth Beissel after she'd sent him a note, he said, "Why? I have nothing to report."

The genial Father Edward "Bud" Blanchard, his mother's youngest sibling, had twigged to his presence in Toronto. For many years a priest on the Prairies, he'd not seen Edward since he was a boy. He dropped by for chats on family history. In San Francisco, Winston Leyland hoped that Edward might translate a gay historical novel from Italian. He did not reply. Undaunted, Winston put us in touch with a gay Toronto doctor who specialized in traumatic injuries. We discussed getting him into a better place, but the prospects were dim. At times, Edward upbraided his female caseworkers and barred them from his room.

Winston flew in, finding that Edward could remember past dealings, but not what had happened a day earlier. He departed, depressed that his author had to live in such a wretched place. Another publisher came to call: in 1978, Ian Young had released Later, Edward's third collection of poems. Ian found him behind drawn blinds, listless but fingers constantly fiddling. From out of town, David Helwig came armed with a contract for *A Magic Prison*. They found a Turkish restaurant, where he discoursed on features of the Turkish language, and, for the waiter's benefit, on how Turkish food differed from Lebanese. David returned two days later, waking Edward, possibly groggy from the Fluoxetine he was taking for his depression and the Lorazepan for his insomnia. No, Edward said, he did not want to go out. If he got up, his sleep would be spoiled. For me, his greeting was sometimes a robust "Fuck off! Go away!" On other occasions, "Hello, Henry" came feebly from the shadows. Possibly, Edward had confused us. More likely, since Henry and I had not always been on easy terms, he was taking the piss out of me. Perhaps he said "Hello, Fraser" to Henry.

Once I took him out for a Chinese meal. Returning, I chose the wrong streetcar, which landed us a few blocks south of his door. When I let him go ahead, he stumbled over a curb and sprawled flat, breaking his glasses, gashing his brow. I hailed a cab to get us back. He meekly accepted the mishap: other lodgers, perhaps thinking I had beat him up, swabbed away the blood. Alison embarked on a week of writing letters, telephone calls, and appointments so Edward could get new glasses. At Christmas, never Edward's favourite time of the year, Rosalyn brought him a gift. He wouldn't open the door. Since Byron had remarked that he'd never known anyone as interested in "eats" as Edward, I gave him M. F. K. Fisher's *The Art of Eating*. He declined our invitation to join us for dinner. The new year brought greetings from the 95-year-old poet Robert Finch. A physical exam showed no sign of the tachycardia about which he'd often complained.

That spring I had major surgery. A few days after the operation, feeling sawn in half, I lay in a hospital bed when Edward, at Alison's behest, suddenly appeared at the door, grinning, clothes disheveled, hair kingfisher-wild. Seeing him was better than the morphine pump my hand clutched. A month later, I took him on an outing. Our cab turned up University Avenue, with the pink sandstone neo-Gothic of Queen's Park, the provincial legislature, looming at the top. Turning left along College Street, the point at which government met academe, we skirted the edge of the University of Toronto campus, within it University College, where Edward had spent four student years.

We drove west into Little Italy, restaurant row, and sat at an outdoor café in the unseasonably warm sun. To my astonishment, Edward accepted a single beer, the first drink he'd taken since his accident. When I said something disparaging about Toronto, he put in a good word for the city — perhaps he was being contrarian as usual, or his mental problems were even graver than I'd thought.

When he was in town, Henry Beissel dropped by. By letter, Ruth recommended that Edward attend the Unitarian Church. "She always drags in religion," he chuckled. Alison and I indulged him in the wishful thinking of a completed passport application. Like other admirers, Sky Gilbert, who had once mounted a dramatized performance centred on Edward's poems, came to view the wrecked revenant whose legend he had followed from afar. From time to time Randy phoned. To Randy, Edward's situation was supremely ironic: A boy grew up to hate Canada. Escape from her had become the motivating force of his life. Yet, in the end, Mother Canada had swept him back into her arms and made her prisoner.

As a memory aid, Edward made entries in a daybook. On May 1: "Change watch to indicate `Mon. 1' rather than `Mon. 31.' Pull on silver marker on right-hand side of dial. Pull it out halfway rather than all the way. Move dial downwards to alter number, upwards to alter week-day." He added an underlined rider that he should ask a worker to do it, "as I find it impossibly complicated."

I took him to Danforth Avenue, the Greek district. We sat at a sidewalk table while he chatted to the waiter about Athens. A string of honking cars went by, with much shouting and waving of Greek flags — clamour about a football match — then a speeding convoy of raucous men, cars, and flags, only these were Turks. For Tuesday, June 20, Edward recorded that around 2 p.m. a worker would come to take him for a walk. "Be dressed for going out." It was the Summer Solstice. *A Magic Prison*, whose cover bore Barker Fairley's portrait of him, would soon be in his hands. Father Blanchard had got the family to sign a birthday card and planned a small party for him on July 12, ruefully aware that his nephew had been born on Orangeman's Day. That month Robert Finch, as old as the century, died.

For Edward in his fetid tomb Wednesday morning, the day after the Solstice, was a day like any other. After a scuffle with a noisy neighbour across the hall, he'd been moved from the second floor to the first: one less set of steep narrow stairs to negotiate to and from the basement dining room. He stumbled down for breakfast. But it was too early; he had lost all sense of time. He dragged himself upstairs and lay down.

Later that morning a cheerful mustached policeman knocked on my door. He told me that a friend of mine, a Mr. Edward Lacey, had died of a heart attack. I was not a praying man, but upstairs I involuntarily sank to my knees and asked God to accept Edward for what he was, to give him what he'd never had. I went down to the morgue. Having watched too much TV, I imagined that a sheet would be swept aside dramatically. But, no, I was to see Edward's face on a closed-circuit monitor. An official warned me that Edward's eyes would be open. But in the event it was not his eyes I noticed, but the strong equine teeth. They were clenched in a grimace.

"Yes," I said, "that is Edward Allan Lacey."

ACKNOWLEDGMENTS

My greatest debt is to the words of Edward Lacey that I have quoted or paraphrased in this book, whether from manuscripts, periodicals, or from his collections *The Forms of Loss; Path of Snow: Poems 1951-73; Later: Poems 1973-1978; Third World: Travel Poems by E.A. Lacey,* as well as from *A Magic Prison: Letters from Edward Lacey,* edited by David Helwig, and the posthumously published *The Collected Poems and Translations of Edward A. Lacey,* edited by myself. Normally, extracting biographical details from a poet's work is a hazardous proceeding, but Lacey was not only an autobiographical poet, but one who was factually scrupulous. This book has been a collaboration.

Among the many people who helped me, I must single out Lacey's great friends, Randy Wicker and the late Ruth (Heydrasch) Beissel: this book could not have been written without their generosity in giving me, or allowing me to copy, letters and other documents. The following persons in Canada, the United States, Germany, India, Indonesia, and Thailand kindly answered my queries in e-mails, phone conversations, letters, or personal interviews, or were helpful in other ways. A few were kind enough to read various phases of the book's manuscript, wholly or in part. My apologies to anyone I may have overlooked.

Haide (Polacsek) Aide; William Aide; Jourdan Arenson; Henry Beissel; Dean Bishop; Walter Bowen; Myrna (Beissel) Bujara; Byron Black; Don Blanchard; the late Edward Blanchard; Janet (Tangney) Brown; John Robert Colombo; Ruth (Brown) Colombo; Reese Copeland; Guy Courteau; the late Marion DeGuerre; James R. Dubro; Angelica (Beissel) Elder; John Forbes; Susanne Forster; Arlette Francière; Monique de Gaye; Billy Hargrove; David Helwig; Ed Jackson; Renate Jürgensen; Lionel Kearns; M. T. Kelly; Adrian King-Edwards; Dennis Lee; Winston Leyland; Jack MacLeod; Jay Macpherson; the late Doug Marshall; Robert McCaldon; Frank Manley; Edith Mirante; Larry Murphy; the late Phyllis (Blanchard) Murtha; Rosalyn Paleff; Susan (Wilford) Schrier; Nik Sheehan; Karen Shenfeld; Carl Spadoni; Alison Sutherland; the late Malcolm Sutherland; the late Bruce Trigger; Reg Truax; Pat Walker; Marg (Tangney) Wansborough; Sandy Wansborough; Paul Weingarden; Gordon Young; Ian Young.

My thanks also to the staff of the William Ready Division of Archives and Research Collections, McMaster University, Hamilton, Ontario, where the Edward Lacey fonds are held, especially the Division's former Director, Carl Spadoni. I am grateful as well to the Canada Council for the Arts, which awarded me a Writing Grant at an opportune point during this book's long composition.

ABOUT THE AUTHOR

Fraser Sutherland is a much travelled Nova Scotian who lives in Toronto, Ontario. His work has appeared worldwide in magazines and anthologies in print and online, and has been translated into French, Italian, Albanian, Serbian, and Farsi. Before he became a freelance writer and editor, Sutherland reported for *The Toronto Star, The*  *Globe and Mail,* and *The Wall Street Journal.* He was a founding editor of *Northern Journey,* a columnist for *Quill & Quire,* and the managing editor of *Books in Canada.* A reviewer for *The Globe and Mail* and other periodicals, Sutherland has written and edited for dictionaries in three countries, and may be the only Canadian writer who is also a lexicographer. As a poet, Sutherland published his tenth collection, *The Philosophy of As If,* last year. *The Style of Innocence: A Study of Hemingway and Callaghan* and *John Glassco: An Essay and Bibliography* are among his other works. *Lost Passport: The Life and Words of Edward Lacey* is his sixteenth book.